DON'T STEP
IN THE
LEADERSHIP

DON'T STEP
IN THE
LEADERSHIP

A DILBERT® BOOK

BY **SCOTT ADAMS**

B⬛XTREE

First published 1999 by Andrews and McMeel a Universal Press Syndicate Company
Kansas City USA

First published in Great Britain 1999 by Boxtree
an imprint of Macmillan Publishers Ltd
25 Eccleston Place London SW1W 9NF
Basingstoke and Oxford

Associated companies throughout the world

ISBN 0 7522 2389 5

www.dilbert.com

9 8 7 6 5 4 3 2 1

A CIP catalogue record for this book is available from
the British Library.

Printed by Butler & Tanner Ltd., Frome and London

For Puzzle Girl

Introduction

Everyone says there's a lack of leadership in the world these days. I think we should all be thankful, because the only reason for leadership is to convince people to do things that are either dangerous (like invading another country) or stupid (working extra hard without extra pay).

Obviously you don't need any leadership to lead you to, for example, eat a warm cookie. But you need a lot of leadership to convince you to march through a desert and shoot strangers. Generally speaking, whenever there is leadership, there is lots of hollering and very few warm cookies. Let's enjoy the lack of leadership while we have it.

Unfortunately, whenever there's a void, someone always fills it. We don't want someone evil being the leader, so I recommend filling the job with a cartoonist. I'd be willing to give it a go. Like any leader, I'll try to get people to do things that are dangerous and stupid, but my plan is to make those things funny for the people who aren't directly involved. That's the best you can hope for when it comes to leadership.

For example, I would limit CEO compensation to whatever the CEO can carry away in his cheeks like a squirrel every night.

To shorten business meetings, I would authorize the invention of special chairs that heat up ten degrees for every minute the occupant talks. If you can make your point in one minute, you get a nicely warmed chair. But if you ramble on for forty minutes, you'll burst into flames to the delight and applause of the other attendees.

I would also encourage a modified version of Scrabble rules for business meetings. If someone uses an acronym or buzzword that sounds suspicious, you can challenge him to define it. If the offender can't define the word, he loses his job. But if he can, he gets to slap the challenger with an appointment calendar.

That's just a sample of the leadership I would provide. This book will give you a good idea of what else is on my agenda. But I consider my leadership temporary, anticipating the day when Dogbert conquers the planet and forces into domestic service everyone who opposed him. You can avoid that fate by joining Dogbert's New Ruling Class (DNRC) now and getting on his good side. All you need to do is sign up for the free *Dilbert* newsletter and you're in the DNRC.

To subscribe, send an e-mail to listserv@listserv.unitedmedia.com in the following format:

subject: newsletter
message: Subscribe Dilbert_News Firstname Lastname

Don't include any other information—your e-mail address will be picked up automatically.

If the automatic method doesn't work for you, you can also subscribe by writing to scottadams@aol.com or via snail mail:

Dilbert Mailing List
United Media
200 Madison Avenue
New York, NY 10016

These methods are much slower than the automatic method so please be patient.

S.Adams

Scott Adams

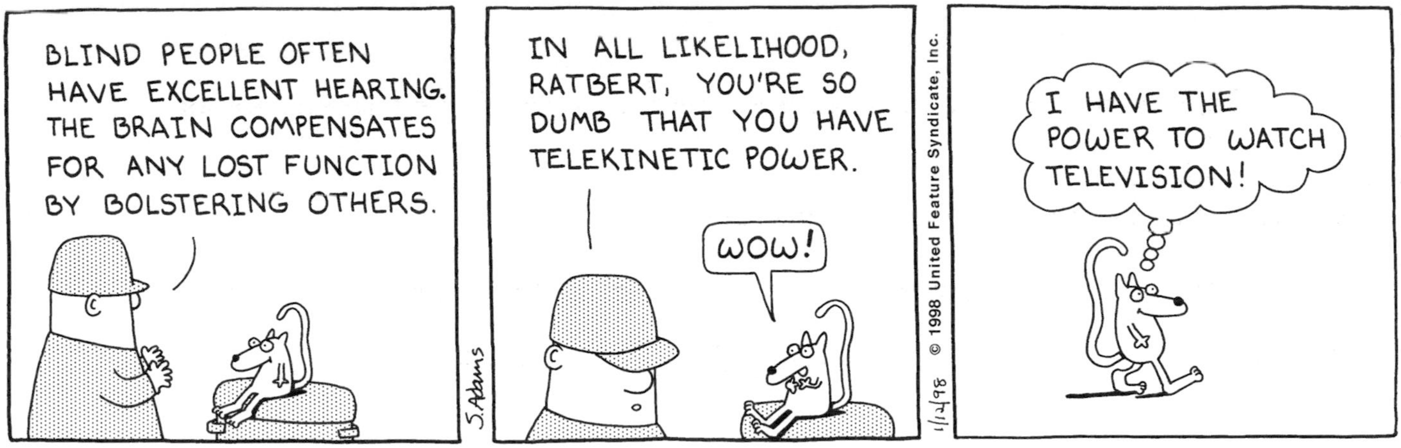
BLIND PEOPLE OFTEN HAVE EXCELLENT HEARING. THE BRAIN COMPENSATES FOR ANY LOST FUNCTION BY BOLSTERING OTHERS.
S. Adams
IN ALL LIKELIHOOD, RATBERT, YOU'RE SO DUMB THAT YOU HAVE TELEKINETIC POWER.
WOW!
1/12/98 © 1998 United Feature Syndicate, Inc.
I HAVE THE POWER TO WATCH TELEVISION!

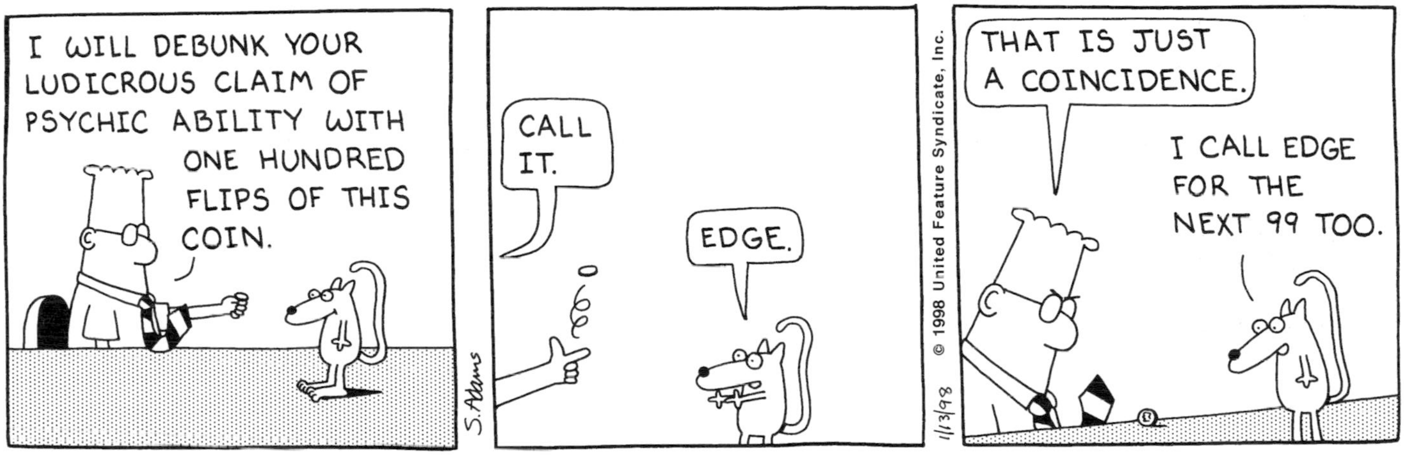
I WILL DEBUNK YOUR LUDICROUS CLAIM OF PSYCHIC ABILITY WITH ONE HUNDRED FLIPS OF THIS COIN.
S. Adams
CALL IT.
EDGE.
1/13/98 © 1998 United Feature Syndicate, Inc.
THAT IS JUST A COINCIDENCE.
I CALL EDGE FOR THE NEXT 99 TOO.

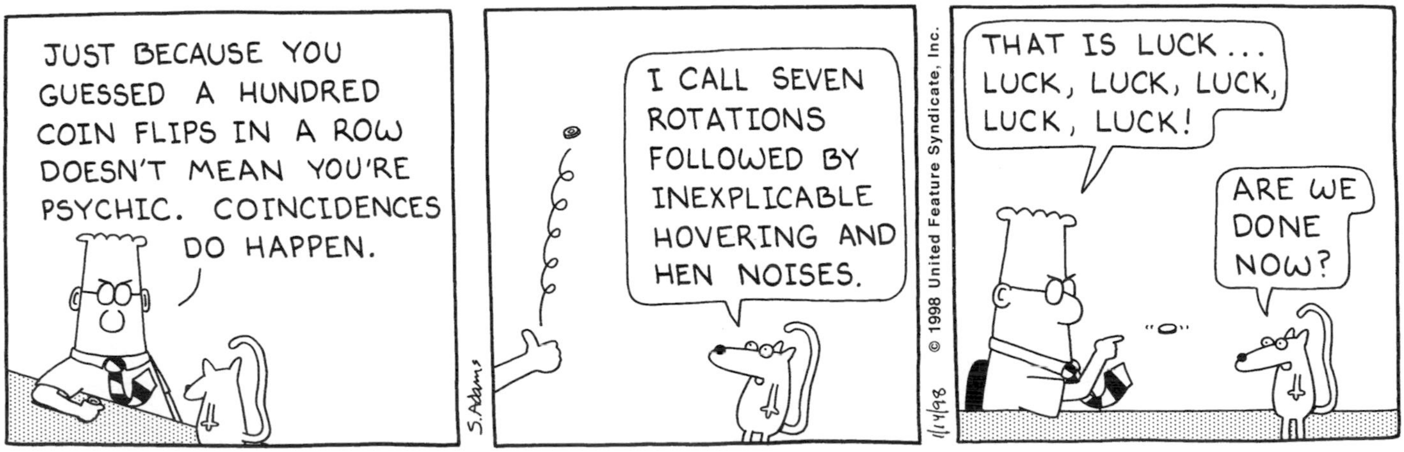
JUST BECAUSE YOU GUESSED A HUNDRED COIN FLIPS IN A ROW DOESN'T MEAN YOU'RE PSYCHIC. COINCIDENCES DO HAPPEN.
S. Adams
I CALL SEVEN ROTATIONS FOLLOWED BY INEXPLICABLE HOVERING AND HEN NOISES.
1/14/98 © 1998 United Feature Syndicate, Inc.
THAT IS LUCK... LUCK, LUCK, LUCK, LUCK, LUCK!
ARE WE DONE NOW?

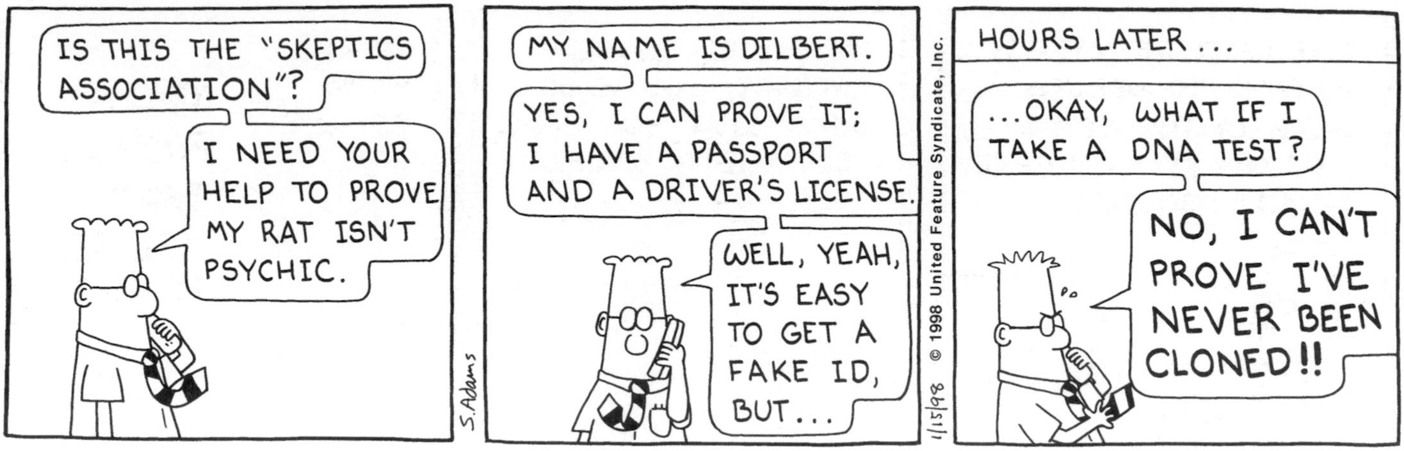
IS THIS THE "SKEPTICS ASSOCIATION"?
I NEED YOUR HELP TO PROVE MY RAT ISN'T PSYCHIC.
S. Adams
MY NAME IS DILBERT.
YES, I CAN PROVE IT; I HAVE A PASSPORT AND A DRIVER'S LICENSE.
WELL, YEAH, IT'S EASY TO GET A FAKE ID, BUT...
1/15/98 © 1998 United Feature Syndicate, Inc.
HOURS LATER...
...OKAY, WHAT IF I TAKE A DNA TEST?
NO, I CAN'T PROVE I'VE NEVER BEEN CLONED!!

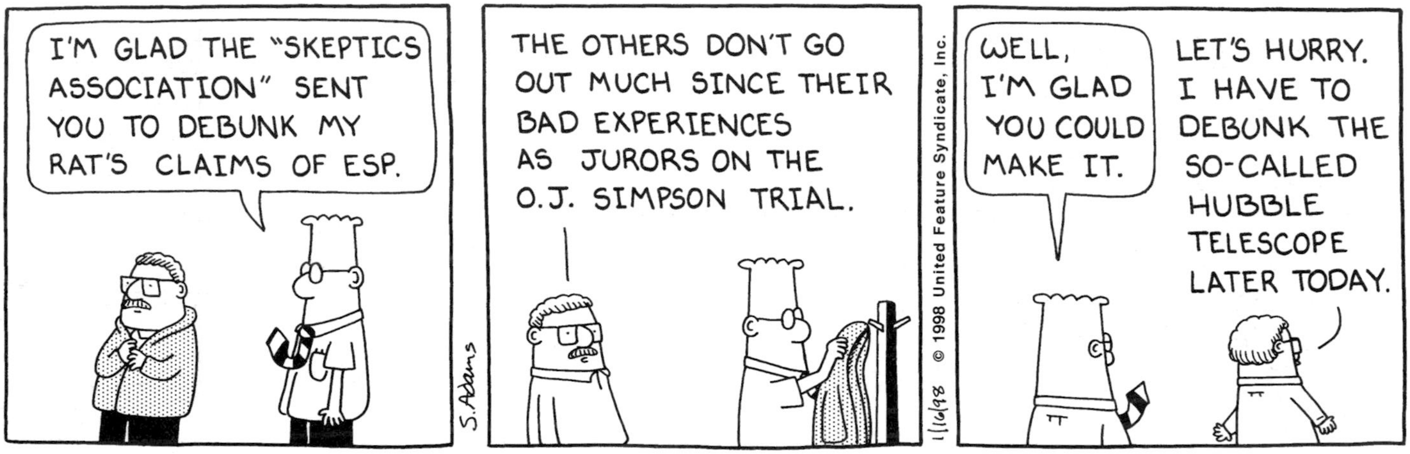
I'M GLAD THE "SKEPTICS ASSOCIATION" SENT YOU TO DEBUNK MY RAT'S CLAIMS OF ESP.
S. Adams
THE OTHERS DON'T GO OUT MUCH SINCE THEIR BAD EXPERIENCES AS JURORS ON THE O.J. SIMPSON TRIAL.
1/16/98 © 1998 United Feature Syndicate, Inc.
WELL, I'M GLAD YOU COULD MAKE IT.
LET'S HURRY. I HAVE TO DEBUNK THE SO-CALLED HUBBLE TELESCOPE LATER TODAY.

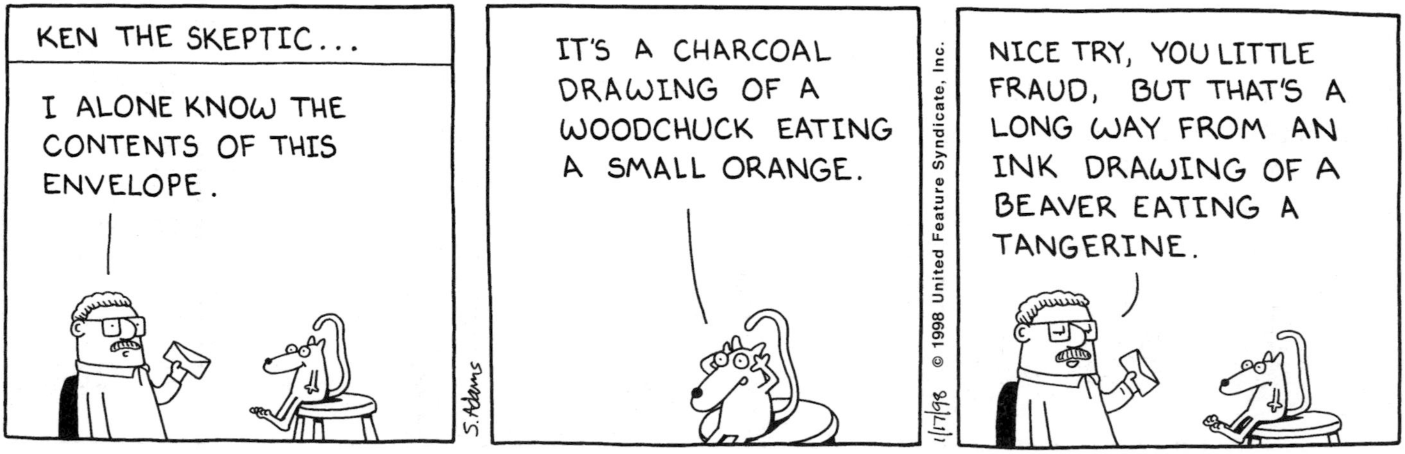
KEN THE SKEPTIC...
I ALONE KNOW THE CONTENTS OF THIS ENVELOPE.
S. Adams
IT'S A CHARCOAL DRAWING OF A WOODCHUCK EATING A SMALL ORANGE.
1/17/98 © 1998 United Feature Syndicate, Inc.
NICE TRY, YOU LITTLE FRAUD, BUT THAT'S A LONG WAY FROM AN INK DRAWING OF A BEAVER EATING A TANGERINE.

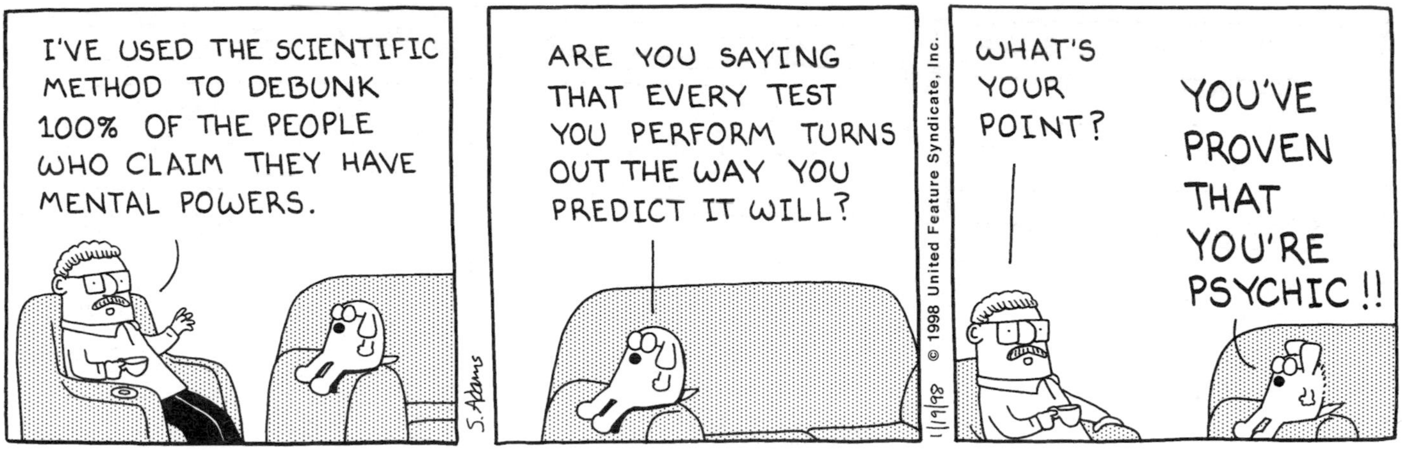
I'VE USED THE SCIENTIFIC METHOD TO DEBUNK 100% OF THE PEOPLE WHO CLAIM THEY HAVE MENTAL POWERS.
ARE YOU SAYING THAT EVERY TEST YOU PERFORM TURNS OUT THE WAY YOU PREDICT IT WILL?
WHAT'S YOUR POINT?
YOU'VE PROVEN THAT YOU'RE PSYCHIC!!
S. Adams
1/19/98
© 1998 United Feature Syndicate, Inc.

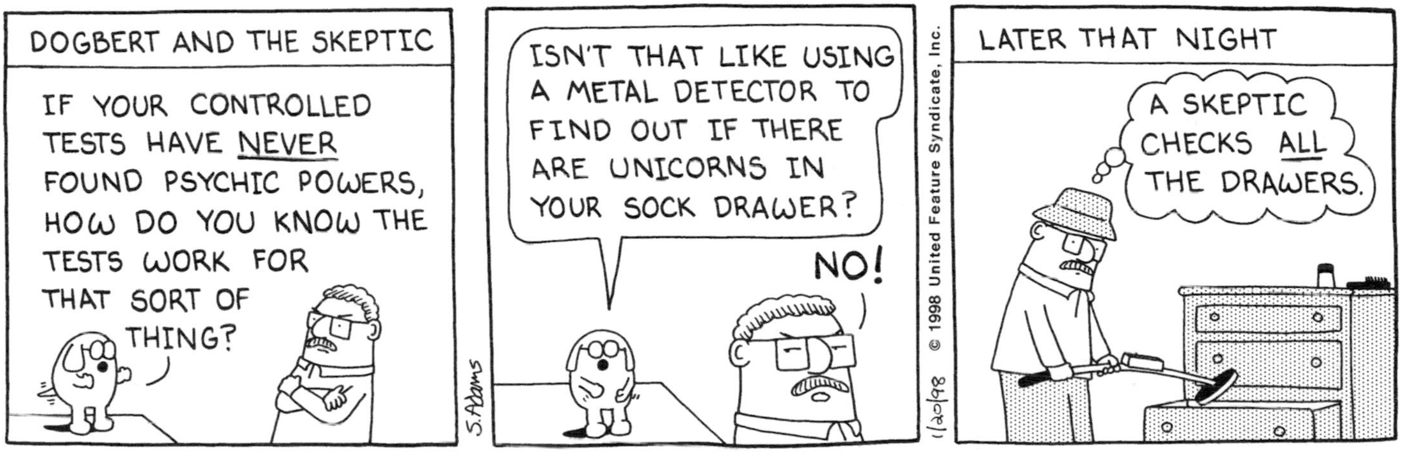
DOGBERT AND THE SKEPTIC
IF YOUR CONTROLLED TESTS HAVE NEVER FOUND PSYCHIC POWERS, HOW DO YOU KNOW THE TESTS WORK FOR THAT SORT OF THING?
ISN'T THAT LIKE USING A METAL DETECTOR TO FIND OUT IF THERE ARE UNICORNS IN YOUR SOCK DRAWER?
NO!
LATER THAT NIGHT
A SKEPTIC CHECKS ALL THE DRAWERS.
S. Adams
1/20/98
© 1998 United Feature Syndicate, Inc.

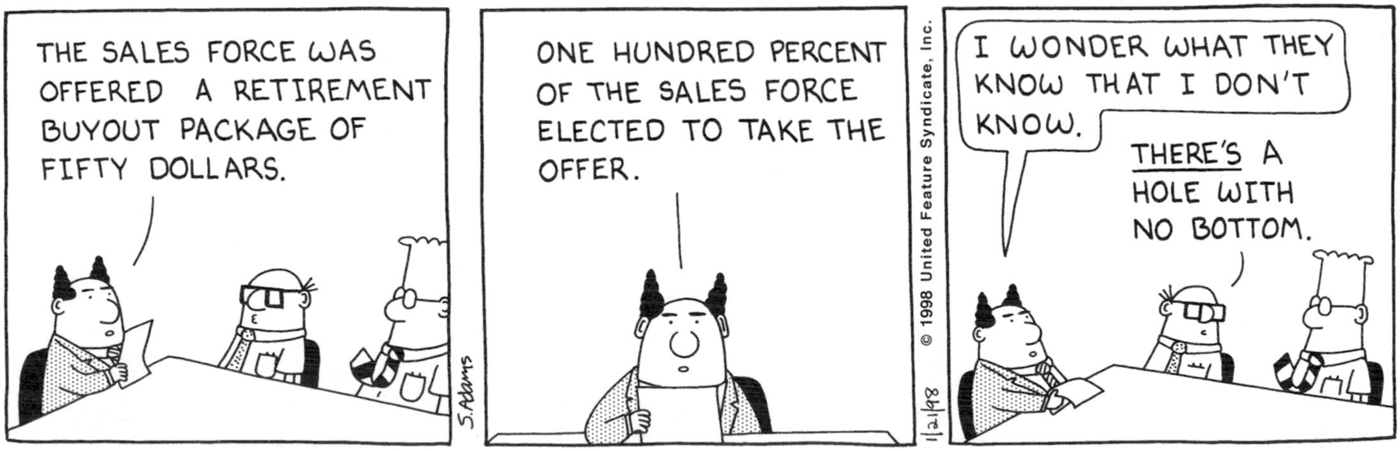
THE SALES FORCE WAS OFFERED A RETIREMENT BUYOUT PACKAGE OF FIFTY DOLLARS.
ONE HUNDRED PERCENT OF THE SALES FORCE ELECTED TO TAKE THE OFFER.
I WONDER WHAT THEY KNOW THAT I DON'T KNOW.
THERE'S A HOLE WITH NO BOTTOM.
S. Adams
1/21/98
© 1998 United Feature Syndicate, Inc.

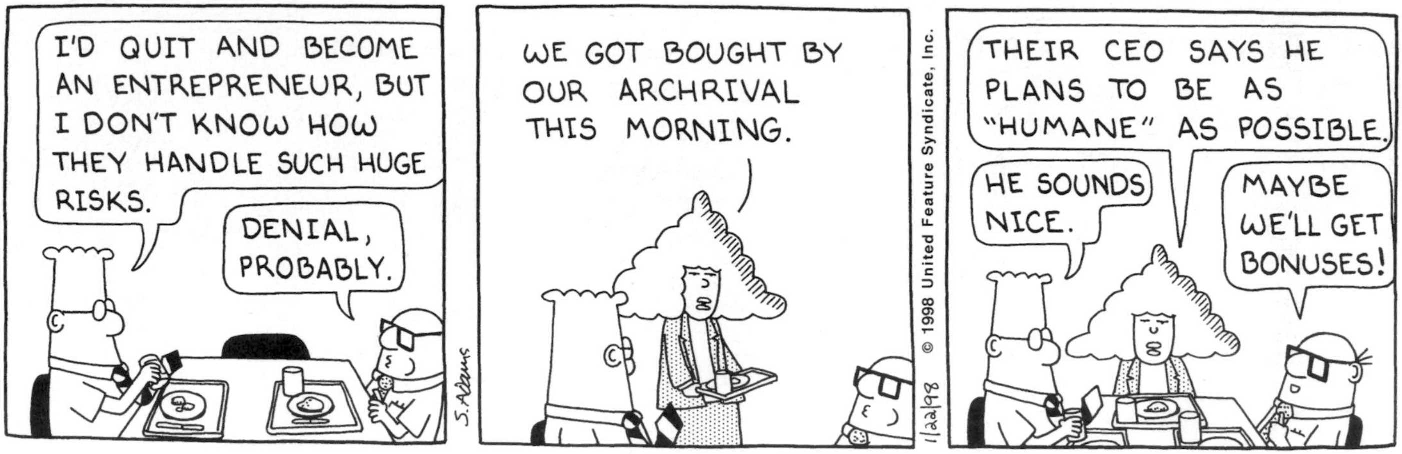
I'D QUIT AND BECOME AN ENTREPRENEUR, BUT I DON'T KNOW HOW THEY HANDLE SUCH HUGE RISKS.
DENIAL, PROBABLY.
WE GOT BOUGHT BY OUR ARCHRIVAL THIS MORNING.
THEIR CEO SAYS HE PLANS TO BE AS "HUMANE" AS POSSIBLE.
HE SOUNDS NICE.
MAYBE WE'LL GET BONUSES!
© 1998 United Feature Syndicate, Inc.

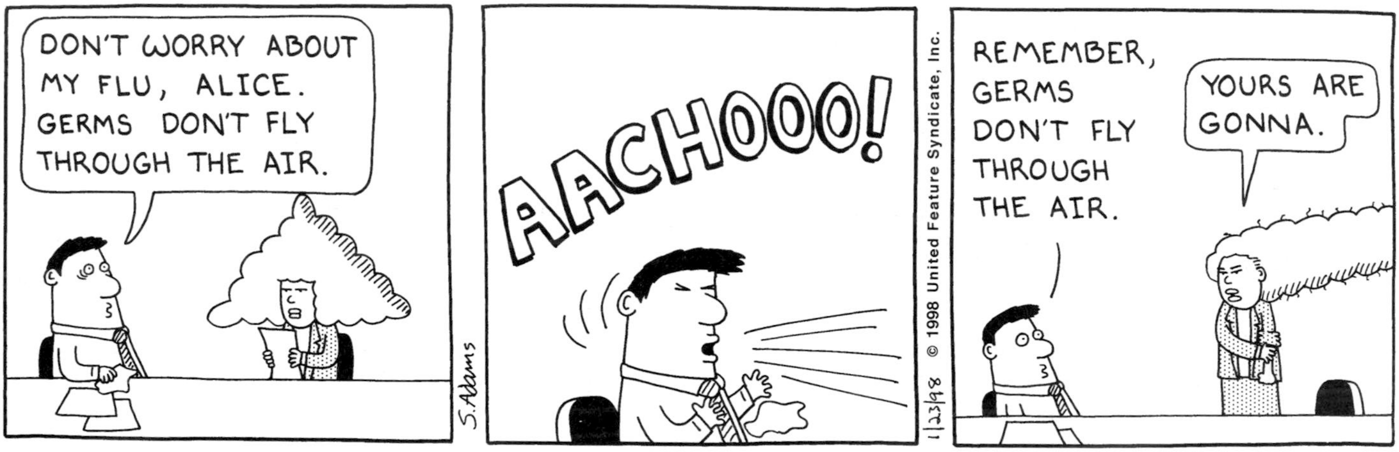
DON'T WORRY ABOUT MY FLU, ALICE. GERMS DON'T FLY THROUGH THE AIR.
AACHOOO!
REMEMBER, GERMS DON'T FLY THROUGH THE AIR.
YOURS ARE GONNA.
© 1998 United Feature Syndicate, Inc.

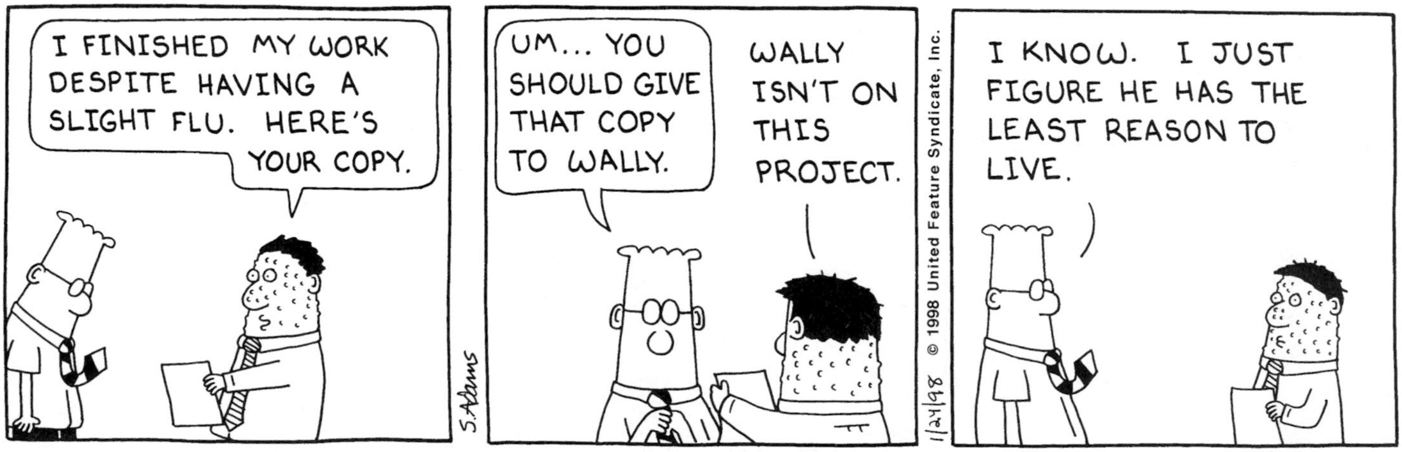
I FINISHED MY WORK DESPITE HAVING A SLIGHT FLU. HERE'S YOUR COPY.
UM... YOU SHOULD GIVE THAT COPY TO WALLY.
WALLY ISN'T ON THIS PROJECT.
I KNOW. I JUST FIGURE HE HAS THE LEAST REASON TO LIVE.
© 1998 United Feature Syndicate, Inc.

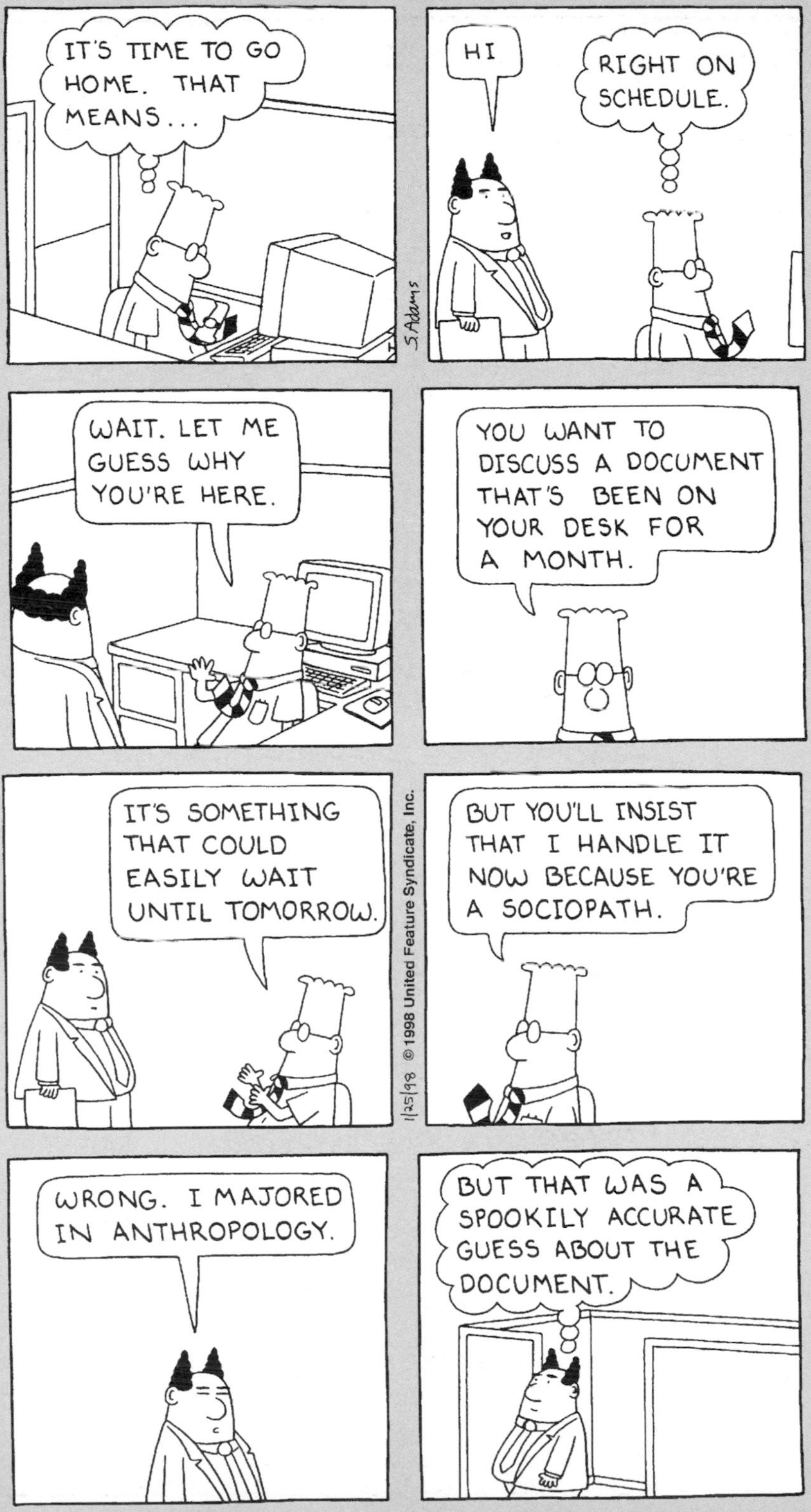
IT'S TIME TO GO HOME. THAT MEANS...
S.Adams
HI
RIGHT ON SCHEDULE.
WAIT. LET ME GUESS WHY YOU'RE HERE.
YOU WANT TO DISCUSS A DOCUMENT THAT'S BEEN ON YOUR DESK FOR A MONTH.
IT'S SOMETHING THAT COULD EASILY WAIT UNTIL TOMORROW.
1/25/98 © 1998 United Feature Syndicate, Inc.
BUT YOU'LL INSIST THAT I HANDLE IT NOW BECAUSE YOU'RE A SOCIOPATH.
WRONG. I MAJORED IN ANTHROPOLOGY.
BUT THAT WAS A SPOOKILY ACCURATE GUESS ABOUT THE DOCUMENT.

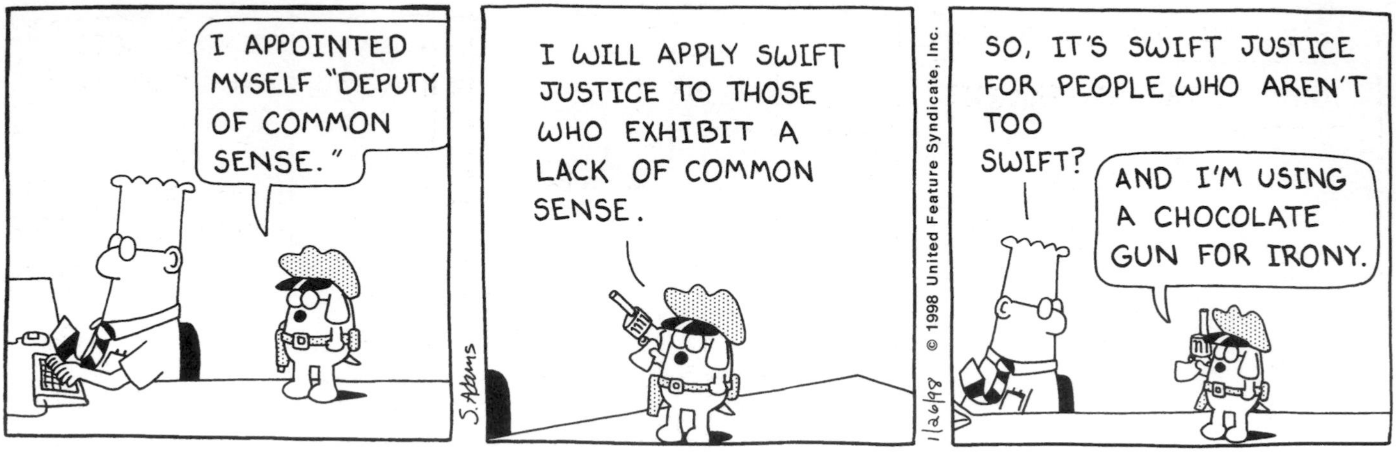
I APPOINTED MYSELF "DEPUTY OF COMMON SENSE."
I WILL APPLY SWIFT JUSTICE TO THOSE WHO EXHIBIT A LACK OF COMMON SENSE.
S. Adams
1/26/98 © 1998 United Feature Syndicate, Inc.
SO, IT'S SWIFT JUSTICE FOR PEOPLE WHO AREN'T TOO SWIFT?
AND I'M USING A CHOCOLATE GUN FOR IRONY.

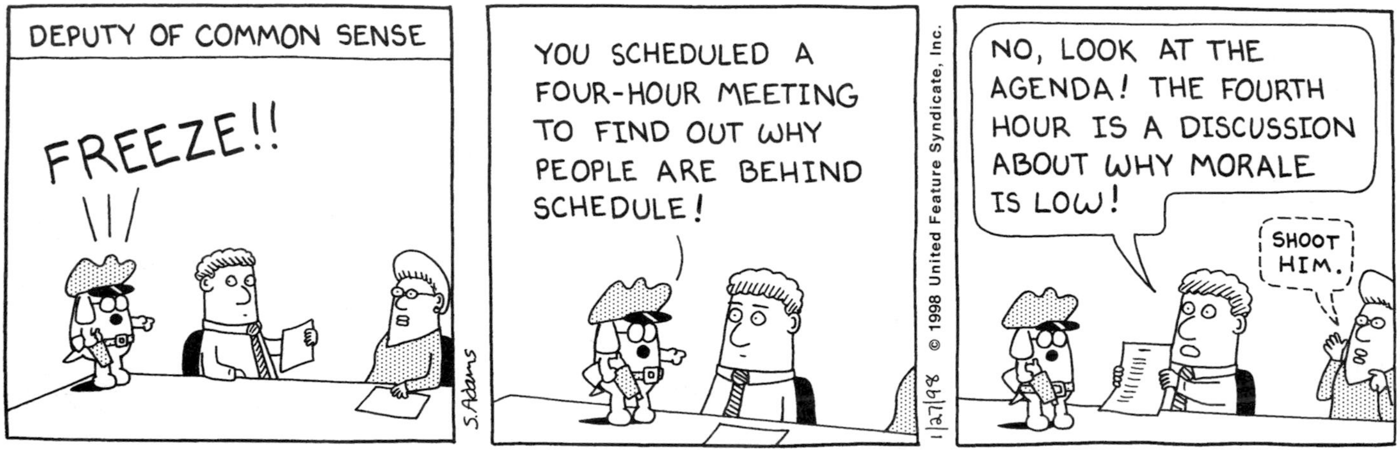
DEPUTY OF COMMON SENSE
FREEZE!!
S. Adams
YOU SCHEDULED A FOUR-HOUR MEETING TO FIND OUT WHY PEOPLE ARE BEHIND SCHEDULE!
1/27/98 © 1998 United Feature Syndicate, Inc.
NO, LOOK AT THE AGENDA! THE FOURTH HOUR IS A DISCUSSION ABOUT WHY MORALE IS LOW!
SHOOT HIM.

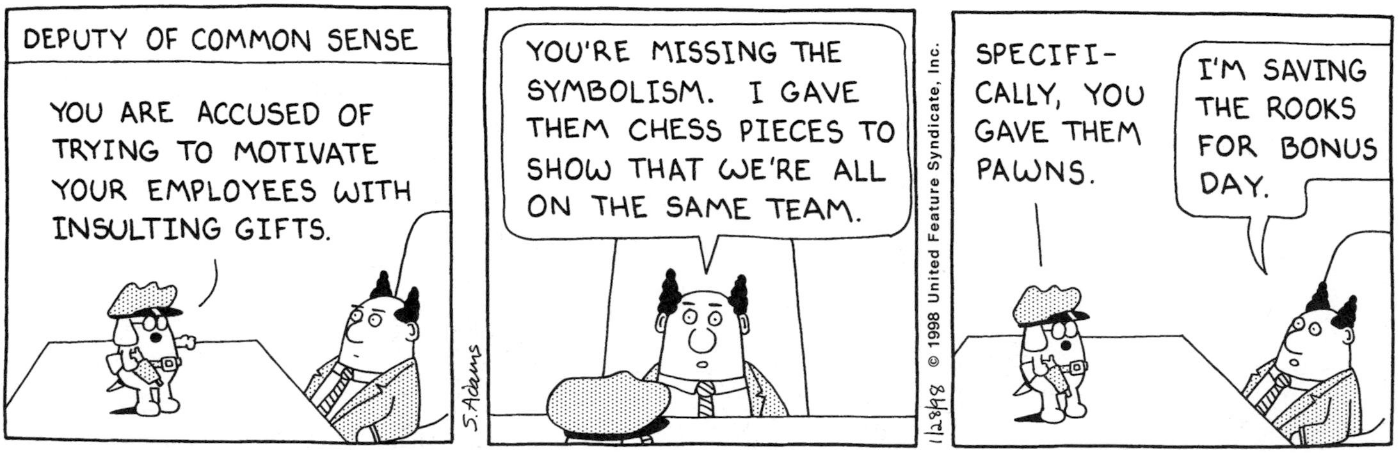
DEPUTY OF COMMON SENSE
YOU ARE ACCUSED OF TRYING TO MOTIVATE YOUR EMPLOYEES WITH INSULTING GIFTS.
S. Adams
YOU'RE MISSING THE SYMBOLISM. I GAVE THEM CHESS PIECES TO SHOW THAT WE'RE ALL ON THE SAME TEAM.
1/28/98 © 1998 United Feature Syndicate, Inc.
SPECIFI- CALLY, YOU GAVE THEM PAWNS.
I'M SAVING THE ROOKS FOR BONUS DAY.

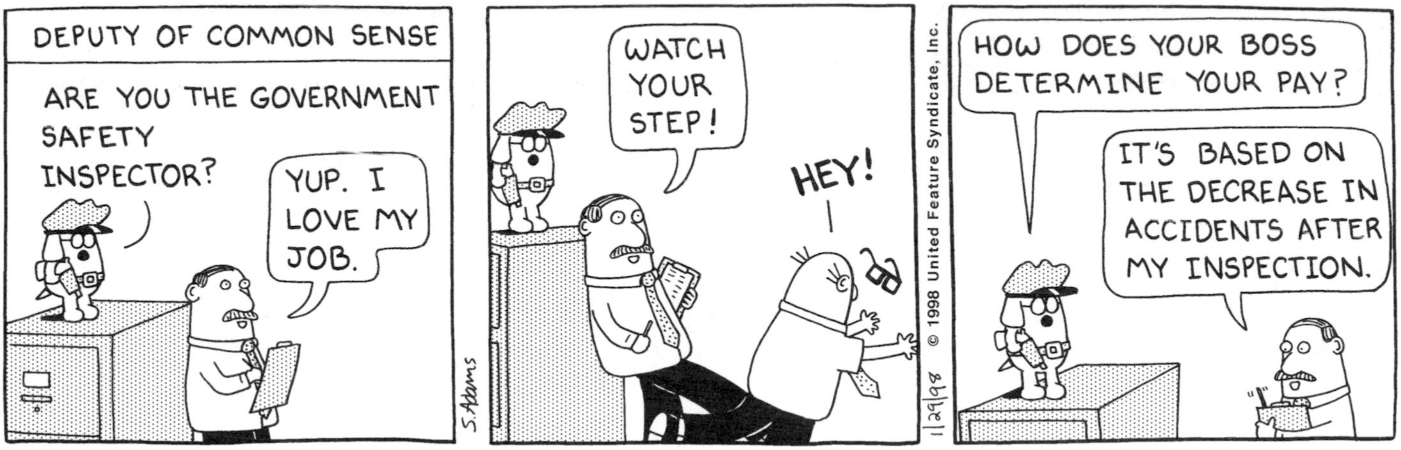
DEPUTY OF COMMON SENSE
ARE YOU THE GOVERNMENT SAFETY INSPECTOR?
YUP. I LOVE MY JOB.
S. Adams
WATCH YOUR STEP!
HEY!
1/29/98 © 1998 United Feature Syndicate, Inc.
HOW DOES YOUR BOSS DETERMINE YOUR PAY?
IT'S BASED ON THE DECREASE IN ACCIDENTS AFTER MY INSPECTION.

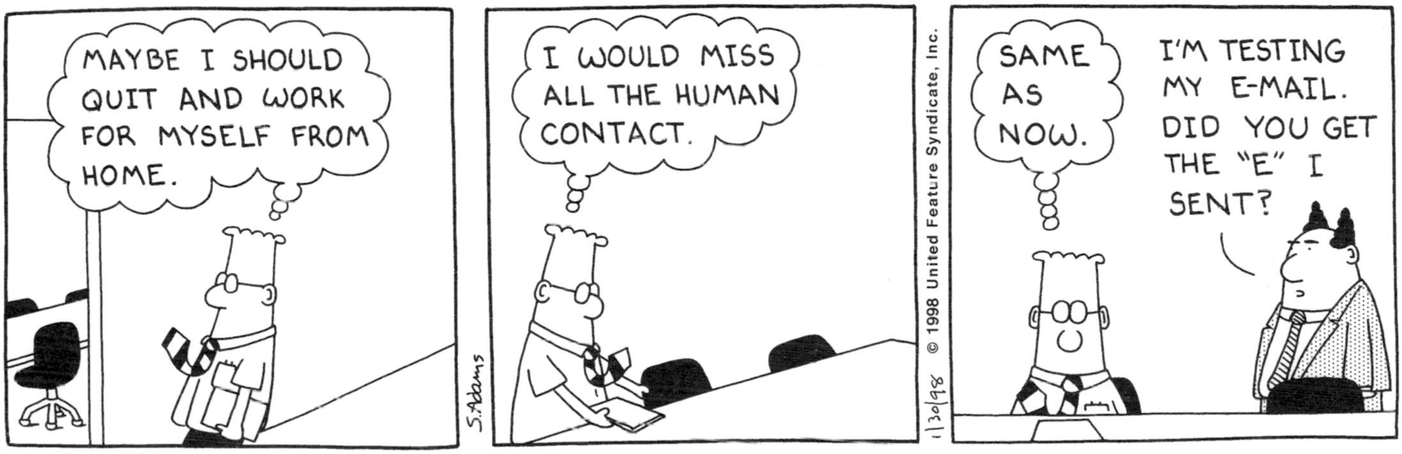
MAYBE I SHOULD QUIT AND WORK FOR MYSELF FROM HOME.
S. Adams
I WOULD MISS ALL THE HUMAN CONTACT.
1/30/98 © 1998 United Feature Syndicate, Inc.
SAME AS NOW.
I'M TESTING MY E-MAIL. DID YOU GET THE "E" I SENT?

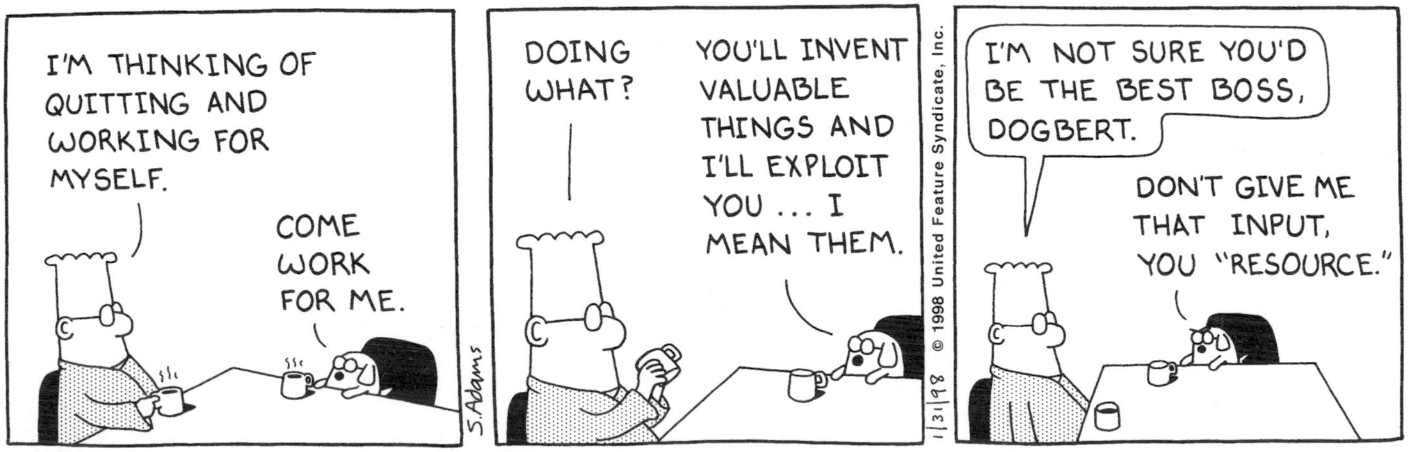
I'M THINKING OF QUITTING AND WORKING FOR MYSELF.
COME WORK FOR ME.
S. Adams
DOING WHAT?
YOU'LL INVENT VALUABLE THINGS AND I'LL EXPLOIT YOU ... I MEAN THEM.
1/31/98 © 1998 United Feature Syndicate, Inc.
I'M NOT SURE YOU'D BE THE BEST BOSS, DOGBERT.
DON'T GIVE ME THAT INPUT, YOU "RESOURCE."

LET'S START BY INTRODUCING OURSELVES.
I'M SUSAN BLOCK FROM I.T.G. I WORK FOR EMILY WOOTEN.
S. Adams
I'M MAX BLUMF. I WORK FOR SUSAN.
I'M ALICE. I WORK FOR... UH... I...
AAAGH!!! I'M FILLED WITH SHAME BY ASSOCIATION!!!
© 1998 United Feature Syndicate, Inc.
2/1/98
WHY ME? WHY WHY WHY
PLEASE TAKE ME TO YOUR GROUP! I'M NOT TAINTED!!!
SOB
CAN WE START OVER? I FORGOT WHO THE FIRST THREE PEOPLE ARE.

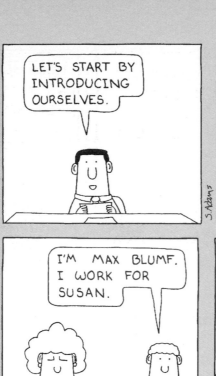

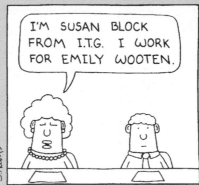

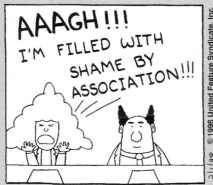

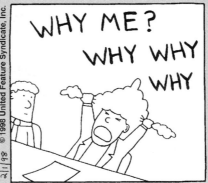

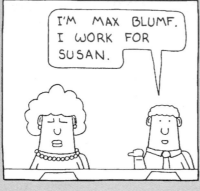

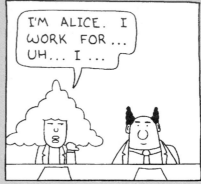

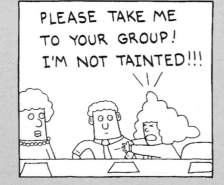

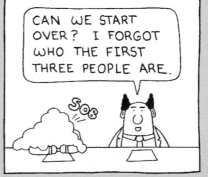

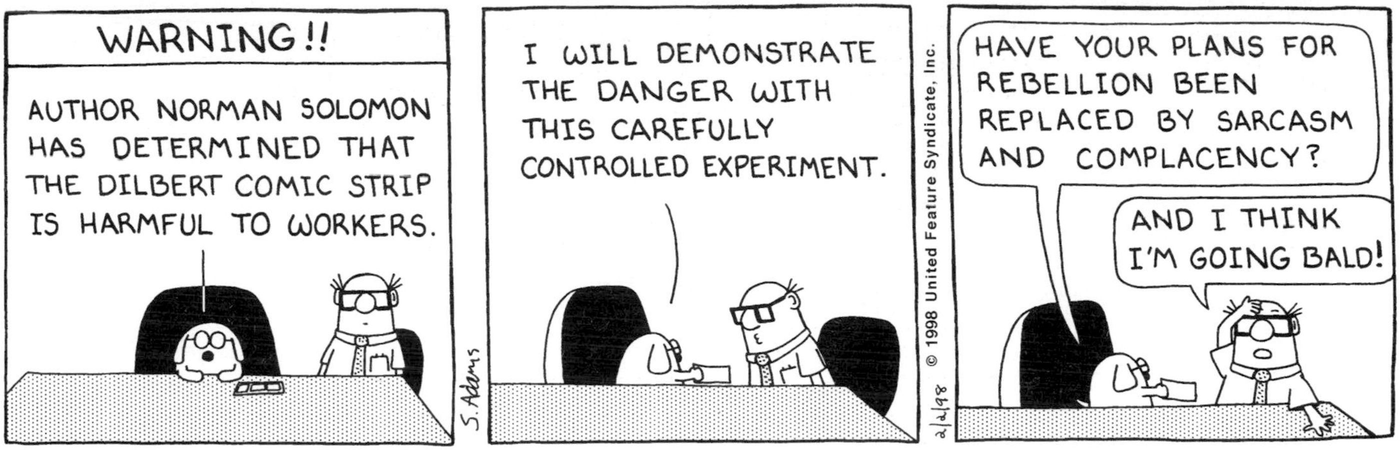
WARNING!!
AUTHOR NORMAN SOLOMON HAS DETERMINED THAT THE DILBERT COMIC STRIP IS HARMFUL TO WORKERS.
S. Adams
I WILL DEMONSTRATE THE DANGER WITH THIS CAREFULLY CONTROLLED EXPERIMENT.
2/2/98
© 1998 United Feature Syndicate, Inc.
HAVE YOUR PLANS FOR REBELLION BEEN REPLACED BY SARCASM AND COMPLACENCY?
AND I THINK I'M GOING BALD!

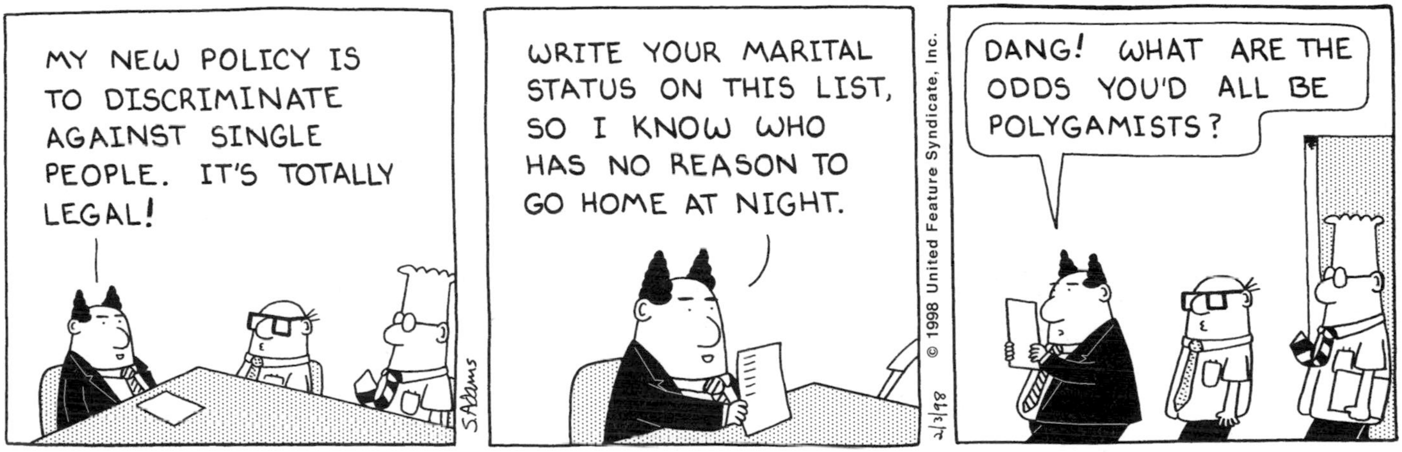
MY NEW POLICY IS TO DISCRIMINATE AGAINST SINGLE PEOPLE. IT'S TOTALLY LEGAL!
S. Adams
WRITE YOUR MARITAL STATUS ON THIS LIST, SO I KNOW WHO HAS NO REASON TO GO HOME AT NIGHT.
2/3/98
© 1998 United Feature Syndicate, Inc.
DANG! WHAT ARE THE ODDS YOU'D ALL BE POLYGAMISTS?

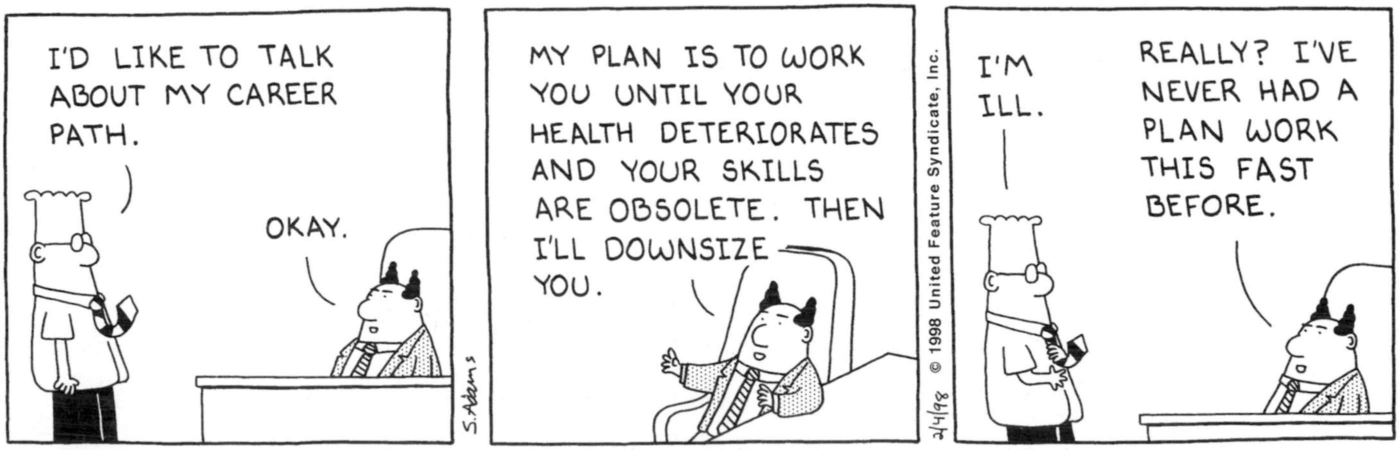
I'D LIKE TO TALK ABOUT MY CAREER PATH.
OKAY.
S. Adams
MY PLAN IS TO WORK YOU UNTIL YOUR HEALTH DETERIORATES AND YOUR SKILLS ARE OBSOLETE. THEN I'LL DOWNSIZE YOU.
2/4/98
© 1998 United Feature Syndicate, Inc.
I'M ILL.
REALLY? I'VE NEVER HAD A PLAN WORK THIS FAST BEFORE.

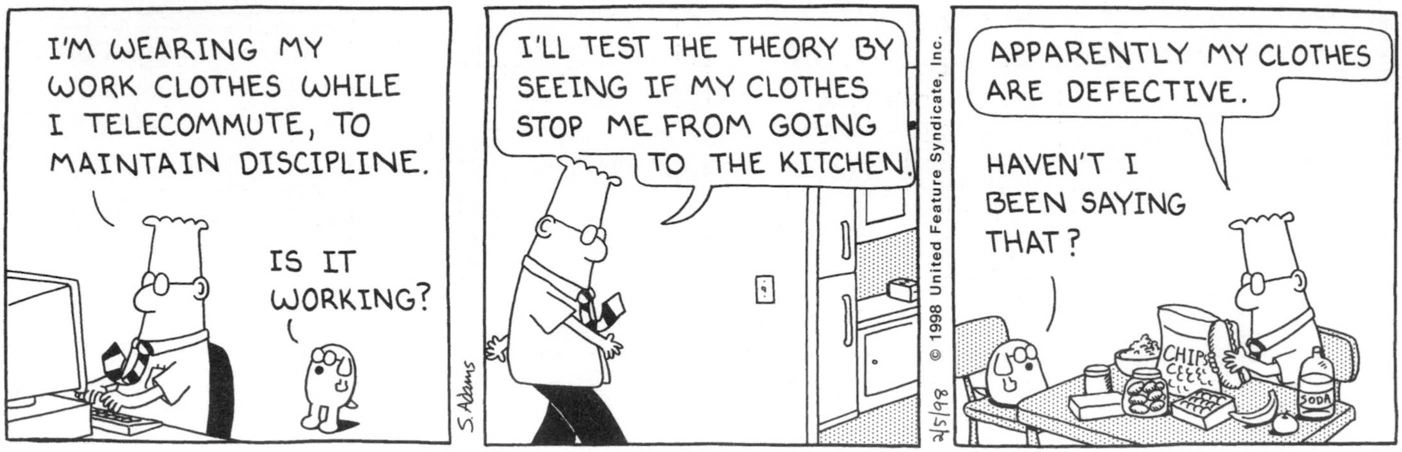
I'M WEARING MY WORK CLOTHES WHILE I TELECOMMUTE, TO MAINTAIN DISCIPLINE.
IS IT WORKING?
I'LL TEST THE THEORY BY SEEING IF MY CLOTHES STOP ME FROM GOING TO THE KITCHEN.
© 1998 United Feature Syndicate, Inc.
2/5/98
APPARENTLY MY CLOTHES ARE DEFECTIVE.
HAVEN'T I BEEN SAYING THAT?
CHIPS
SODA

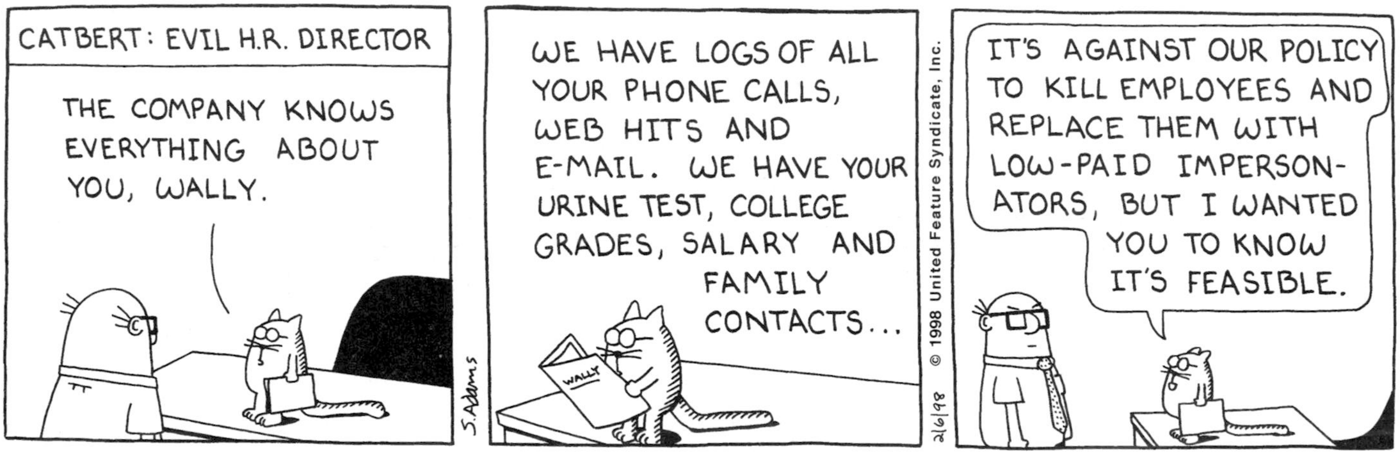
CATBERT: EVIL H.R. DIRECTOR
THE COMPANY KNOWS EVERYTHING ABOUT YOU, WALLY.
WE HAVE LOGS OF ALL YOUR PHONE CALLS, WEB HITS AND E-MAIL. WE HAVE YOUR URINE TEST, COLLEGE GRADES, SALARY AND FAMILY CONTACTS...
WALLY
© 1998 United Feature Syndicate, Inc.
2/6/98
IT'S AGAINST OUR POLICY TO KILL EMPLOYEES AND REPLACE THEM WITH LOW-PAID IMPERSON-ATORS, BUT I WANTED YOU TO KNOW IT'S FEASIBLE.

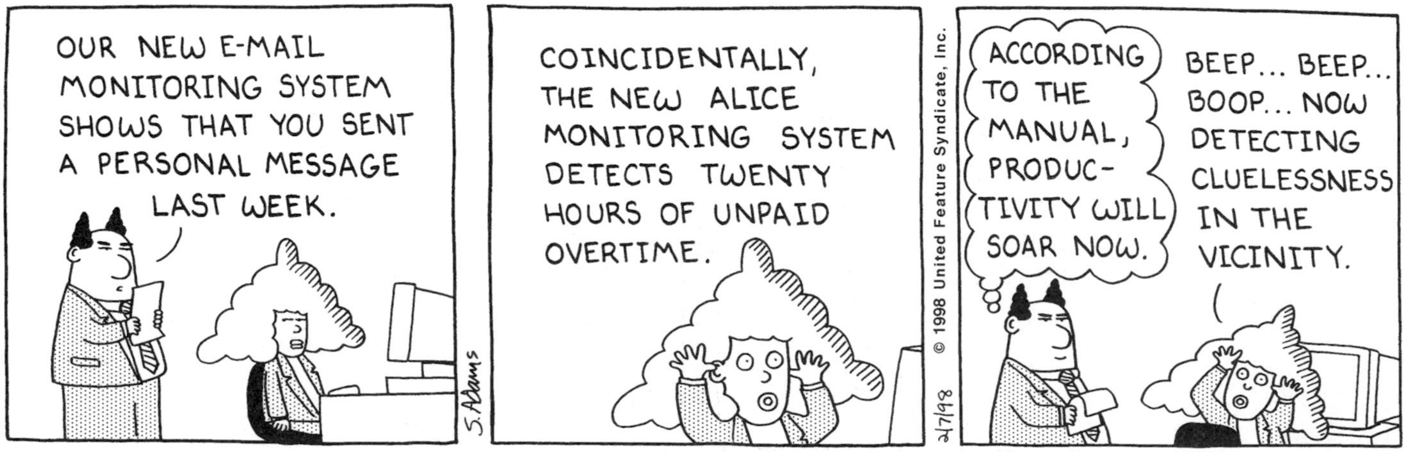
OUR NEW E-MAIL MONITORING SYSTEM SHOWS THAT YOU SENT A PERSONAL MESSAGE LAST WEEK.
COINCIDENTALLY, THE NEW ALICE MONITORING SYSTEM DETECTS TWENTY HOURS OF UNPAID OVERTIME.
© 1998 United Feature Syndicate, Inc.
2/7/98
ACCORDING TO THE MANUAL, PRODUC-TIVITY WILL SOAR NOW.
BEEP... BEEP... BOOP... NOW DETECTING CLUELESSNESS IN THE VICINITY.

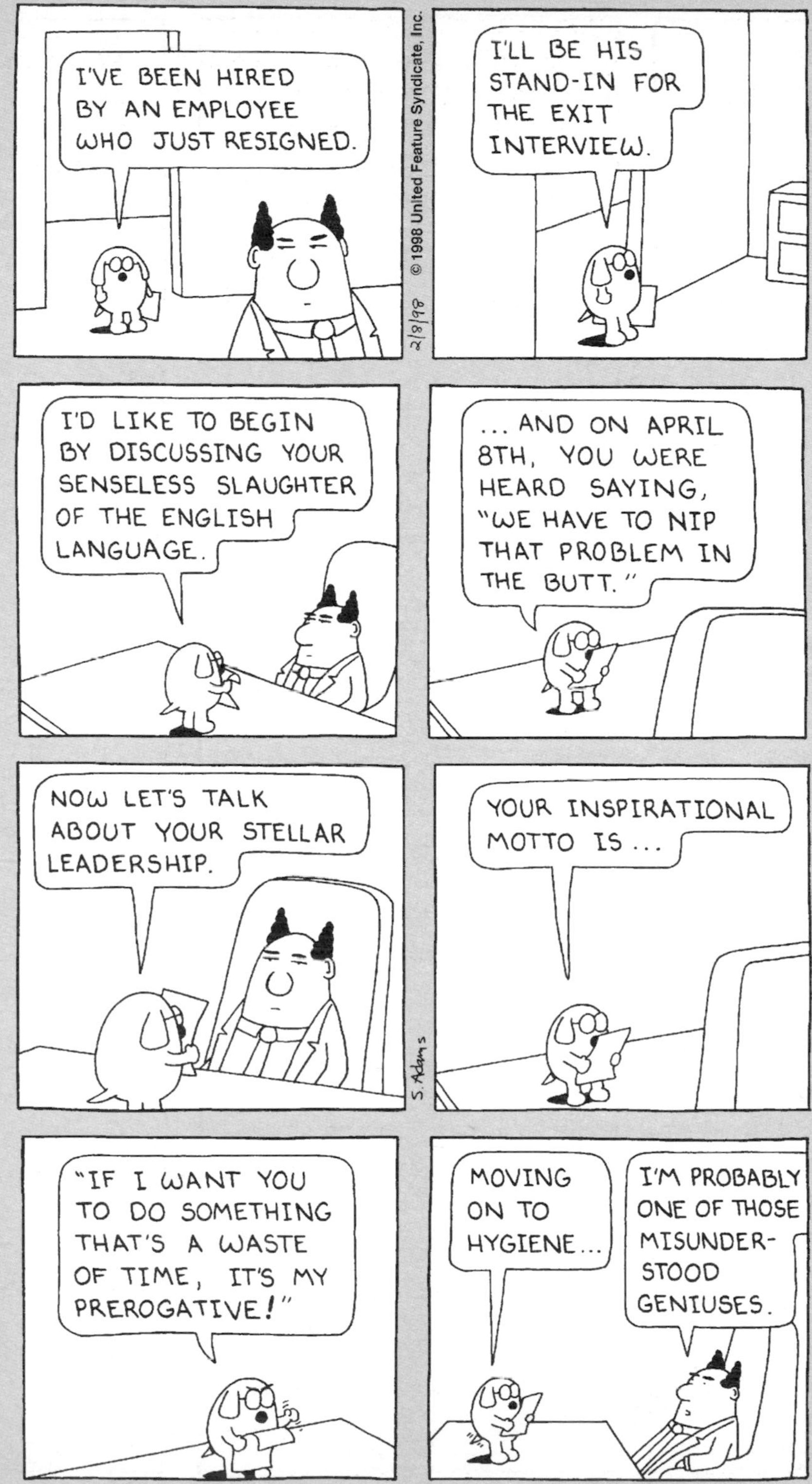
I'VE BEEN HIRED BY AN EMPLOYEE WHO JUST RESIGNED.
© 1998 United Feature Syndicate, Inc.
2/8/98
I'LL BE HIS STAND-IN FOR THE EXIT INTERVIEW.
I'D LIKE TO BEGIN BY DISCUSSING YOUR SENSELESS SLAUGHTER OF THE ENGLISH LANGUAGE.
... AND ON APRIL 8TH, YOU WERE HEARD SAYING, "WE HAVE TO NIP THAT PROBLEM IN THE BUTT."
NOW LET'S TALK ABOUT YOUR STELLAR LEADERSHIP.
S. Adams
YOUR INSPIRATIONAL MOTTO IS ...
"IF I WANT YOU TO DO SOMETHING THAT'S A WASTE OF TIME, IT'S MY PREROGATIVE!"
MOVING ON TO HYGIENE...
I'M PROBABLY ONE OF THOSE MISUNDER-STOOD GENIUSES.

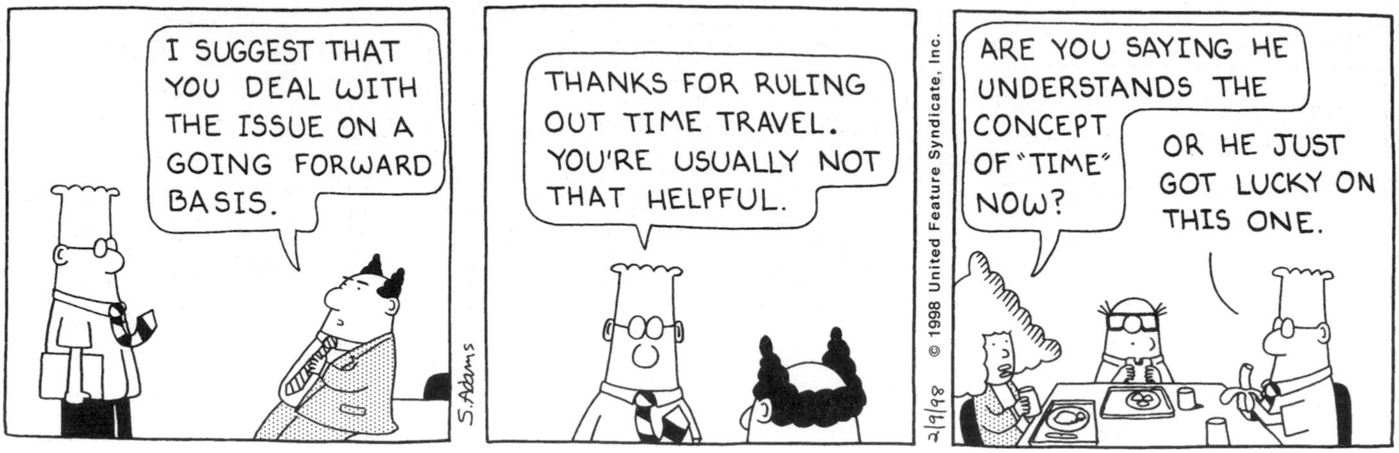
I SUGGEST THAT YOU DEAL WITH THE ISSUE ON A GOING FORWARD BASIS.
S. Adams
THANKS FOR RULING OUT TIME TRAVEL. YOU'RE USUALLY NOT THAT HELPFUL.
2/9/98 © 1998 United Feature Syndicate, Inc.
ARE YOU SAYING HE UNDERSTANDS THE CONCEPT OF "TIME" NOW?
OR HE JUST GOT LUCKY ON THIS ONE.

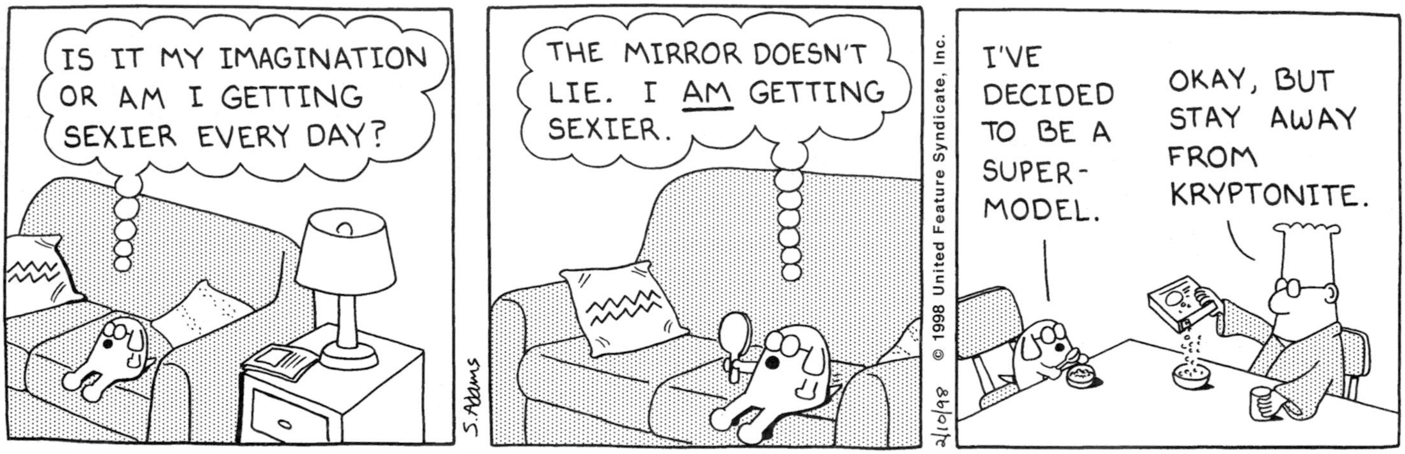
IS IT MY IMAGINATION OR AM I GETTING SEXIER EVERY DAY?
S. Adams
THE MIRROR DOESN'T LIE. I AM GETTING SEXIER.
2/10/98 © 1998 United Feature Syndicate, Inc.
I'VE DECIDED TO BE A SUPER-MODEL.
OKAY, BUT STAY AWAY FROM KRYPTONITE.

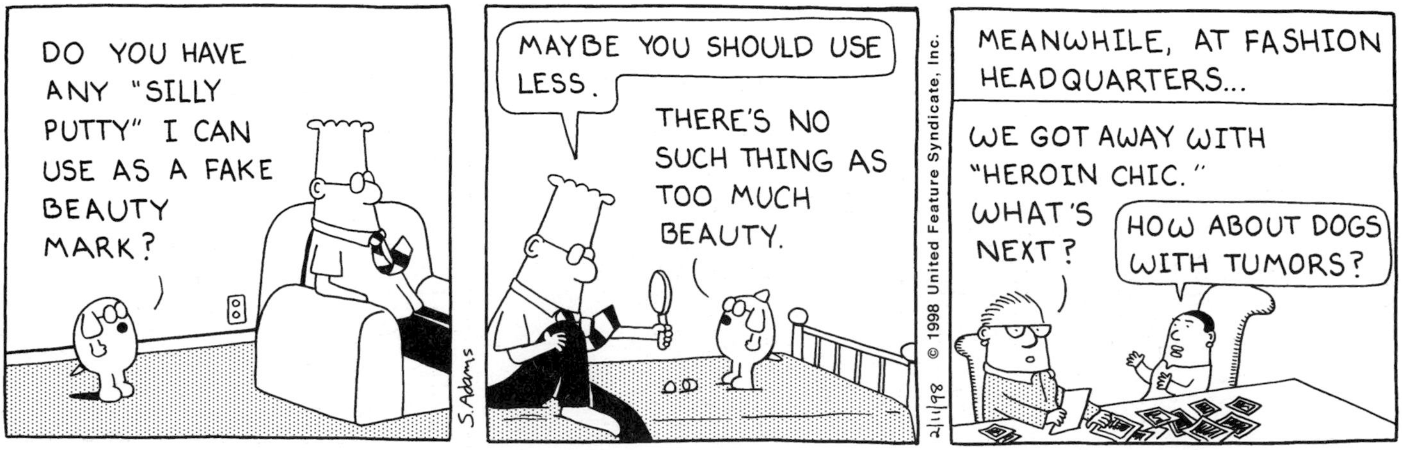
DO YOU HAVE ANY "SILLY PUTTY" I CAN USE AS A FAKE BEAUTY MARK?
S. Adams
MAYBE YOU SHOULD USE LESS.
THERE'S NO SUCH THING AS TOO MUCH BEAUTY.
2/11/98 © 1998 United Feature Syndicate, Inc.
MEANWHILE, AT FASHION HEADQUARTERS...
WE GOT AWAY WITH "HEROIN CHIC." WHAT'S NEXT?
HOW ABOUT DOGS WITH TUMORS?

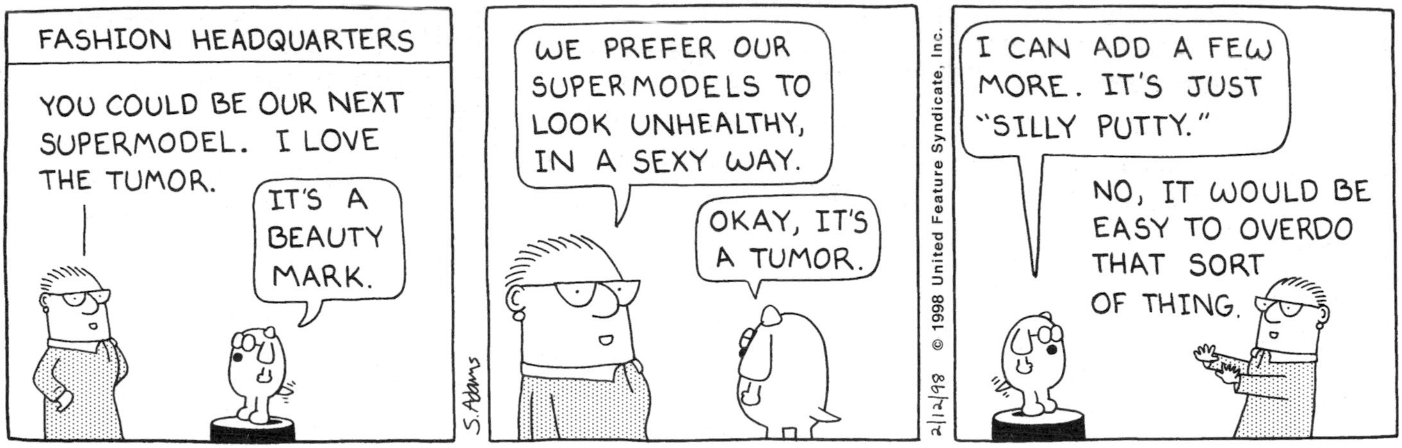
FASHION HEADQUARTERS
YOU COULD BE OUR NEXT SUPERMODEL. I LOVE THE TUMOR.
IT'S A BEAUTY MARK.
S. Adams
WE PREFER OUR SUPERMODELS TO LOOK UNHEALTHY, IN A SEXY WAY.
OKAY, IT'S A TUMOR.
2/12/98 © 1998 United Feature Syndicate, Inc.
I CAN ADD A FEW MORE. IT'S JUST "SILLY PUTTY."
NO, IT WOULD BE EASY TO OVERDO THAT SORT OF THING.

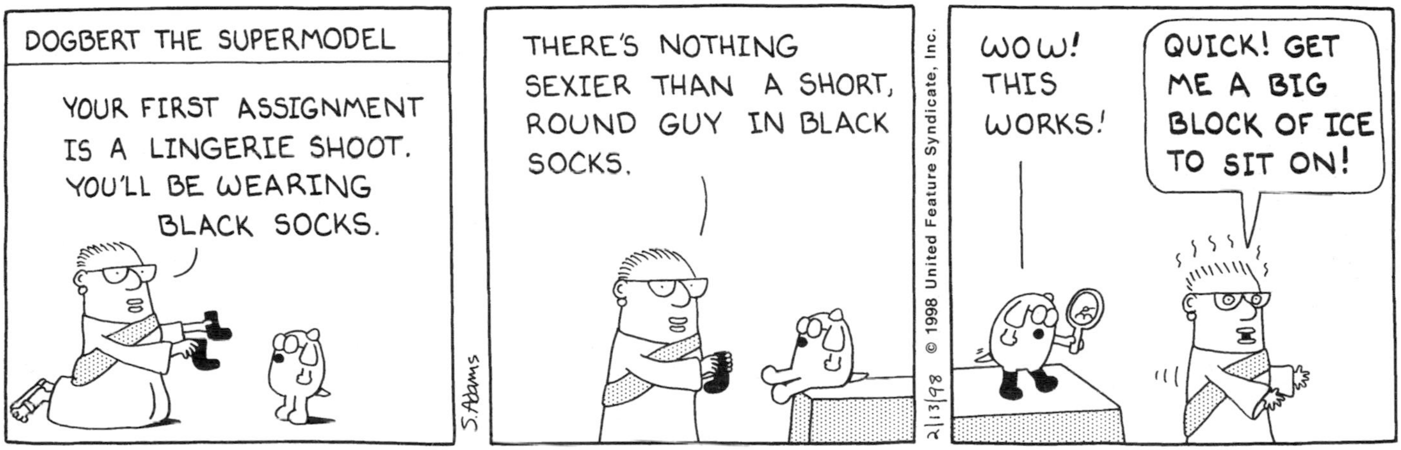
DOGBERT THE SUPERMODEL
YOUR FIRST ASSIGNMENT IS A LINGERIE SHOOT. YOU'LL BE WEARING BLACK SOCKS.
S. Adams
THERE'S NOTHING SEXIER THAN A SHORT, ROUND GUY IN BLACK SOCKS.
2/13/98 © 1998 United Feature Syndicate, Inc.
WOW! THIS WORKS!
QUICK! GET ME A BIG BLOCK OF ICE TO SIT ON!

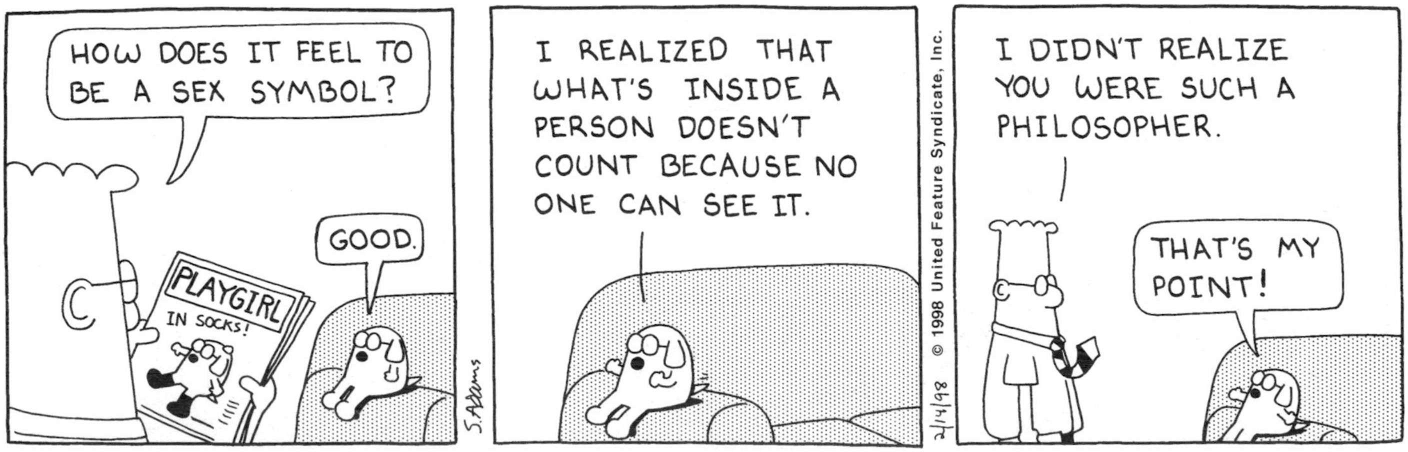
HOW DOES IT FEEL TO BE A SEX SYMBOL?
PLAYGIRL
IN SOCKS!
GOOD.
S. Adams
I REALIZED THAT WHAT'S INSIDE A PERSON DOESN'T COUNT BECAUSE NO ONE CAN SEE IT.
2/14/98 © 1998 United Feature Syndicate, Inc.
I DIDN'T REALIZE YOU WERE SUCH A PHILOSOPHER.
THAT'S MY POINT!

I FINISHED THE TECHNICAL RECOMMENDATION YOU REQUESTED.
S. Adams
AT FIRST I WAS MIFFED THAT YOU TOLD ME WHAT RECOMMENDATION YOU WANTED.
IT MADE ME FEEL USELESS AND WEAK.
BUT RATHER THAN DWELL ON MY POWERLESSNESS...
I DECIDED TO FIND JOY IN THE ONE DECISION I CAN MAKE.
2/15/98 © 1998 United Feature Syndicate, Inc.
I CHOSE A HELVETICA TYPE FONT.
AND I NEVER LOOKED BACK.
OH, SO THAT'S WHAT'S WRONG WITH IT.
I COACH AND I COACH, BUT THEY STILL WALK OUT OF HERE ALL RUBBER-LEGGED.

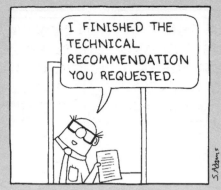

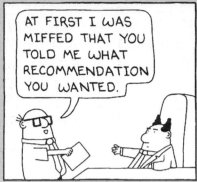

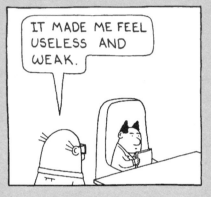

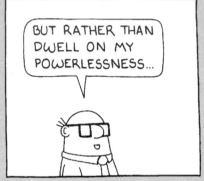

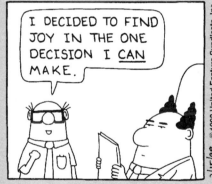

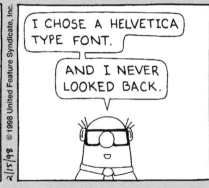

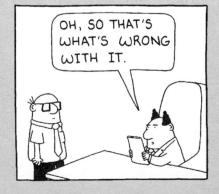

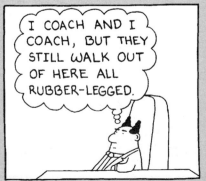

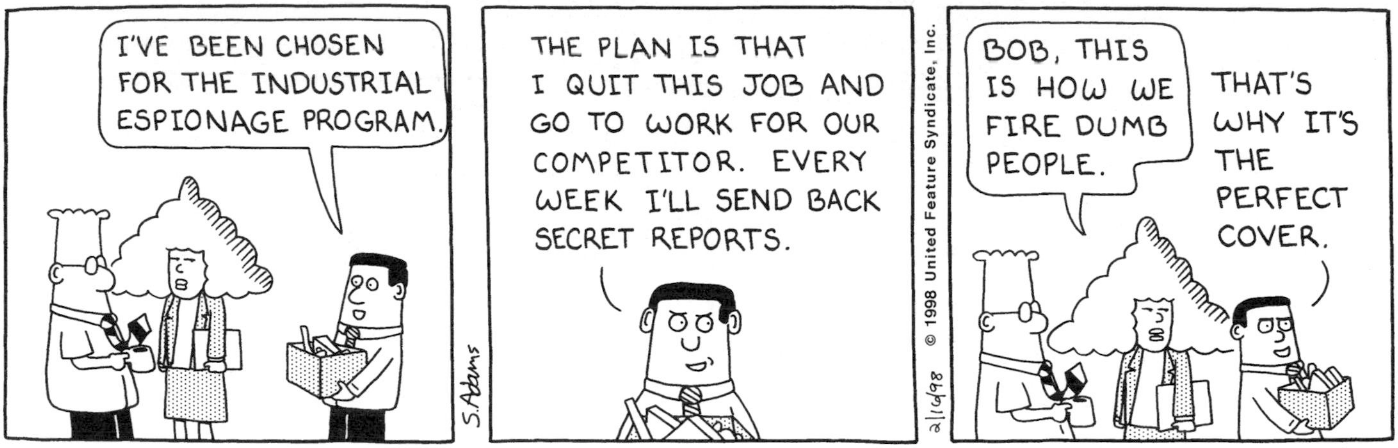
I'VE BEEN CHOSEN FOR THE INDUSTRIAL ESPIONAGE PROGRAM.
THE PLAN IS THAT I QUIT THIS JOB AND GO TO WORK FOR OUR COMPETITOR. EVERY WEEK I'LL SEND BACK SECRET REPORTS.
BOB, THIS IS HOW WE FIRE DUMB PEOPLE.
THAT'S WHY IT'S THE PERFECT COVER.
S. Adams
2/16/98
© 1998 United Feature Syndicate, Inc.

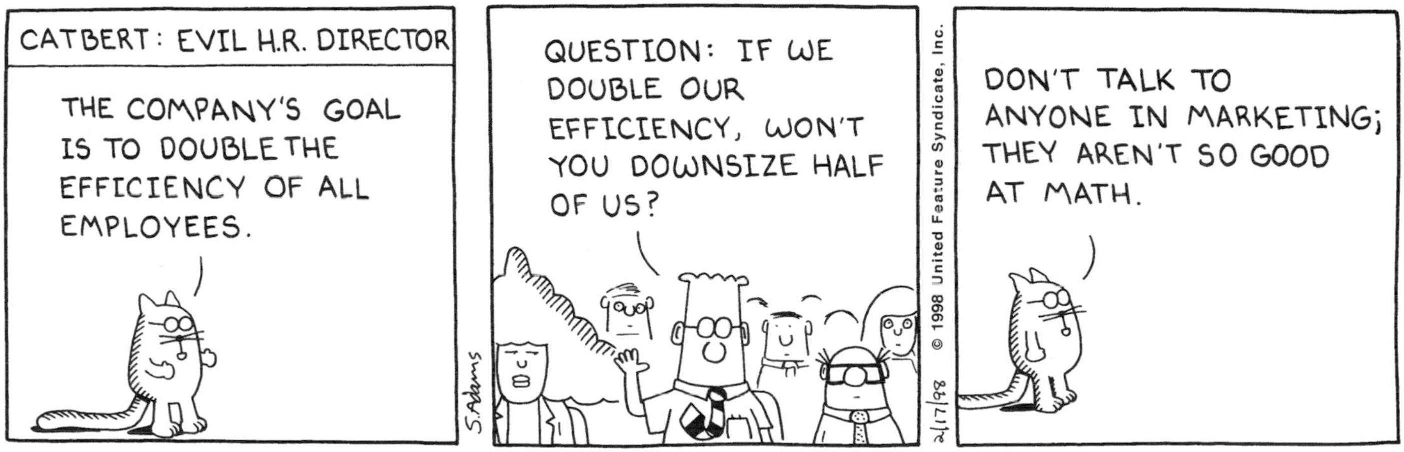
CATBERT: EVIL H.R. DIRECTOR
THE COMPANY'S GOAL IS TO DOUBLE THE EFFICIENCY OF ALL EMPLOYEES.
QUESTION: IF WE DOUBLE OUR EFFICIENCY, WON'T YOU DOWNSIZE HALF OF US?
DON'T TALK TO ANYONE IN MARKETING; THEY AREN'T SO GOOD AT MATH.
S. Adams
2/17/98
© 1998 United Feature Syndicate, Inc.

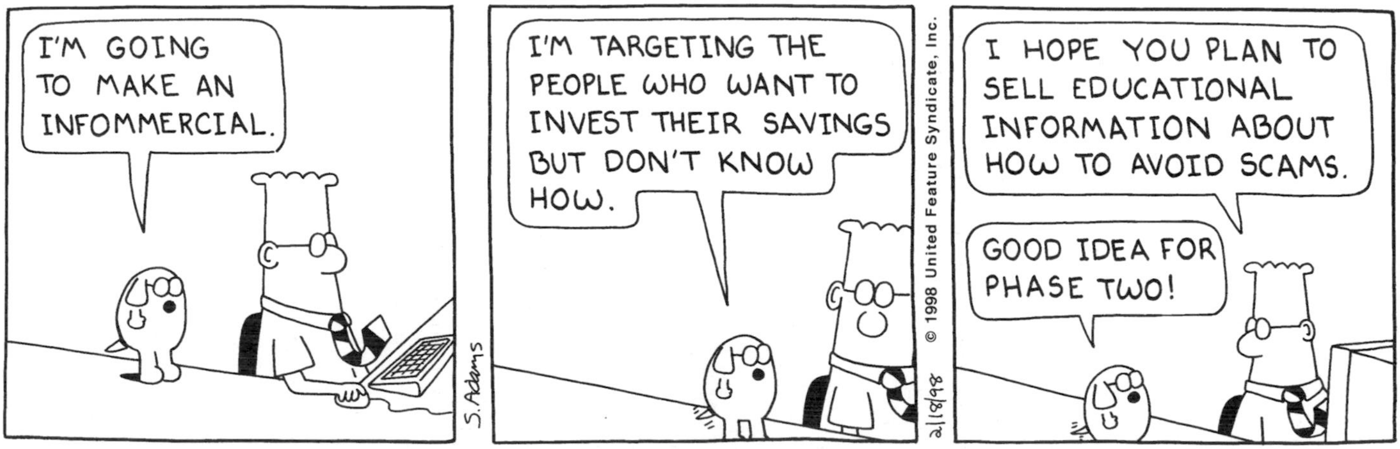
I'M GOING TO MAKE AN INFOMMERCIAL.
I'M TARGETING THE PEOPLE WHO WANT TO INVEST THEIR SAVINGS BUT DON'T KNOW HOW.
I HOPE YOU PLAN TO SELL EDUCATIONAL INFORMATION ABOUT HOW TO AVOID SCAMS.
GOOD IDEA FOR PHASE TWO!
S. Adams
2/18/98
© 1998 United Feature Syndicate, Inc.

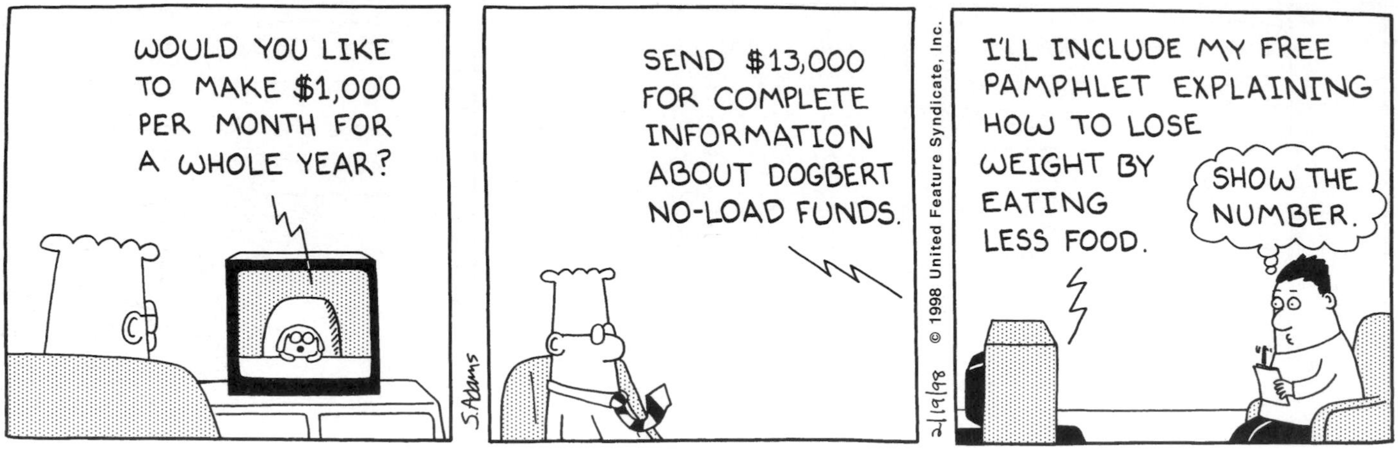
WOULD YOU LIKE TO MAKE $1,000 PER MONTH FOR A WHOLE YEAR?
S. Adams
SEND $13,000 FOR COMPLETE INFORMATION ABOUT DOGBERT NO-LOAD FUNDS.
2/19/98 © 1998 United Feature Syndicate, Inc.
I'LL INCLUDE MY FREE PAMPHLET EXPLAINING HOW TO LOSE WEIGHT BY EATING LESS FOOD.
SHOW THE NUMBER.

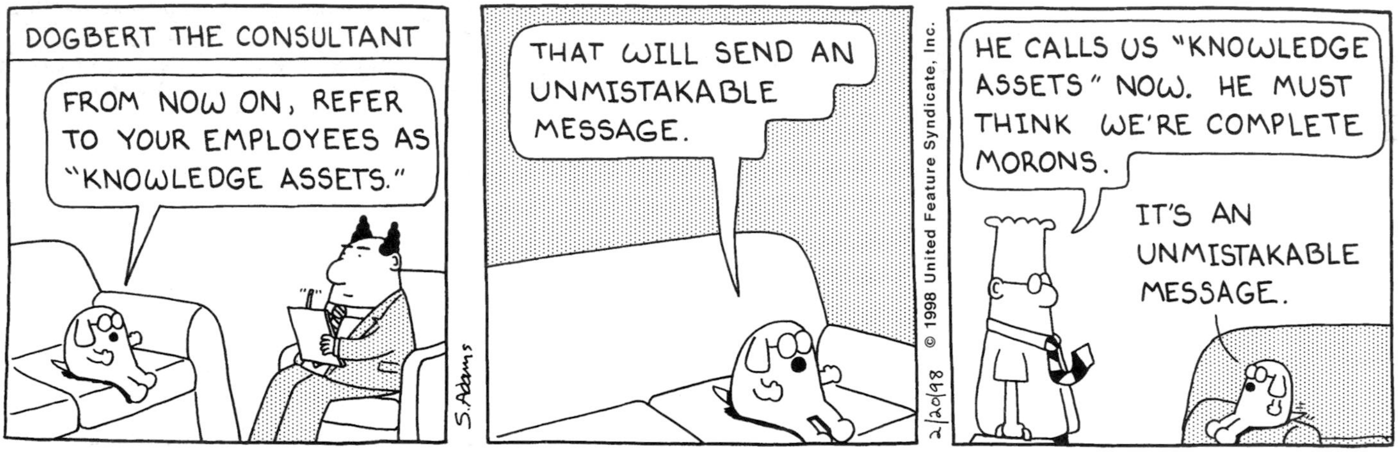
DOGBERT THE CONSULTANT
FROM NOW ON, REFER TO YOUR EMPLOYEES AS "KNOWLEDGE ASSETS."
S. Adams
THAT WILL SEND AN UNMISTAKABLE MESSAGE.
2/20/98 © 1998 United Feature Syndicate, Inc.
HE CALLS US "KNOWLEDGE ASSETS" NOW. HE MUST THINK WE'RE COMPLETE MORONS.
IT'S AN UNMISTAKABLE MESSAGE.

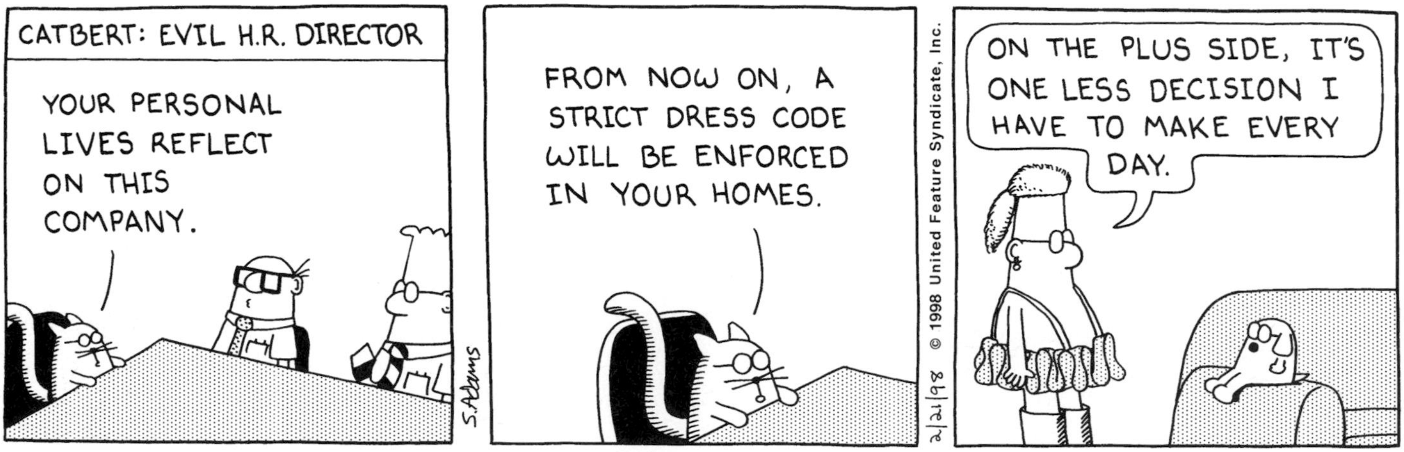
CATBERT: EVIL H.R. DIRECTOR
YOUR PERSONAL LIVES REFLECT ON THIS COMPANY.
S. Adams
FROM NOW ON, A STRICT DRESS CODE WILL BE ENFORCED IN YOUR HOMES.
2/21/98 © 1998 United Feature Syndicate, Inc.
ON THE PLUS SIDE, IT'S ONE LESS DECISION I HAVE TO MAKE EVERY DAY.

HAPPY BIRTHDAY, ALICE!
I WAS PLANNING TO GET A GIFT...
BUT THEN I THOUGHT...
WHY NOT GIVE THE MONEY TO CHARITY IN ALICE'S NAME?
REALLY? WHICH CHARITY?
UMM... "THE UNITED SOCIETY OF POOR PEOPLE WITH MAJOR HEALTH PROBLEMS."
S.Adams
2/22/98 © 1998 United Feature Syndicate, Inc.

...AND DILBERT GOT ME AN ASHTRAY, EVEN THOUGH I DON'T SMOKE.
YOU DON'T?
THEY SAY THIS SORT OF THING BUILDS TEAM SPIRIT.
IT MUST BE GRADUAL.

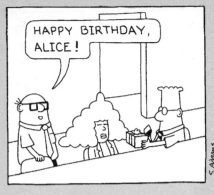

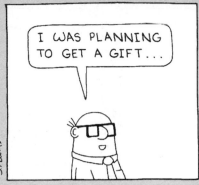

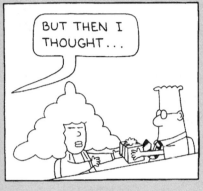

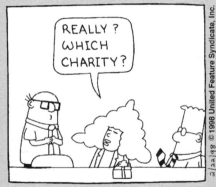

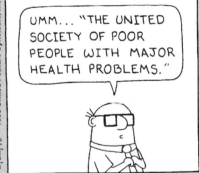

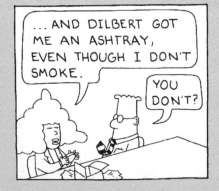

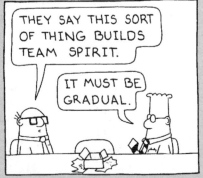

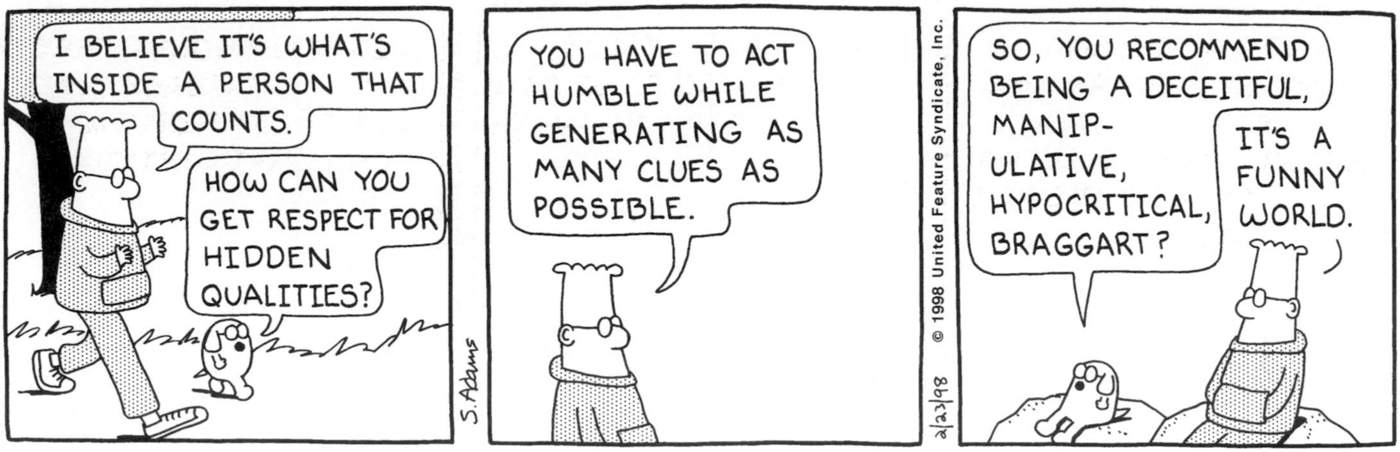
I BELIEVE IT'S WHAT'S INSIDE A PERSON THAT COUNTS.
HOW CAN YOU GET RESPECT FOR HIDDEN QUALITIES?
S. Adams
YOU HAVE TO ACT HUMBLE WHILE GENERATING AS MANY CLUES AS POSSIBLE.
2/23/98 © 1998 United Feature Syndicate, Inc.
SO, YOU RECOMMEND BEING A DECEITFUL, MANIP-ULATIVE, HYPOCRITICAL, BRAGGART?
IT'S A FUNNY WORLD.

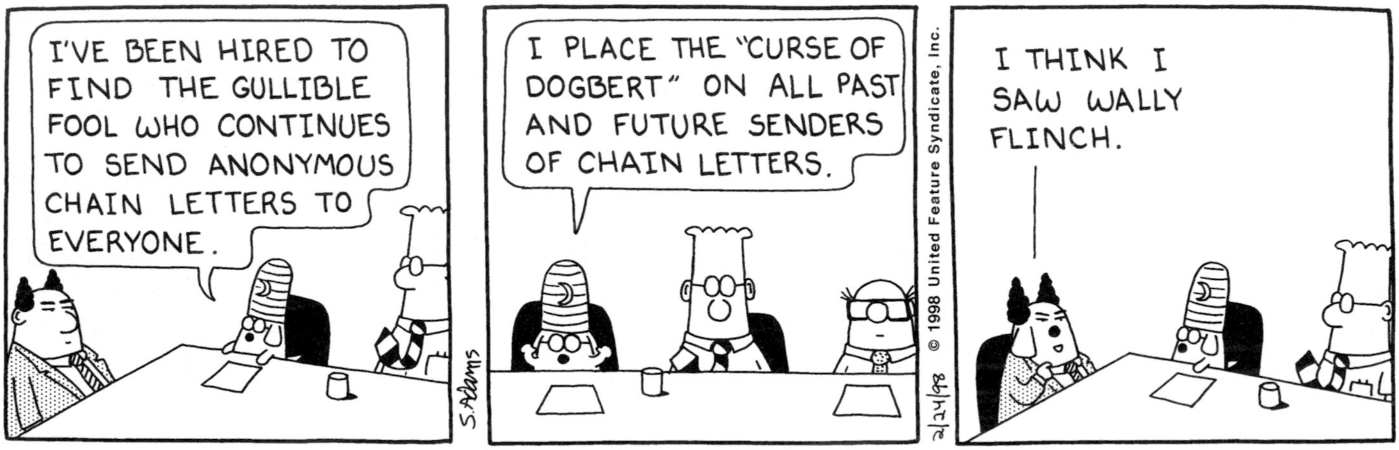
I'VE BEEN HIRED TO FIND THE GULLIBLE FOOL WHO CONTINUES TO SEND ANONYMOUS CHAIN LETTERS TO EVERYONE.
S. Adams
I PLACE THE "CURSE OF DOGBERT" ON ALL PAST AND FUTURE SENDERS OF CHAIN LETTERS.
2/24/98 © 1998 United Feature Syndicate, Inc.
I THINK I SAW WALLY FLINCH.

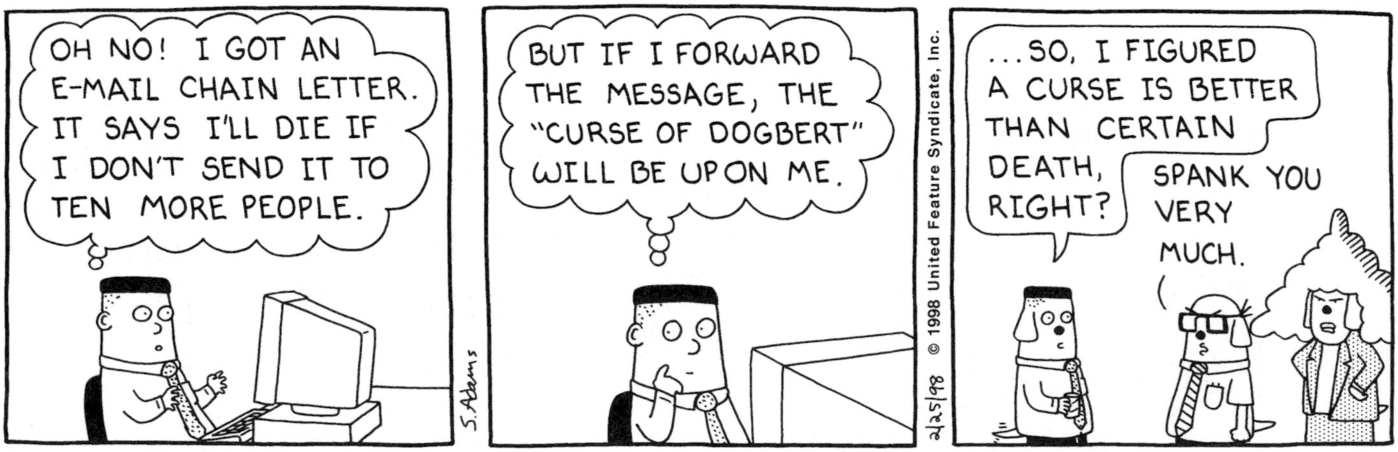
OH NO! I GOT AN E-MAIL CHAIN LETTER. IT SAYS I'LL DIE IF I DON'T SEND IT TO TEN MORE PEOPLE.
S. Adams
BUT IF I FORWARD THE MESSAGE, THE "CURSE OF DOGBERT" WILL BE UPON ME.
2/25/98 © 1998 United Feature Syndicate, Inc.
...SO, I FIGURED A CURSE IS BETTER THAN CERTAIN DEATH, RIGHT?
SPANK YOU VERY MUCH.

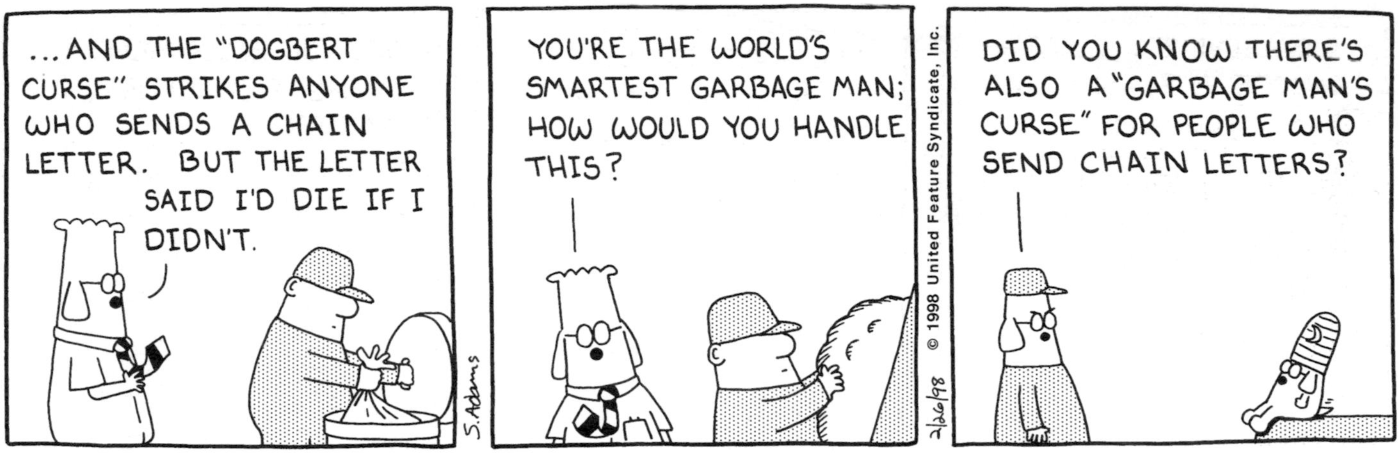
...AND THE "DOGBERT CURSE" STRIKES ANYONE WHO SENDS A CHAIN LETTER. BUT THE LETTER SAID I'D DIE IF I DIDN'T.
S. Adams
YOU'RE THE WORLD'S SMARTEST GARBAGE MAN; HOW WOULD YOU HANDLE THIS?
2/26/98 © 1998 United Feature Syndicate, Inc.
DID YOU KNOW THERE'S ALSO A "GARBAGE MAN'S CURSE" FOR PEOPLE WHO SEND CHAIN LETTERS?

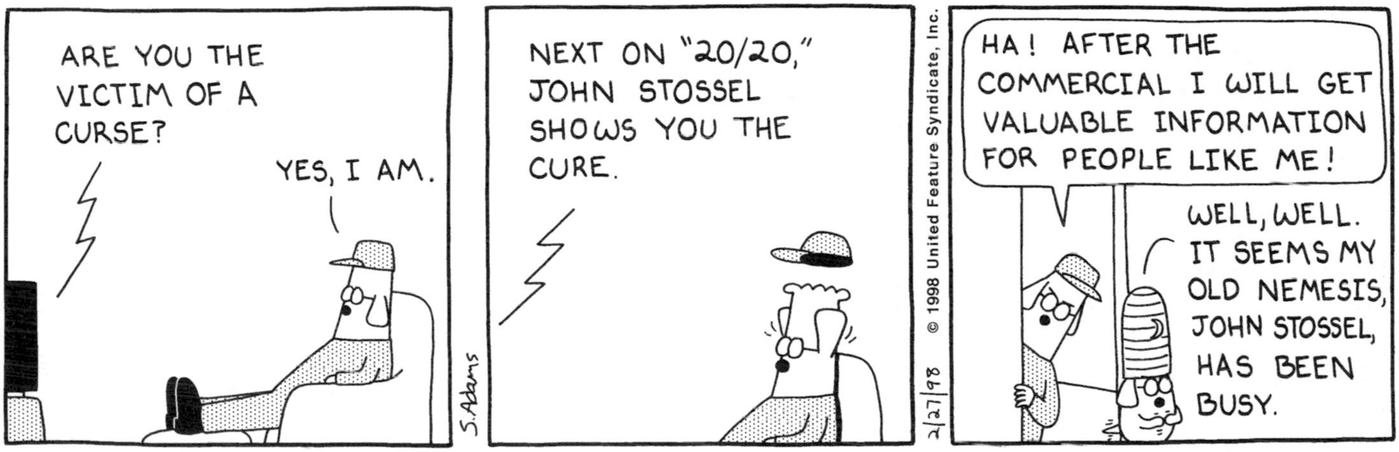
ARE YOU THE VICTIM OF A CURSE?
YES, I AM.
S. Adams
NEXT ON "20/20," JOHN STOSSEL SHOWS YOU THE CURE.
2/27/98 © 1998 United Feature Syndicate, Inc.
HA! AFTER THE COMMERCIAL I WILL GET VALUABLE INFORMATION FOR PEOPLE LIKE ME!
WELL, WELL. IT SEEMS MY OLD NEMESIS, JOHN STOSSEL, HAS BEEN BUSY.

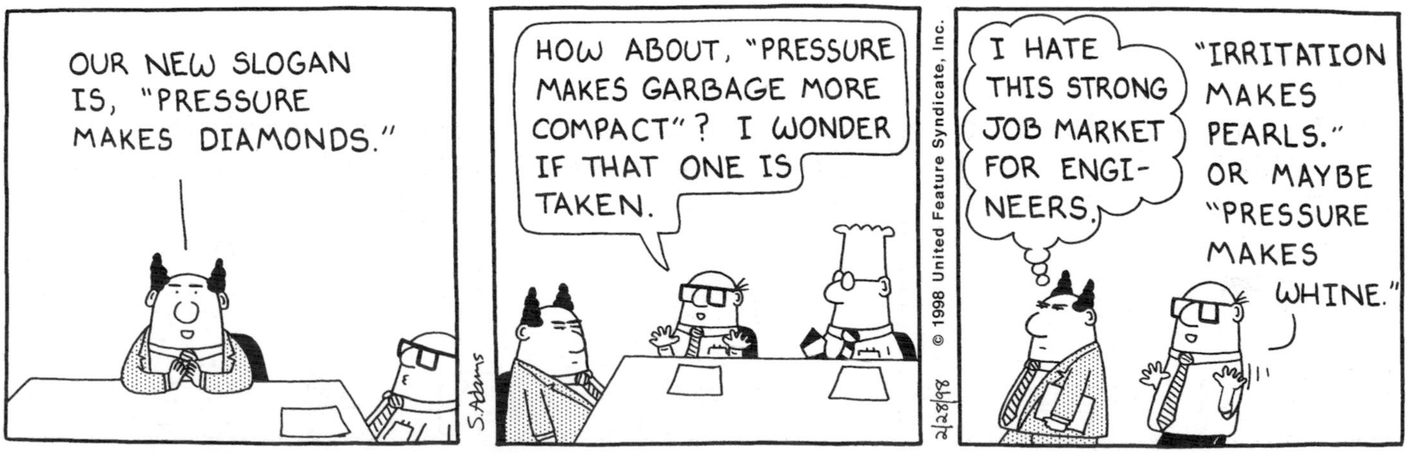
OUR NEW SLOGAN IS, "PRESSURE MAKES DIAMONDS."
S. Adams
HOW ABOUT, "PRESSURE MAKES GARBAGE MORE COMPACT"? I WONDER IF THAT ONE IS TAKEN.
2/28/98 © 1998 United Feature Syndicate, Inc.
I HATE THIS STRONG JOB MARKET FOR ENGINEERS.
"IRRITATION MAKES PEARLS." OR MAYBE "PRESSURE MAKES WHINE."

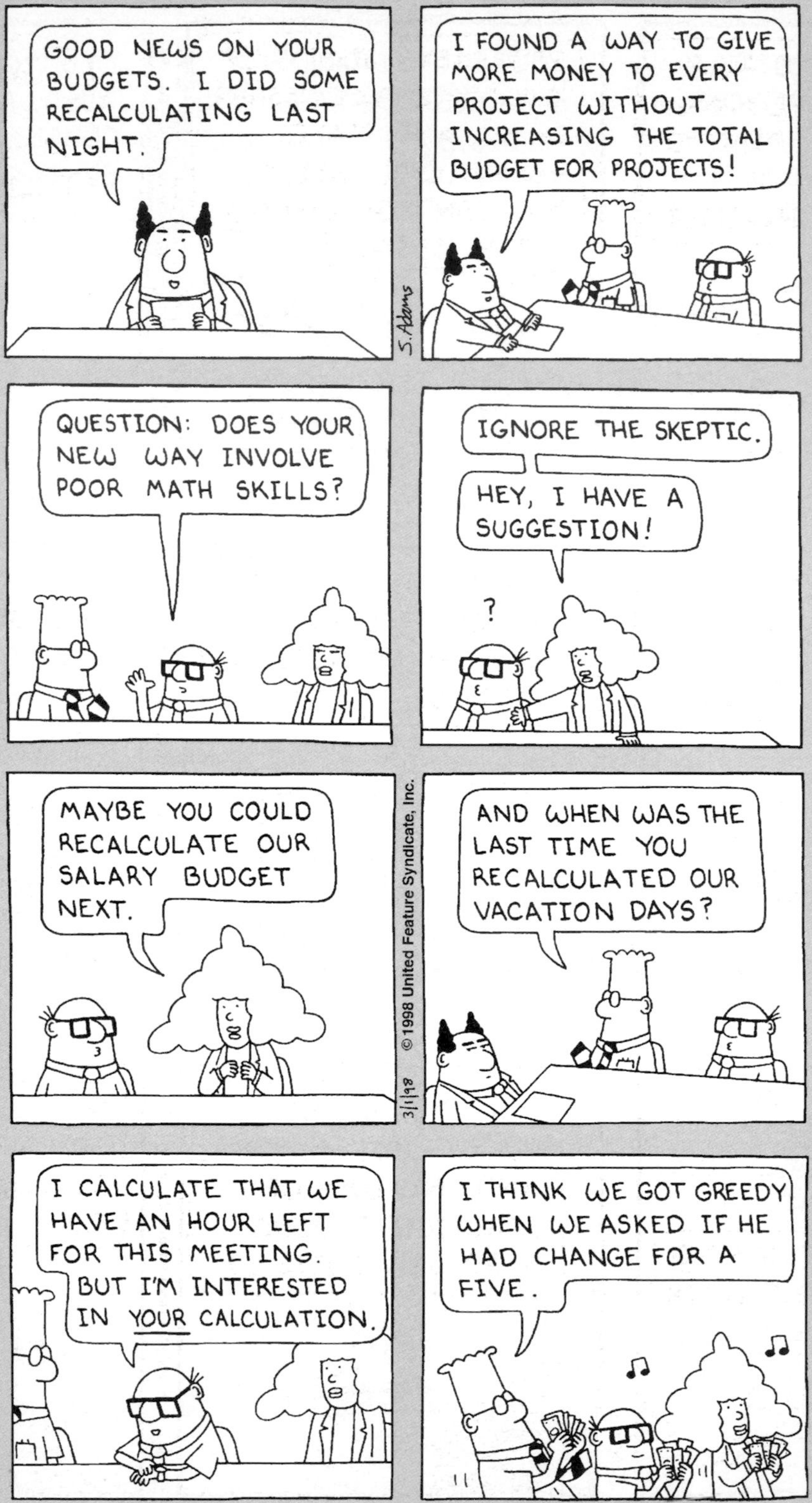
GOOD NEWS ON YOUR BUDGETS. I DID SOME RECALCULATING LAST NIGHT.
I FOUND A WAY TO GIVE MORE MONEY TO EVERY PROJECT WITHOUT INCREASING THE TOTAL BUDGET FOR PROJECTS!
S. Adams
QUESTION: DOES YOUR NEW WAY INVOLVE POOR MATH SKILLS?
IGNORE THE SKEPTIC.
HEY, I HAVE A SUGGESTION!
?
MAYBE YOU COULD RECALCULATE OUR SALARY BUDGET NEXT.
© 1998 United Feature Syndicate, Inc.
3/1/98
AND WHEN WAS THE LAST TIME YOU RECALCULATED OUR VACATION DAYS?
I CALCULATE THAT WE HAVE AN HOUR LEFT FOR THIS MEETING.
BUT I'M INTERESTED IN YOUR CALCULATION.
I THINK WE GOT GREEDY WHEN WE ASKED IF HE HAD CHANGE FOR A FIVE.

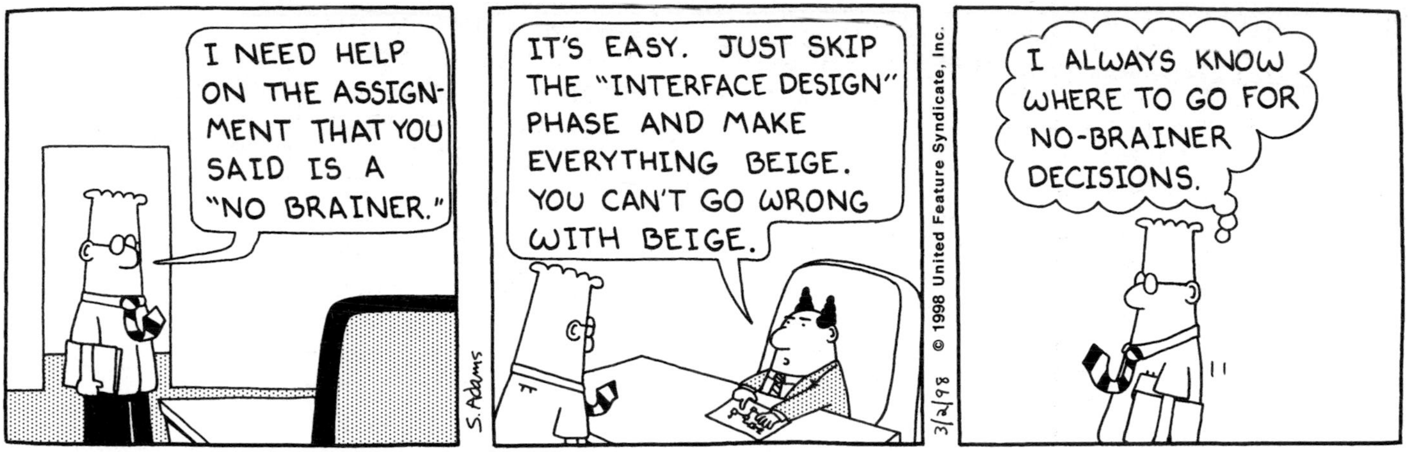
I NEED HELP ON THE ASSIGNMENT THAT YOU SAID IS A "NO BRAINER."
S. Adams
IT'S EASY. JUST SKIP THE "INTERFACE DESIGN" PHASE AND MAKE EVERYTHING BEIGE. YOU CAN'T GO WRONG WITH BEIGE.
3/2/98 © 1998 United Feature Syndicate, Inc.
I ALWAYS KNOW WHERE TO GO FOR NO-BRAINER DECISIONS.

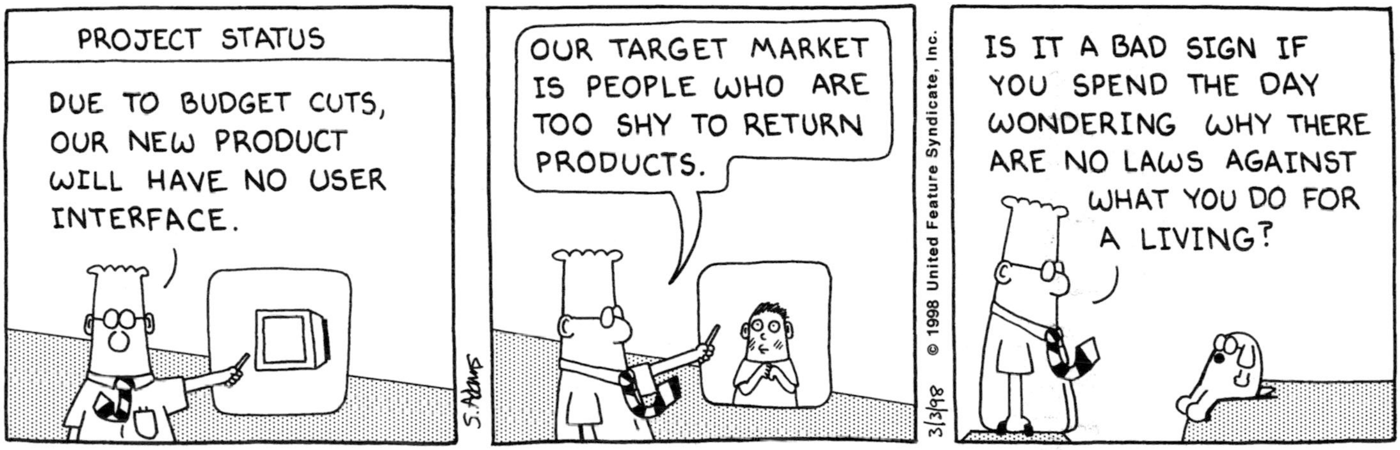
PROJECT STATUS
DUE TO BUDGET CUTS, OUR NEW PRODUCT WILL HAVE NO USER INTERFACE.
S. Adams
OUR TARGET MARKET IS PEOPLE WHO ARE TOO SHY TO RETURN PRODUCTS.
3/3/98 © 1998 United Feature Syndicate, Inc.
IS IT A BAD SIGN IF YOU SPEND THE DAY WONDERING WHY THERE ARE NO LAWS AGAINST WHAT YOU DO FOR A LIVING?

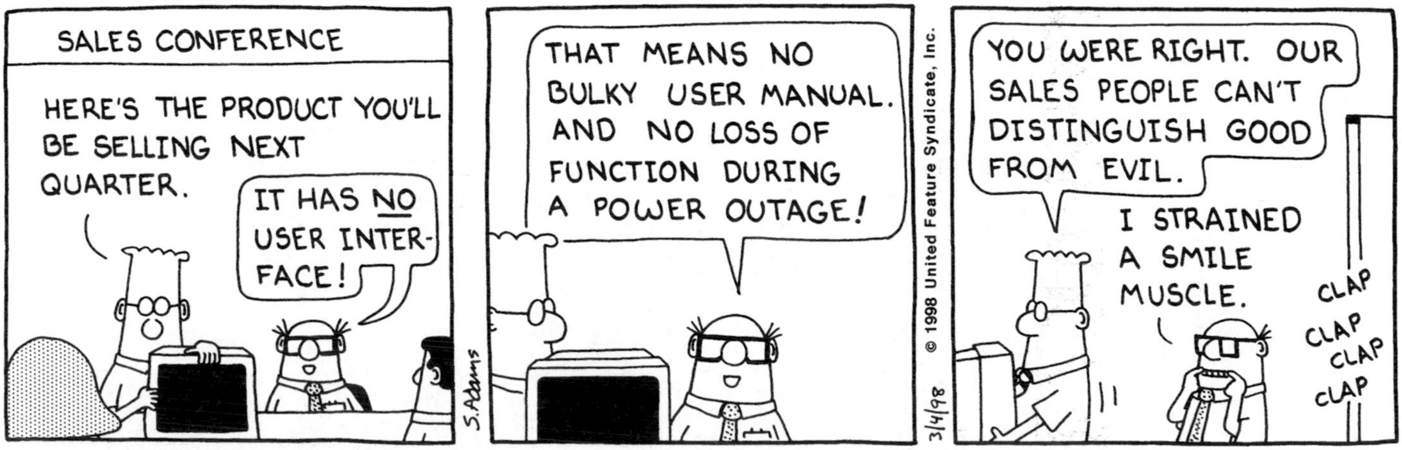
SALES CONFERENCE
HERE'S THE PRODUCT YOU'LL BE SELLING NEXT QUARTER.
IT HAS NO USER INTERFACE!
S. Adams
THAT MEANS NO BULKY USER MANUAL. AND NO LOSS OF FUNCTION DURING A POWER OUTAGE!
3/4/98 © 1998 United Feature Syndicate, Inc.
YOU WERE RIGHT. OUR SALES PEOPLE CAN'T DISTINGUISH GOOD FROM EVIL.
I STRAINED A SMILE MUSCLE.
CLAP
CLAP
CLAP
CLAP

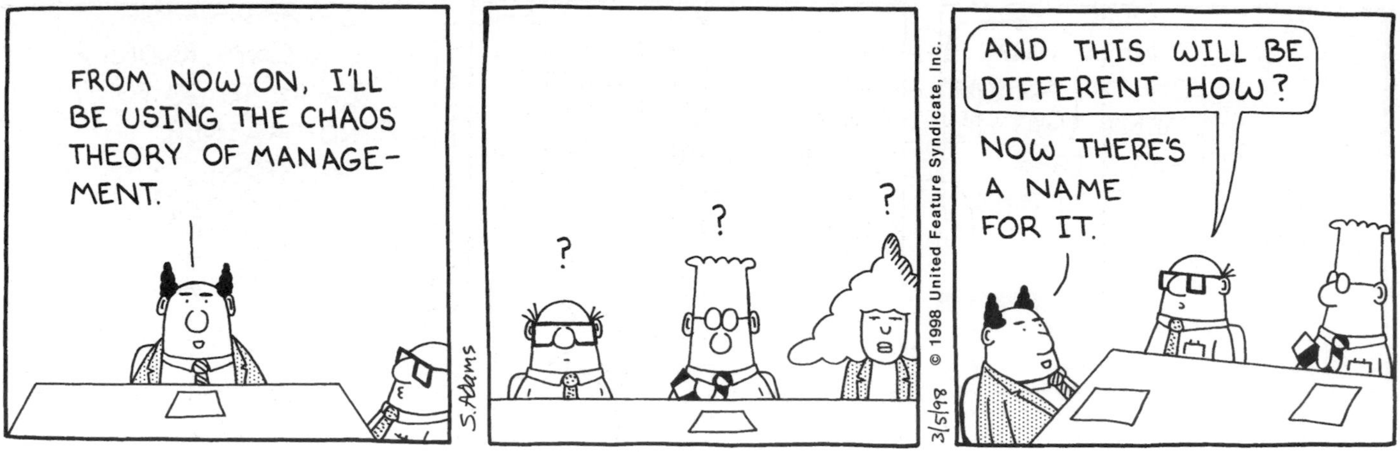
FROM NOW ON, I'LL BE USING THE CHAOS THEORY OF MANAGEMENT.
?
?
?
S. Adams
© 1998 United Feature Syndicate, Inc.
3/5/98
NOW THERE'S A NAME FOR IT.
AND THIS WILL BE DIFFERENT HOW?

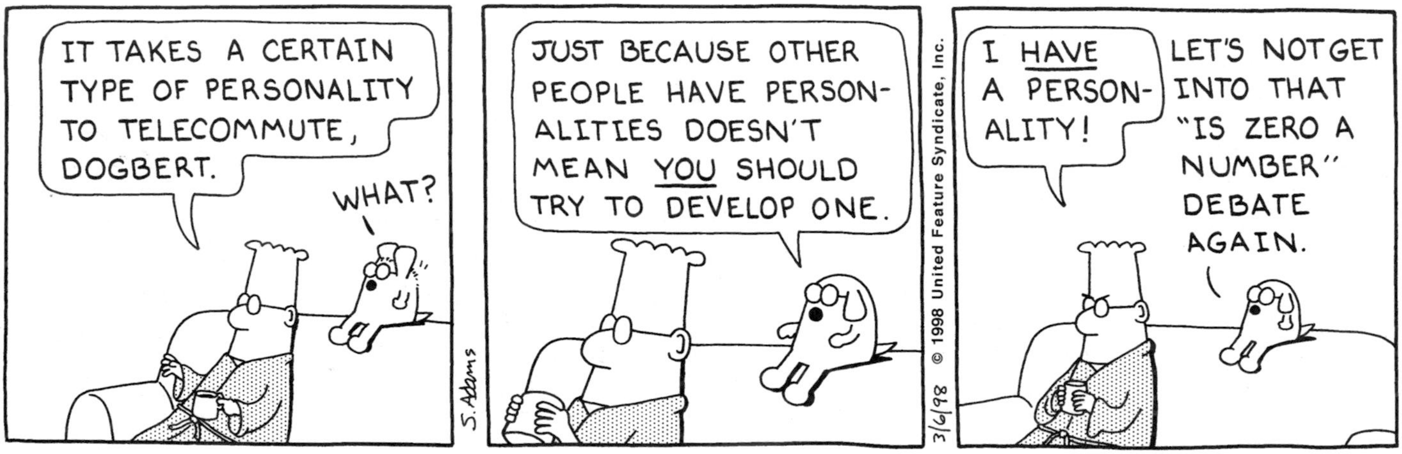
IT TAKES A CERTAIN TYPE OF PERSONALITY TO TELECOMMUTE, DOGBERT.
WHAT?
S. Adams
JUST BECAUSE OTHER PEOPLE HAVE PERSONALITIES DOESN'T MEAN YOU SHOULD TRY TO DEVELOP ONE.
© 1998 United Feature Syndicate, Inc.
3/6/98
I HAVE A PERSONALITY!
LET'S NOT GET INTO THAT "IS ZERO A NUMBER" DEBATE AGAIN.

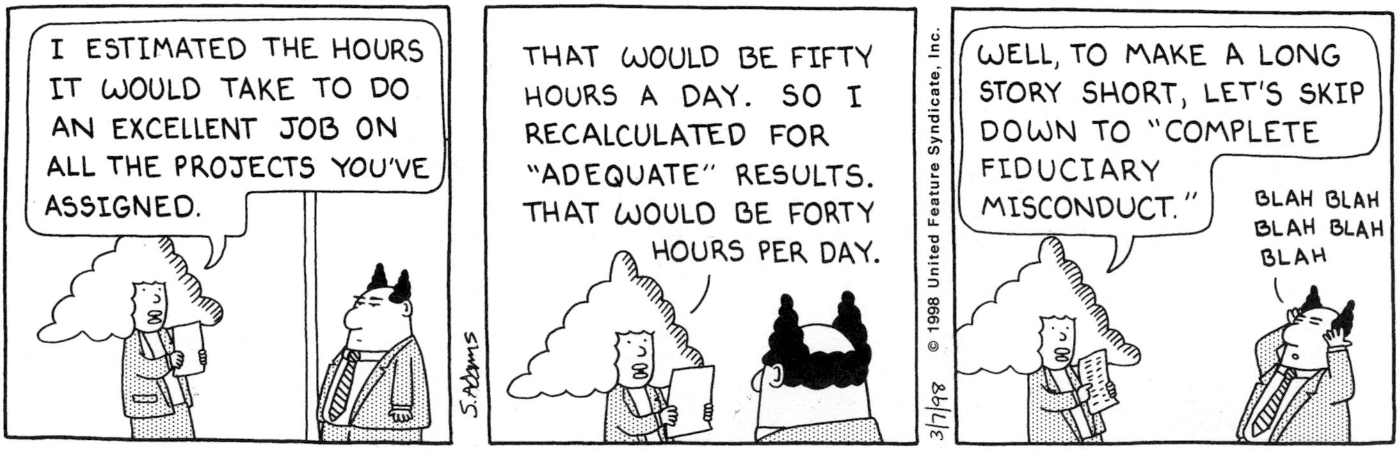
I ESTIMATED THE HOURS IT WOULD TAKE TO DO AN EXCELLENT JOB ON ALL THE PROJECTS YOU'VE ASSIGNED.
S. Adams
THAT WOULD BE FIFTY HOURS A DAY. SO I RECALCULATED FOR "ADEQUATE" RESULTS. THAT WOULD BE FORTY HOURS PER DAY.
© 1998 United Feature Syndicate, Inc.
3/7/98
WELL, TO MAKE A LONG STORY SHORT, LET'S SKIP DOWN TO "COMPLETE FIDUCIARY MISCONDUCT."
BLAH BLAH BLAH BLAH BLAH

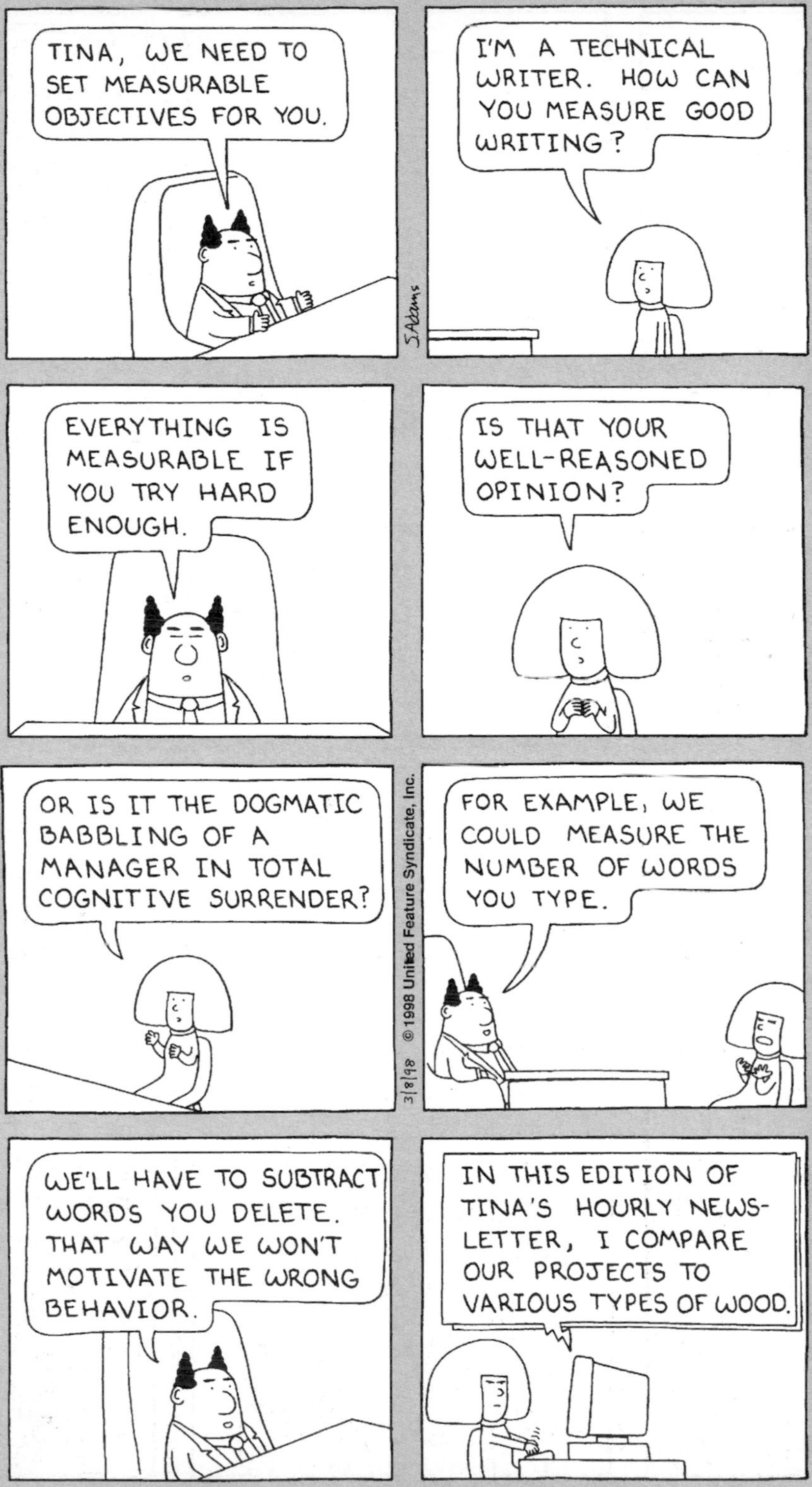
TINA, WE NEED TO SET MEASURABLE OBJECTIVES FOR YOU.
I'M A TECHNICAL WRITER. HOW CAN YOU MEASURE GOOD WRITING?
EVERYTHING IS MEASURABLE IF YOU TRY HARD ENOUGH.
IS THAT YOUR WELL-REASONED OPINION?
OR IS IT THE DOGMATIC BABBLING OF A MANAGER IN TOTAL COGNITIVE SURRENDER?
FOR EXAMPLE, WE COULD MEASURE THE NUMBER OF WORDS YOU TYPE.
WE'LL HAVE TO SUBTRACT WORDS YOU DELETE. THAT WAY WE WON'T MOTIVATE THE WRONG BEHAVIOR.
IN THIS EDITION OF TINA'S HOURLY NEWS-LETTER, I COMPARE OUR PROJECTS TO VARIOUS TYPES OF WOOD.
S.Adams
3/8/98 © 1998 United Feature Syndicate, Inc.

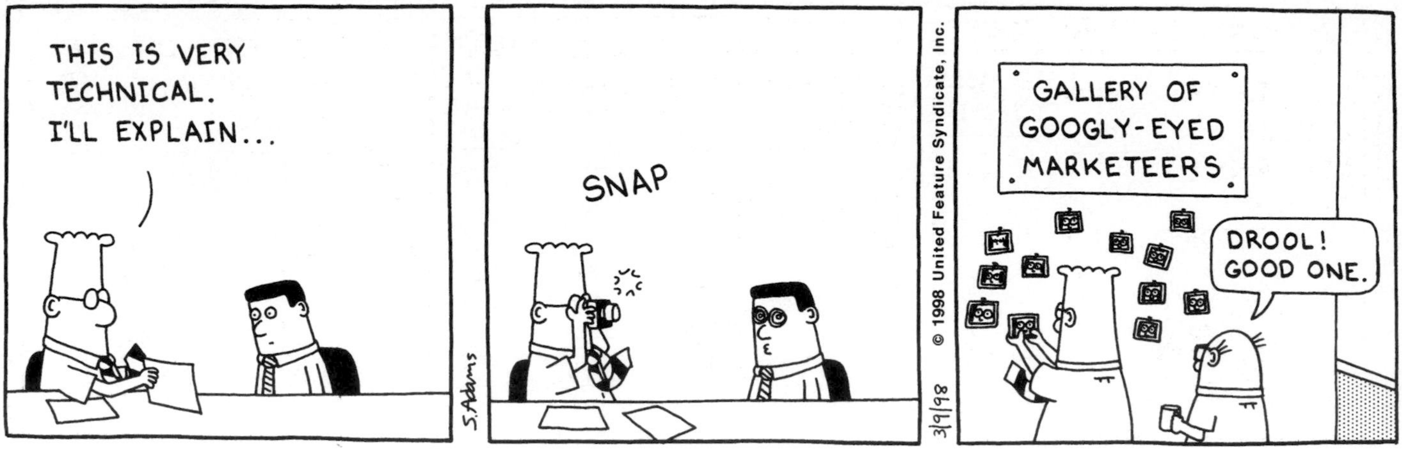
THIS IS VERY TECHNICAL. I'LL EXPLAIN...
SNAP
GALLERY OF GOOGLY-EYED MARKETEERS
DROOL! GOOD ONE.
S. Adams
3/9/98 © 1998 United Feature Syndicate, Inc.

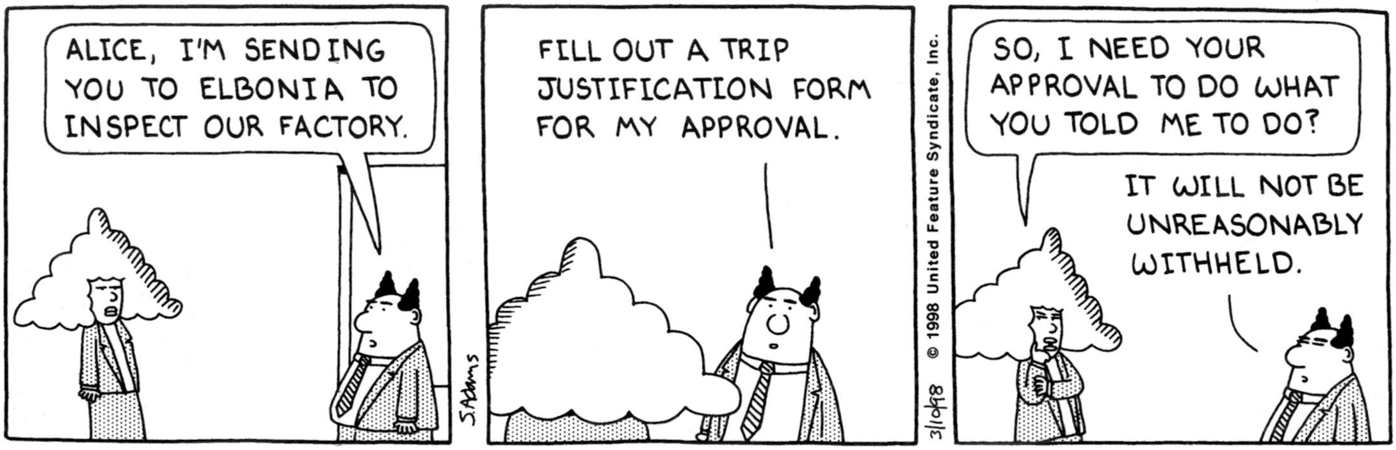
ALICE, I'M SENDING YOU TO ELBONIA TO INSPECT OUR FACTORY.
FILL OUT A TRIP JUSTIFICATION FORM FOR MY APPROVAL.
SO, I NEED YOUR APPROVAL TO DO WHAT YOU TOLD ME TO DO?
IT WILL NOT BE UNREASONABLY WITHHELD.
S. Adams
3/10/98 © 1998 United Feature Syndicate, Inc.

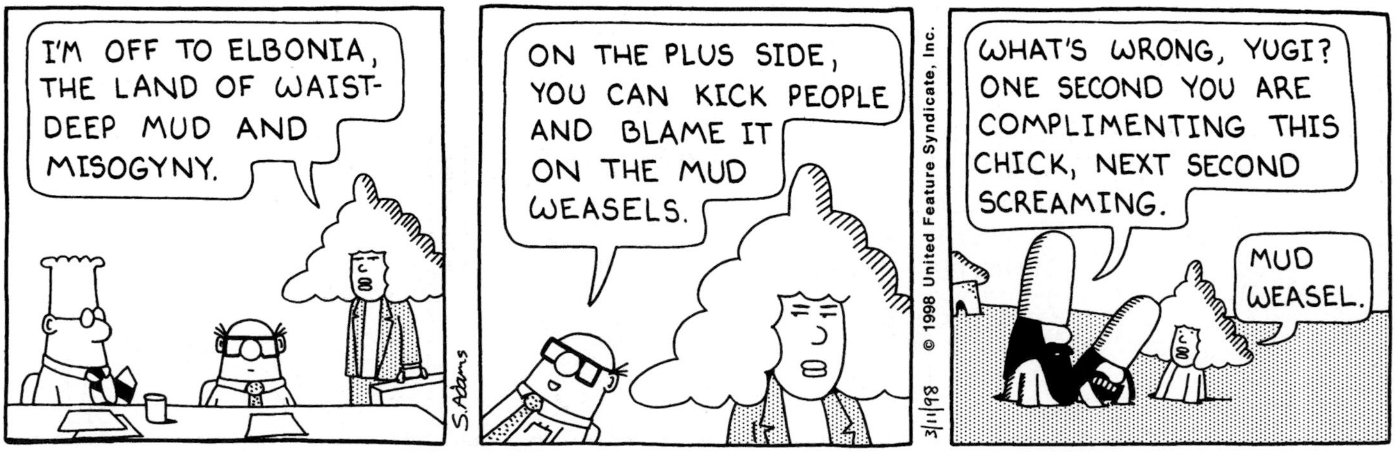
I'M OFF TO ELBONIA, THE LAND OF WAIST-DEEP MUD AND MISOGYNY.
ON THE PLUS SIDE, YOU CAN KICK PEOPLE AND BLAME IT ON THE MUD WEASELS.
WHAT'S WRONG, YUGI? ONE SECOND YOU ARE COMPLIMENTING THIS CHICK, NEXT SECOND SCREAMING.
MUD WEASEL.
S. Adams
3/11/98 © 1998 United Feature Syndicate, Inc.

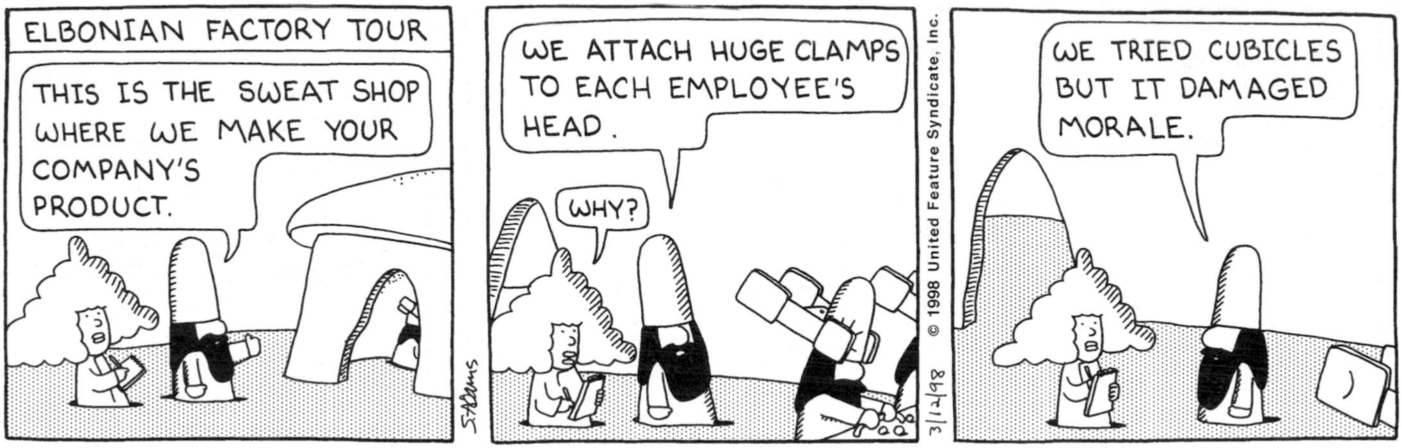
ELBONIAN FACTORY TOUR
THIS IS THE SWEAT SHOP WHERE WE MAKE YOUR COMPANY'S PRODUCT.
WE ATTACH HUGE CLAMPS TO EACH EMPLOYEE'S HEAD.
WHY?
WE TRIED CUBICLES BUT IT DAMAGED MORALE.
© 1998 United Feature Syndicate, Inc.
3/12/98

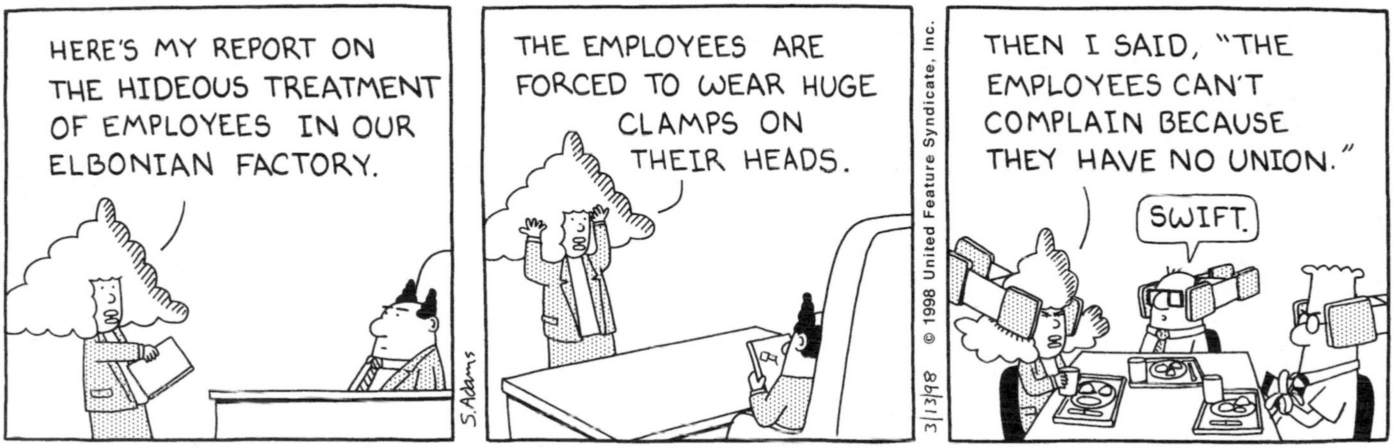
HERE'S MY REPORT ON THE HIDEOUS TREATMENT OF EMPLOYEES IN OUR ELBONIAN FACTORY.
THE EMPLOYEES ARE FORCED TO WEAR HUGE CLAMPS ON THEIR HEADS.
THEN I SAID, "THE EMPLOYEES CAN'T COMPLAIN BECAUSE THEY HAVE NO UNION."
SWIFT.
© 1998 United Feature Syndicate, Inc.
3/13/98

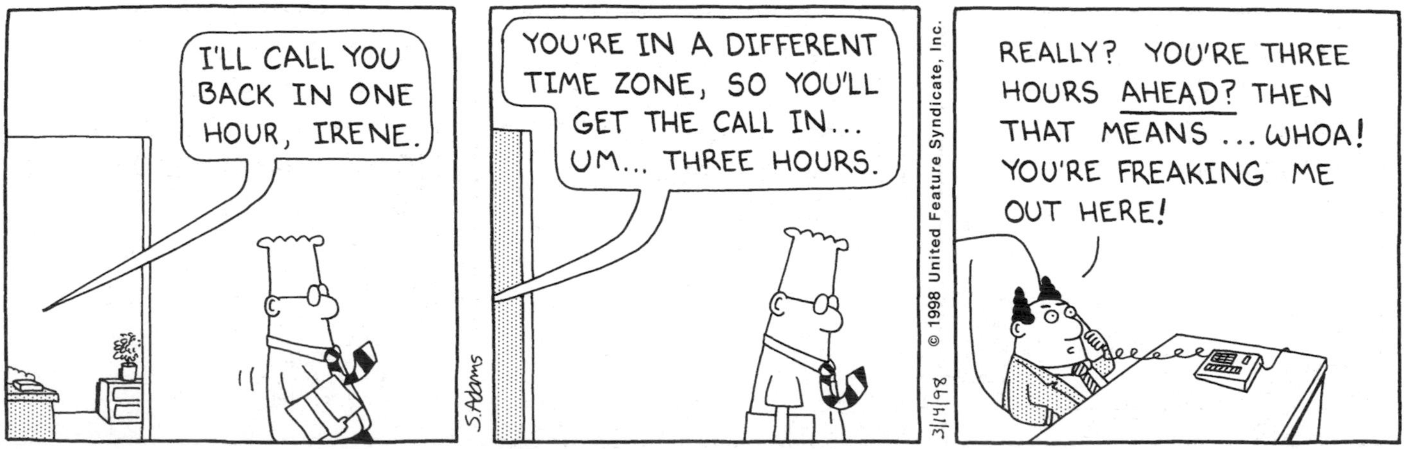
I'LL CALL YOU BACK IN ONE HOUR, IRENE.
YOU'RE IN A DIFFERENT TIME ZONE, SO YOU'LL GET THE CALL IN... UM... THREE HOURS.
REALLY? YOU'RE THREE HOURS AHEAD? THEN THAT MEANS ... WHOA! YOU'RE FREAKING ME OUT HERE!
© 1998 United Feature Syndicate, Inc.
3/14/98

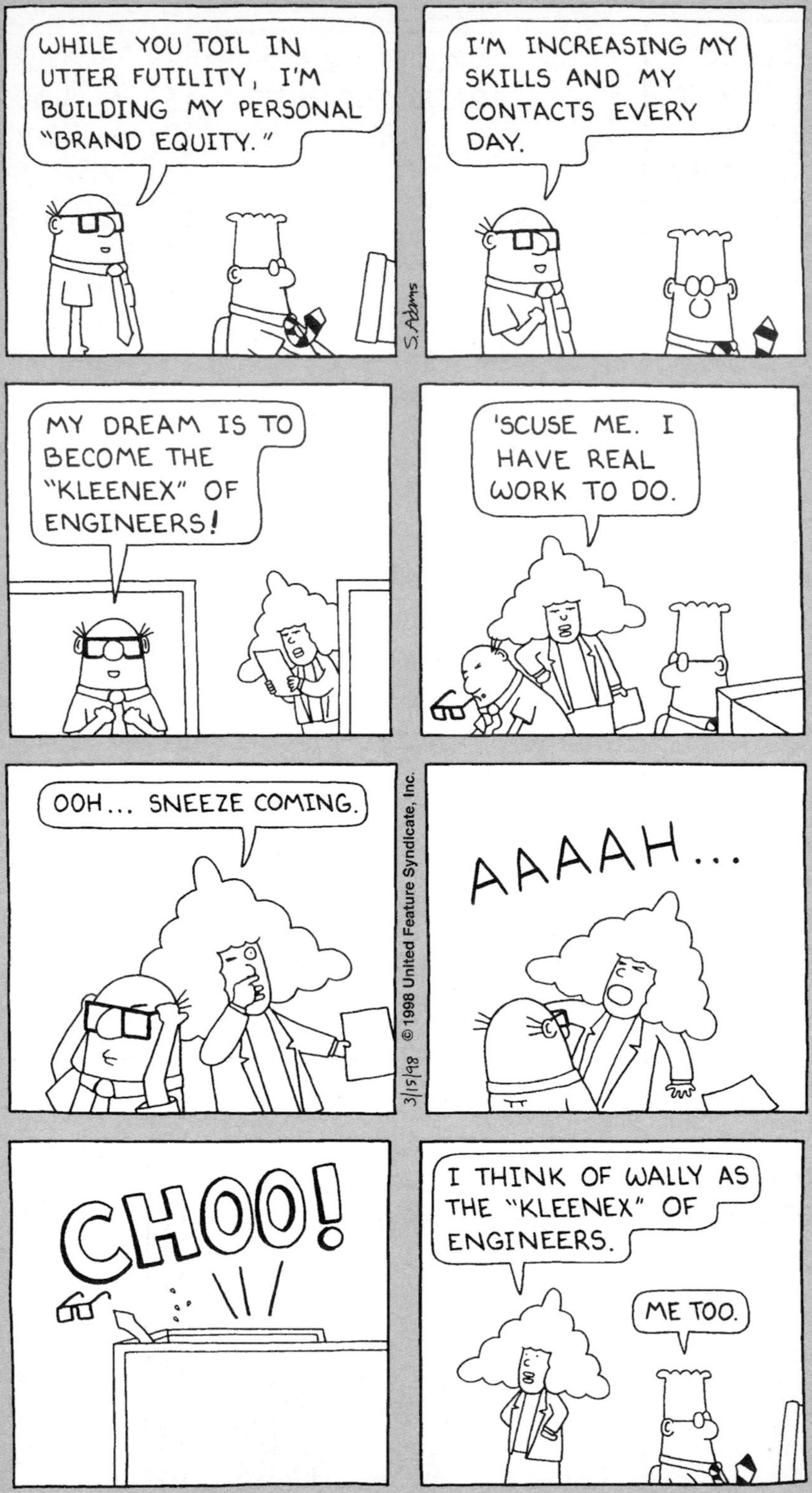
WHILE YOU TOIL IN UTTER FUTILITY, I'M BUILDING MY PERSONAL "BRAND EQUITY."
S. Adams
I'M INCREASING MY SKILLS AND MY CONTACTS EVERY DAY.
MY DREAM IS TO BECOME THE "KLEENEX" OF ENGINEERS!
'SCUSE ME. I HAVE REAL WORK TO DO.
OOH... SNEEZE COMING.
3/15/98 © 1998 United Feature Syndicate, Inc.
AAAAH...
CHOO!
I THINK OF WALLY AS THE "KLEENEX" OF ENGINEERS.
ME TOO.

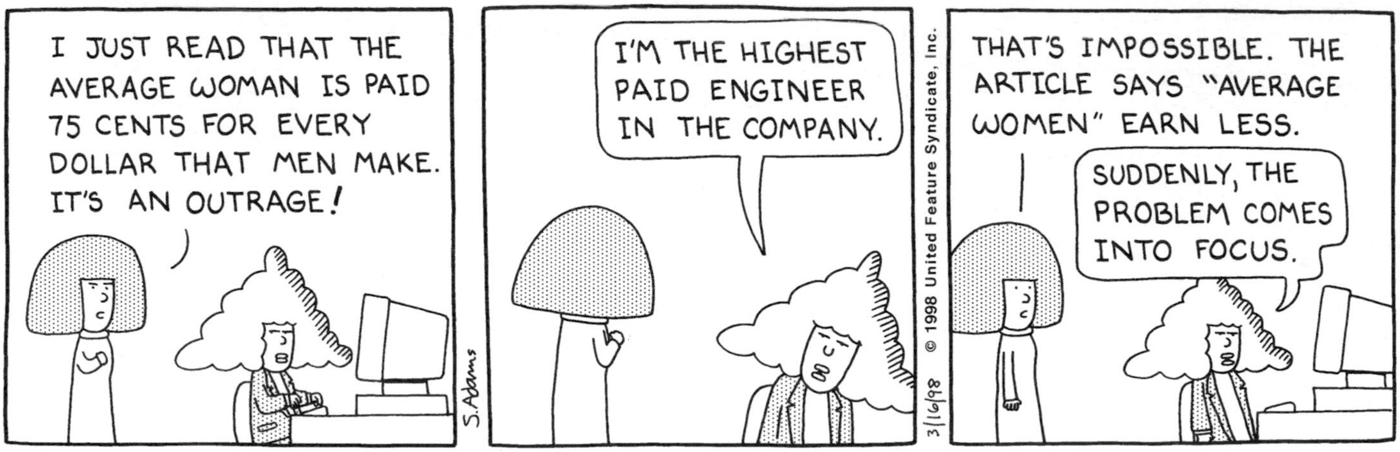
I JUST READ THAT THE AVERAGE WOMAN IS PAID 75 CENTS FOR EVERY DOLLAR THAT MEN MAKE. IT'S AN OUTRAGE!
S. Adams
I'M THE HIGHEST PAID ENGINEER IN THE COMPANY.
3/16/98 © 1998 United Feature Syndicate, Inc.
THAT'S IMPOSSIBLE. THE ARTICLE SAYS "AVERAGE WOMEN" EARN LESS.
SUDDENLY, THE PROBLEM COMES INTO FOCUS.

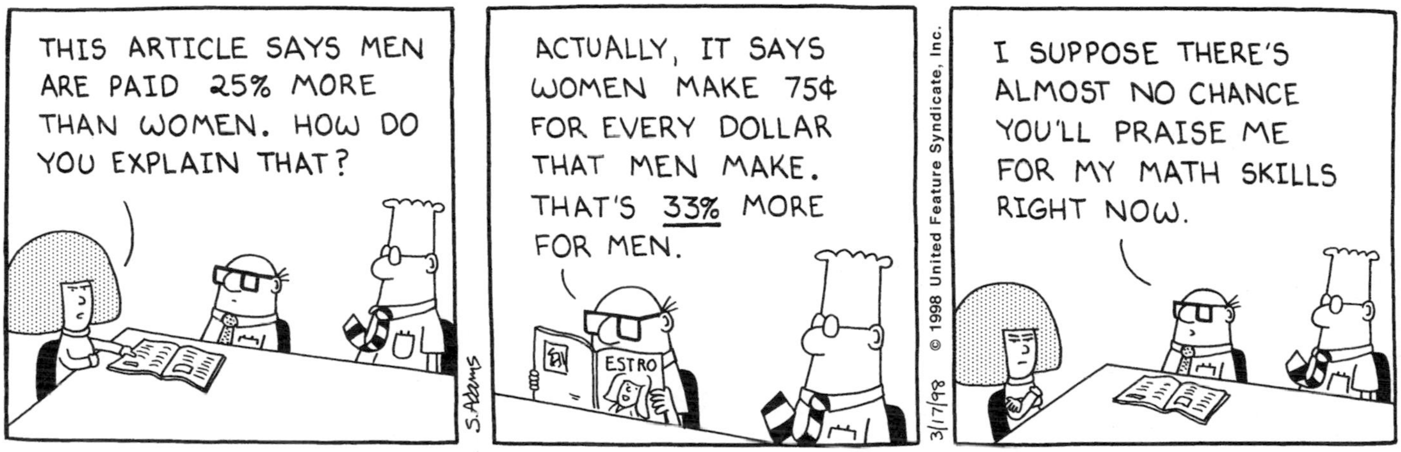
THIS ARTICLE SAYS MEN ARE PAID 25% MORE THAN WOMEN. HOW DO YOU EXPLAIN THAT?
S. Adams
ACTUALLY, IT SAYS WOMEN MAKE 75¢ FOR EVERY DOLLAR THAT MEN MAKE. THAT'S 33% MORE FOR MEN.
ESTRO
3/17/98 © 1998 United Feature Syndicate, Inc.
I SUPPOSE THERE'S ALMOST NO CHANCE YOU'LL PRAISE ME FOR MY MATH SKILLS RIGHT NOW.

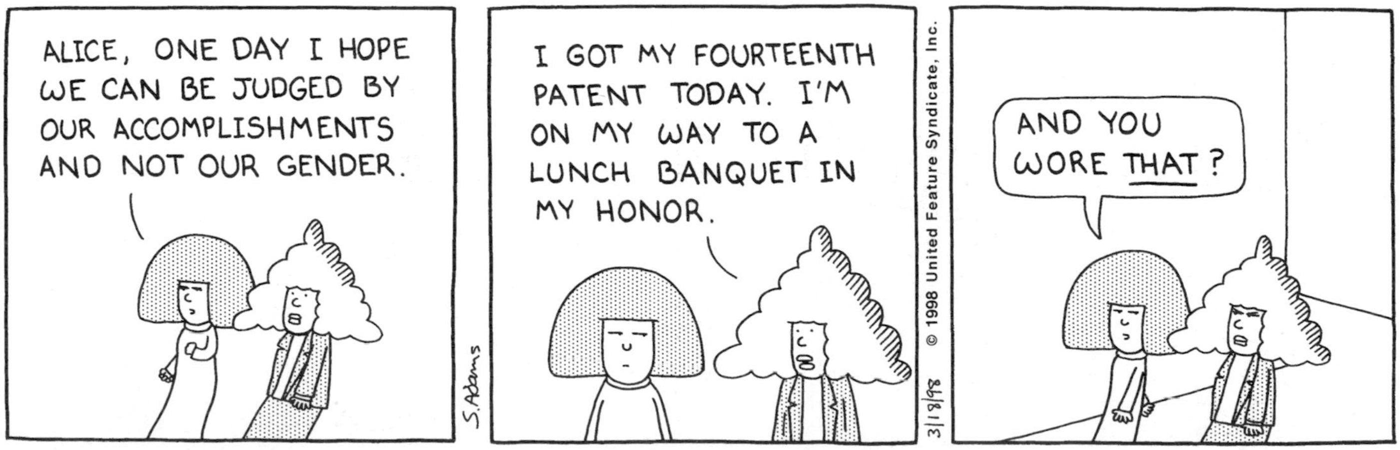
ALICE, ONE DAY I HOPE WE CAN BE JUDGED BY OUR ACCOMPLISHMENTS AND NOT OUR GENDER.
S. Adams
I GOT MY FOURTEENTH PATENT TODAY. I'M ON MY WAY TO A LUNCH BANQUET IN MY HONOR.
3/18/98 © 1998 United Feature Syndicate, Inc.
AND YOU WORE THAT?

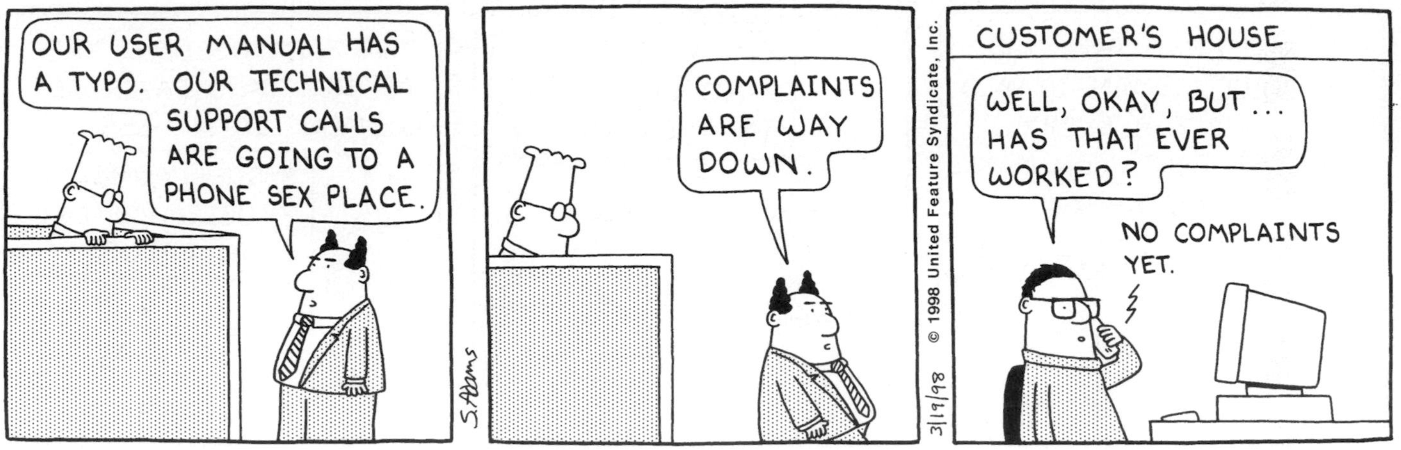
OUR USER MANUAL HAS A TYPO. OUR TECHNICAL SUPPORT CALLS ARE GOING TO A PHONE SEX PLACE.
S. Adams
COMPLAINTS ARE WAY DOWN.
3/19/98 © 1998 United Feature Syndicate, Inc.
CUSTOMER'S HOUSE
WELL, OKAY, BUT... HAS THAT EVER WORKED?
NO COMPLAINTS YET.

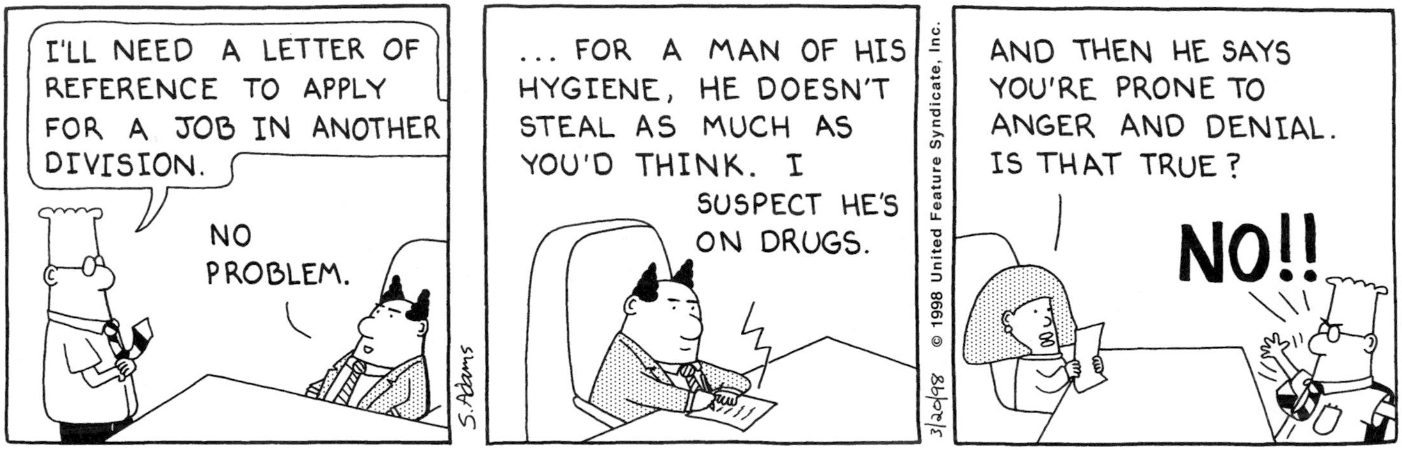
I'LL NEED A LETTER OF REFERENCE TO APPLY FOR A JOB IN ANOTHER DIVISION.
NO PROBLEM.
S. Adams
... FOR A MAN OF HIS HYGIENE, HE DOESN'T STEAL AS MUCH AS YOU'D THINK. I
SUSPECT HE'S ON DRUGS.
3/20/98 © 1998 United Feature Syndicate, Inc.
AND THEN HE SAYS YOU'RE PRONE TO ANGER AND DENIAL. IS THAT TRUE?
NO!!

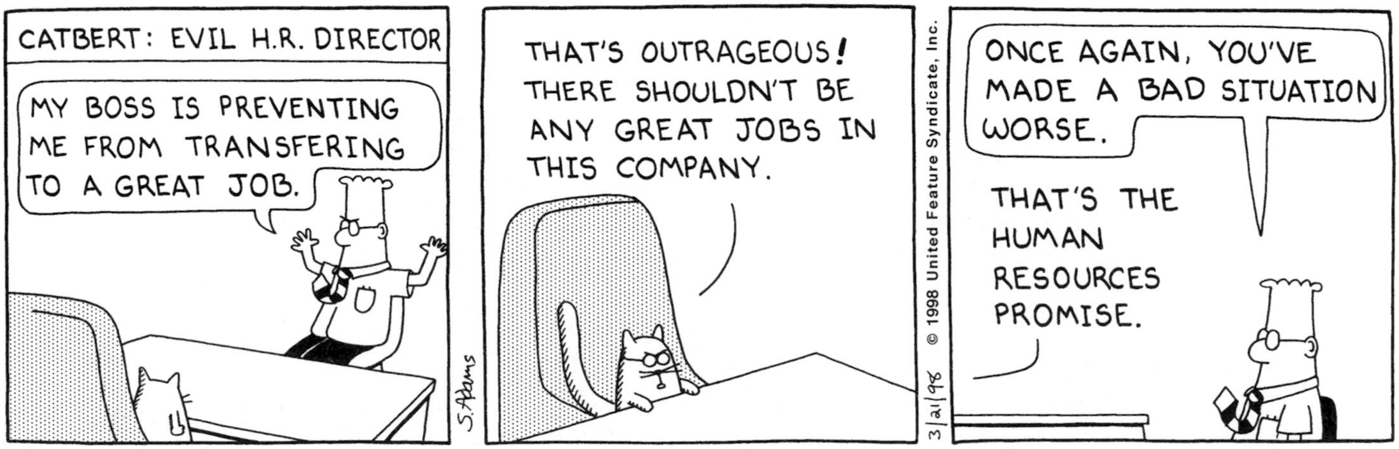
CATBERT: EVIL H.R. DIRECTOR
MY BOSS IS PREVENTING ME FROM TRANSFERING TO A GREAT JOB.
S. Adams
THAT'S OUTRAGEOUS! THERE SHOULDN'T BE ANY GREAT JOBS IN THIS COMPANY.
3/21/98 © 1998 United Feature Syndicate, Inc.
ONCE AGAIN, YOU'VE MADE A BAD SITUATION WORSE.
THAT'S THE HUMAN RESOURCES PROMISE.

CATBERT: EVIL H.R. DIRECTOR
S. Adams
THERE'S BEEN A SLIGHT CHANGE IN THE VACATION POLICY.
ARE WE GETTING MORE VACATION DAYS?
YOU MUST BE NEW HERE.
AS YOU KNOW, ALL VACATION TIME MUST BE USED IN THE YEAR IT IS EARNED.
© 1998 United Feature Syndicate, Inc.
3/22/98
I REALIZE THIS IS NOT ALWAYS CONVENIENT. SO I'VE DECIDED TO BE FLEXIBLE.
FROM NOW ON, ANY TIME YOU SPEND IN THE RESTROOM WILL COUNT AS VACATION.
WE SHOULD COMPLAIN.
IF YOU NEED ME, I'LL BE TAKING A PORCELAIN CRUISE.

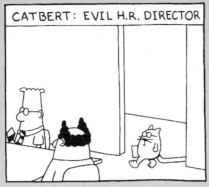

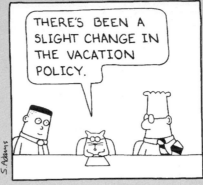

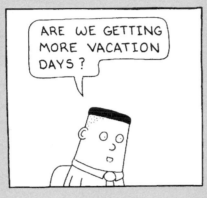

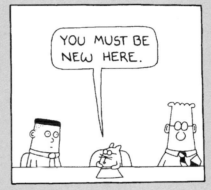

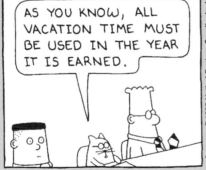

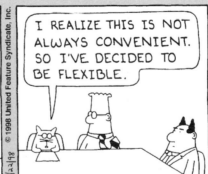

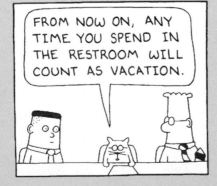

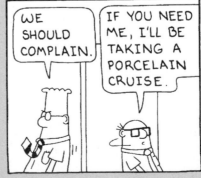

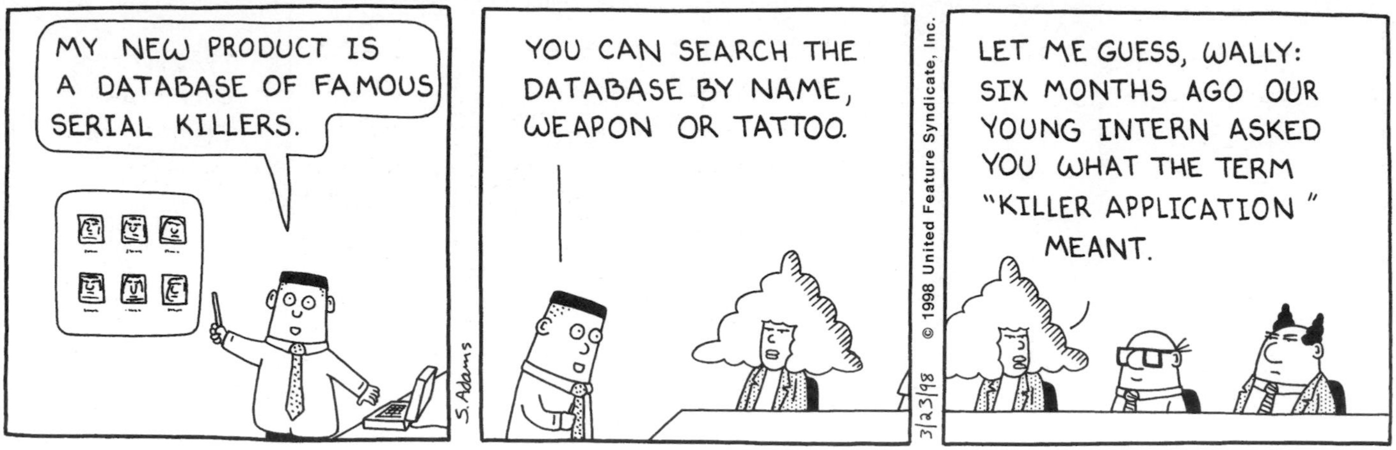
MY NEW PRODUCT IS A DATABASE OF FAMOUS SERIAL KILLERS.
YOU CAN SEARCH THE DATABASE BY NAME, WEAPON OR TATTOO.
LET ME GUESS, WALLY: SIX MONTHS AGO OUR YOUNG INTERN ASKED YOU WHAT THE TERM "KILLER APPLICATION" MEANT.
S. Adams
3/23/98
© 1998 United Feature Syndicate, Inc.

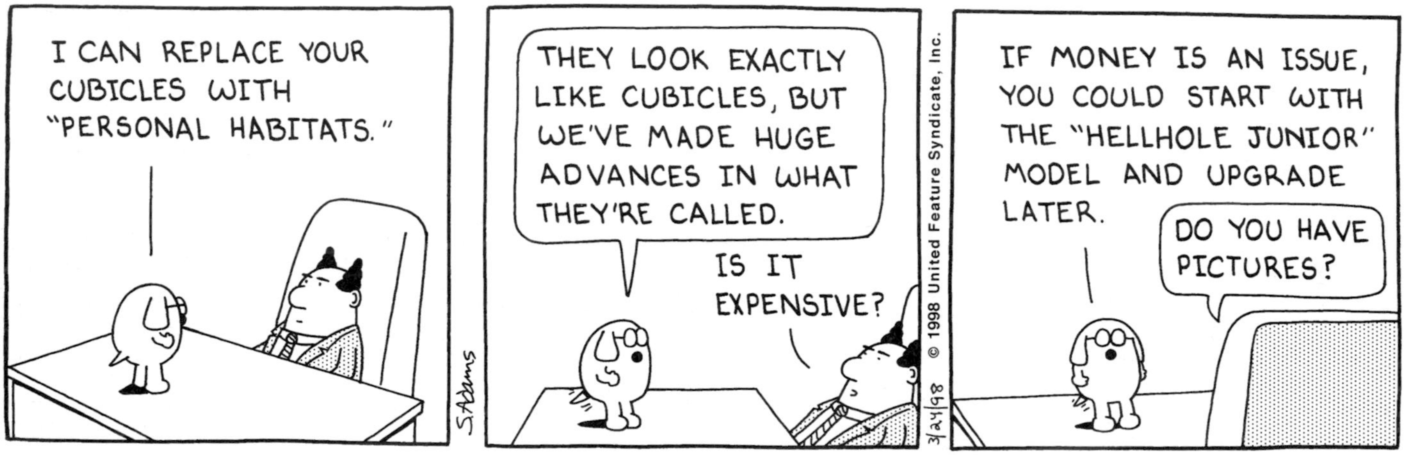
I CAN REPLACE YOUR CUBICLES WITH "PERSONAL HABITATS."
THEY LOOK EXACTLY LIKE CUBICLES, BUT WE'VE MADE HUGE ADVANCES IN WHAT THEY'RE CALLED.
IS IT EXPENSIVE?
IF MONEY IS AN ISSUE, YOU COULD START WITH THE "HELLHOLE JUNIOR" MODEL AND UPGRADE LATER.
DO YOU HAVE PICTURES?
S. Adams
3/24/98
© 1998 United Feature Syndicate, Inc.

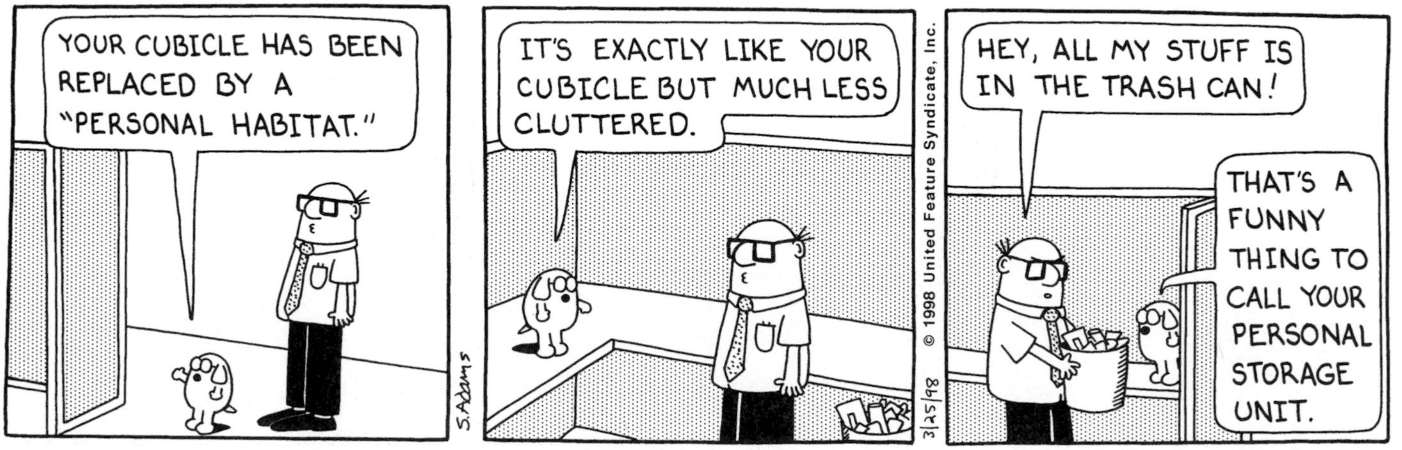
YOUR CUBICLE HAS BEEN REPLACED BY A "PERSONAL HABITAT."
IT'S EXACTLY LIKE YOUR CUBICLE BUT MUCH LESS CLUTTERED.
HEY, ALL MY STUFF IS IN THE TRASH CAN!
THAT'S A FUNNY THING TO CALL YOUR PERSONAL STORAGE UNIT.
S. Adams
3/25/98
© 1998 United Feature Syndicate, Inc.

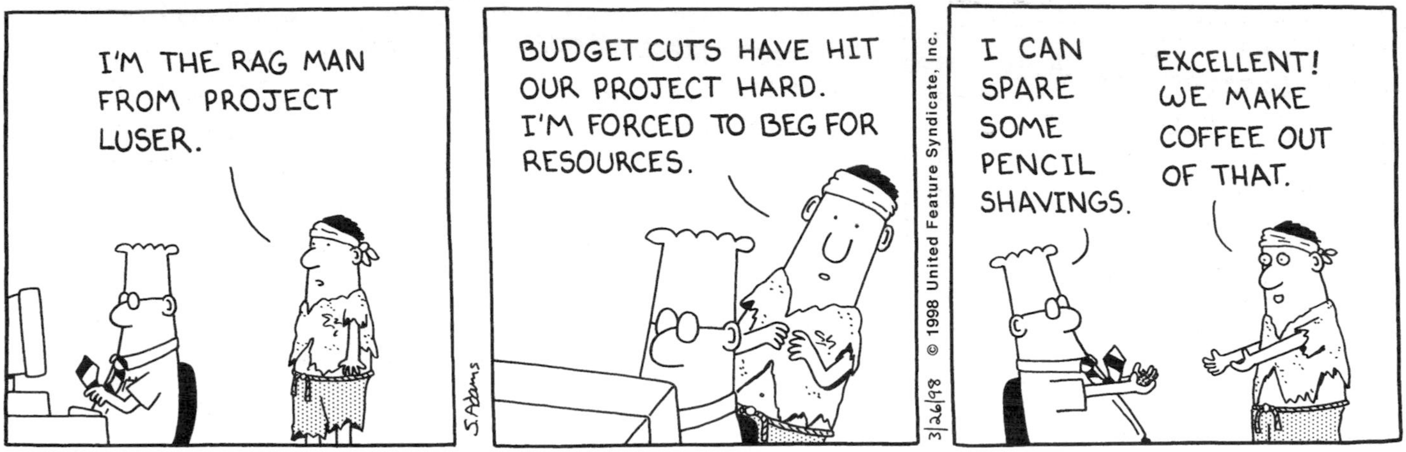
I'M THE RAG MAN FROM PROJECT LUSER.
BUDGET CUTS HAVE HIT OUR PROJECT HARD. I'M FORCED TO BEG FOR RESOURCES.
S.Adams
3/26/98 © 1998 United Feature Syndicate, Inc.
I CAN SPARE SOME PENCIL SHAVINGS.
EXCELLENT! WE MAKE COFFEE OUT OF THAT.

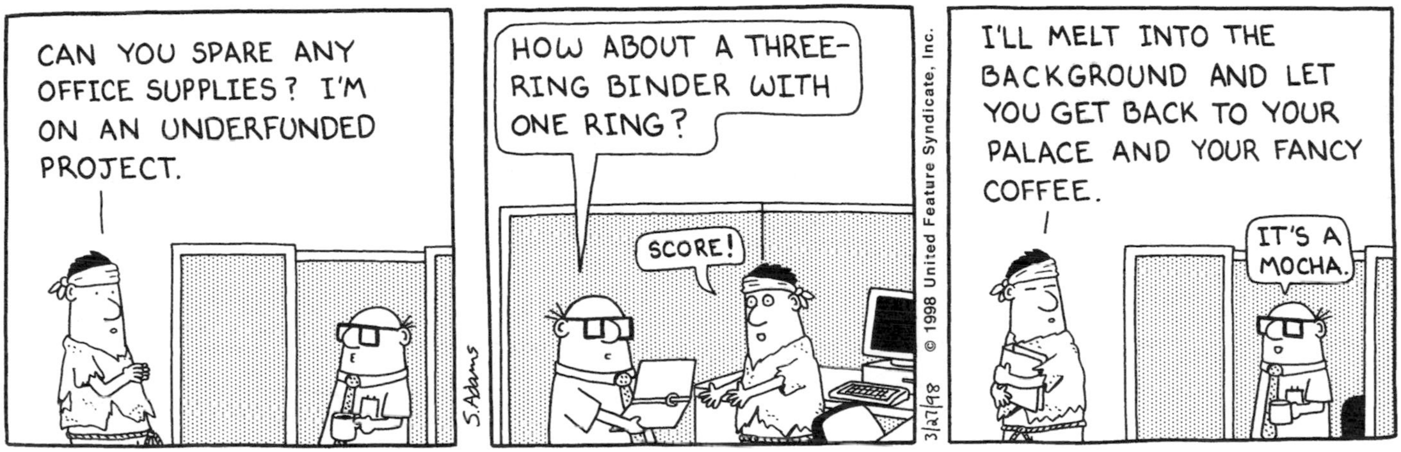
CAN YOU SPARE ANY OFFICE SUPPLIES? I'M ON AN UNDERFUNDED PROJECT.
HOW ABOUT A THREE-RING BINDER WITH ONE RING?
SCORE!
S.Adams
3/27/98 © 1998 United Feature Syndicate, Inc.
I'LL MELT INTO THE BACKGROUND AND LET YOU GET BACK TO YOUR PALACE AND YOUR FANCY COFFEE.
IT'S A MOCHA.

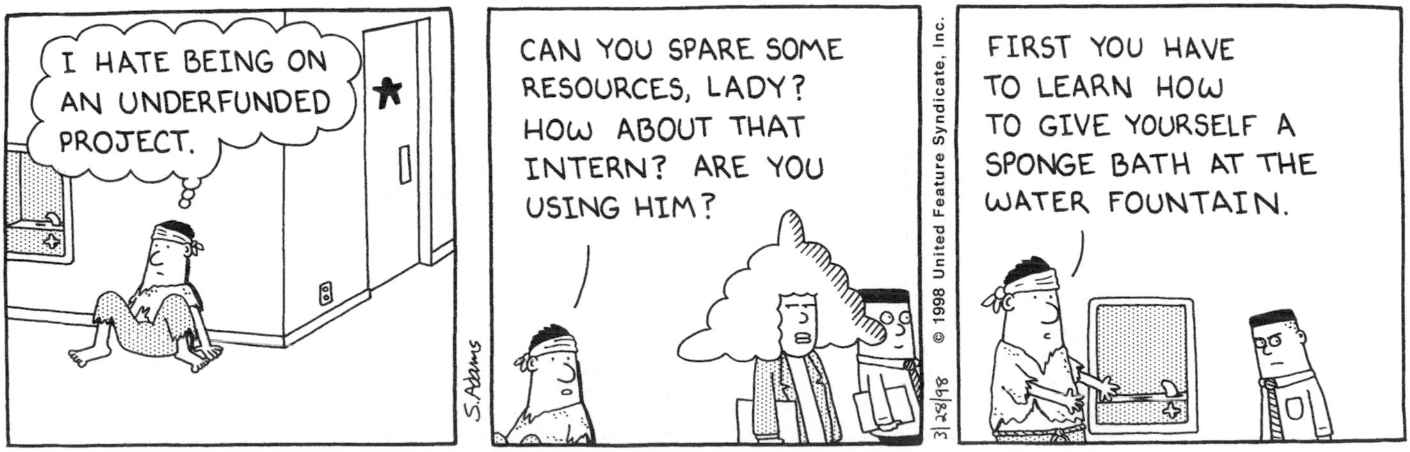
I HATE BEING ON AN UNDERFUNDED PROJECT.
CAN YOU SPARE SOME RESOURCES, LADY? HOW ABOUT THAT INTERN? ARE YOU USING HIM?
S.Adams
3/28/98 © 1998 United Feature Syndicate, Inc.
FIRST YOU HAVE TO LEARN HOW TO GIVE YOURSELF A SPONGE BATH AT THE WATER FOUNTAIN.

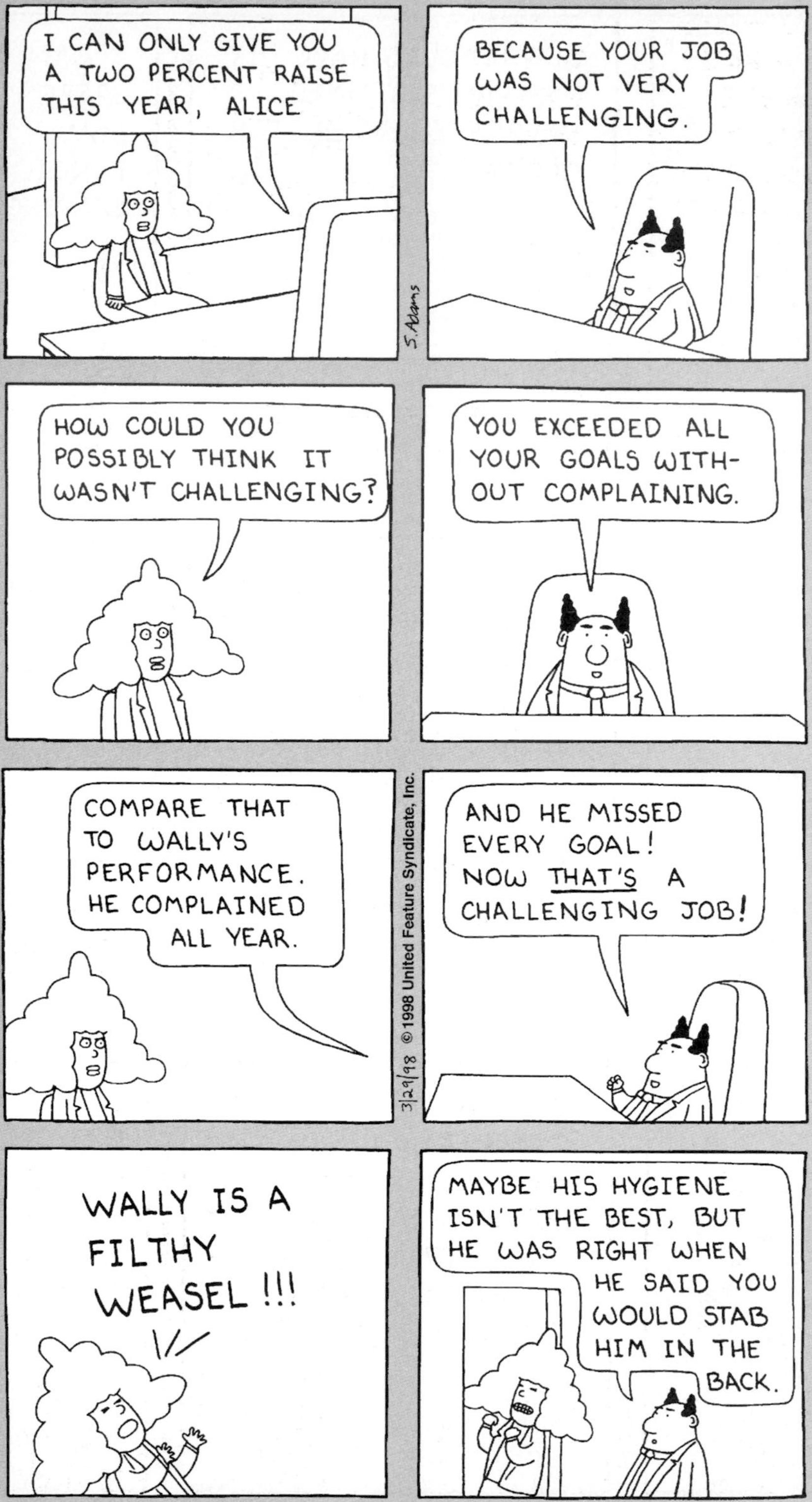
I CAN ONLY GIVE YOU A TWO PERCENT RAISE THIS YEAR, ALICE
BECAUSE YOUR JOB WAS NOT VERY CHALLENGING.
S. Adams
HOW COULD YOU POSSIBLY THINK IT WASN'T CHALLENGING?
YOU EXCEEDED ALL YOUR GOALS WITH-OUT COMPLAINING.
COMPARE THAT TO WALLY'S PERFORMANCE. HE COMPLAINED ALL YEAR.
AND HE MISSED EVERY GOAL! NOW THAT'S A CHALLENGING JOB!
WALLY IS A FILTHY WEASEL !!!
MAYBE HIS HYGIENE ISN'T THE BEST, BUT HE WAS RIGHT WHEN HE SAID YOU WOULD STAB HIM IN THE BACK.

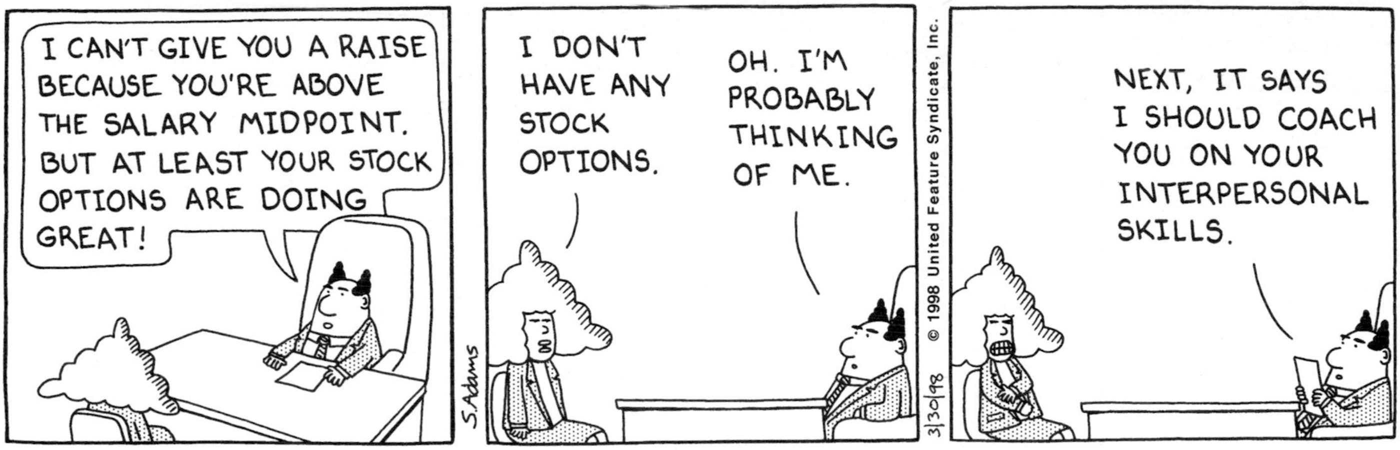
I CAN'T GIVE YOU A RAISE BECAUSE YOU'RE ABOVE THE SALARY MIDPOINT. BUT AT LEAST YOUR STOCK OPTIONS ARE DOING GREAT!
S.Adams
I DON'T HAVE ANY STOCK OPTIONS.
OH. I'M PROBABLY THINKING OF ME.
3/30/98 © 1998 United Feature Syndicate, Inc.
NEXT, IT SAYS I SHOULD COACH YOU ON YOUR INTERPERSONAL SKILLS.

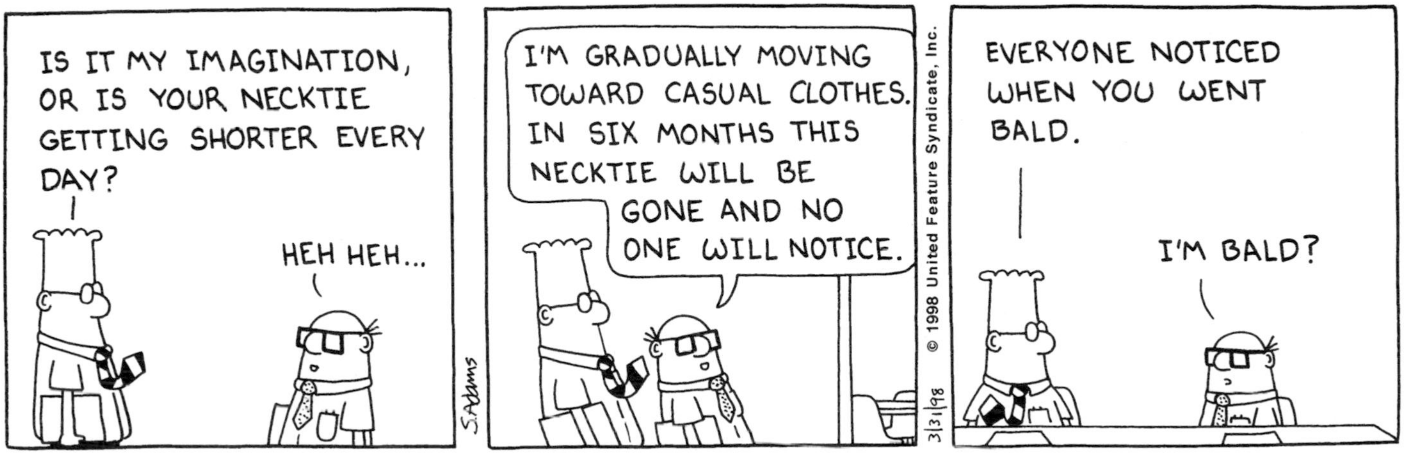
IS IT MY IMAGINATION, OR IS YOUR NECKTIE GETTING SHORTER EVERY DAY?
HEH HEH...
S.Adams
I'M GRADUALLY MOVING TOWARD CASUAL CLOTHES. IN SIX MONTHS THIS NECKTIE WILL BE GONE AND NO ONE WILL NOTICE.
3/31/98 © 1998 United Feature Syndicate, Inc.
EVERYONE NOTICED WHEN YOU WENT BALD.
I'M BALD?

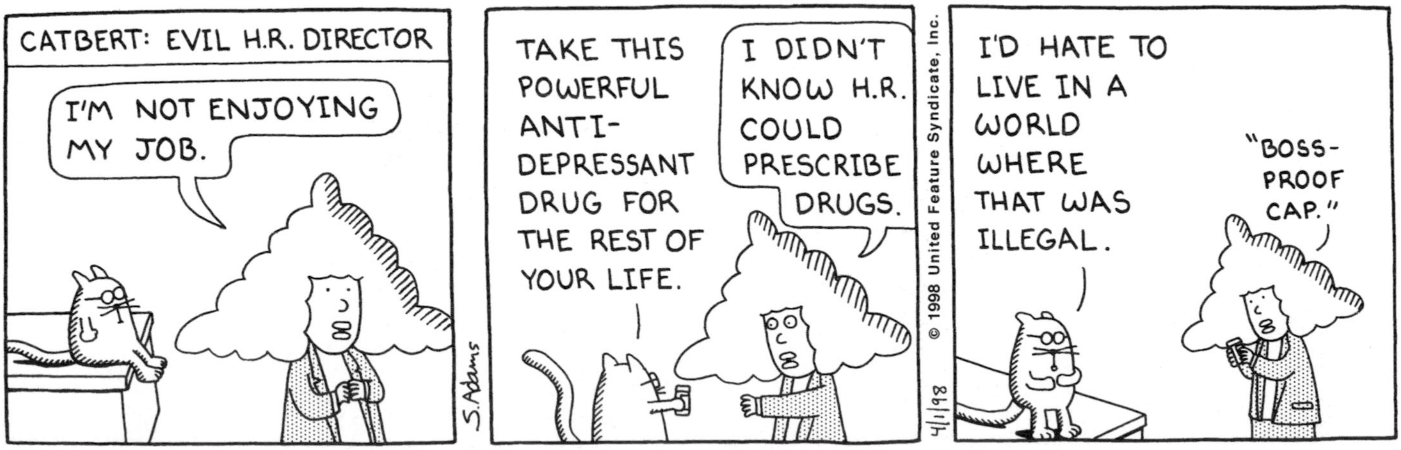
CATBERT: EVIL H.R. DIRECTOR
I'M NOT ENJOYING MY JOB.
S.Adams
TAKE THIS POWERFUL ANTI-DEPRESSANT DRUG FOR THE REST OF YOUR LIFE.
I DIDN'T KNOW H.R. COULD PRESCRIBE DRUGS.
4/1/98 © 1998 United Feature Syndicate, Inc.
I'D HATE TO LIVE IN A WORLD WHERE THAT WAS ILLEGAL.
"BOSS-PROOF CAP."

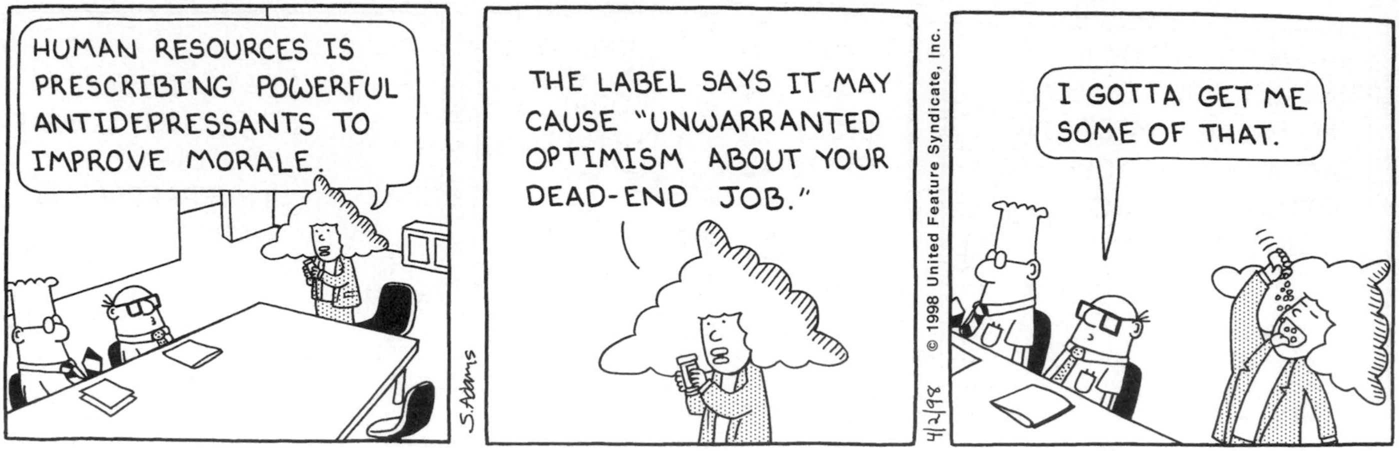
HUMAN RESOURCES IS PRESCRIBING POWERFUL ANTIDEPRESSANTS TO IMPROVE MORALE.
THE LABEL SAYS IT MAY CAUSE "UNWARRANTED OPTIMISM ABOUT YOUR DEAD-END JOB."
I GOTTA GET ME SOME OF THAT.
S. Adams
4/2/98
© 1998 United Feature Syndicate, Inc.

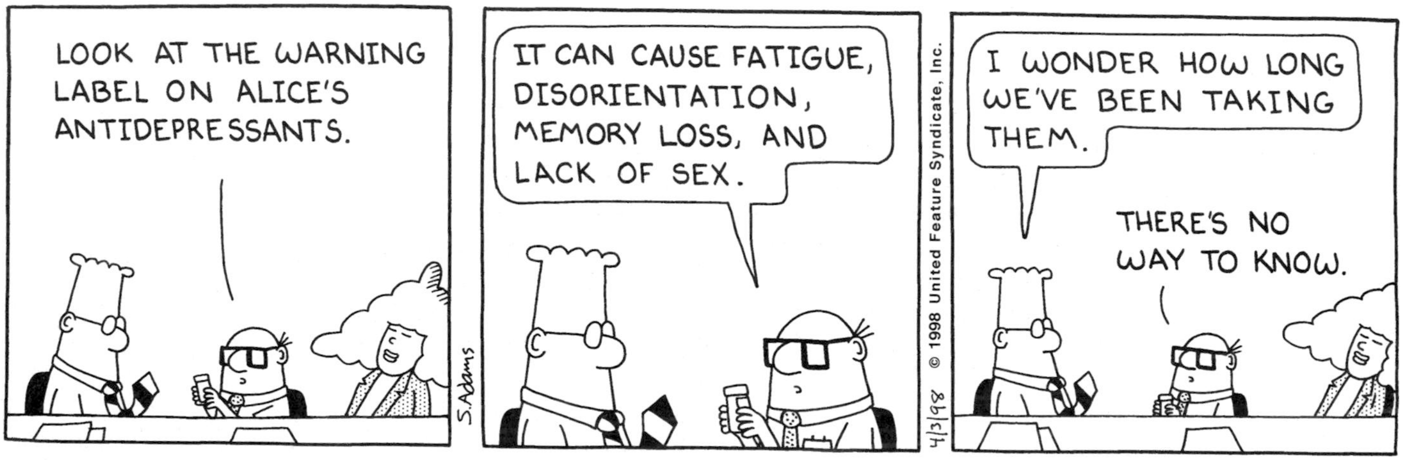
LOOK AT THE WARNING LABEL ON ALICE'S ANTIDEPRESSANTS.
IT CAN CAUSE FATIGUE, DISORIENTATION, MEMORY LOSS, AND LACK OF SEX.
I WONDER HOW LONG WE'VE BEEN TAKING THEM.
THERE'S NO WAY TO KNOW.
S. Adams
4/3/98
© 1998 United Feature Syndicate, Inc.

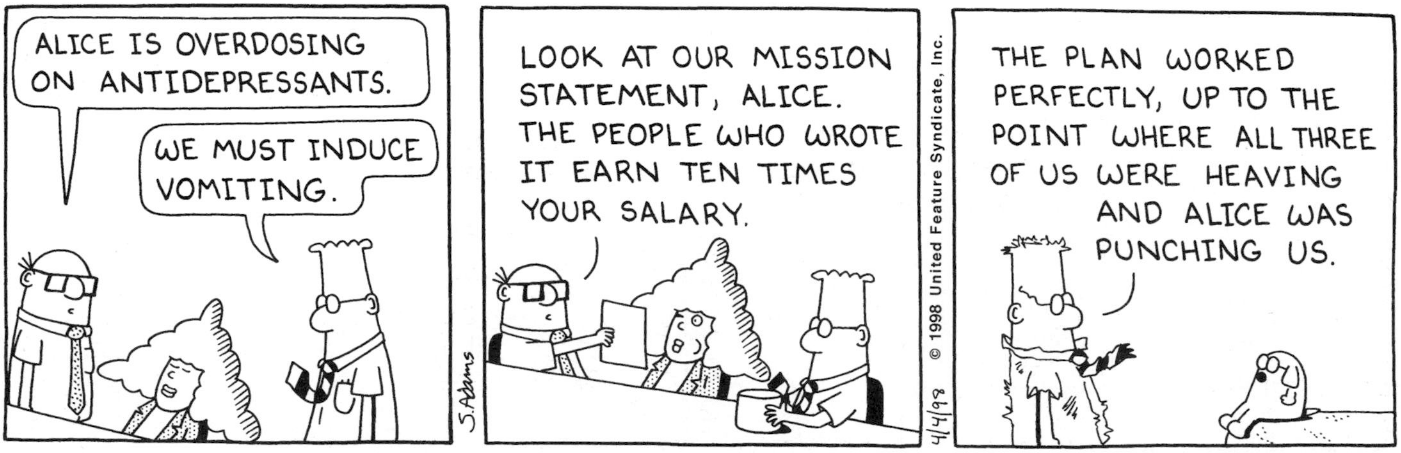
ALICE IS OVERDOSING ON ANTIDEPRESSANTS.
WE MUST INDUCE VOMITING.
LOOK AT OUR MISSION STATEMENT, ALICE. THE PEOPLE WHO WROTE IT EARN TEN TIMES YOUR SALARY.
THE PLAN WORKED PERFECTLY, UP TO THE POINT WHERE ALL THREE OF US WERE HEAVING AND ALICE WAS PUNCHING US.
S. Adams
4/4/98
© 1998 United Feature Syndicate, Inc.

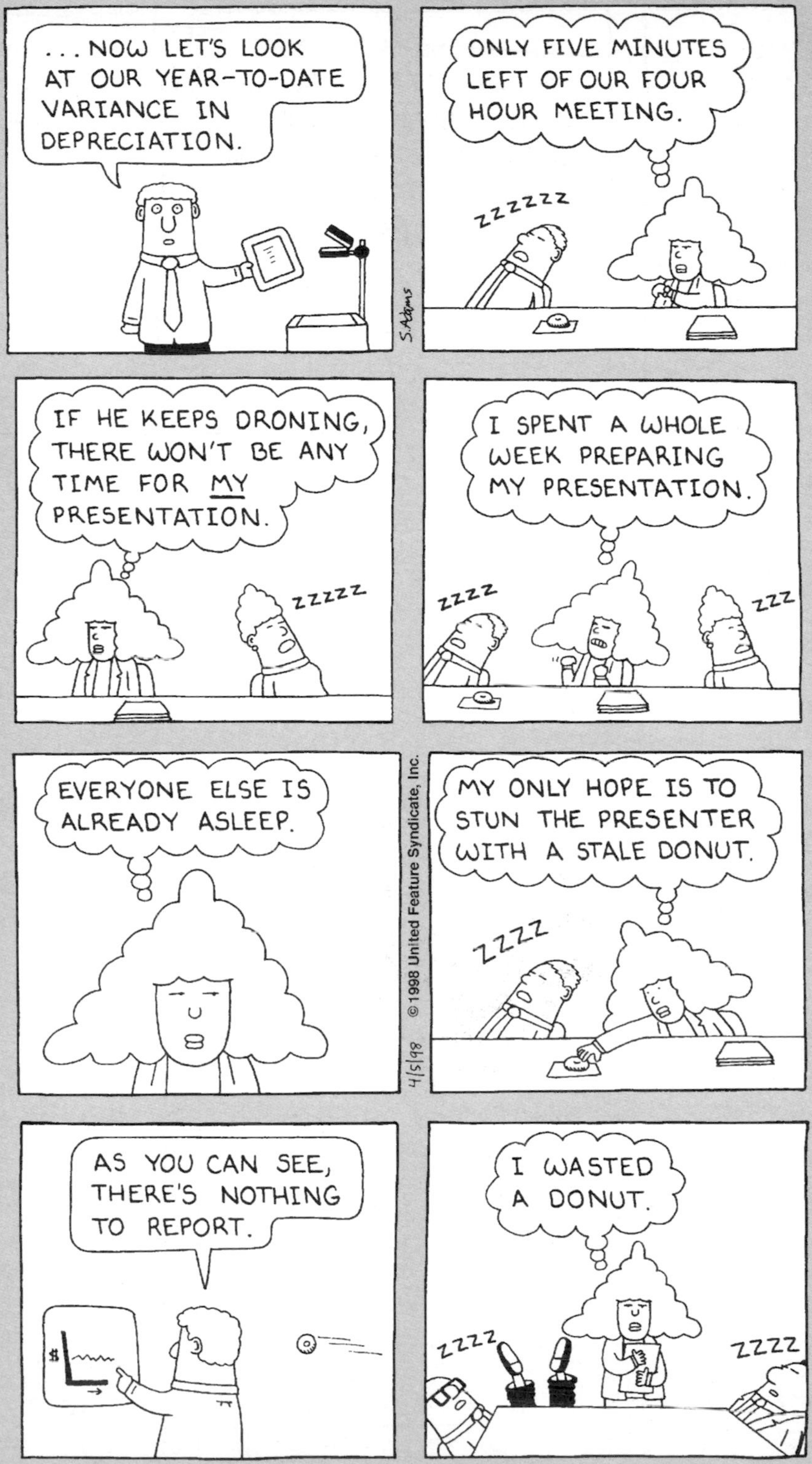
...NOW LET'S LOOK AT OUR YEAR-TO-DATE VARIANCE IN DEPRECIATION.
S.Adams
ONLY FIVE MINUTES LEFT OF OUR FOUR HOUR MEETING.
ZZZZZZ
IF HE KEEPS DRONING, THERE WON'T BE ANY TIME FOR MY PRESENTATION.
ZZZZZ
I SPENT A WHOLE WEEK PREPARING MY PRESENTATION.
ZZZZ
ZZZ
EVERYONE ELSE IS ALREADY ASLEEP.
© 1998 United Feature Syndicate, Inc.
4/5/98
MY ONLY HOPE IS TO STUN THE PRESENTER WITH A STALE DONUT.
ZZZZ
AS YOU CAN SEE, THERE'S NOTHING TO REPORT.
$
I WASTED A DONUT.
ZZZZ
ZZZZ

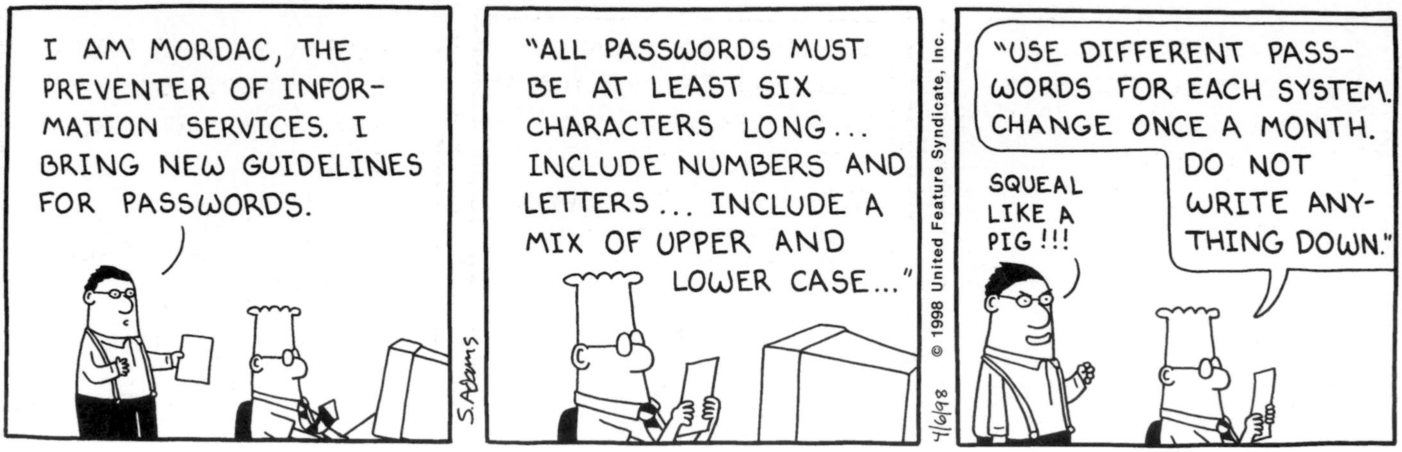
I AM MORDAC, THE PREVENTER OF INFORMATION SERVICES. I BRING NEW GUIDELINES FOR PASSWORDS.
S. Adams
"ALL PASSWORDS MUST BE AT LEAST SIX CHARACTERS LONG... INCLUDE NUMBERS AND LETTERS... INCLUDE A MIX OF UPPER AND LOWER CASE..."
4/6/98
© 1998 United Feature Syndicate, Inc.
"USE DIFFERENT PASSWORDS FOR EACH SYSTEM. CHANGE ONCE A MONTH. DO NOT WRITE ANYTHING DOWN."
SQUEAL LIKE A PIG!!!

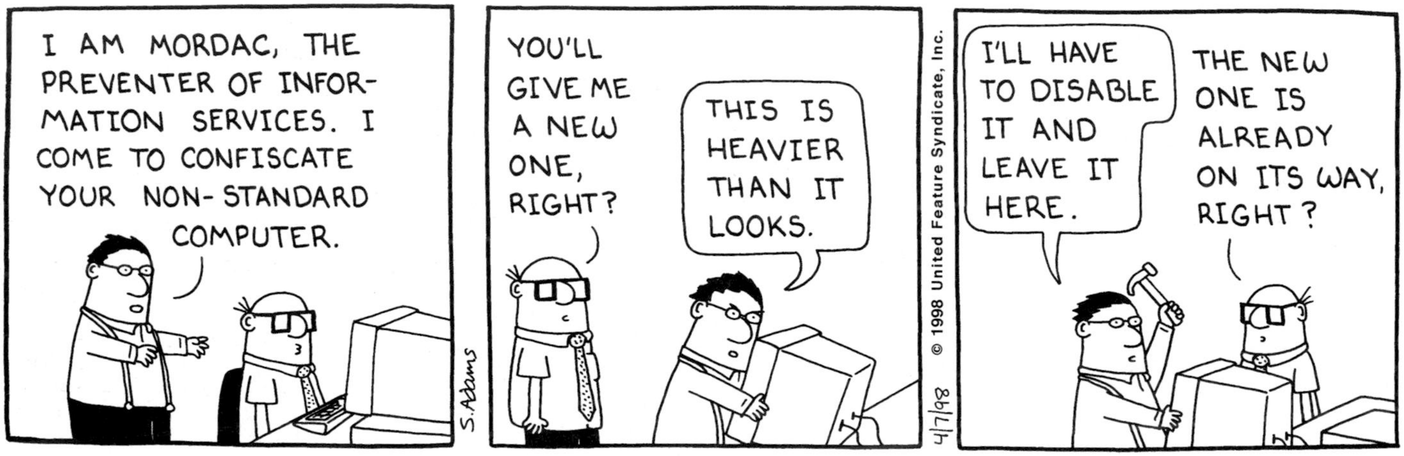
I AM MORDAC, THE PREVENTER OF INFORMATION SERVICES. I COME TO CONFISCATE YOUR NON-STANDARD COMPUTER.
S. Adams
YOU'LL GIVE ME A NEW ONE, RIGHT?
THIS IS HEAVIER THAN IT LOOKS.
4/7/98
© 1998 United Feature Syndicate, Inc.
I'LL HAVE TO DISABLE IT AND LEAVE IT HERE.
THE NEW ONE IS ALREADY ON ITS WAY, RIGHT?

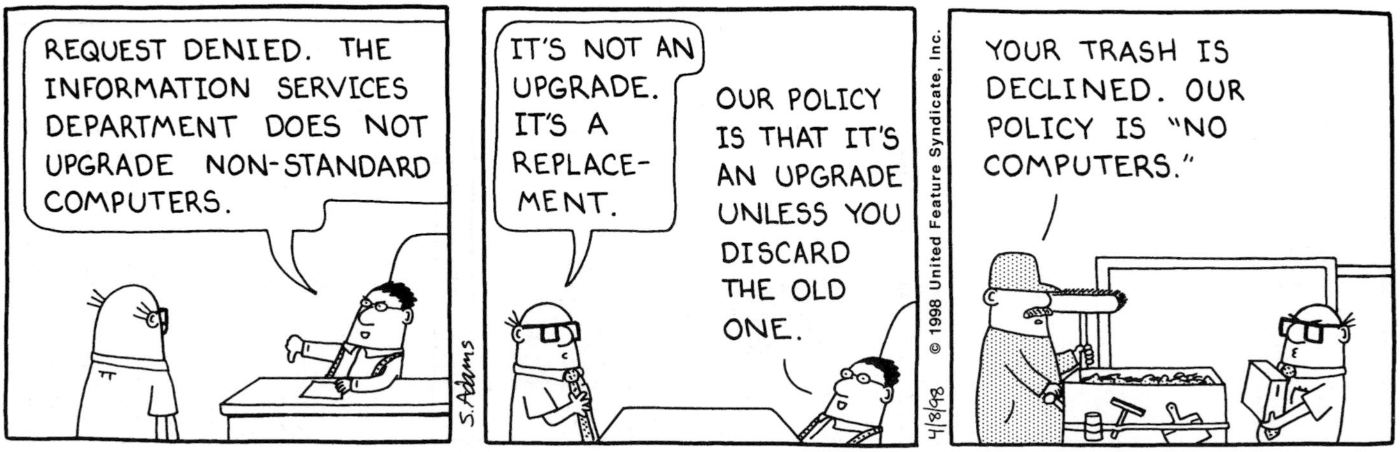
REQUEST DENIED. THE INFORMATION SERVICES DEPARTMENT DOES NOT UPGRADE NON-STANDARD COMPUTERS.
S. Adams
IT'S NOT AN UPGRADE. IT'S A REPLACEMENT.
OUR POLICY IS THAT IT'S AN UPGRADE UNLESS YOU DISCARD THE OLD ONE.
4/8/98
© 1998 United Feature Syndicate, Inc.
YOUR TRASH IS DECLINED. OUR POLICY IS "NO COMPUTERS."

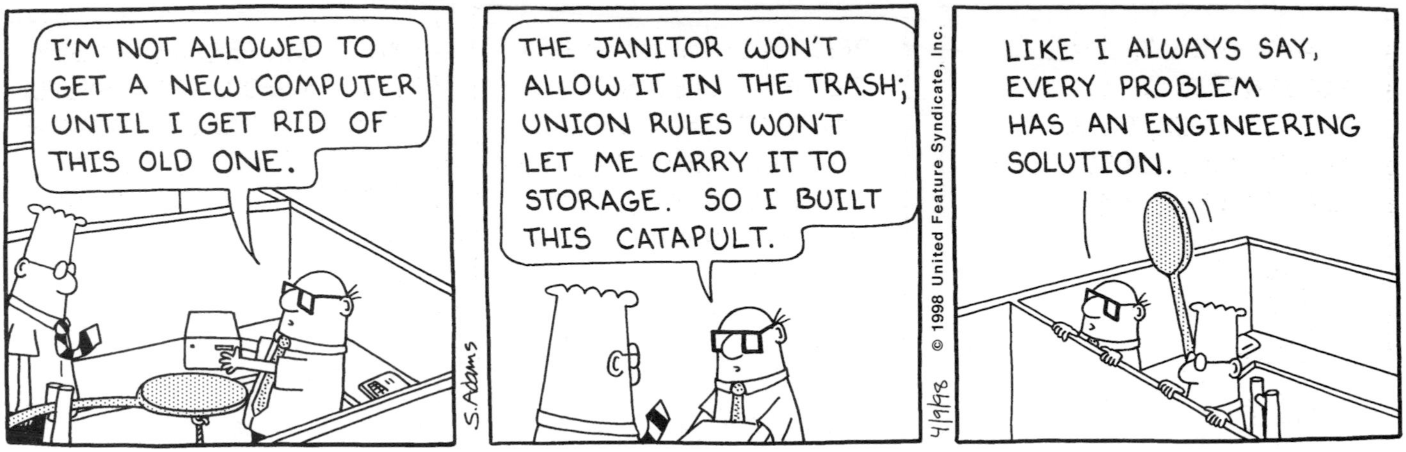
I'M NOT ALLOWED TO GET A NEW COMPUTER UNTIL I GET RID OF THIS OLD ONE.
S. Adams
THE JANITOR WON'T ALLOW IT IN THE TRASH; UNION RULES WON'T LET ME CARRY IT TO STORAGE. SO I BUILT THIS CATAPULT.
4/9/98 © 1998 United Feature Syndicate, Inc.
LIKE I ALWAYS SAY, EVERY PROBLEM HAS AN ENGINEERING SOLUTION.

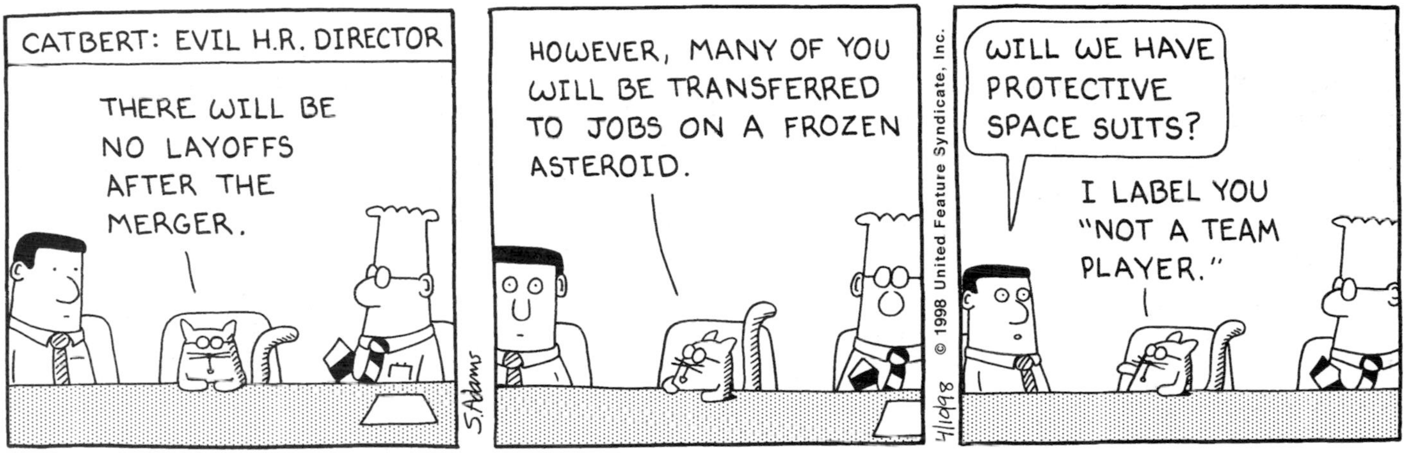
CATBERT: EVIL H.R. DIRECTOR
THERE WILL BE NO LAYOFFS AFTER THE MERGER.
S. Adams
HOWEVER, MANY OF YOU WILL BE TRANSFERRED TO JOBS ON A FROZEN ASTEROID.
4/10/98 © 1998 United Feature Syndicate, Inc.
WILL WE HAVE PROTECTIVE SPACE SUITS?
I LABEL YOU "NOT A TEAM PLAYER."

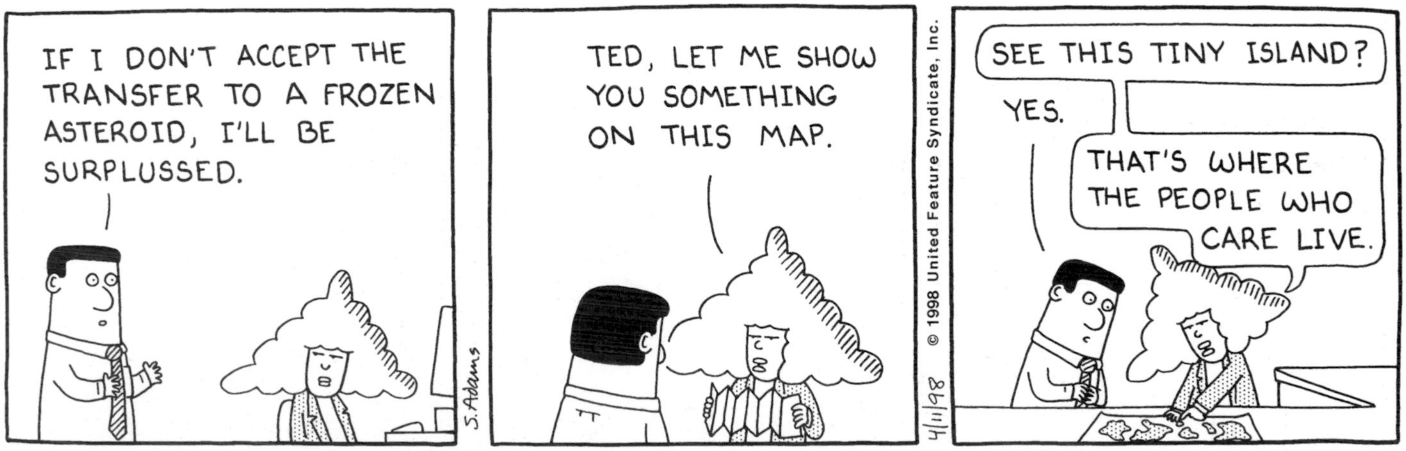
IF I DON'T ACCEPT THE TRANSFER TO A FROZEN ASTEROID, I'LL BE SURPLUSSED.
S. Adams
TED, LET ME SHOW YOU SOMETHING ON THIS MAP.
4/11/98 © 1998 United Feature Syndicate, Inc.
SEE THIS TINY ISLAND?
YES.
THAT'S WHERE THE PEOPLE WHO CARE LIVE.

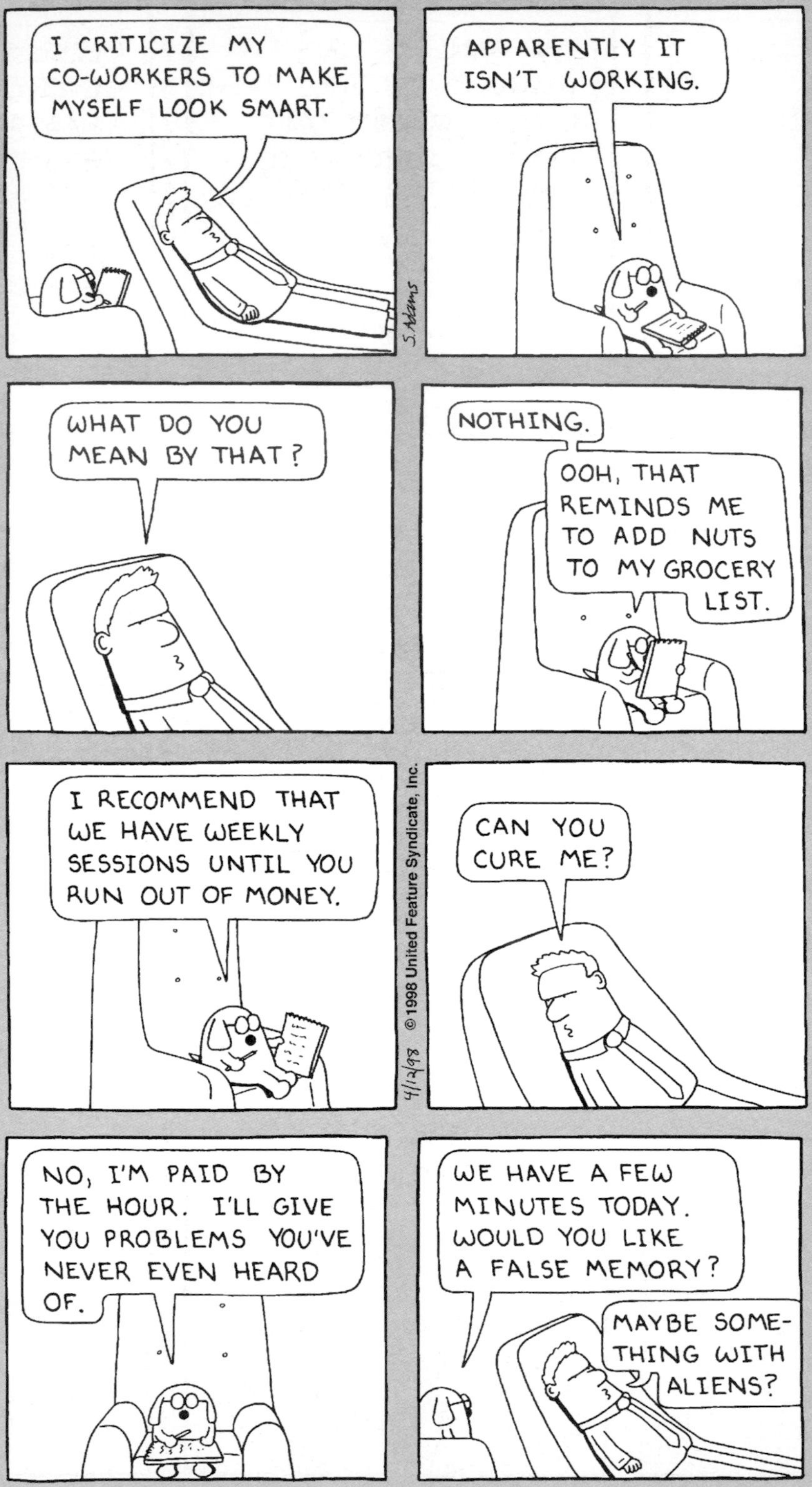
I CRITICIZE MY CO-WORKERS TO MAKE MYSELF LOOK SMART.
APPARENTLY IT ISN'T WORKING.
S. Adams
WHAT DO YOU MEAN BY THAT?
NOTHING.
OOH, THAT REMINDS ME TO ADD NUTS TO MY GROCERY LIST.
I RECOMMEND THAT WE HAVE WEEKLY SESSIONS UNTIL YOU RUN OUT OF MONEY.
© 1998 United Feature Syndicate, Inc.
4/12/98
CAN YOU CURE ME?
NO, I'M PAID BY THE HOUR. I'LL GIVE YOU PROBLEMS YOU'VE NEVER EVEN HEARD OF.
WE HAVE A FEW MINUTES TODAY. WOULD YOU LIKE A FALSE MEMORY?
MAYBE SOMETHING WITH ALIENS?

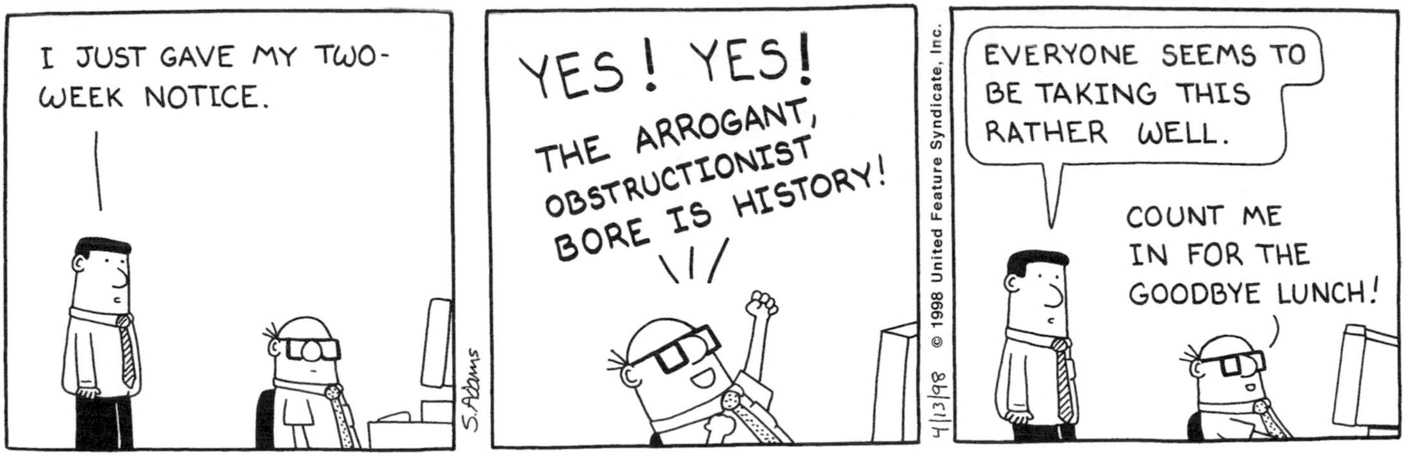
I JUST GAVE MY TWO-WEEK NOTICE.
S. Adams
YES! YES!
THE ARROGANT, OBSTRUCTIONIST BORE IS HISTORY!
4/13/98 © 1998 United Feature Syndicate, Inc.
EVERYONE SEEMS TO BE TAKING THIS RATHER WELL.
COUNT ME IN FOR THE GOODBYE LUNCH!

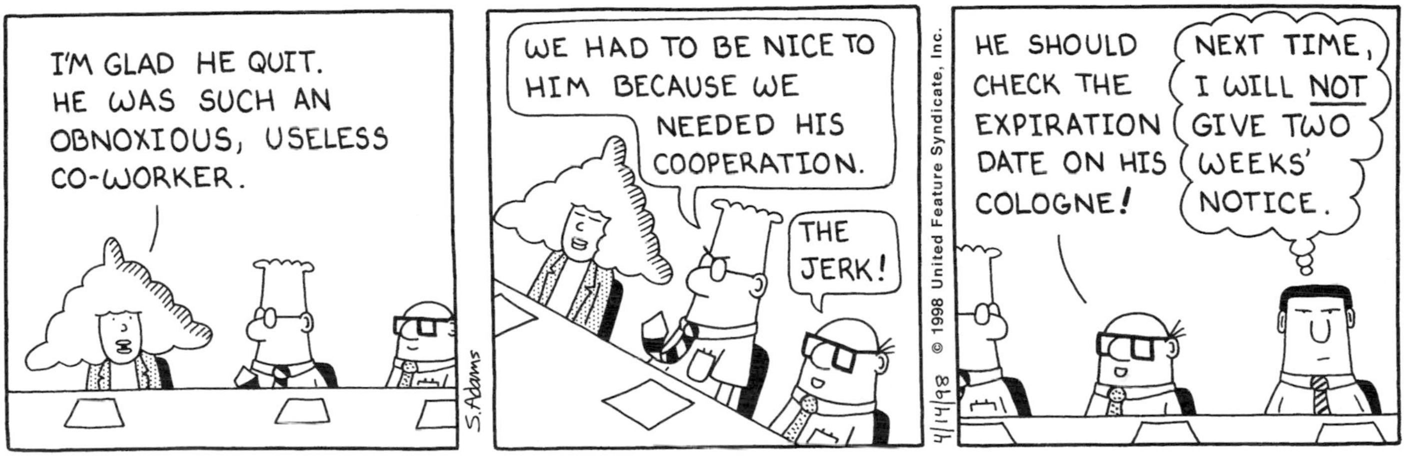
I'M GLAD HE QUIT. HE WAS SUCH AN OBNOXIOUS, USELESS CO-WORKER.
S. Adams
WE HAD TO BE NICE TO HIM BECAUSE WE NEEDED HIS COOPERATION.
THE JERK!
4/14/98 © 1998 United Feature Syndicate, Inc.
HE SHOULD CHECK THE EXPIRATION DATE ON HIS COLOGNE!
NEXT TIME, I WILL NOT GIVE TWO WEEKS' NOTICE.

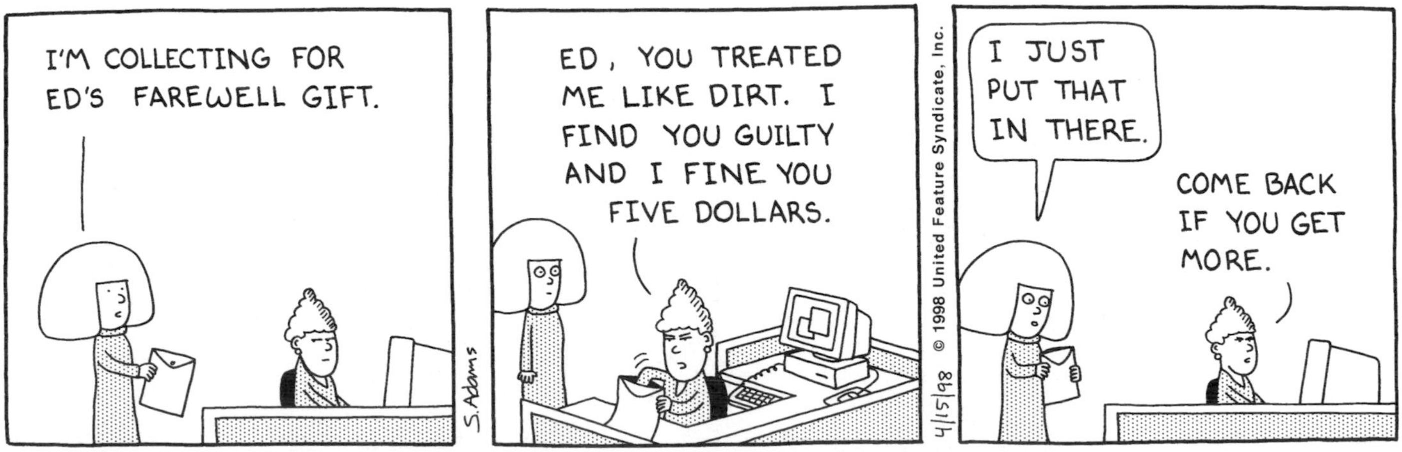
I'M COLLECTING FOR ED'S FAREWELL GIFT.
S. Adams
ED, YOU TREATED ME LIKE DIRT. I FIND YOU GUILTY AND I FINE YOU FIVE DOLLARS.
4/15/98 © 1998 United Feature Syndicate, Inc.
I JUST PUT THAT IN THERE.
COME BACK IF YOU GET MORE.

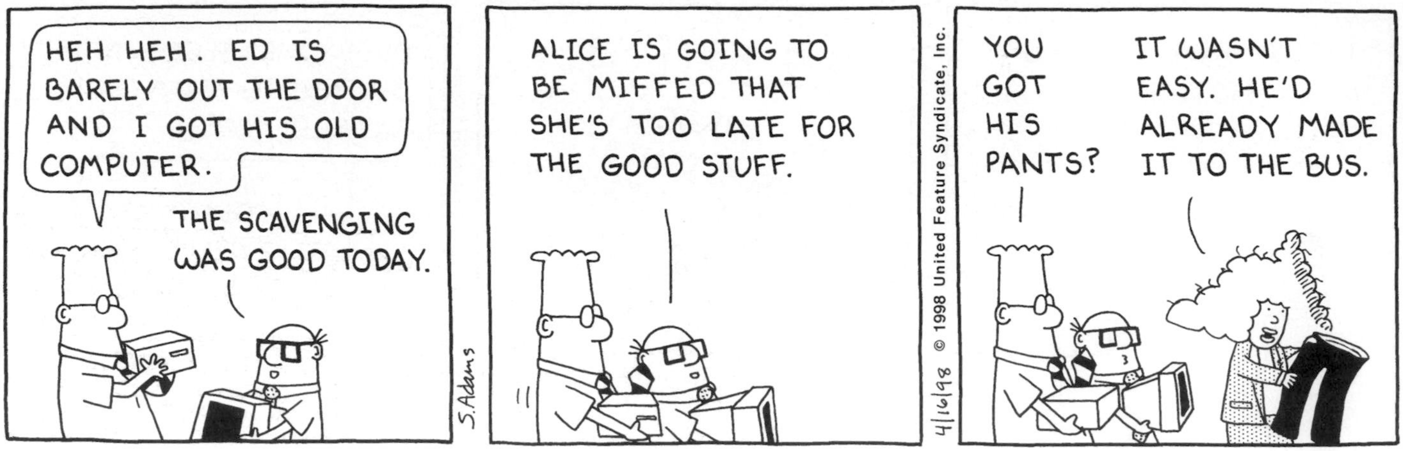
HEH HEH. ED IS BARELY OUT THE DOOR AND I GOT HIS OLD COMPUTER.
THE SCAVENGING WAS GOOD TODAY.
S. Adams
ALICE IS GOING TO BE MIFFED THAT SHE'S TOO LATE FOR THE GOOD STUFF.
4/16/98 © 1998 United Feature Syndicate, Inc.
YOU GOT HIS PANTS?
IT WASN'T EASY. HE'D ALREADY MADE IT TO THE BUS.

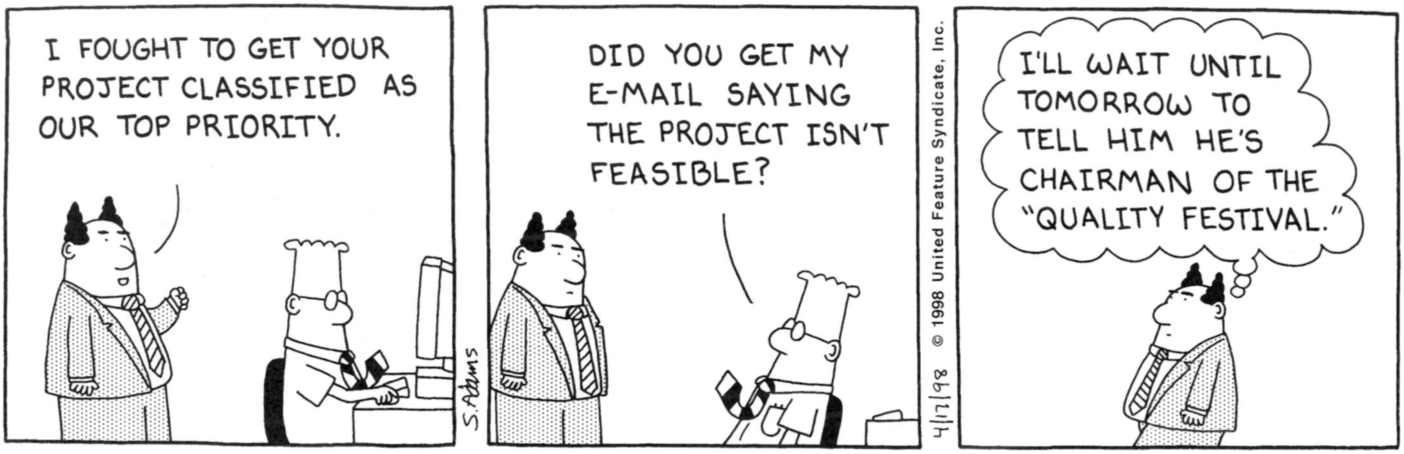
I FOUGHT TO GET YOUR PROJECT CLASSIFIED AS OUR TOP PRIORITY.
S. Adams
DID YOU GET MY E-MAIL SAYING THE PROJECT ISN'T FEASIBLE?
4/17/98 © 1998 United Feature Syndicate, Inc.
I'LL WAIT UNTIL TOMORROW TO TELL HIM HE'S CHAIRMAN OF THE "QUALITY FESTIVAL."

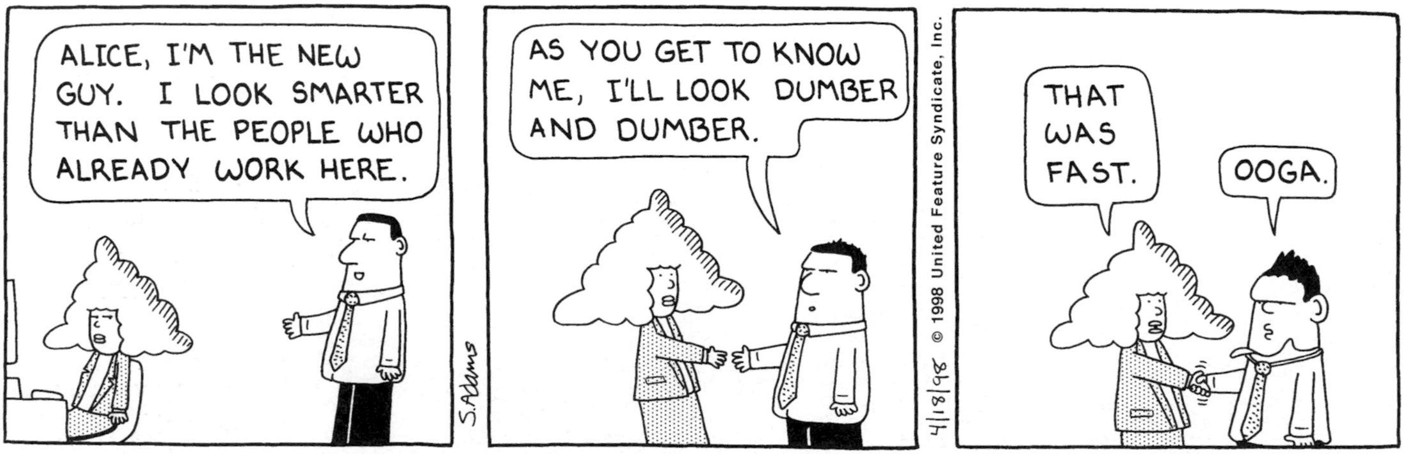
ALICE, I'M THE NEW GUY. I LOOK SMARTER THAN THE PEOPLE WHO ALREADY WORK HERE.
S. Adams
AS YOU GET TO KNOW ME, I'LL LOOK DUMBER AND DUMBER.
4/18/98 © 1998 United Feature Syndicate, Inc.
THAT WAS FAST.
OOGA.

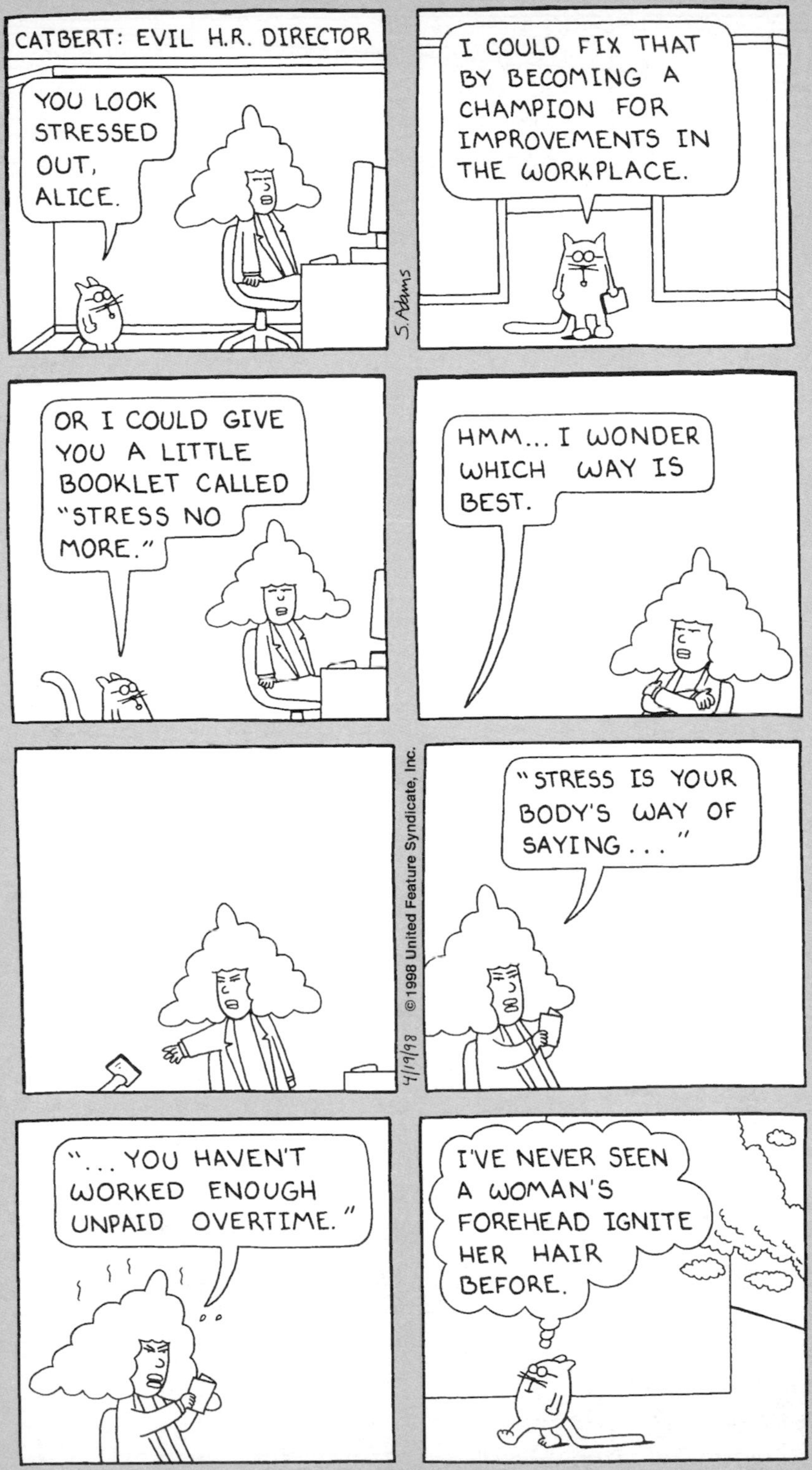
CATBERT: EVIL H.R. DIRECTOR
YOU LOOK STRESSED OUT, ALICE.
S. Adams
I COULD FIX THAT BY BECOMING A CHAMPION FOR IMPROVEMENTS IN THE WORKPLACE.
OR I COULD GIVE YOU A LITTLE BOOKLET CALLED "STRESS NO MORE."
HMM... I WONDER WHICH WAY IS BEST.
© 1998 United Feature Syndicate, Inc.
4/19/98
"STRESS IS YOUR BODY'S WAY OF SAYING..."
"...YOU HAVEN'T WORKED ENOUGH UNPAID OVERTIME."
I'VE NEVER SEEN A WOMAN'S FOREHEAD IGNITE HER HAIR BEFORE.

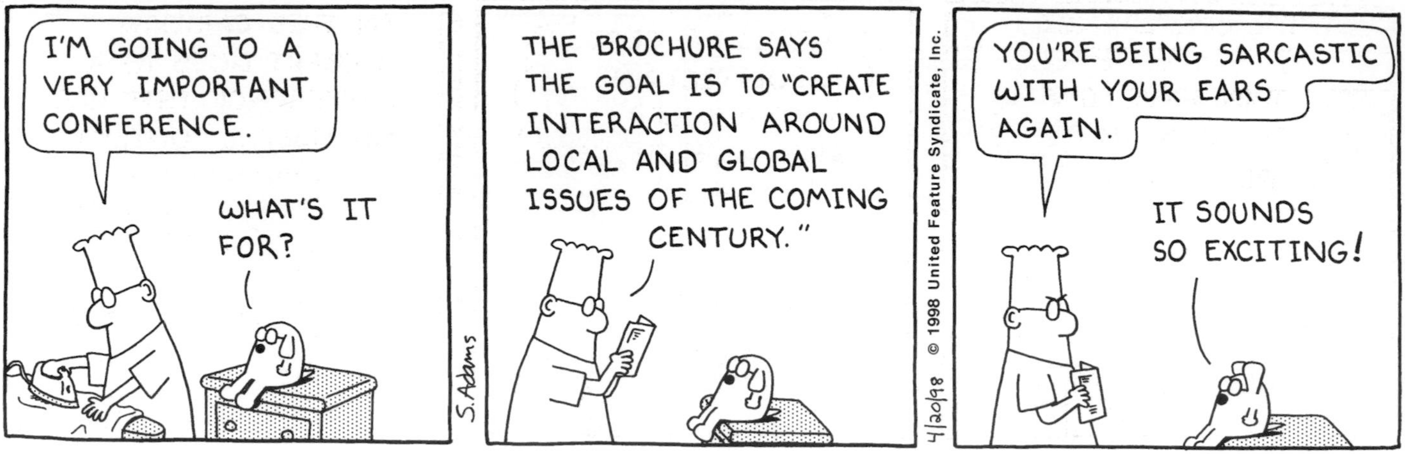
I'M GOING TO A VERY IMPORTANT CONFERENCE.
WHAT'S IT FOR?
S. Adams
THE BROCHURE SAYS THE GOAL IS TO "CREATE INTERACTION AROUND LOCAL AND GLOBAL ISSUES OF THE COMING CENTURY."
4/20/98 © 1998 United Feature Syndicate, Inc.
YOU'RE BEING SARCASTIC WITH YOUR EARS AGAIN.
IT SOUNDS SO EXCITING!

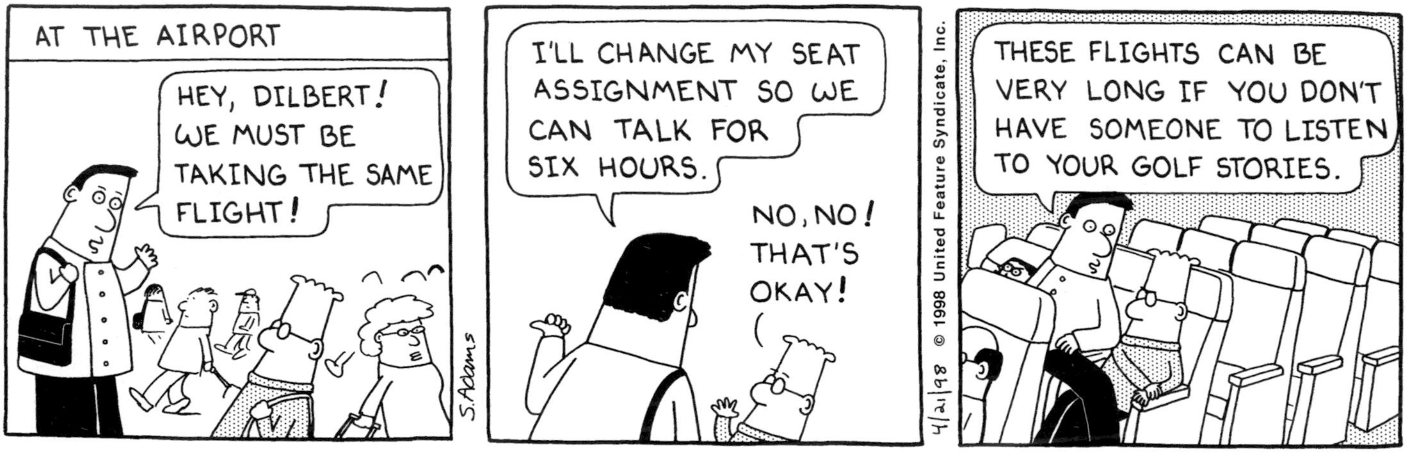
AT THE AIRPORT
HEY, DILBERT! WE MUST BE TAKING THE SAME FLIGHT!
S. Adams
I'LL CHANGE MY SEAT ASSIGNMENT SO WE CAN TALK FOR SIX HOURS.
NO, NO! THAT'S OKAY!
4/21/98 © 1998 United Feature Syndicate, Inc.
THESE FLIGHTS CAN BE VERY LONG IF YOU DON'T HAVE SOMEONE TO LISTEN TO YOUR GOLF STORIES.

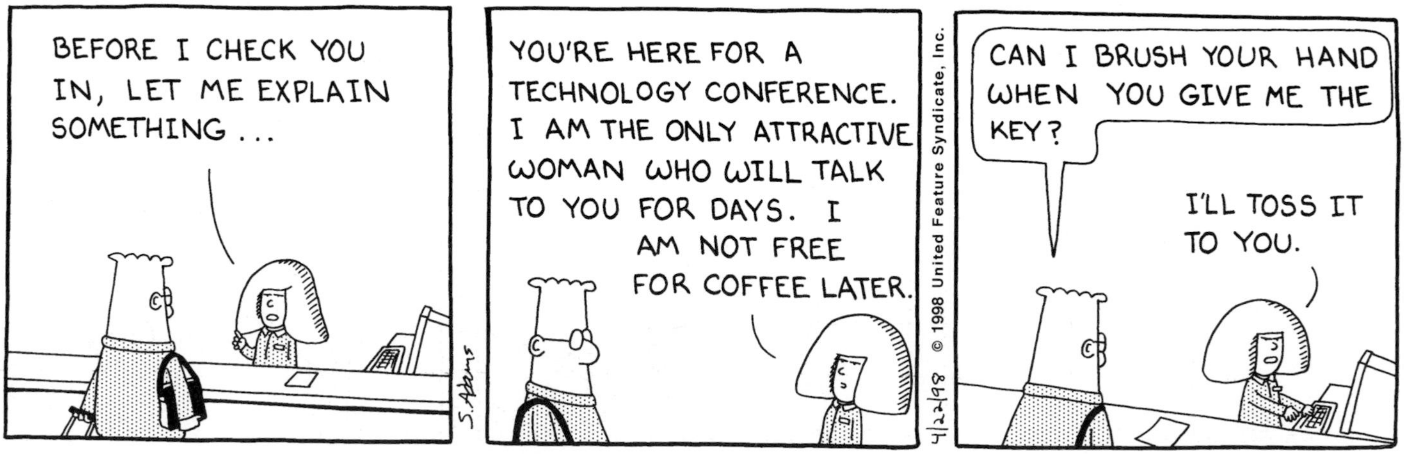
BEFORE I CHECK YOU IN, LET ME EXPLAIN SOMETHING . . .
S. Adams
YOU'RE HERE FOR A TECHNOLOGY CONFERENCE. I AM THE ONLY ATTRACTIVE WOMAN WHO WILL TALK TO YOU FOR DAYS. I AM NOT FREE FOR COFFEE LATER.
4/22/98 © 1998 United Feature Syndicate, Inc.
CAN I BRUSH YOUR HAND WHEN YOU GIVE ME THE KEY?
I'LL TOSS IT TO YOU.

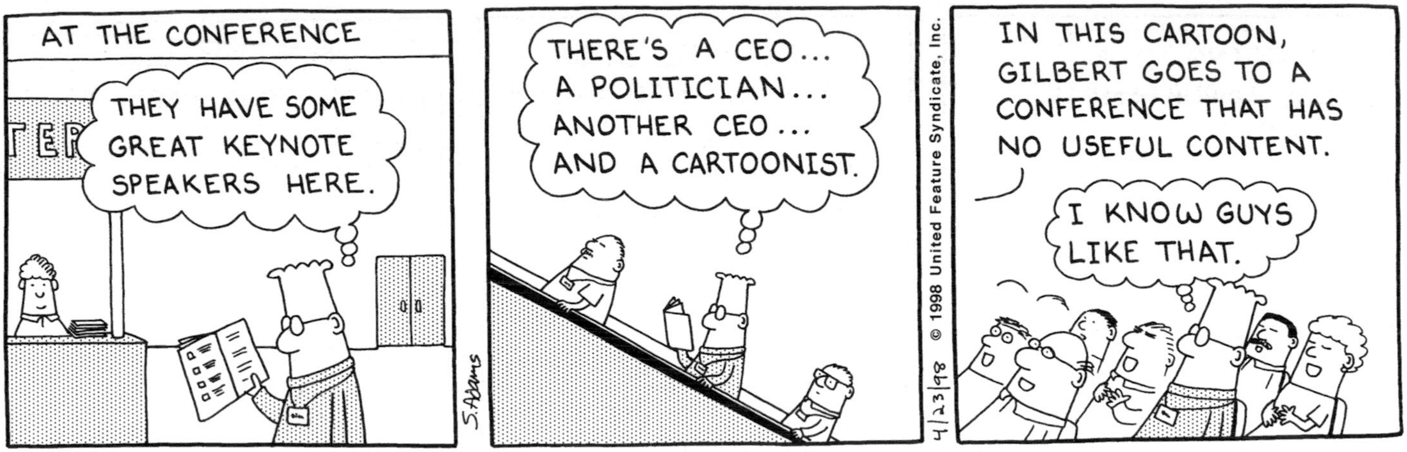
AT THE CONFERENCE
THEY HAVE SOME GREAT KEYNOTE SPEAKERS HERE.
THERE'S A CEO... A POLITICIAN... ANOTHER CEO... AND A CARTOONIST.
IN THIS CARTOON, GILBERT GOES TO A CONFERENCE THAT HAS NO USEFUL CONTENT.
I KNOW GUYS LIKE THAT.
© 1998 United Feature Syndicate, Inc.

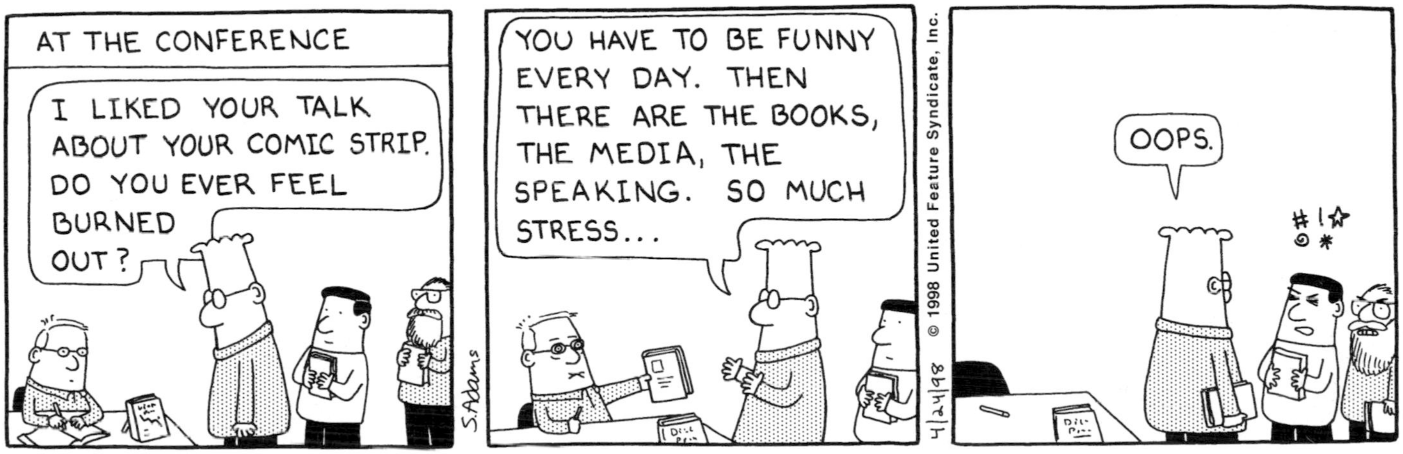
AT THE CONFERENCE
I LIKED YOUR TALK ABOUT YOUR COMIC STRIP. DO YOU EVER FEEL BURNED OUT?
YOU HAVE TO BE FUNNY EVERY DAY. THEN THERE ARE THE BOOKS, THE MEDIA, THE SPEAKING. SO MUCH STRESS...
OOPS.
© 1998 United Feature Syndicate, Inc.

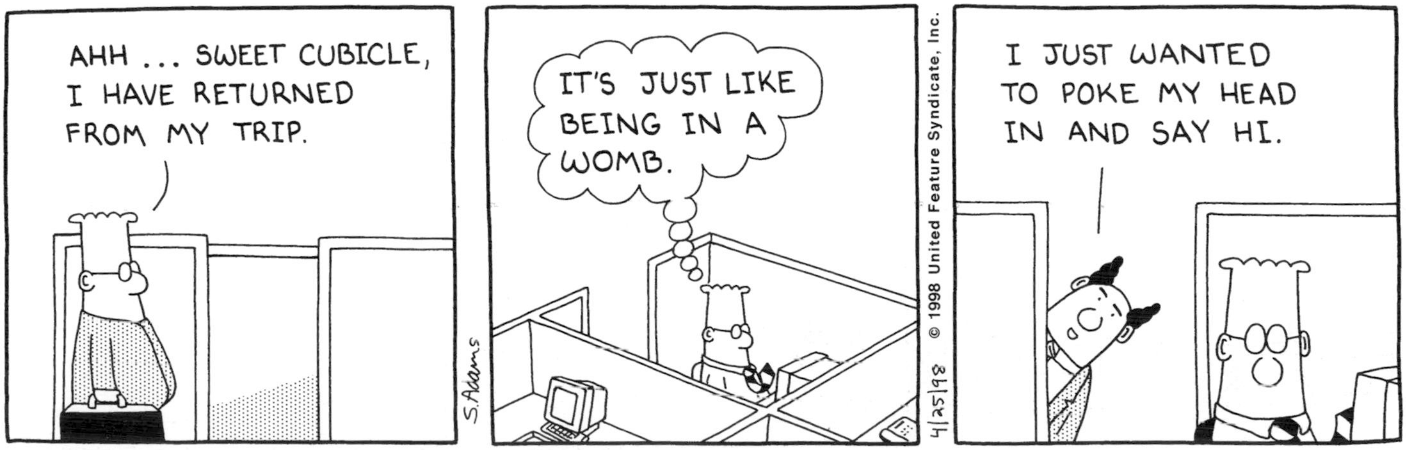
AHH ... SWEET CUBICLE, I HAVE RETURNED FROM MY TRIP.
IT'S JUST LIKE BEING IN A WOMB.
I JUST WANTED TO POKE MY HEAD IN AND SAY HI.
© 1998 United Feature Syndicate, Inc.

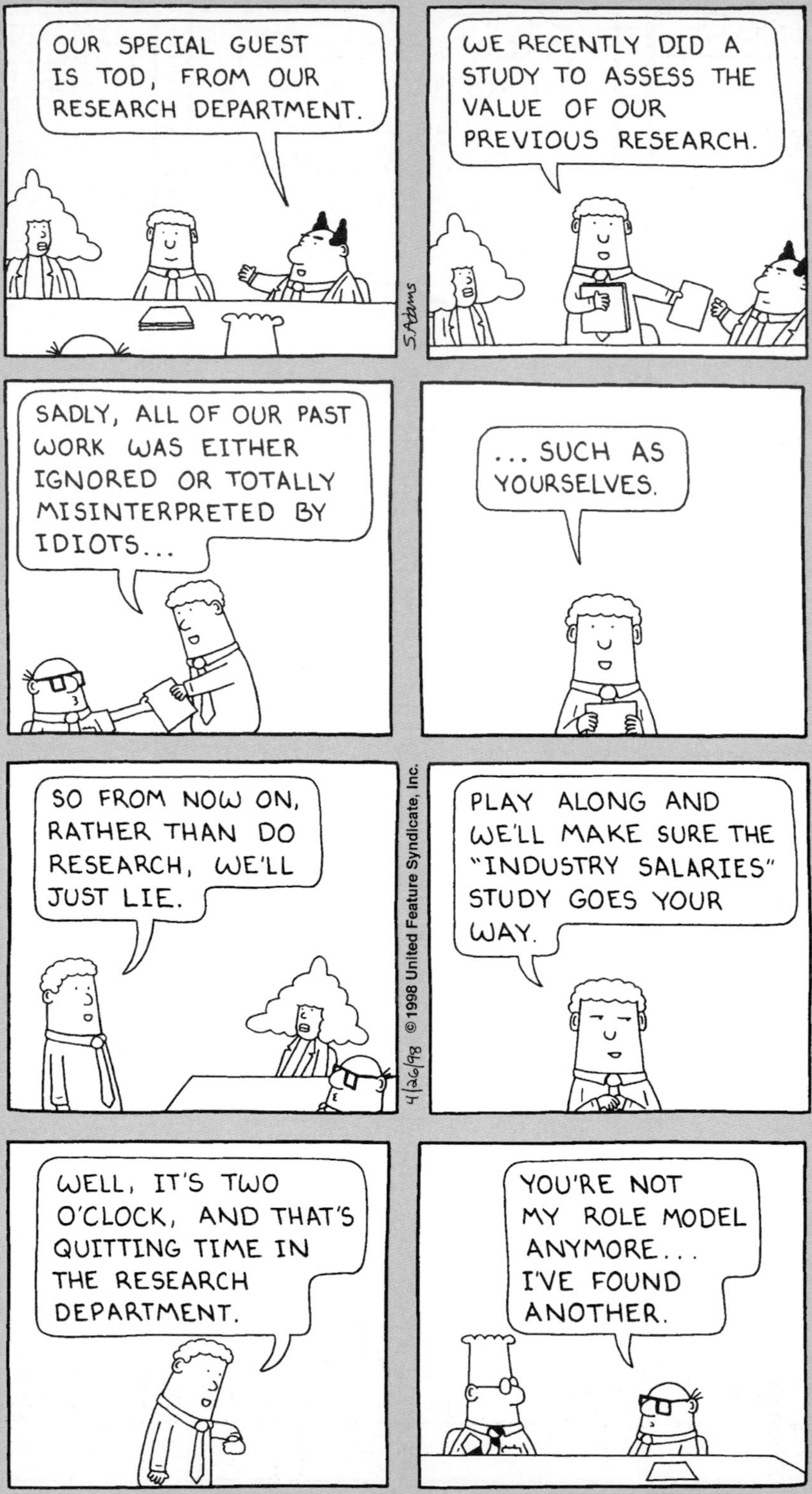
OUR SPECIAL GUEST IS TOD, FROM OUR RESEARCH DEPARTMENT.
WE RECENTLY DID A STUDY TO ASSESS THE VALUE OF OUR PREVIOUS RESEARCH.
S.Adams
SADLY, ALL OF OUR PAST WORK WAS EITHER IGNORED OR TOTALLY MISINTERPRETED BY IDIOTS...
... SUCH AS YOURSELVES.
SO FROM NOW ON, RATHER THAN DO RESEARCH, WE'LL JUST LIE.
4/26/98 © 1998 United Feature Syndicate, Inc.
PLAY ALONG AND WE'LL MAKE SURE THE "INDUSTRY SALARIES" STUDY GOES YOUR WAY.
WELL, IT'S TWO O'CLOCK, AND THAT'S QUITTING TIME IN THE RESEARCH DEPARTMENT.
YOU'RE NOT MY ROLE MODEL ANYMORE... I'VE FOUND ANOTHER.

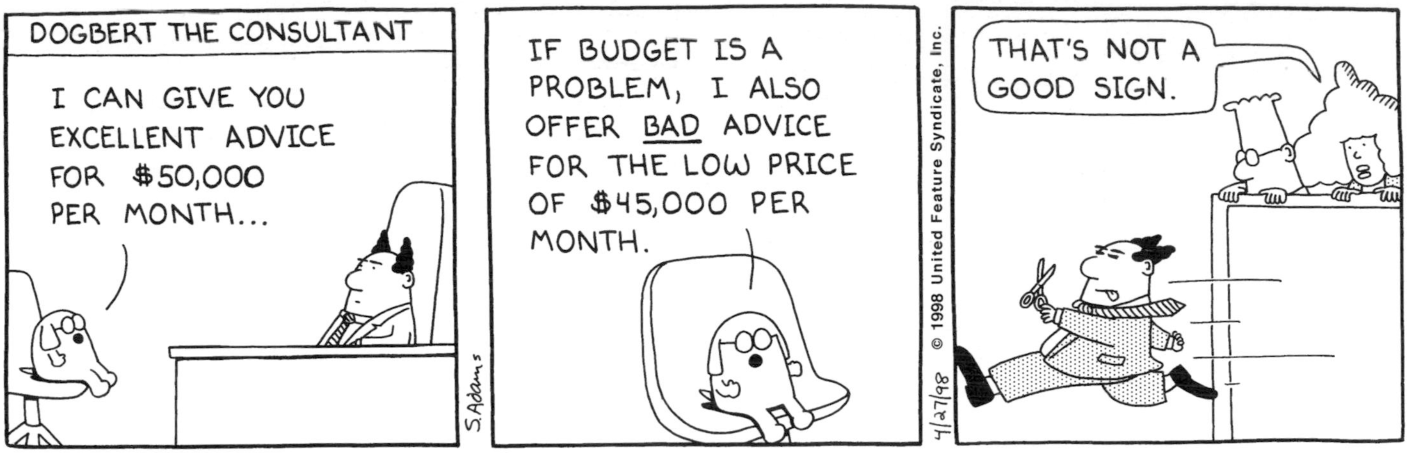
DOGBERT THE CONSULTANT
I CAN GIVE YOU EXCELLENT ADVICE FOR $50,000 PER MONTH...
IF BUDGET IS A PROBLEM, I ALSO OFFER BAD ADVICE FOR THE LOW PRICE OF $45,000 PER MONTH.
THAT'S NOT A GOOD SIGN.
S. Adams
4/27/98 © 1998 United Feature Syndicate, Inc.

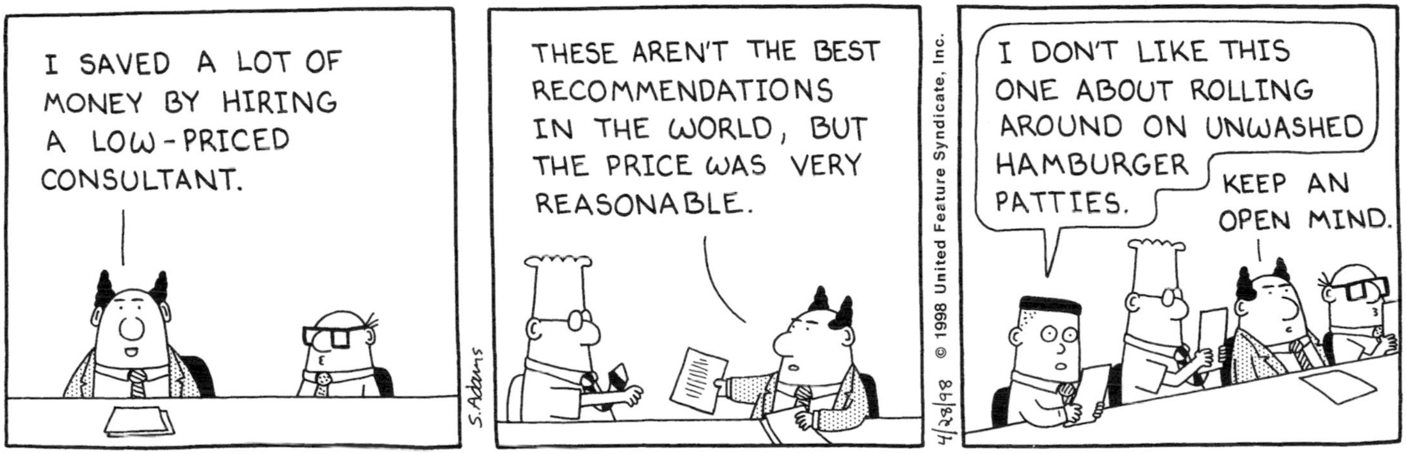
I SAVED A LOT OF MONEY BY HIRING A LOW-PRICED CONSULTANT.
THESE AREN'T THE BEST RECOMMENDATIONS IN THE WORLD, BUT THE PRICE WAS VERY REASONABLE.
I DON'T LIKE THIS ONE ABOUT ROLLING AROUND ON UNWASHED HAMBURGER PATTIES.
KEEP AN OPEN MIND.
S. Adams
4/28/98 © 1998 United Feature Syndicate, Inc.

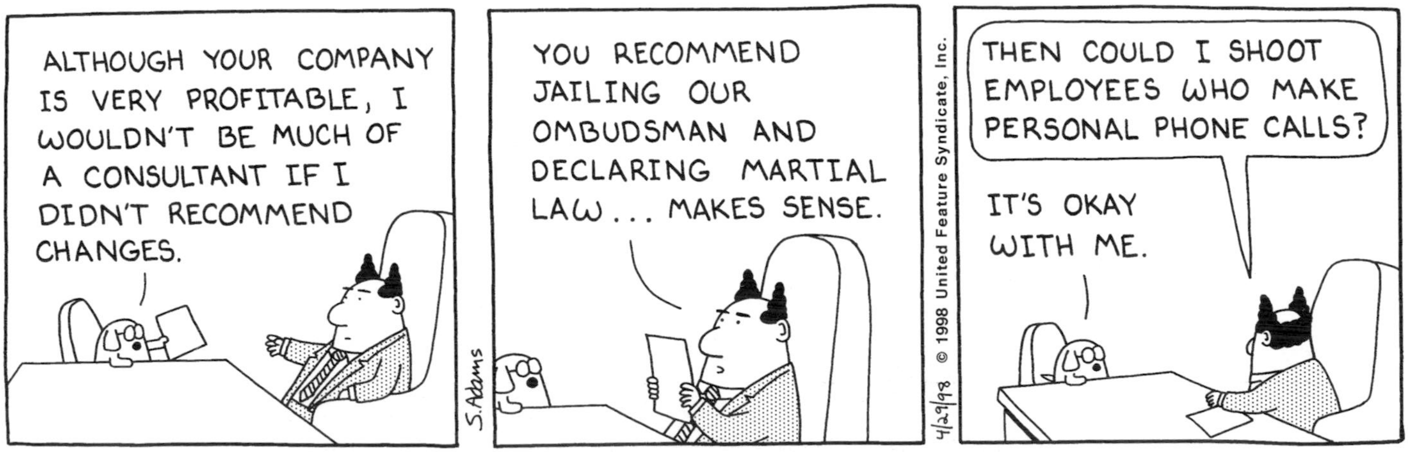
ALTHOUGH YOUR COMPANY IS VERY PROFITABLE, I WOULDN'T BE MUCH OF A CONSULTANT IF I DIDN'T RECOMMEND CHANGES.
YOU RECOMMEND JAILING OUR OMBUDSMAN AND DECLARING MARTIAL LAW... MAKES SENSE.
THEN COULD I SHOOT EMPLOYEES WHO MAKE PERSONAL PHONE CALLS?
IT'S OKAY WITH ME.
S. Adams
4/29/98 © 1998 United Feature Syndicate, Inc.

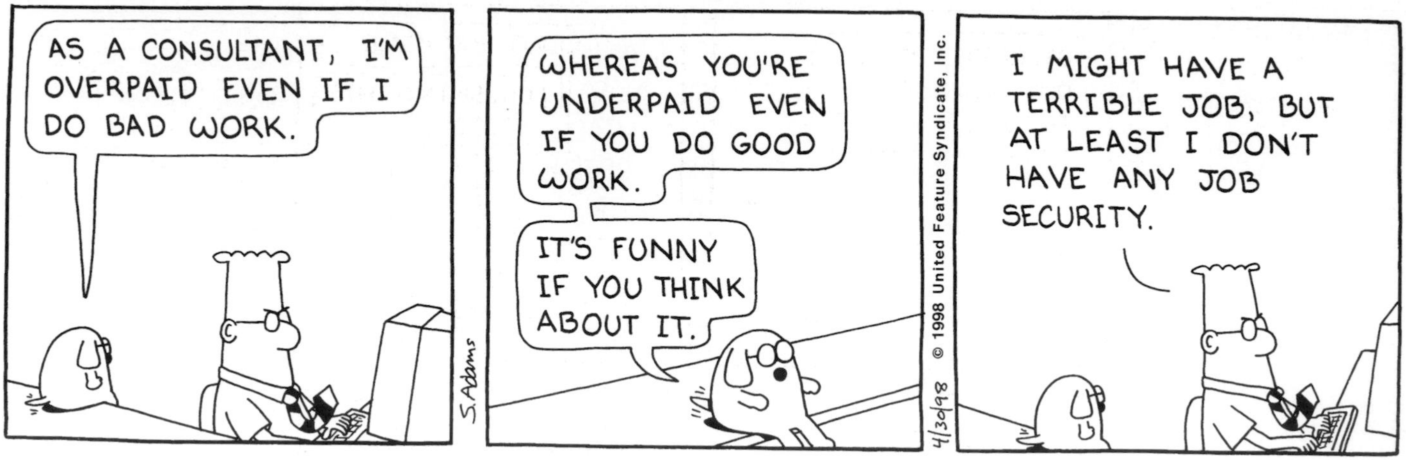
AS A CONSULTANT, I'M OVERPAID EVEN IF I DO BAD WORK.
WHEREAS YOU'RE UNDERPAID EVEN IF YOU DO GOOD WORK.
IT'S FUNNY IF YOU THINK ABOUT IT.
I MIGHT HAVE A TERRIBLE JOB, BUT AT LEAST I DON'T HAVE ANY JOB SECURITY.
S. Adams
4/30/98 © 1998 United Feature Syndicate, Inc.

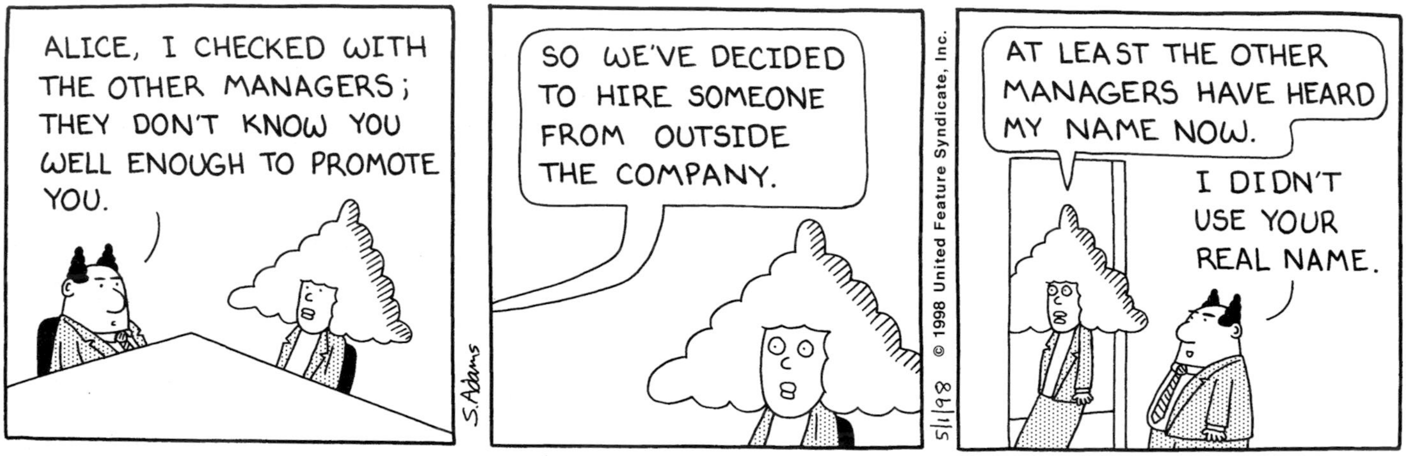
ALICE, I CHECKED WITH THE OTHER MANAGERS; THEY DON'T KNOW YOU WELL ENOUGH TO PROMOTE YOU.
SO WE'VE DECIDED TO HIRE SOMEONE FROM OUTSIDE THE COMPANY.
AT LEAST THE OTHER MANAGERS HAVE HEARD MY NAME NOW.
I DIDN'T USE YOUR REAL NAME.
S. Adams
5/1/98 © 1998 United Feature Syndicate, Inc.

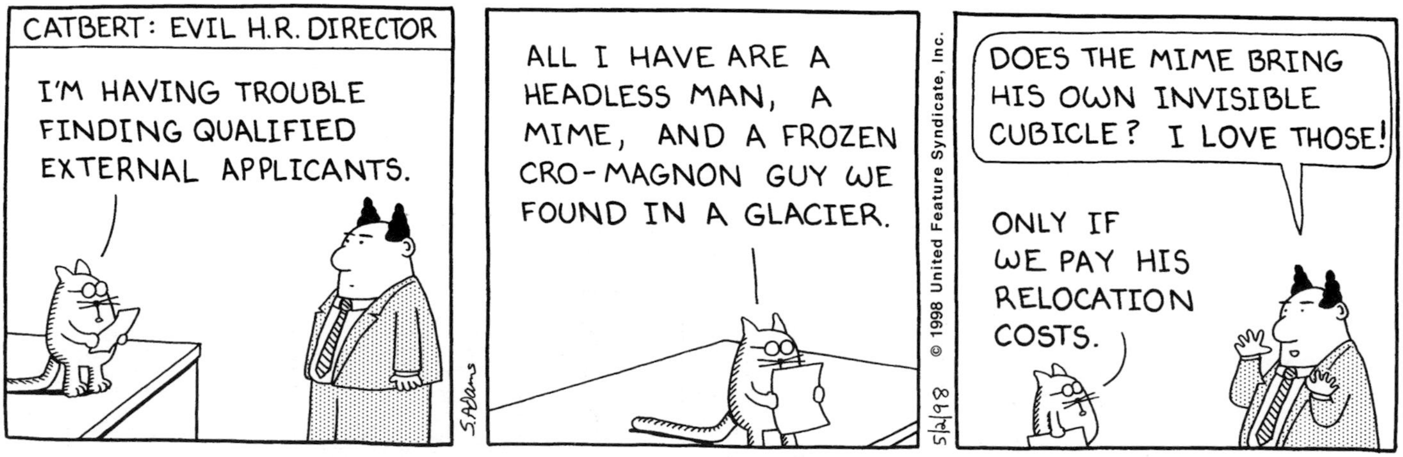
CATBERT: EVIL H.R. DIRECTOR
I'M HAVING TROUBLE FINDING QUALIFIED EXTERNAL APPLICANTS.
ALL I HAVE ARE A HEADLESS MAN, A MIME, AND A FROZEN CRO-MAGNON GUY WE FOUND IN A GLACIER.
DOES THE MIME BRING HIS OWN INVISIBLE CUBICLE? I LOVE THOSE!
ONLY IF WE PAY HIS RELOCATION COSTS.
S. Adams
5/2/98 © 1998 United Feature Syndicate, Inc.

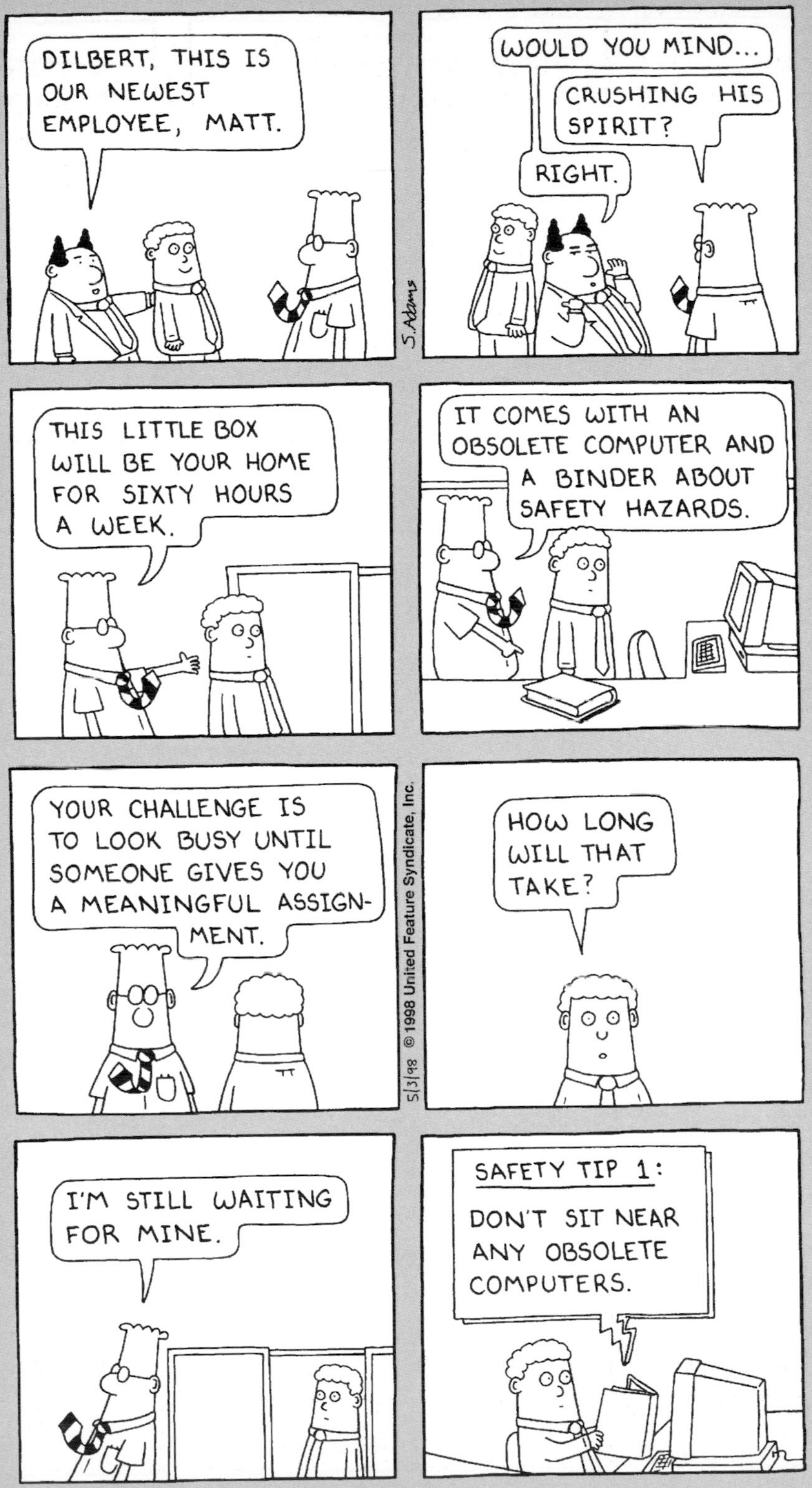
DILBERT, THIS IS OUR NEWEST EMPLOYEE, MATT.
S. Adams
WOULD YOU MIND...
CRUSHING HIS SPIRIT?
RIGHT.
THIS LITTLE BOX WILL BE YOUR HOME FOR SIXTY HOURS A WEEK.
IT COMES WITH AN OBSOLETE COMPUTER AND A BINDER ABOUT SAFETY HAZARDS.
YOUR CHALLENGE IS TO LOOK BUSY UNTIL SOMEONE GIVES YOU A MEANINGFUL ASSIGNMENT.
5/3/98 © 1998 United Feature Syndicate, Inc.
HOW LONG WILL THAT TAKE?
I'M STILL WAITING FOR MINE.
SAFETY TIP 1:
DON'T SIT NEAR ANY OBSOLETE COMPUTERS.

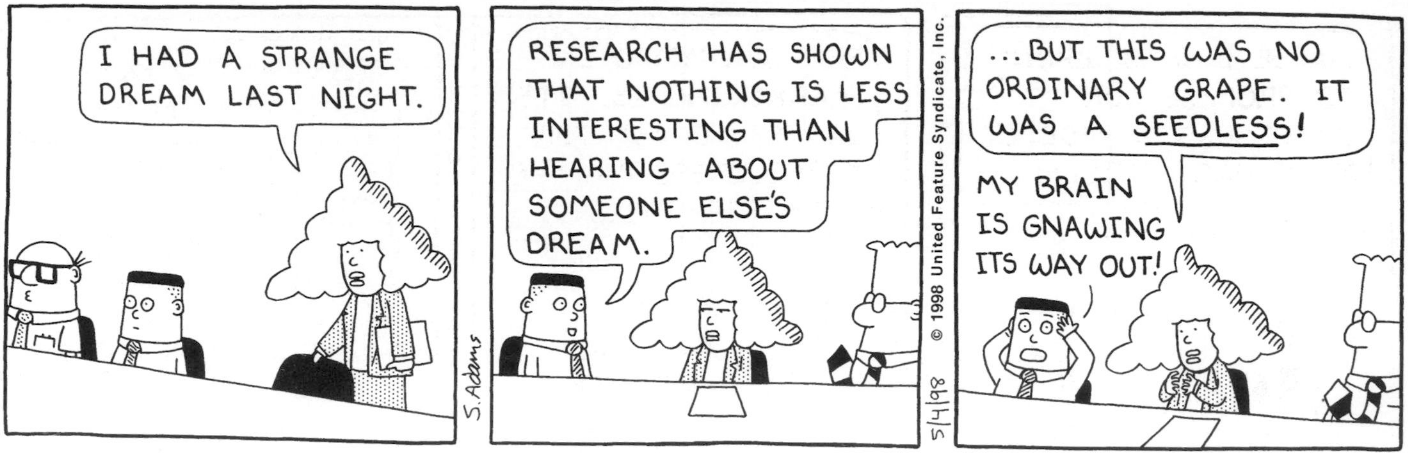
I HAD A STRANGE DREAM LAST NIGHT.
S. Adams
RESEARCH HAS SHOWN THAT NOTHING IS LESS INTERESTING THAN HEARING ABOUT SOMEONE ELSE'S DREAM.
5/4/98
© 1998 United Feature Syndicate, Inc.
...BUT THIS WAS NO ORDINARY GRAPE. IT WAS A SEEDLESS!
MY BRAIN IS GNAWING ITS WAY OUT!

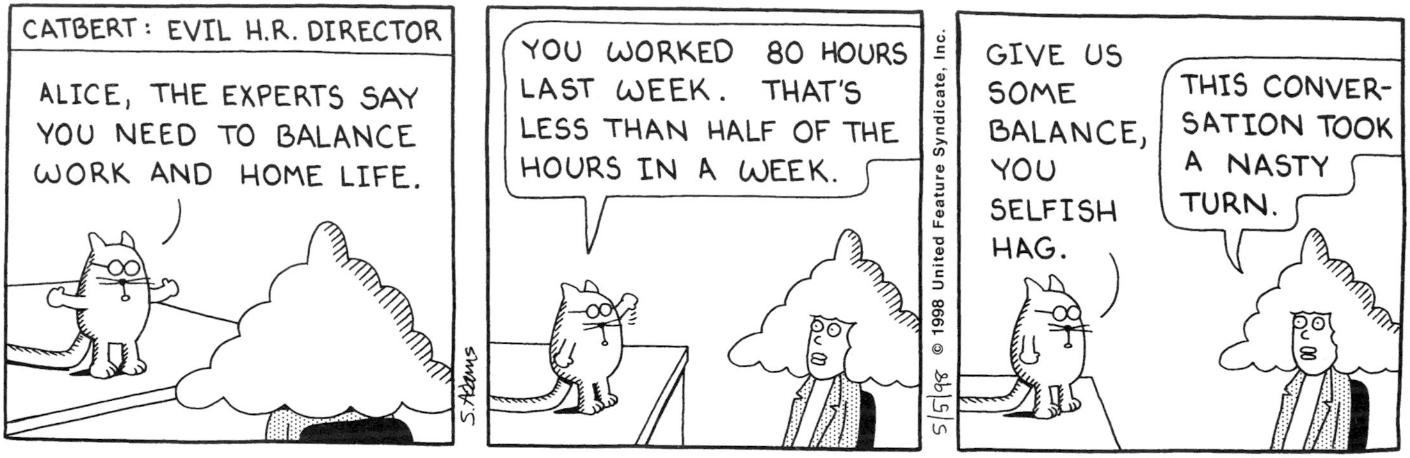
CATBERT: EVIL H.R. DIRECTOR
ALICE, THE EXPERTS SAY YOU NEED TO BALANCE WORK AND HOME LIFE.
S. Adams
YOU WORKED 80 HOURS LAST WEEK. THAT'S LESS THAN HALF OF THE HOURS IN A WEEK.
5/5/98
© 1998 United Feature Syndicate, Inc.
GIVE US SOME BALANCE, YOU SELFISH HAG.
THIS CONVERSATION TOOK A NASTY TURN.

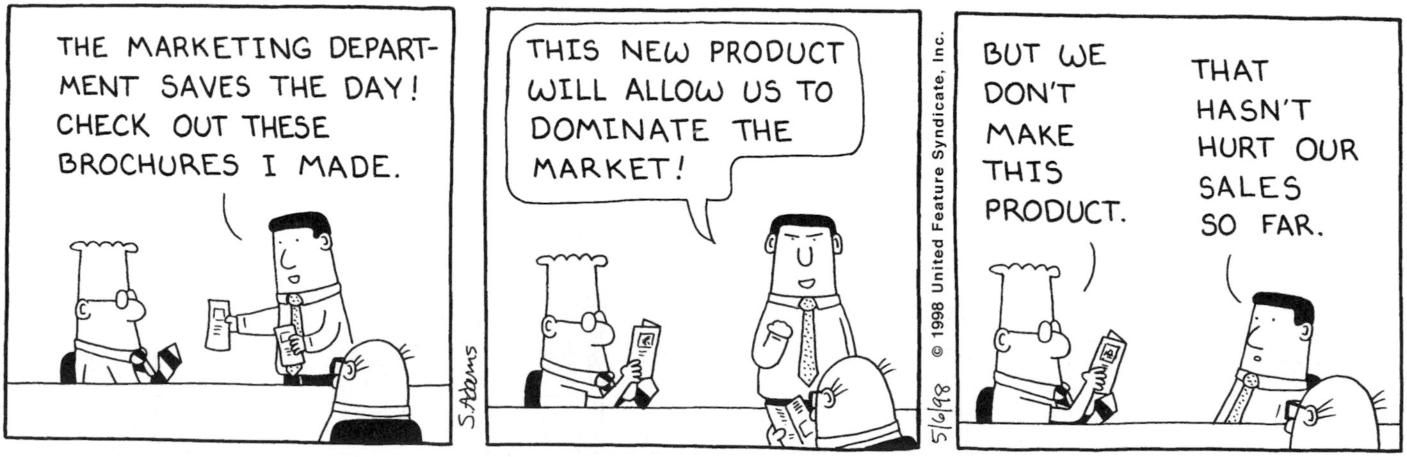
THE MARKETING DEPARTMENT SAVES THE DAY! CHECK OUT THESE BROCHURES I MADE.
S. Adams
THIS NEW PRODUCT WILL ALLOW US TO DOMINATE THE MARKET!
5/6/98
© 1998 United Feature Syndicate, Inc.
BUT WE DON'T MAKE THIS PRODUCT.
THAT HASN'T HURT OUR SALES SO FAR.

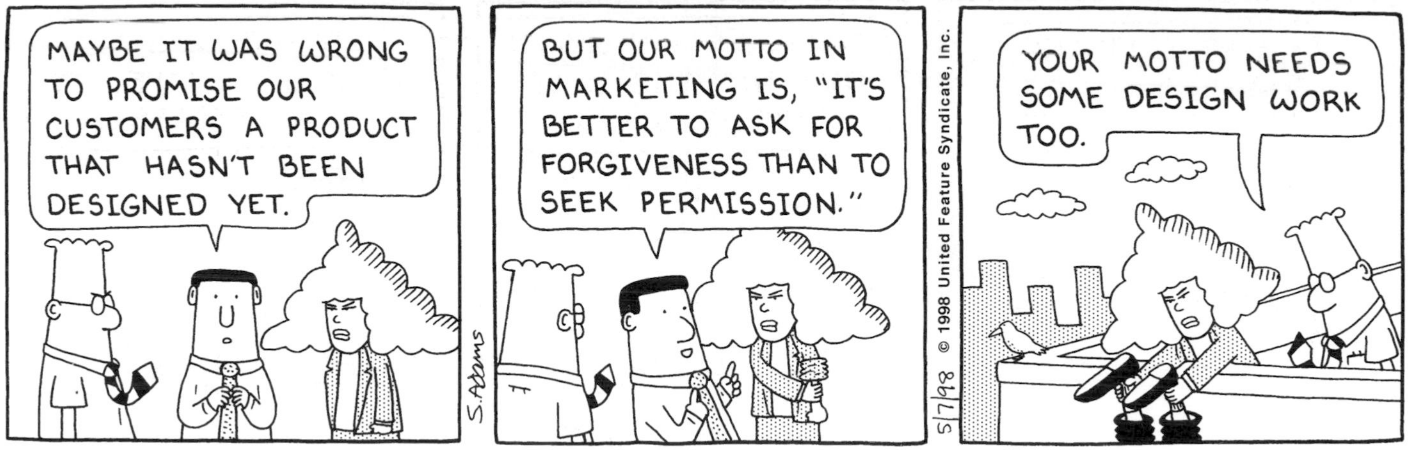
MAYBE IT WAS WRONG TO PROMISE OUR CUSTOMERS A PRODUCT THAT HASN'T BEEN DESIGNED YET.
S. Adams
BUT OUR MOTTO IN MARKETING IS, "IT'S BETTER TO ASK FOR FORGIVENESS THAN TO SEEK PERMISSION."
5/7/98 © 1998 United Feature Syndicate, Inc.
YOUR MOTTO NEEDS SOME DESIGN WORK TOO.

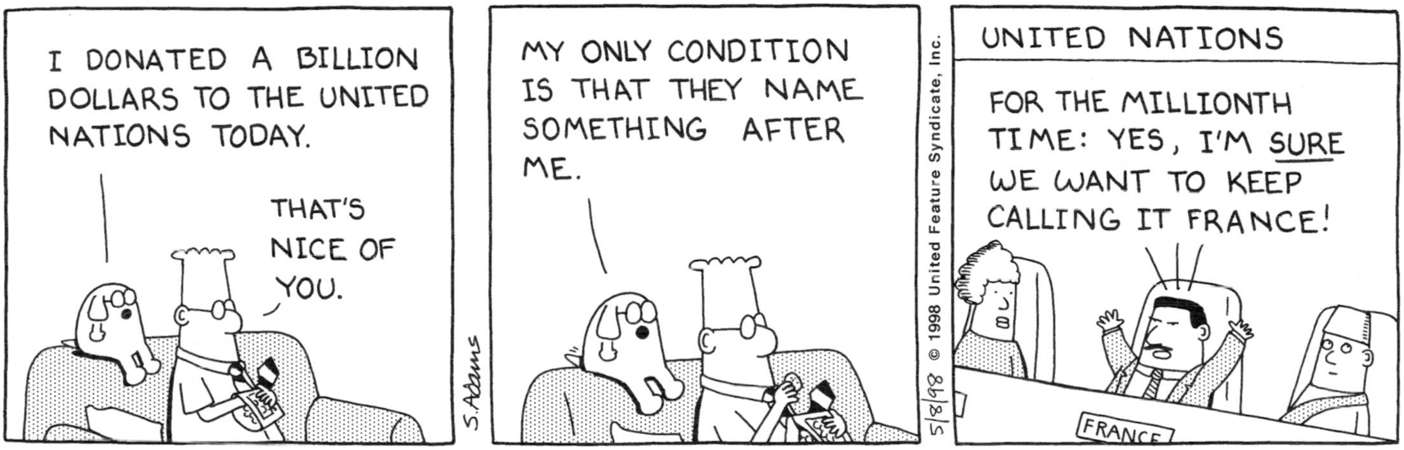
I DONATED A BILLION DOLLARS TO THE UNITED NATIONS TODAY.
THAT'S NICE OF YOU.
S. Adams
MY ONLY CONDITION IS THAT THEY NAME SOMETHING AFTER ME.
5/8/98 © 1998 United Feature Syndicate, Inc.
UNITED NATIONS
FOR THE MILLIONTH TIME: YES, I'M SURE WE WANT TO KEEP CALLING IT FRANCE!
FRANCE

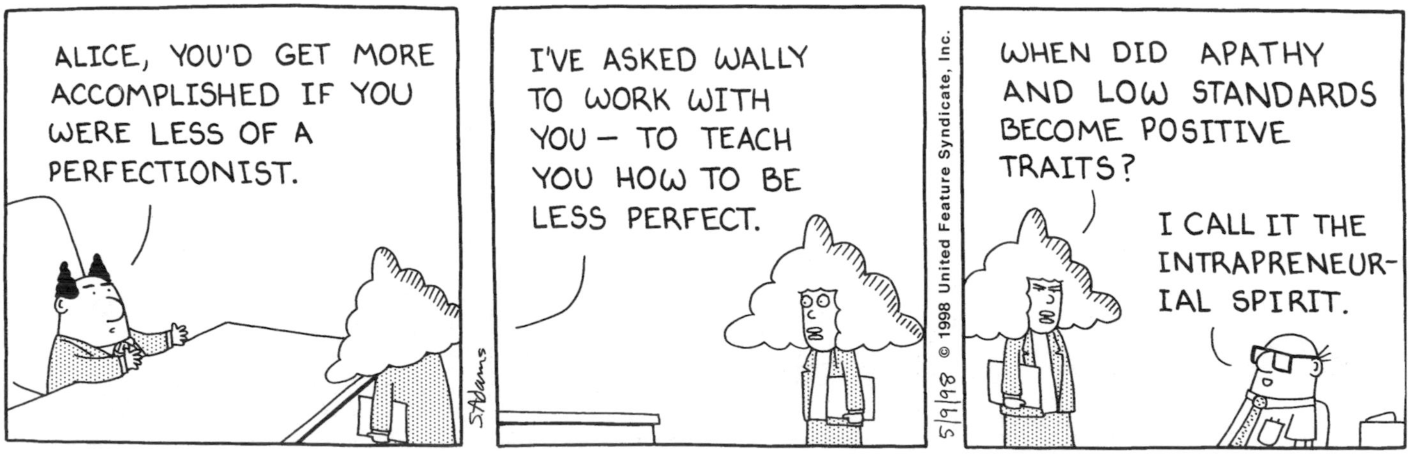
ALICE, YOU'D GET MORE ACCOMPLISHED IF YOU WERE LESS OF A PERFECTIONIST.
S. Adams
I'VE ASKED WALLY TO WORK WITH YOU – TO TEACH YOU HOW TO BE LESS PERFECT.
5/9/98 © 1998 United Feature Syndicate, Inc.
WHEN DID APATHY AND LOW STANDARDS BECOME POSITIVE TRAITS?
I CALL IT THE INTRAPRENEURIAL SPIRIT.

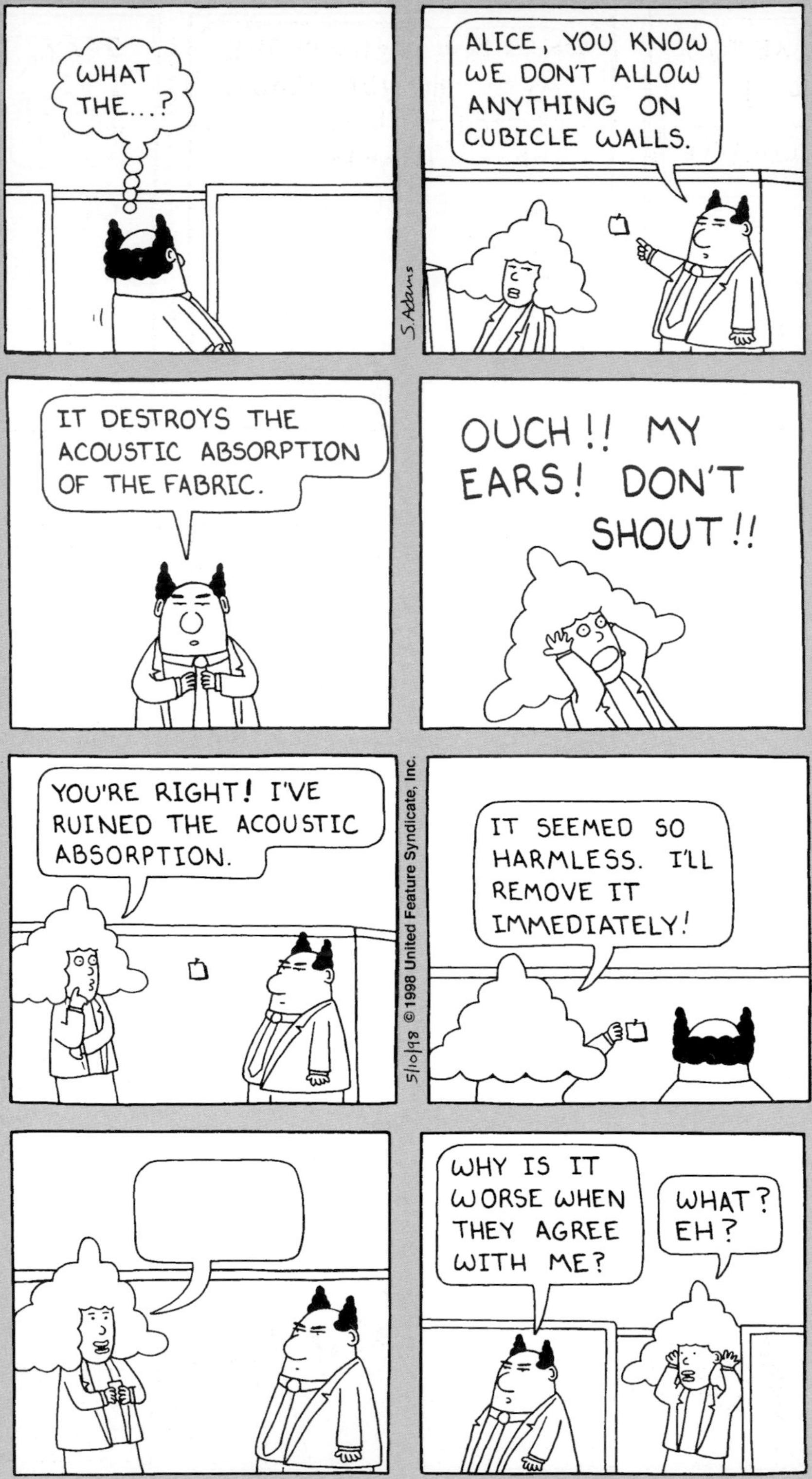
WHAT THE...?
ALICE, YOU KNOW WE DON'T ALLOW ANYTHING ON CUBICLE WALLS.
S. Adams
IT DESTROYS THE ACOUSTIC ABSORPTION OF THE FABRIC.
OUCH!! MY EARS! DON'T SHOUT!!
YOU'RE RIGHT! I'VE RUINED THE ACOUSTIC ABSORPTION.
5/10/98 © 1998 United Feature Syndicate, Inc.
IT SEEMED SO HARMLESS. I'LL REMOVE IT IMMEDIATELY!
WHY IS IT WORSE WHEN THEY AGREE WITH ME?
WHAT? EH?

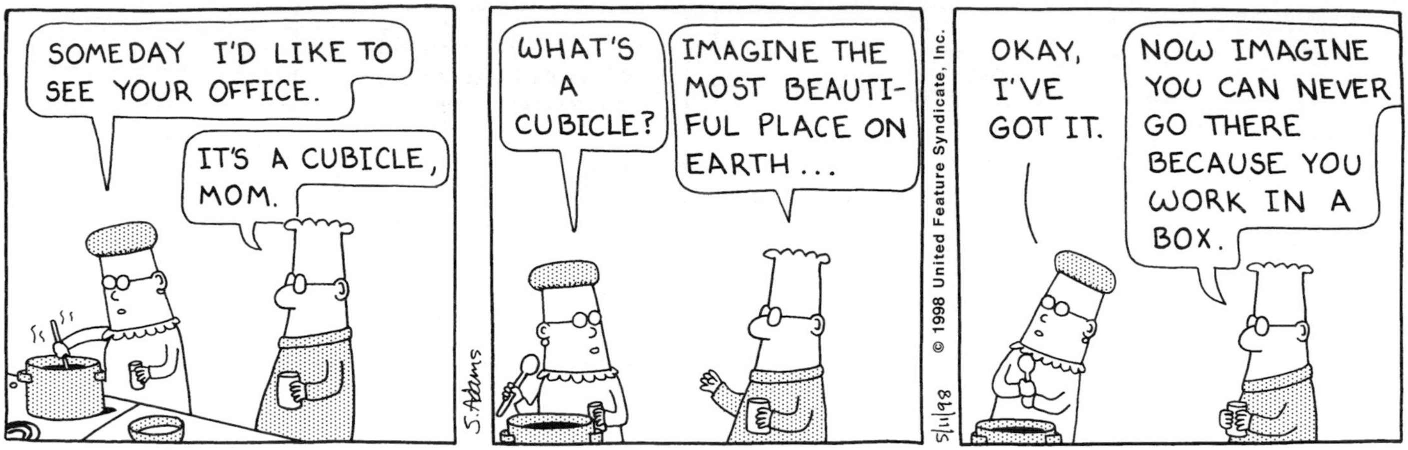
SOMEDAY I'D LIKE TO SEE YOUR OFFICE.
IT'S A CUBICLE, MOM.
WHAT'S A CUBICLE?
IMAGINE THE MOST BEAUTIFUL PLACE ON EARTH ...
OKAY, I'VE GOT IT.
NOW IMAGINE YOU CAN NEVER GO THERE BECAUSE YOU WORK IN A BOX.
S. Adams
5/11/98
© 1998 United Feature Syndicate, Inc.

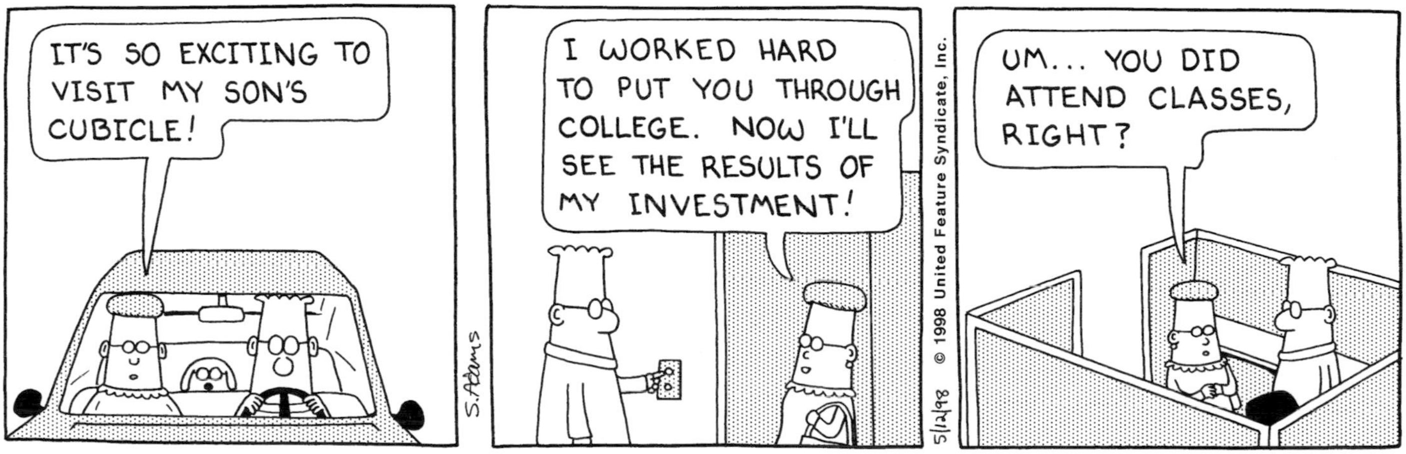
IT'S SO EXCITING TO VISIT MY SON'S CUBICLE!
I WORKED HARD TO PUT YOU THROUGH COLLEGE. NOW I'LL SEE THE RESULTS OF MY INVESTMENT!
UM... YOU DID ATTEND CLASSES, RIGHT?
S. Adams
5/12/98
© 1998 United Feature Syndicate, Inc.

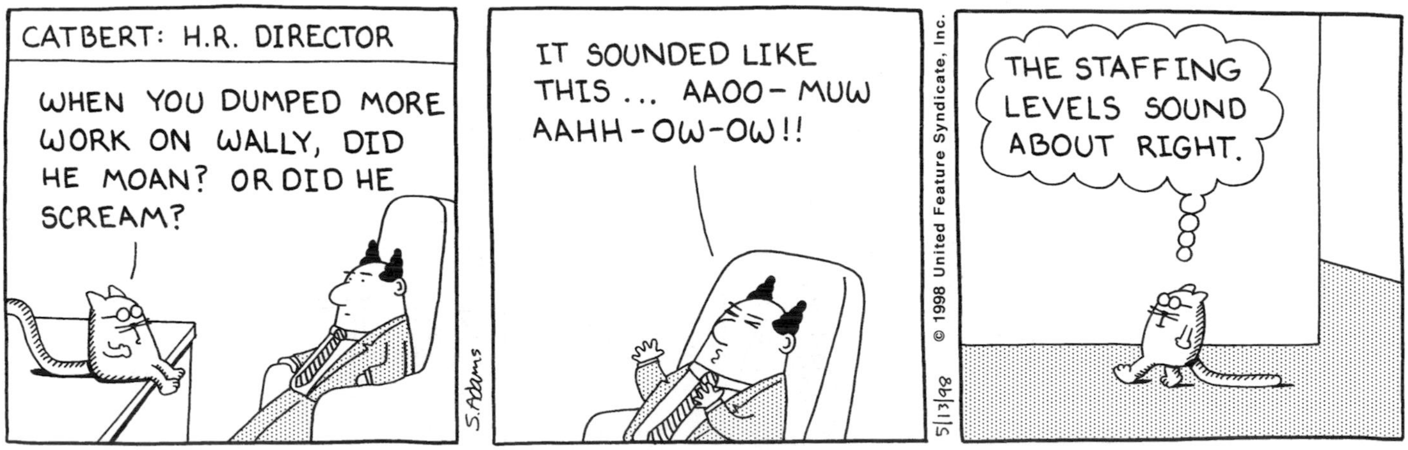
CATBERT: H.R. DIRECTOR
WHEN YOU DUMPED MORE WORK ON WALLY, DID HE MOAN? OR DID HE SCREAM?
IT SOUNDED LIKE THIS ... AAOO-MUW AAHH-OW-OW!!
THE STAFFING LEVELS SOUND ABOUT RIGHT.
S. Adams
5/13/98
© 1998 United Feature Syndicate, Inc.

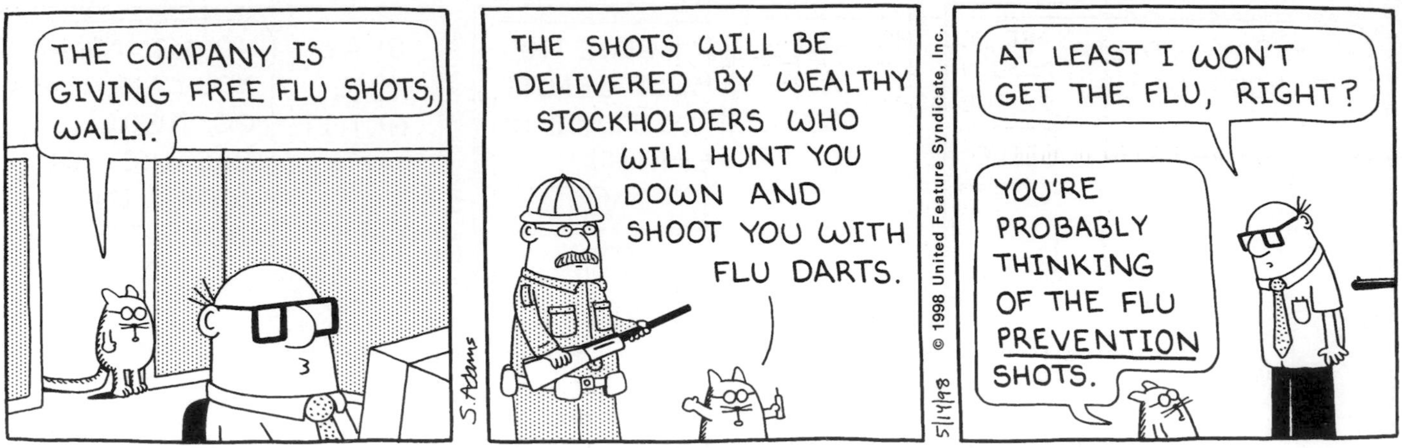
THE COMPANY IS GIVING FREE FLU SHOTS, WALLY.
S. Adams
THE SHOTS WILL BE DELIVERED BY WEALTHY STOCKHOLDERS WHO WILL HUNT YOU DOWN AND SHOOT YOU WITH FLU DARTS.
5/14/98 © 1998 United Feature Syndicate, Inc.
AT LEAST I WON'T GET THE FLU, RIGHT?
YOU'RE PROBABLY THINKING OF THE FLU PREVENTION SHOTS.

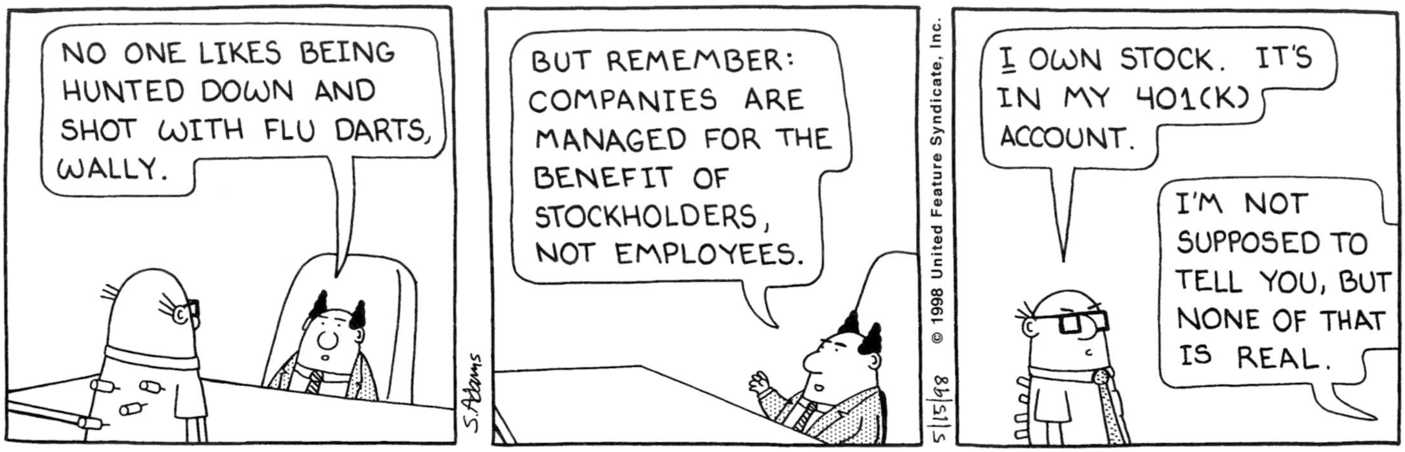
NO ONE LIKES BEING HUNTED DOWN AND SHOT WITH FLU DARTS, WALLY.
S. Adams
BUT REMEMBER: COMPANIES ARE MANAGED FOR THE BENEFIT OF STOCKHOLDERS, NOT EMPLOYEES.
5/15/98 © 1998 United Feature Syndicate, Inc.
I OWN STOCK. IT'S IN MY 401(K) ACCOUNT.
I'M NOT SUPPOSED TO TELL YOU, BUT NONE OF THAT IS REAL.

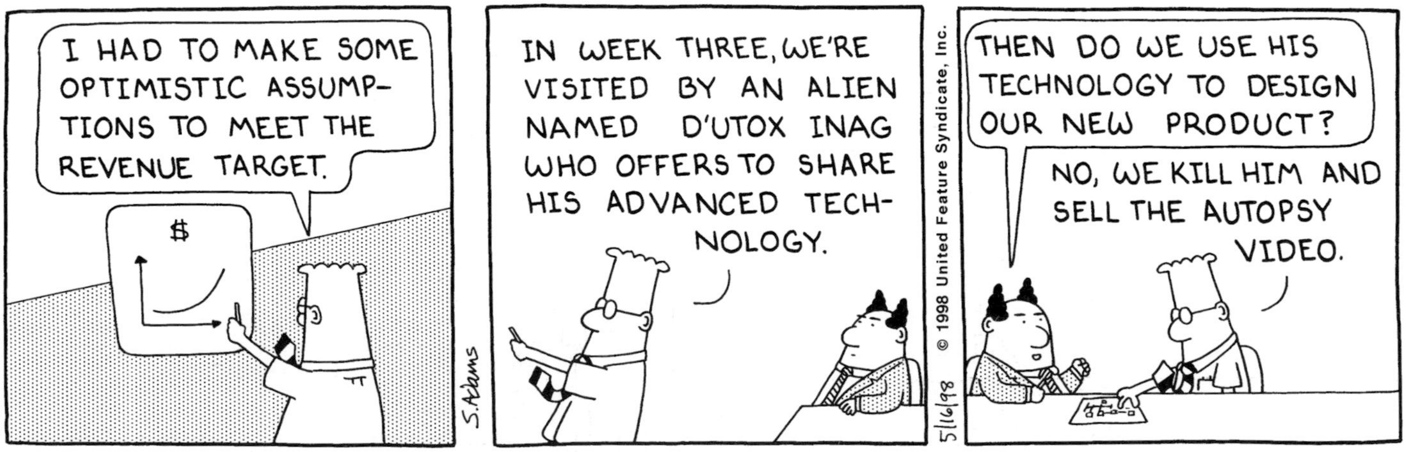
I HAD TO MAKE SOME OPTIMISTIC ASSUMPTIONS TO MEET THE REVENUE TARGET.
$
S. Adams
IN WEEK THREE, WE'RE VISITED BY AN ALIEN NAMED D'UTOX INAG WHO OFFERS TO SHARE HIS ADVANCED TECHNOLOGY.
5/16/98 © 1998 United Feature Syndicate, Inc.
THEN DO WE USE HIS TECHNOLOGY TO DESIGN OUR NEW PRODUCT?
NO, WE KILL HIM AND SELL THE AUTOPSY VIDEO.

ARE YOU THE POMPOUS AIRBAG OF THE OFFICE?
INDEED.
S. Adams
I'VE BEEN ASKED TO DEFLATE YOU.
MY SOURCES TELL ME THAT YOU COMBINE ARROGANCE WITH TRIVIA AND TRY TO PASS IT OFF AS INTELLIGENCE.
THAT'S BECAUSE I'M SURROUNDED BY FOOLS WHO DON'T EVEN KNOW THE CAPITAL OF ELBONIA!
5/17/98 © 1998 United Feature Syndicate, Inc.
I HAVE A SIGNED STATEMENT FROM YOUR WIFE...
...THAT YOU PUT WET LAUNDRY IN THE OVEN LAST NIGHT.
THAT EXPLAINS THE CHEWY CASSEROLE SHE SERVED ME THIS MORNING.

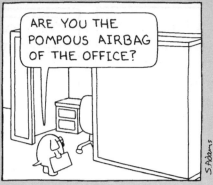

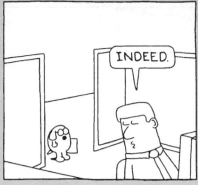

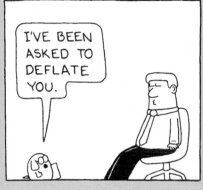

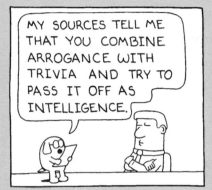

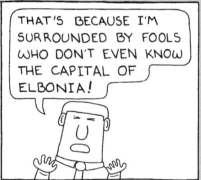

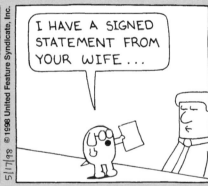

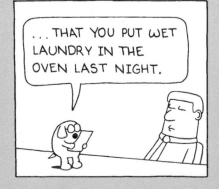

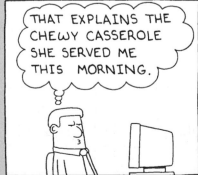

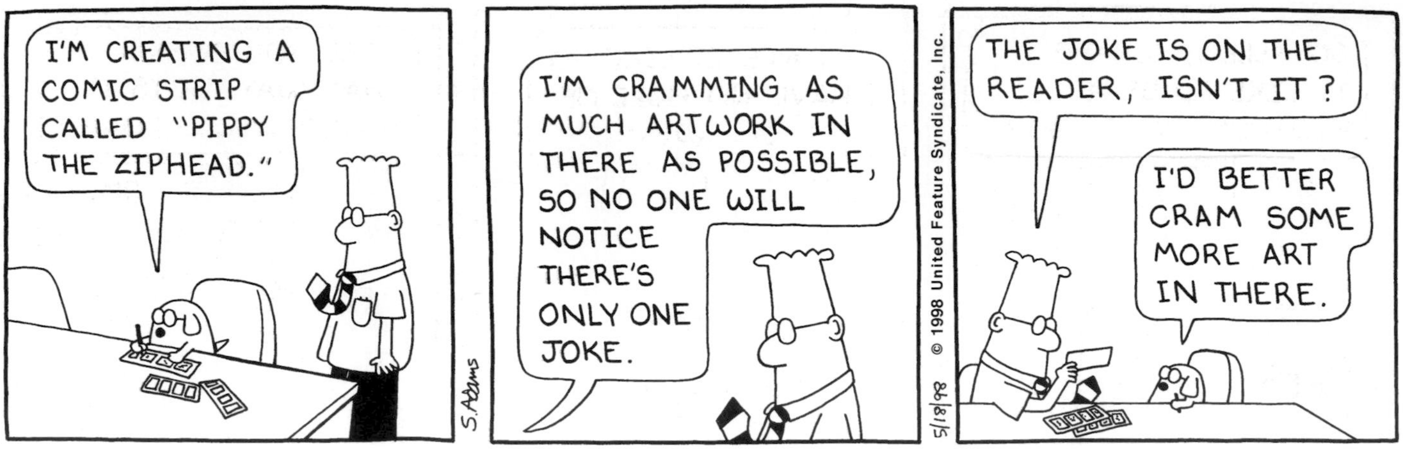
I'M CREATING A COMIC STRIP CALLED "PIPPY THE ZIPHEAD."
I'M CRAMMING AS MUCH ARTWORK IN THERE AS POSSIBLE, SO NO ONE WILL NOTICE THERE'S ONLY ONE JOKE.
THE JOKE IS ON THE READER, ISN'T IT?
I'D BETTER CRAM SOME MORE ART IN THERE.
S. Adams
5/18/98 © 1998 United Feature Syndicate, Inc.

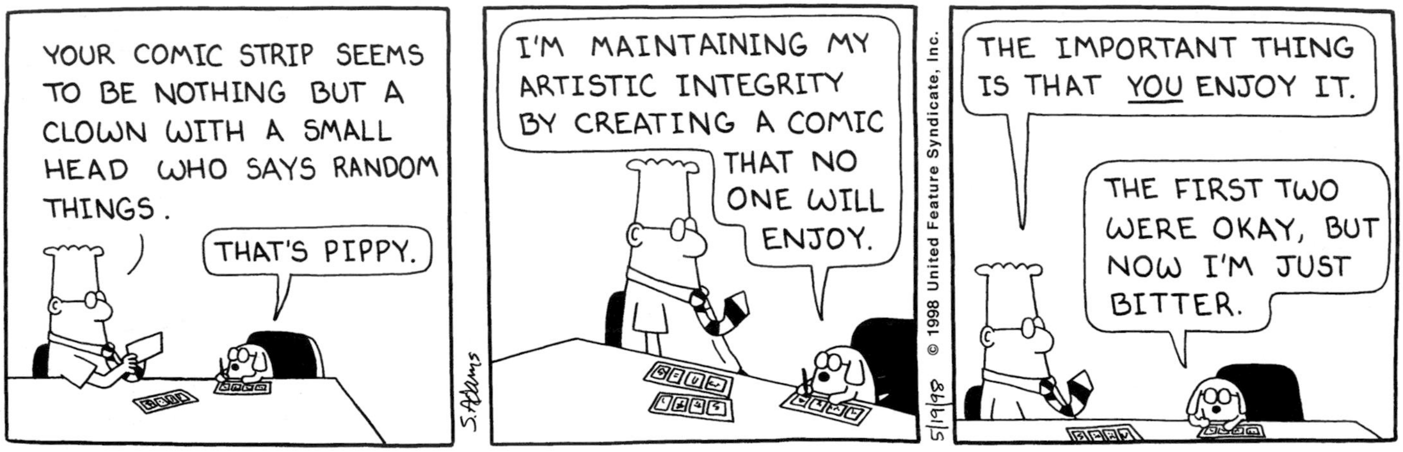
YOUR COMIC STRIP SEEMS TO BE NOTHING BUT A CLOWN WITH A SMALL HEAD WHO SAYS RANDOM THINGS.
THAT'S PIPPY.
I'M MAINTAINING MY ARTISTIC INTEGRITY BY CREATING A COMIC THAT NO ONE WILL ENJOY.
THE IMPORTANT THING IS THAT YOU ENJOY IT.
THE FIRST TWO WERE OKAY, BUT NOW I'M JUST BITTER.
S. Adams
5/19/98 © 1998 United Feature Syndicate, Inc.

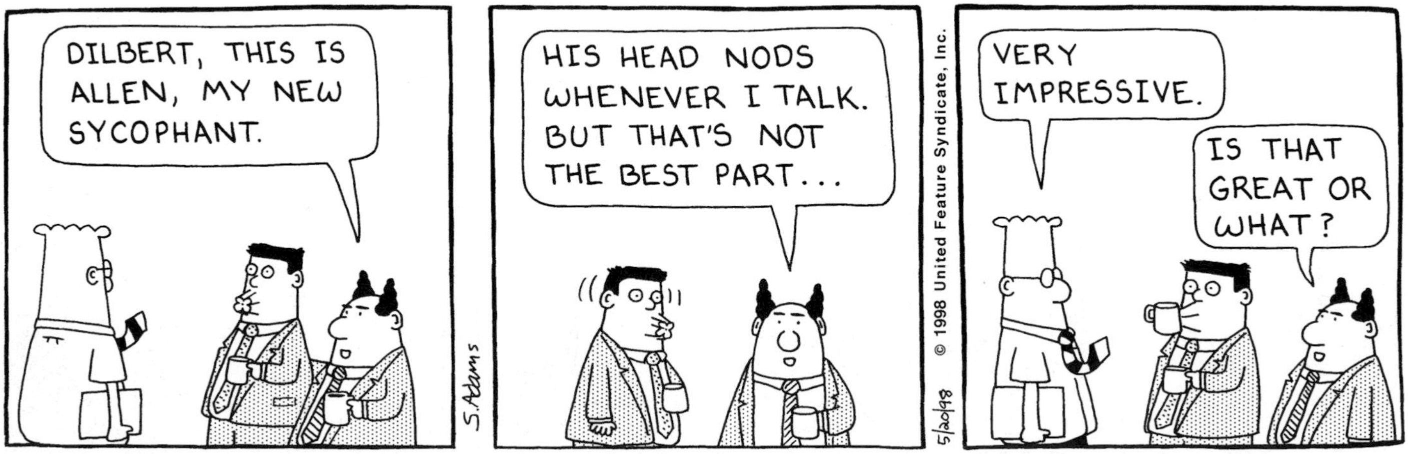
DILBERT, THIS IS ALLEN, MY NEW SYCOPHANT.
HIS HEAD NODS WHENEVER I TALK. BUT THAT'S NOT THE BEST PART...
VERY IMPRESSIVE.
IS THAT GREAT OR WHAT?
S. Adams
5/20/98 © 1998 United Feature Syndicate, Inc.

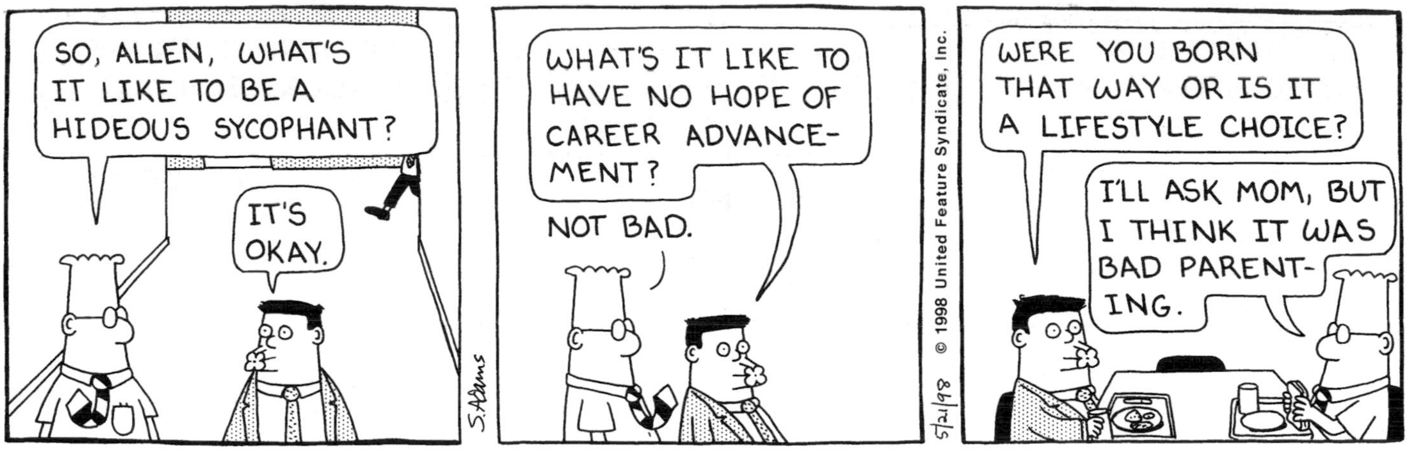
SO, ALLEN, WHAT'S IT LIKE TO BE A HIDEOUS SYCOPHANT?
IT'S OKAY.
WHAT'S IT LIKE TO HAVE NO HOPE OF CAREER ADVANCE-MENT?
NOT BAD.
WERE YOU BORN THAT WAY OR IS IT A LIFESTYLE CHOICE?
I'LL ASK MOM, BUT I THINK IT WAS BAD PARENT-ING.
S. Adams
5/21/98 © 1998 United Feature Syndicate, Inc.

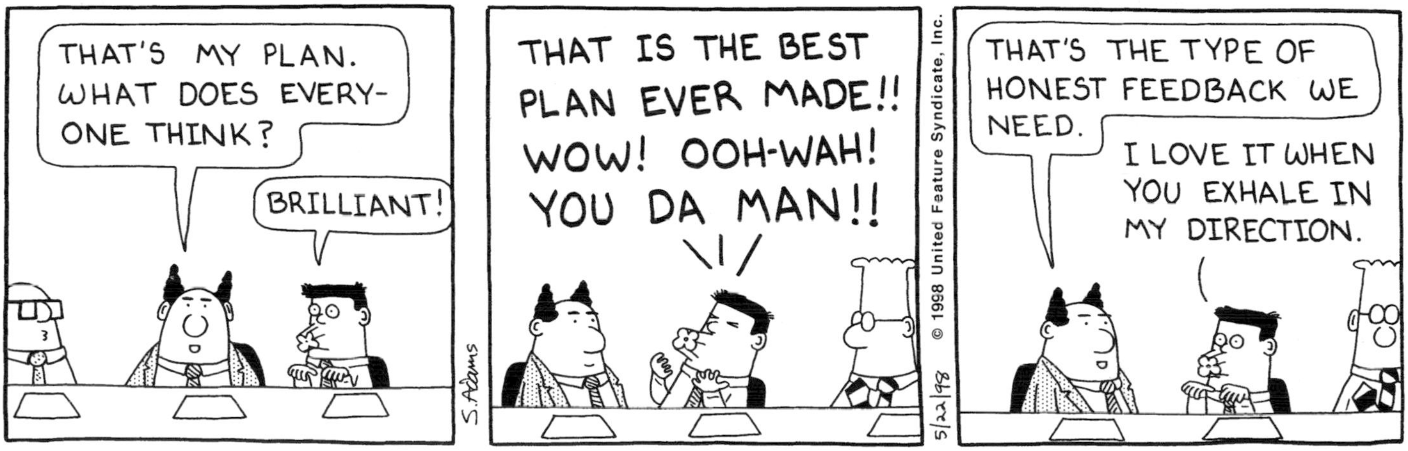
THAT'S MY PLAN. WHAT DOES EVERY-ONE THINK?
BRILLIANT!
THAT IS THE BEST PLAN EVER MADE!! WOW! OOH-WAH! YOU DA MAN!!
THAT'S THE TYPE OF HONEST FEEDBACK WE NEED.
I LOVE IT WHEN YOU EXHALE IN MY DIRECTION.
S. Adams
5/22/98 © 1998 United Feature Syndicate, Inc.

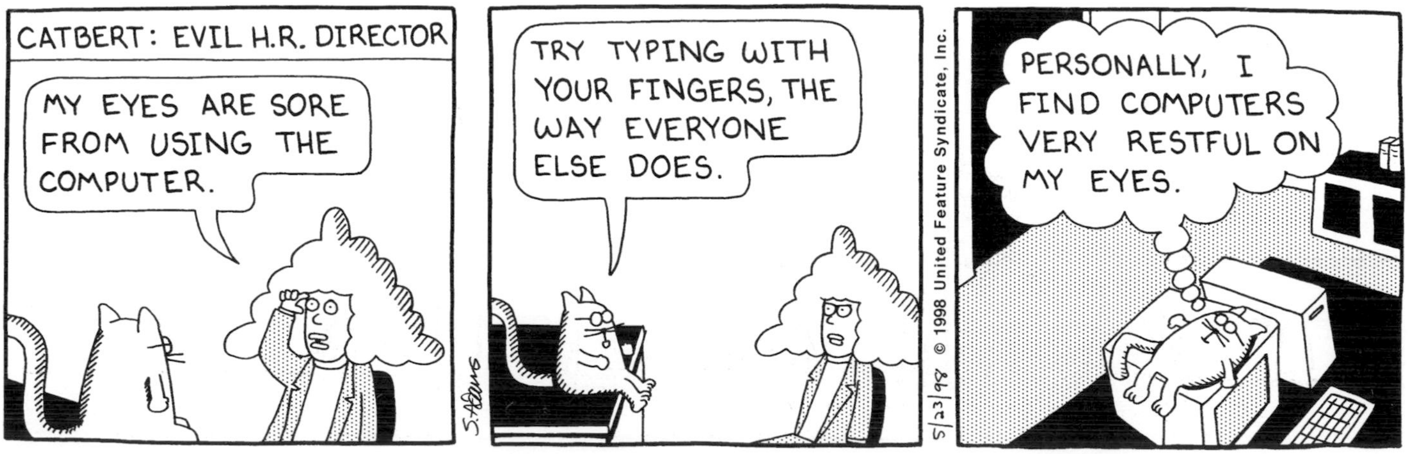
CATBERT: EVIL H.R. DIRECTOR
MY EYES ARE SORE FROM USING THE COMPUTER.
TRY TYPING WITH YOUR FINGERS, THE WAY EVERYONE ELSE DOES.
PERSONALLY, I FIND COMPUTERS VERY RESTFUL ON MY EYES.
S. Adams
5/23/98 © 1998 United Feature Syndicate, Inc.

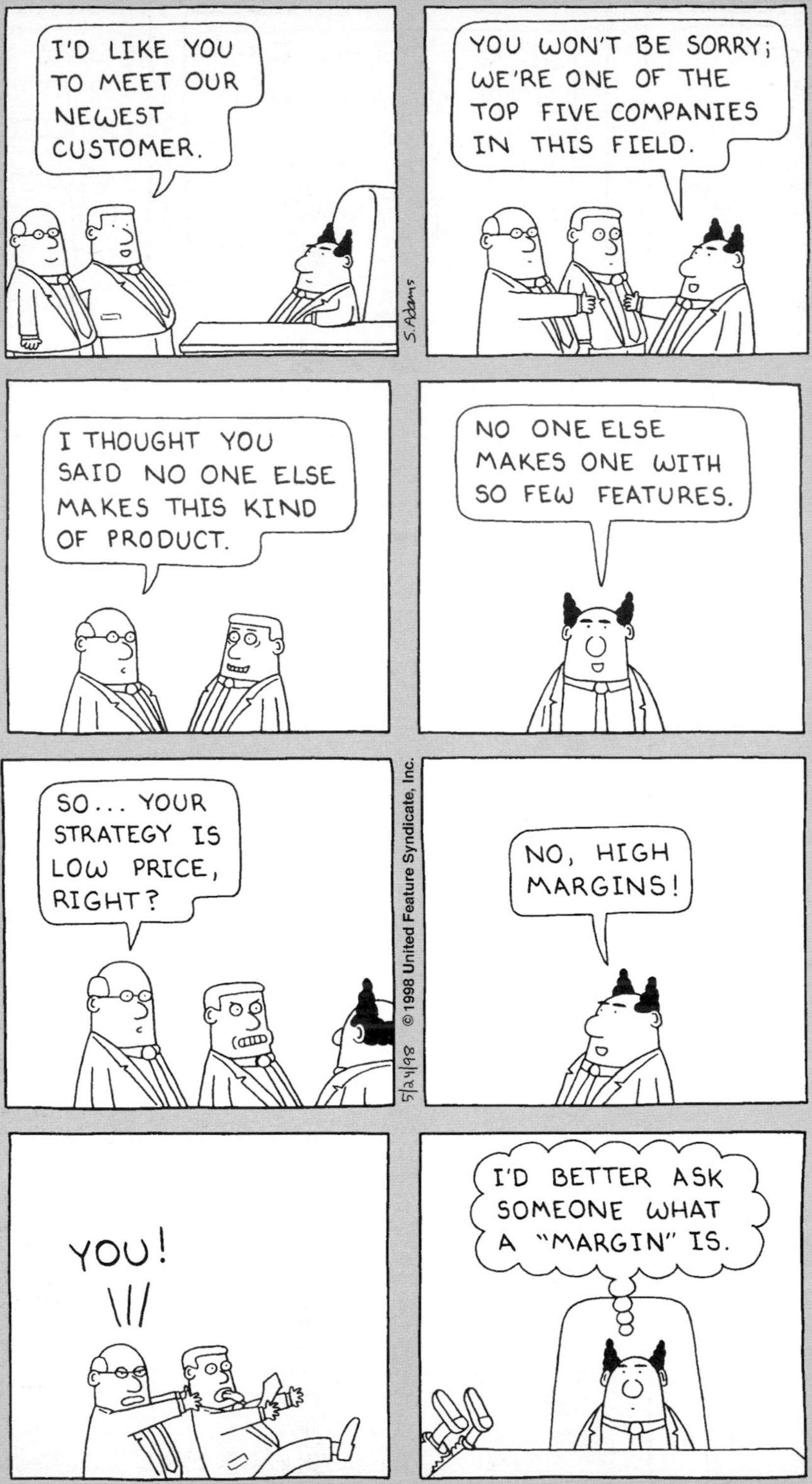
I'D LIKE YOU TO MEET OUR NEWEST CUSTOMER.
S. Adams
YOU WON'T BE SORRY; WE'RE ONE OF THE TOP FIVE COMPANIES IN THIS FIELD.
I THOUGHT YOU SAID NO ONE ELSE MAKES THIS KIND OF PRODUCT.
NO ONE ELSE MAKES ONE WITH SO FEW FEATURES.
SO... YOUR STRATEGY IS LOW PRICE, RIGHT?
© 1998 United Feature Syndicate, Inc.
5/24/98
NO, HIGH MARGINS!
YOU!
I'D BETTER ASK SOMEONE WHAT A "MARGIN" IS.

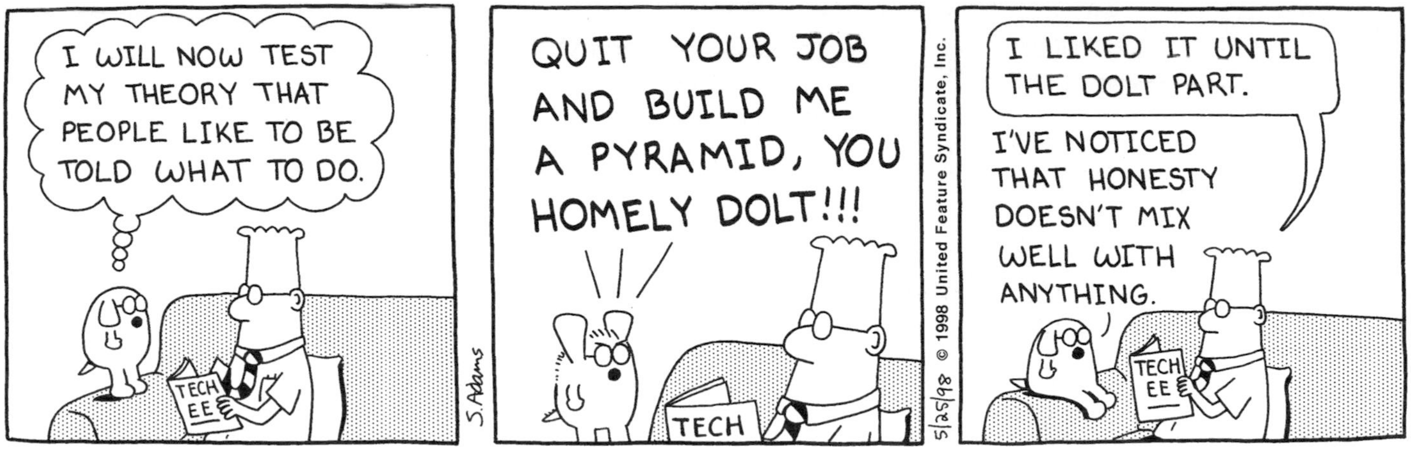
I WILL NOW TEST MY THEORY THAT PEOPLE LIKE TO BE TOLD WHAT TO DO.
TECH EE
S. Adams
QUIT YOUR JOB AND BUILD ME A PYRAMID, YOU HOMELY DOLT!!!
TECH
5/25/98 © 1998 United Feature Syndicate, Inc.
I LIKED IT UNTIL THE DOLT PART.
I'VE NOTICED THAT HONESTY DOESN'T MIX WELL WITH ANYTHING.
TECH EE

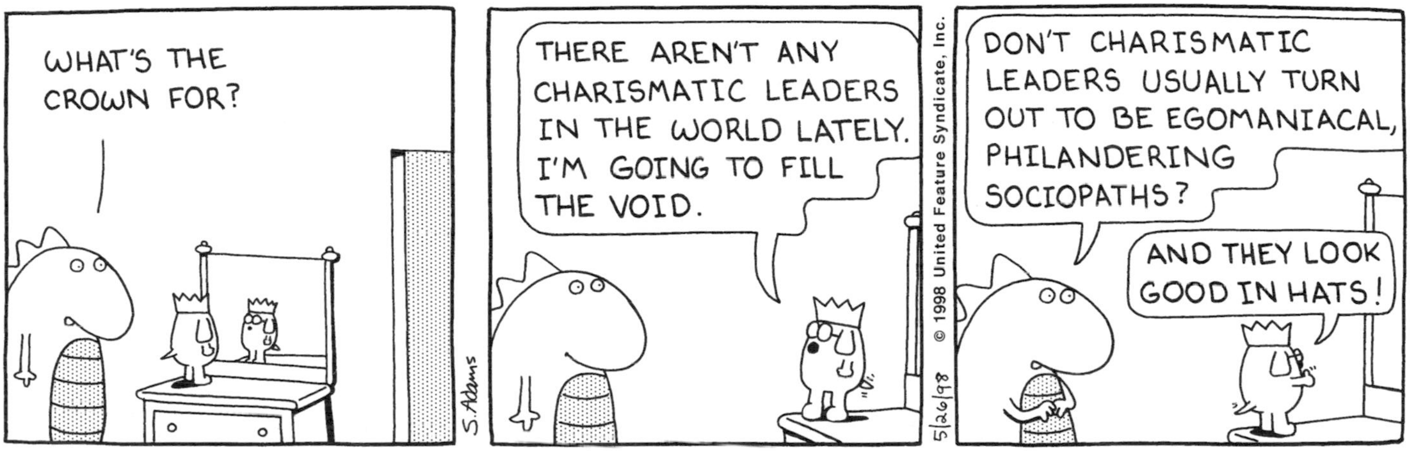
WHAT'S THE CROWN FOR?
S. Adams
THERE AREN'T ANY CHARISMATIC LEADERS IN THE WORLD LATELY. I'M GOING TO FILL THE VOID.
5/26/98 © 1998 United Feature Syndicate, Inc.
DON'T CHARISMATIC LEADERS USUALLY TURN OUT TO BE EGOMANIACAL, PHILANDERING SOCIOPATHS?
AND THEY LOOK GOOD IN HATS!

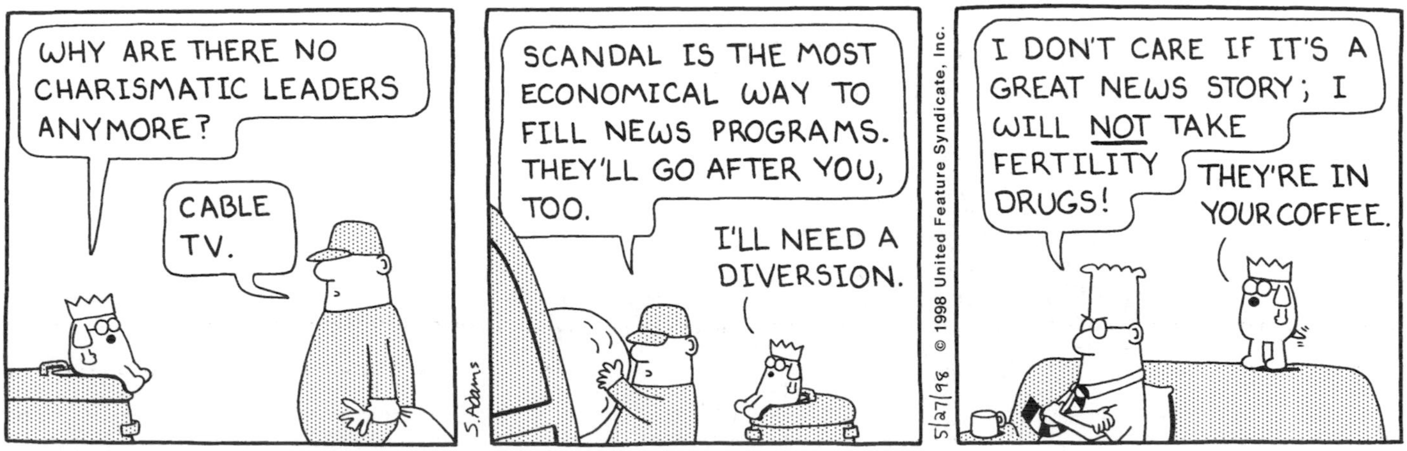
WHY ARE THERE NO CHARISMATIC LEADERS ANYMORE?
CABLE TV.
S. Adams
SCANDAL IS THE MOST ECONOMICAL WAY TO FILL NEWS PROGRAMS. THEY'LL GO AFTER YOU, TOO.
I'LL NEED A DIVERSION.
5/27/98 © 1998 United Feature Syndicate, Inc.
I DON'T CARE IF IT'S A GREAT NEWS STORY; I WILL NOT TAKE FERTILITY DRUGS!
THEY'RE IN YOUR COFFEE.

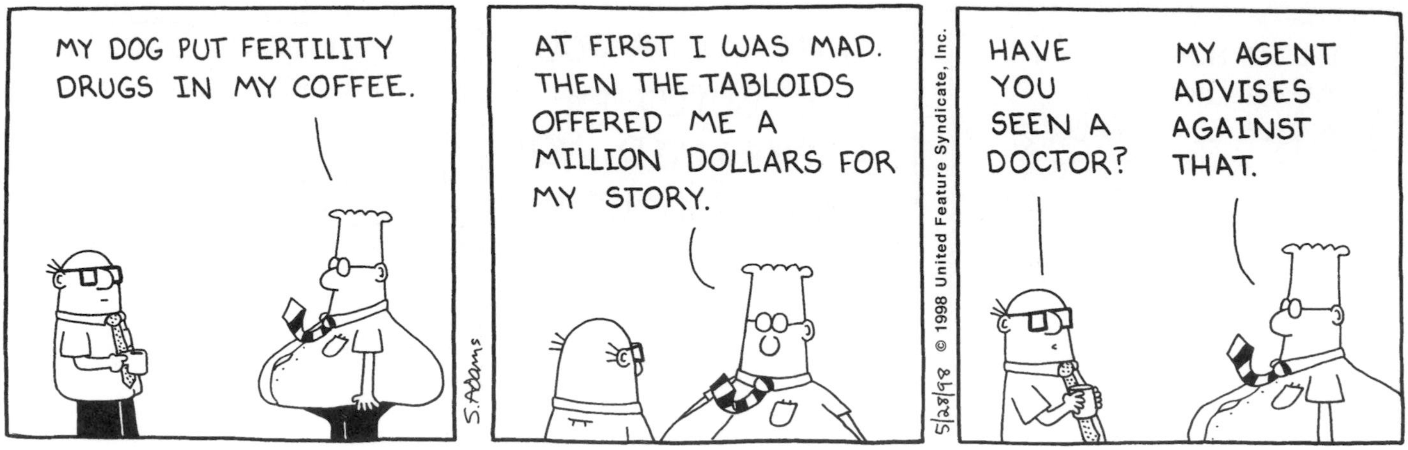
MY DOG PUT FERTILITY DRUGS IN MY COFFEE.
S. Adams
AT FIRST I WAS MAD. THEN THE TABLOIDS OFFERED ME A MILLION DOLLARS FOR MY STORY.
5/28/98 © 1998 United Feature Syndicate, Inc.
HAVE YOU SEEN A DOCTOR?
MY AGENT ADVISES AGAINST THAT.

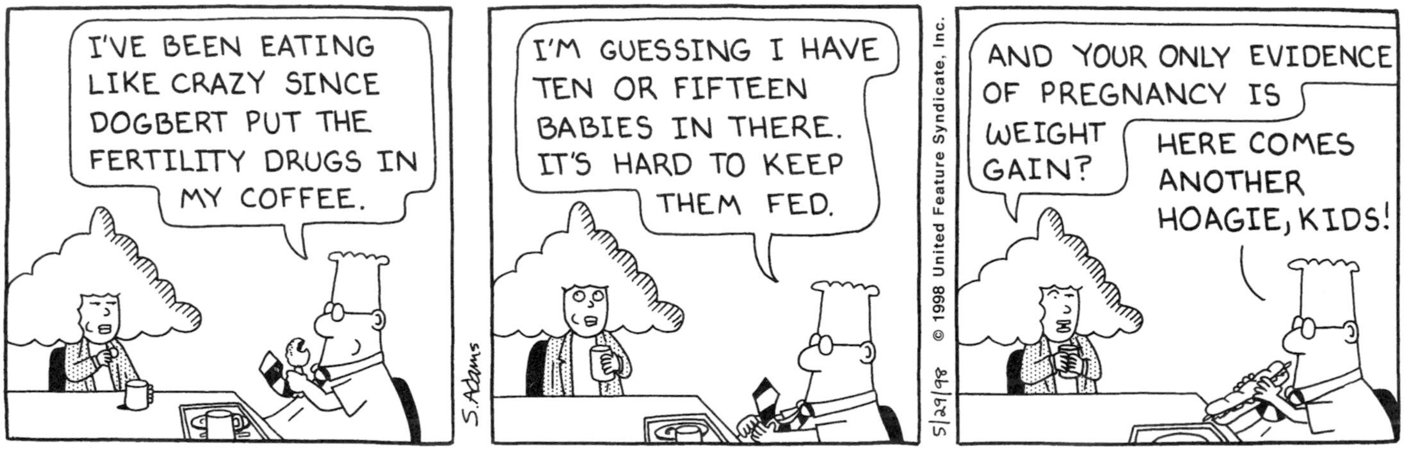
I'VE BEEN EATING LIKE CRAZY SINCE DOGBERT PUT THE FERTILITY DRUGS IN MY COFFEE.
S. Adams
I'M GUESSING I HAVE TEN OR FIFTEEN BABIES IN THERE. IT'S HARD TO KEEP THEM FED.
5/29/98 © 1998 United Feature Syndicate, Inc.
AND YOUR ONLY EVIDENCE OF PREGNANCY IS WEIGHT GAIN?
HERE COMES ANOTHER HOAGIE, KIDS!

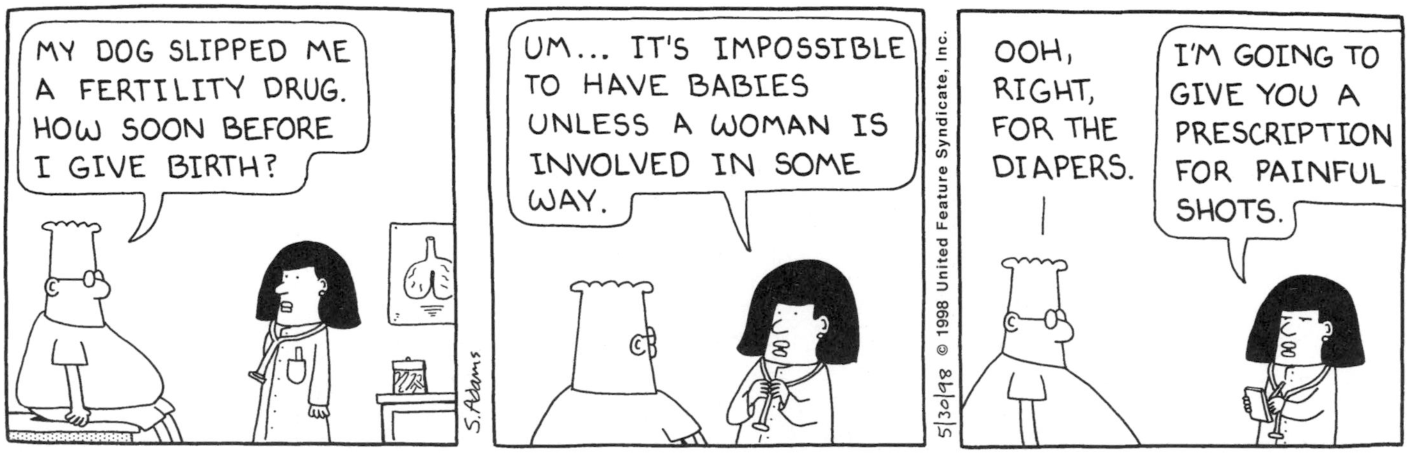
MY DOG SLIPPED ME A FERTILITY DRUG. HOW SOON BEFORE I GIVE BIRTH?
S. Adams
UM... IT'S IMPOSSIBLE TO HAVE BABIES UNLESS A WOMAN IS INVOLVED IN SOME WAY.
5/30/98 © 1998 United Feature Syndicate, Inc.
OOH, RIGHT, FOR THE DIAPERS.
I'M GOING TO GIVE YOU A PRESCRIPTION FOR PAINFUL SHOTS.

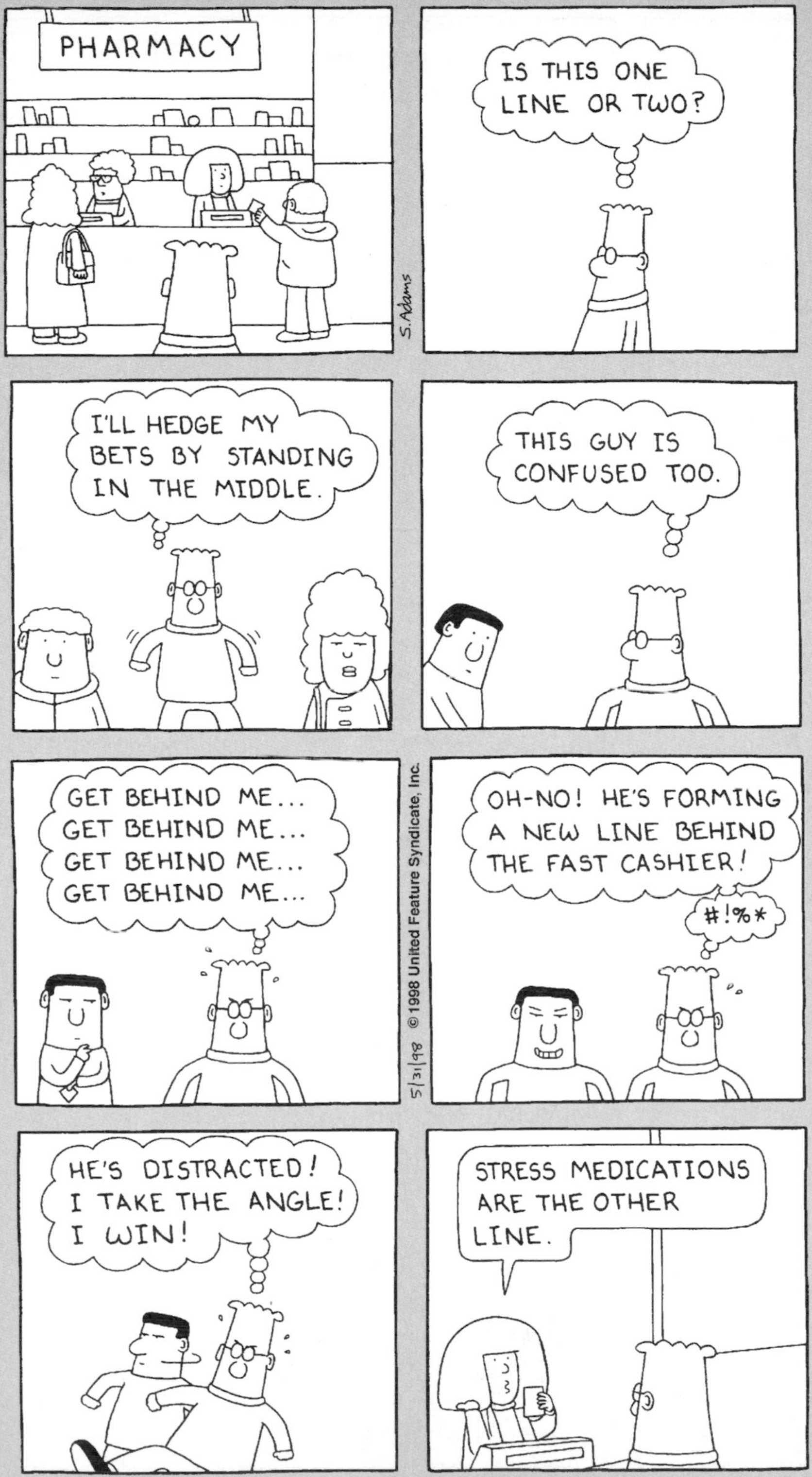
PHARMACY
S. Adams
IS THIS ONE LINE OR TWO?
I'LL HEDGE MY BETS BY STANDING IN THE MIDDLE.
THIS GUY IS CONFUSED TOO.
GET BEHIND ME... GET BEHIND ME... GET BEHIND ME... GET BEHIND ME...
5/31/98 © 1998 United Feature Syndicate, Inc.
OH-NO! HE'S FORMING A NEW LINE BEHIND THE FAST CASHIER!
#!%*
HE'S DISTRACTED! I TAKE THE ANGLE! I WIN!
STRESS MEDICATIONS ARE THE OTHER LINE.

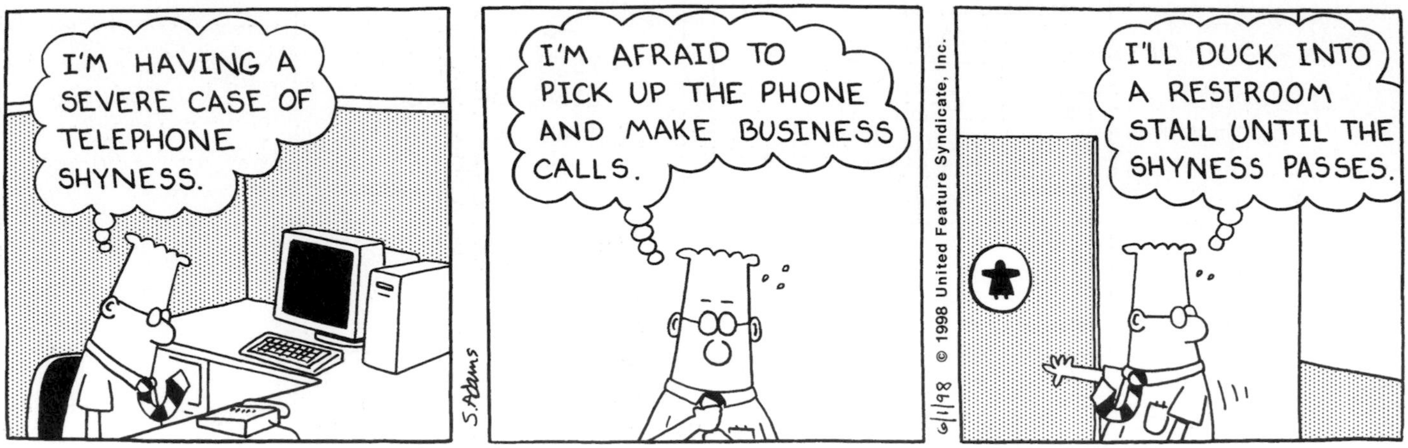
I'M HAVING A SEVERE CASE OF TELEPHONE SHYNESS.
I'M AFRAID TO PICK UP THE PHONE AND MAKE BUSINESS CALLS.
I'LL DUCK INTO A RESTROOM STALL UNTIL THE SHYNESS PASSES.
S. Adams
6/1/98 © 1998 United Feature Syndicate, Inc.

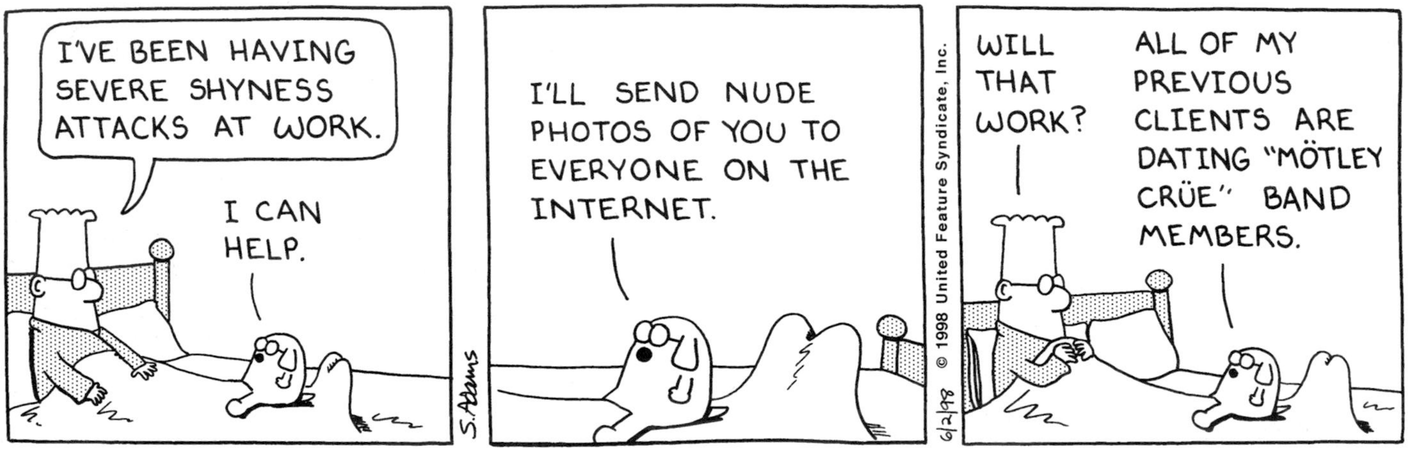
I'VE BEEN HAVING SEVERE SHYNESS ATTACKS AT WORK.
I CAN HELP.
I'LL SEND NUDE PHOTOS OF YOU TO EVERYONE ON THE INTERNET.
WILL THAT WORK?
ALL OF MY PREVIOUS CLIENTS ARE DATING "MÖTLEY CRÜE" BAND MEMBERS.
S. Adams
6/2/98 © 1998 United Feature Syndicate, Inc.

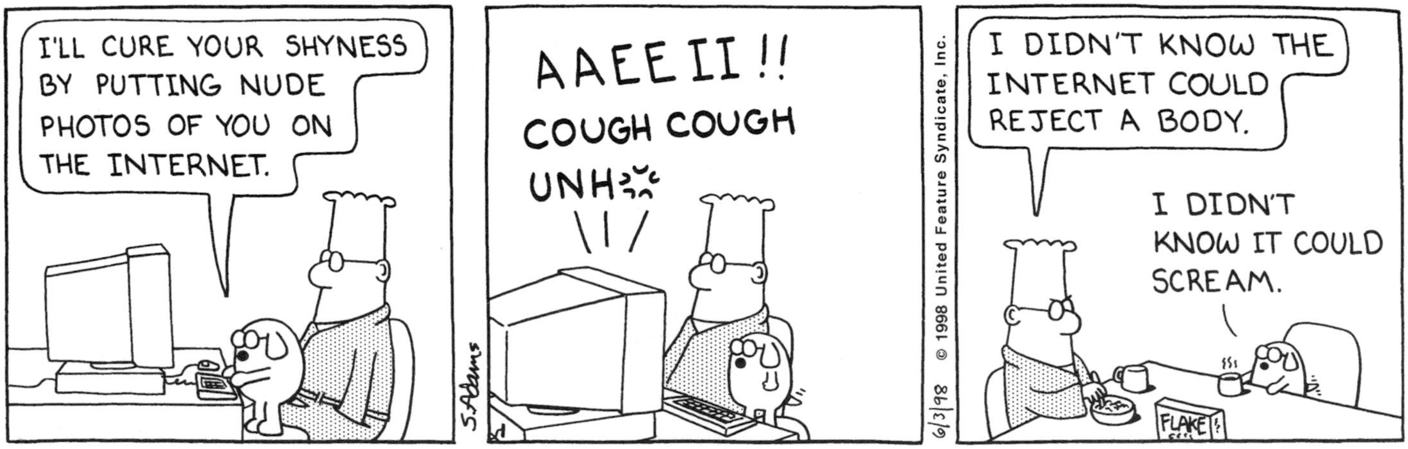
I'LL CURE YOUR SHYNESS BY PUTTING NUDE PHOTOS OF YOU ON THE INTERNET.
AAEEII!!
COUGH COUGH
UNH
I DIDN'T KNOW THE INTERNET COULD REJECT A BODY.
I DIDN'T KNOW IT COULD SCREAM.
FLAKES
S. Adams
6/3/98 © 1998 United Feature Syndicate, Inc.

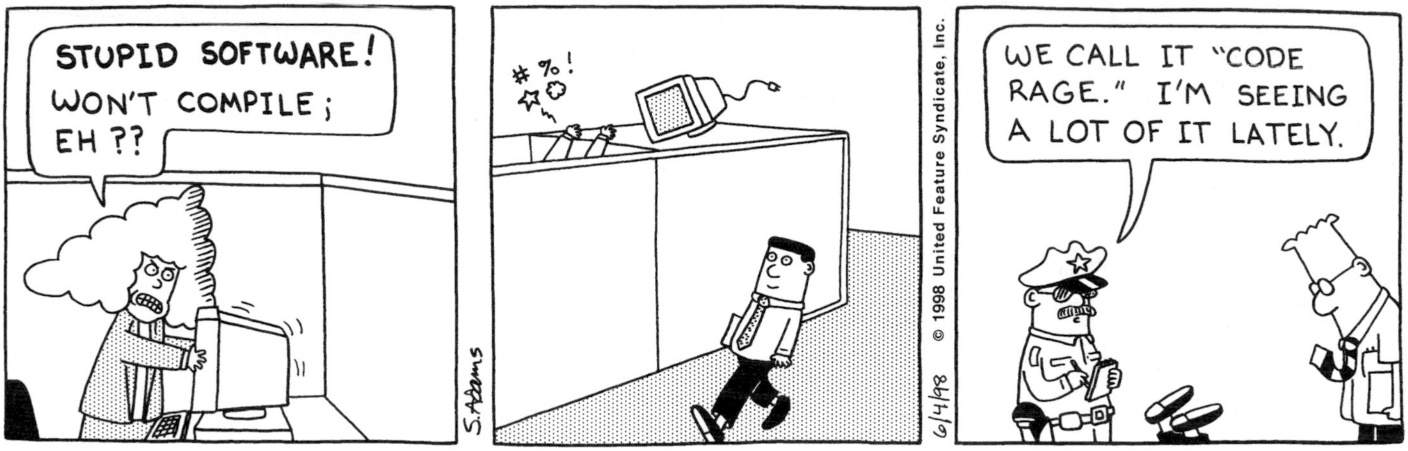
STUPID SOFTWARE! WON'T COMPILE; EH??
% !
S. Adams
© 1998 United Feature Syndicate, Inc.
6/4/98
WE CALL IT "CODE RAGE." I'M SEEING A LOT OF IT LATELY.

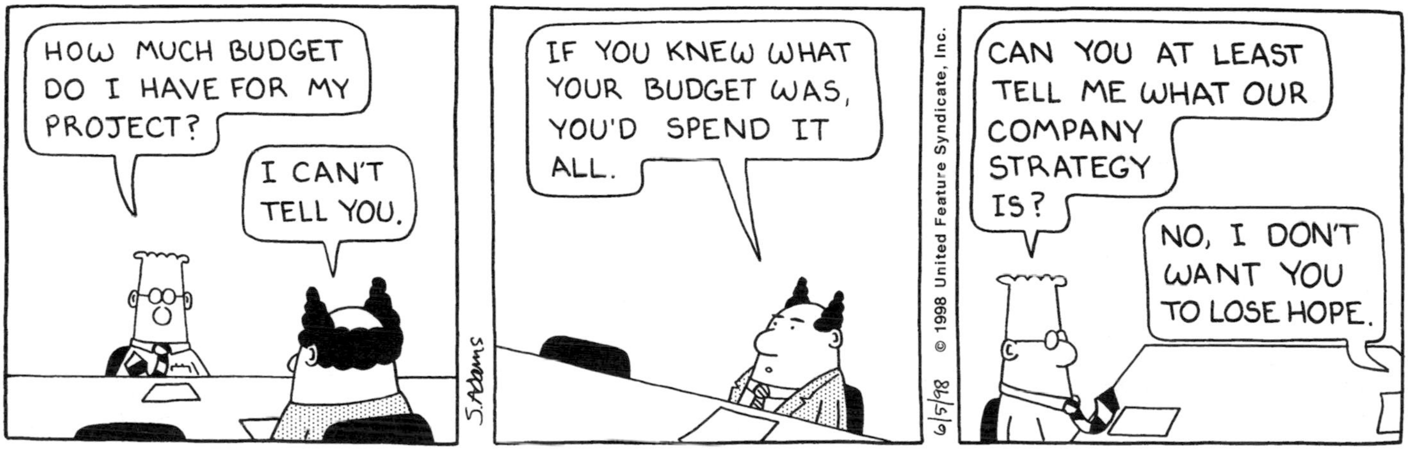
HOW MUCH BUDGET DO I HAVE FOR MY PROJECT?
I CAN'T TELL YOU.
S. Adams
IF YOU KNEW WHAT YOUR BUDGET WAS, YOU'D SPEND IT ALL.
© 1998 United Feature Syndicate, Inc.
6/5/98
CAN YOU AT LEAST TELL ME WHAT OUR COMPANY STRATEGY IS?
NO, I DON'T WANT YOU TO LOSE HOPE.

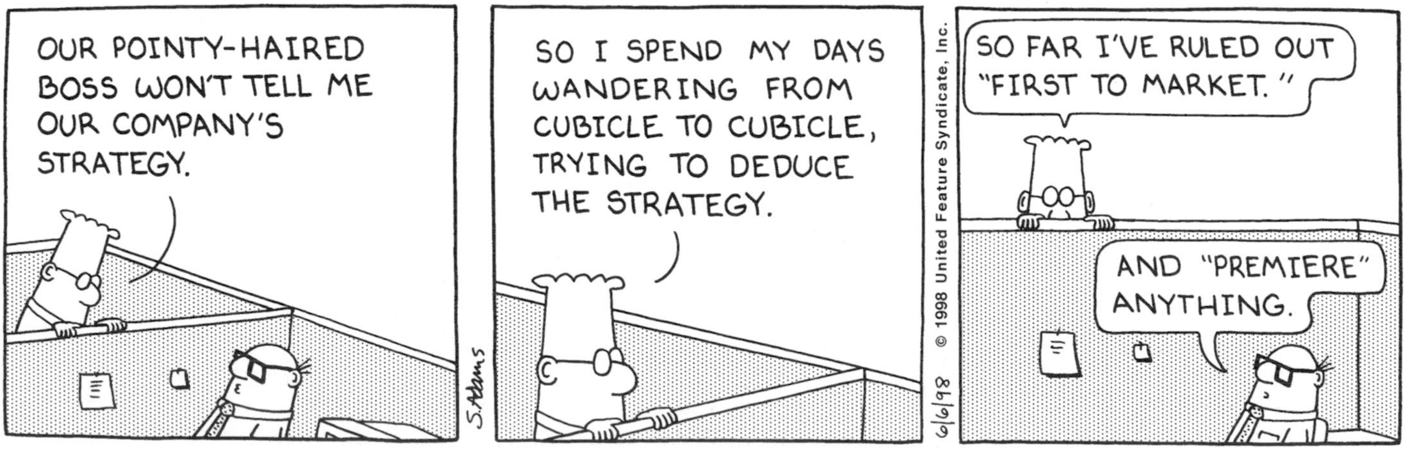
OUR POINTY-HAIRED BOSS WON'T TELL ME OUR COMPANY'S STRATEGY.
S. Adams
SO I SPEND MY DAYS WANDERING FROM CUBICLE TO CUBICLE, TRYING TO DEDUCE THE STRATEGY.
© 1998 United Feature Syndicate, Inc.
6/6/98
SO FAR I'VE RULED OUT "FIRST TO MARKET."
AND "PREMIERE" ANYTHING.

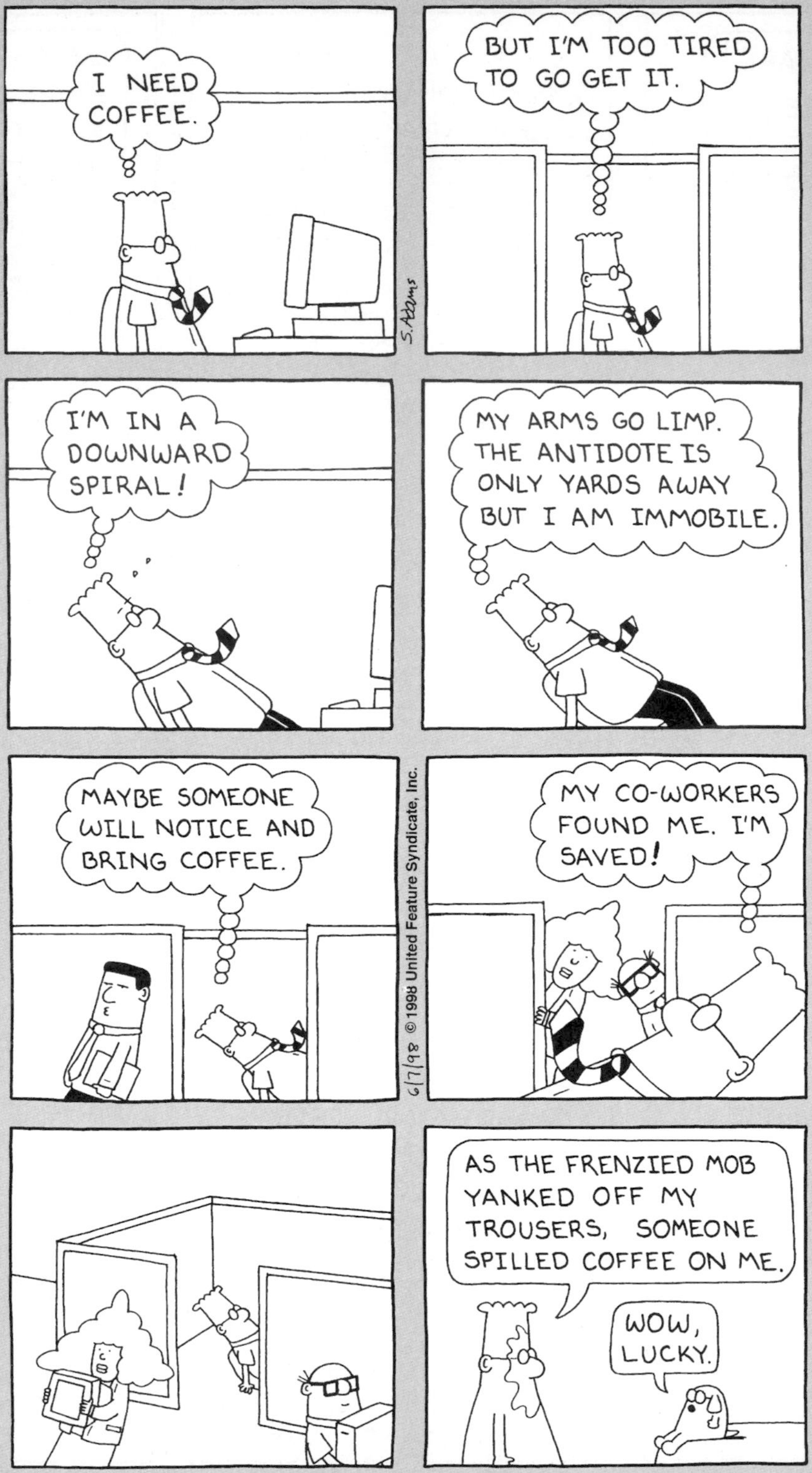
I NEED COFFEE.
BUT I'M TOO TIRED TO GO GET IT.
S. Adams
I'M IN A DOWNWARD SPIRAL!
MY ARMS GO LIMP. THE ANTIDOTE IS ONLY YARDS AWAY BUT I AM IMMOBILE.
MAYBE SOMEONE WILL NOTICE AND BRING COFFEE.
6/7/98 © 1998 United Feature Syndicate, Inc.
MY CO-WORKERS FOUND ME. I'M SAVED!
AS THE FRENZIED MOB YANKED OFF MY TROUSERS, SOMEONE SPILLED COFFEE ON ME.
WOW, LUCKY.

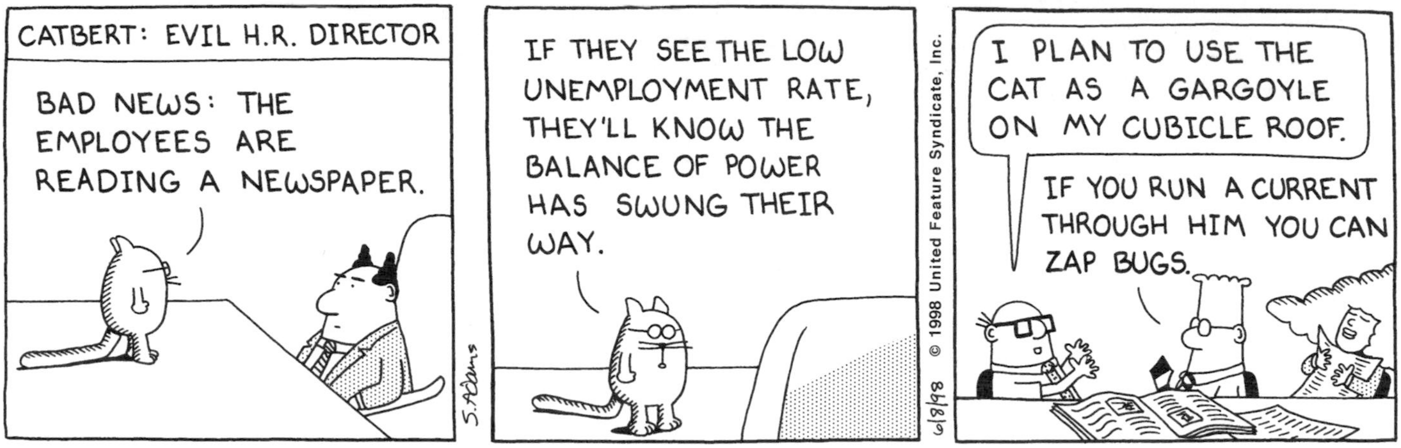
CATBERT: EVIL H.R. DIRECTOR
BAD NEWS: THE EMPLOYEES ARE READING A NEWSPAPER.
IF THEY SEE THE LOW UNEMPLOYMENT RATE, THEY'LL KNOW THE BALANCE OF POWER HAS SWUNG THEIR WAY.
S. Adams
6/8/98 © 1998 United Feature Syndicate, Inc.
I PLAN TO USE THE CAT AS A GARGOYLE ON MY CUBICLE ROOF.
IF YOU RUN A CURRENT THROUGH HIM YOU CAN ZAP BUGS.

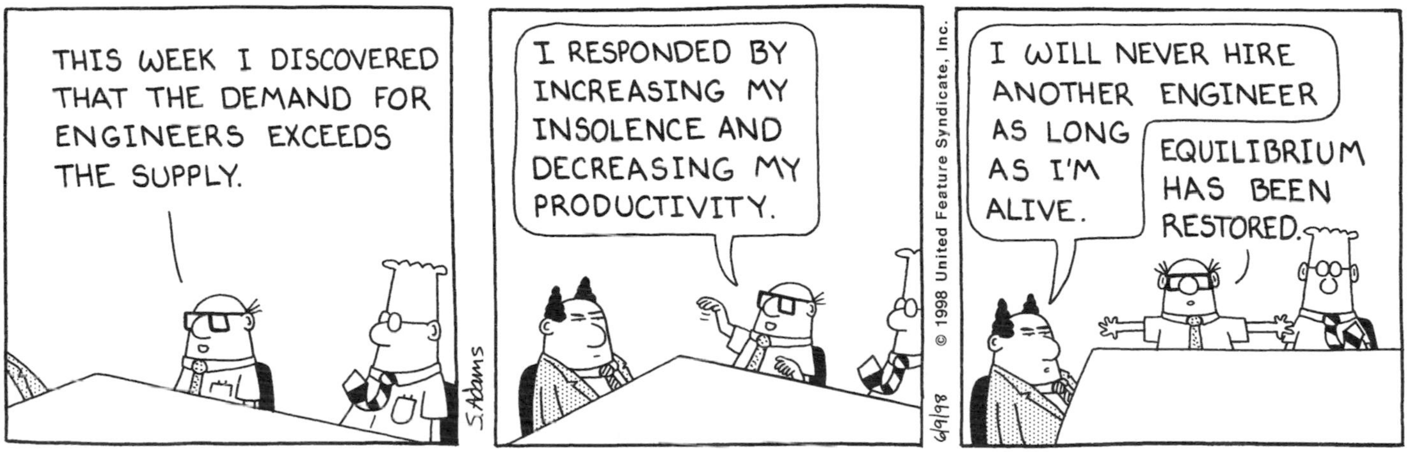
THIS WEEK I DISCOVERED THAT THE DEMAND FOR ENGINEERS EXCEEDS THE SUPPLY.
S. Adams
I RESPONDED BY INCREASING MY INSOLENCE AND DECREASING MY PRODUCTIVITY.
6/9/98 © 1998 United Feature Syndicate, Inc.
I WILL NEVER HIRE ANOTHER ENGINEER AS LONG AS I'M ALIVE.
EQUILIBRIUM HAS BEEN RESTORED.

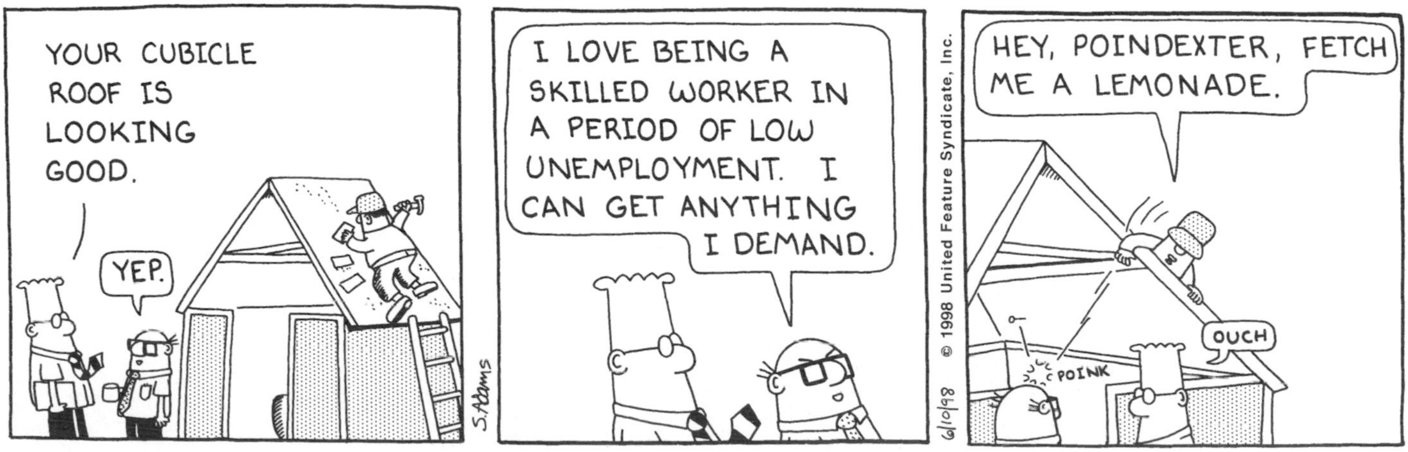
YOUR CUBICLE ROOF IS LOOKING GOOD.
YEP.
S. Adams
I LOVE BEING A SKILLED WORKER IN A PERIOD OF LOW UNEMPLOYMENT. I CAN GET ANYTHING I DEMAND.
6/10/98 © 1998 United Feature Syndicate, Inc.
HEY, POINDEXTER, FETCH ME A LEMONADE.
POINK
OUCH

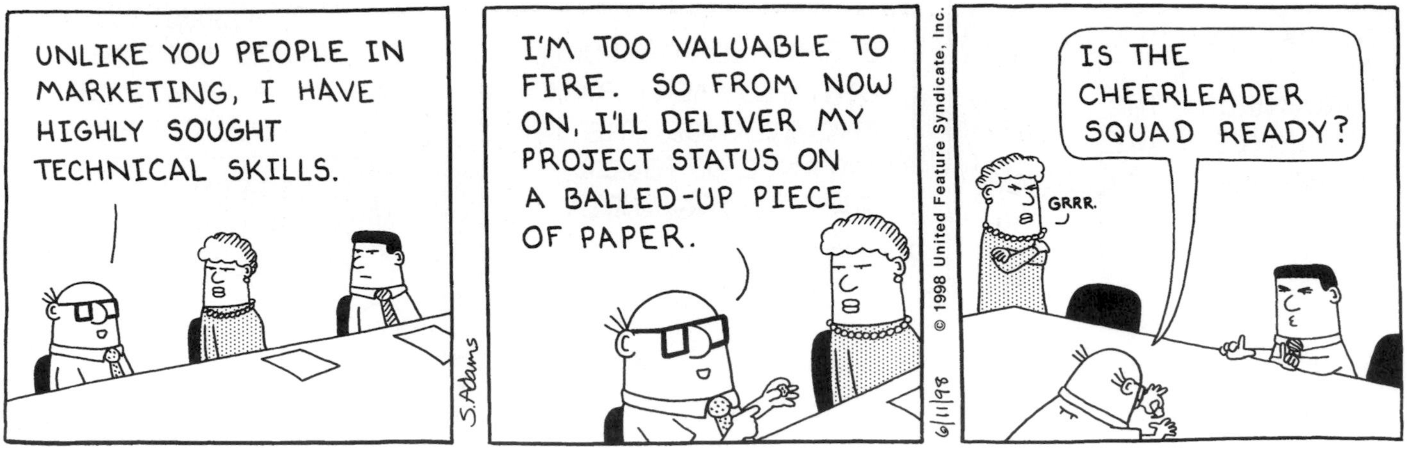
UNLIKE YOU PEOPLE IN MARKETING, I HAVE HIGHLY SOUGHT TECHNICAL SKILLS.
S. Adams
I'M TOO VALUABLE TO FIRE. SO FROM NOW ON, I'LL DELIVER MY PROJECT STATUS ON A BALLED-UP PIECE OF PAPER.
6/11/98 © 1998 United Feature Syndicate, Inc.
IS THE CHEERLEADER SQUAD READY?
GRRR.

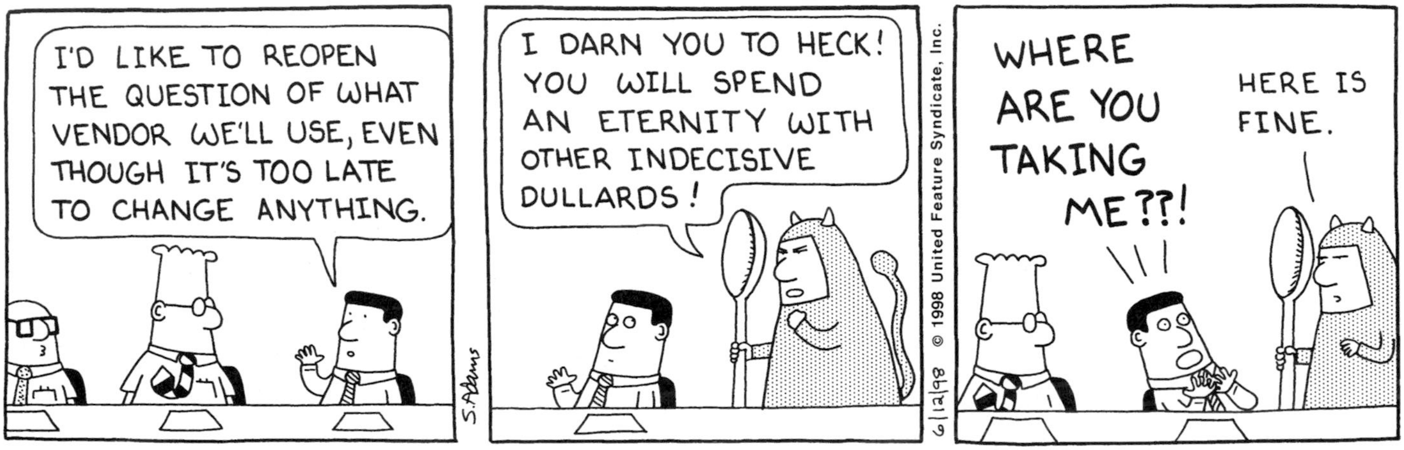
I'D LIKE TO REOPEN THE QUESTION OF WHAT VENDOR WE'LL USE, EVEN THOUGH IT'S TOO LATE TO CHANGE ANYTHING.
S. Adams
I DARN YOU TO HECK! YOU WILL SPEND AN ETERNITY WITH OTHER INDECISIVE DULLARDS!
6/12/98 © 1998 United Feature Syndicate, Inc.
WHERE ARE YOU TAKING ME??!
HERE IS FINE.

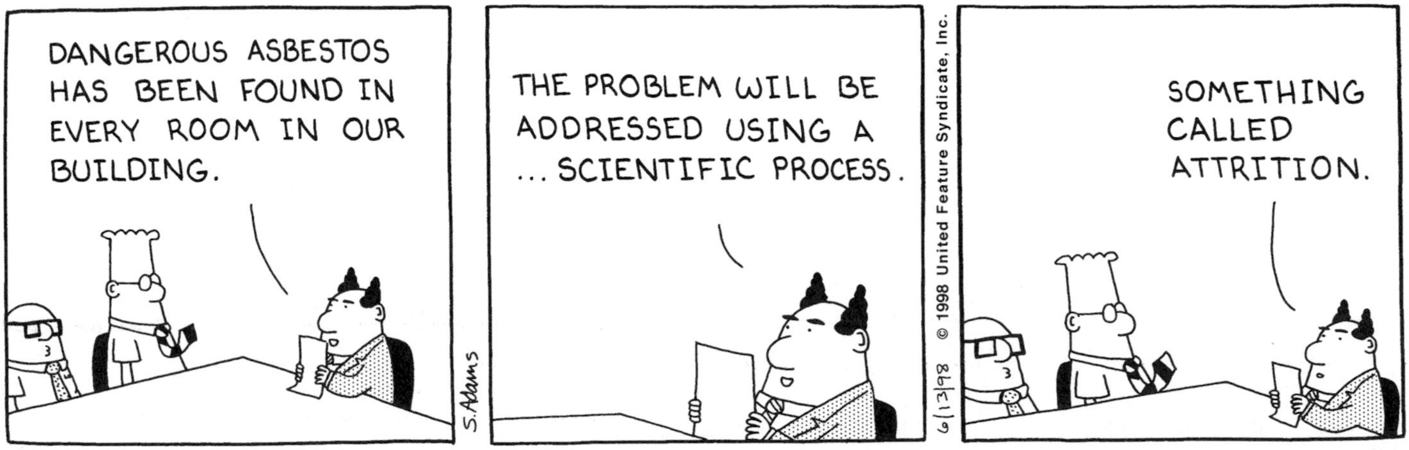
DANGEROUS ASBESTOS HAS BEEN FOUND IN EVERY ROOM IN OUR BUILDING.
S. Adams
THE PROBLEM WILL BE ADDRESSED USING A ... SCIENTIFIC PROCESS.
6/13/98 © 1998 United Feature Syndicate, Inc.
SOMETHING CALLED ATTRITION.

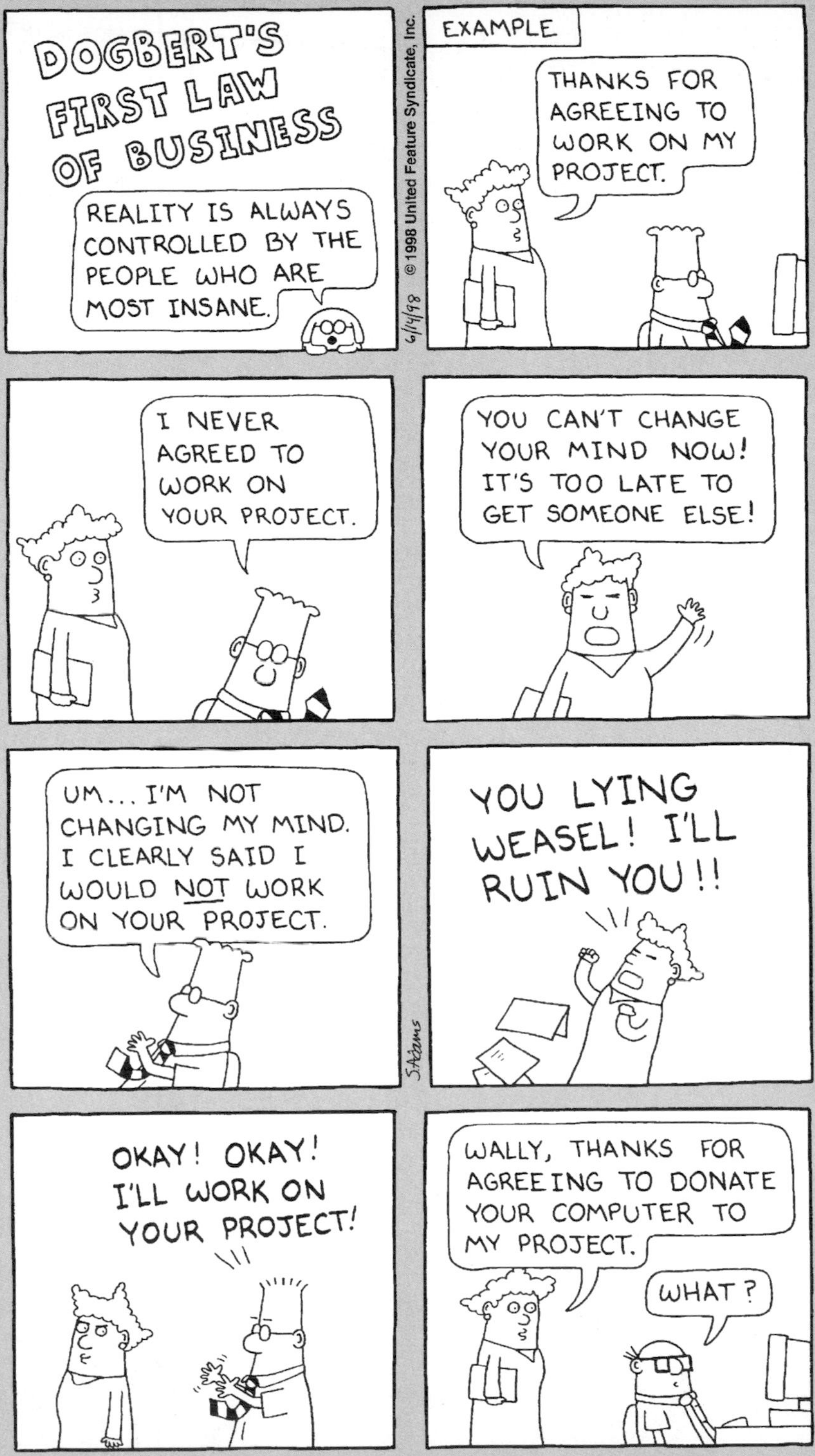
DOGBERT'S FIRST LAW OF BUSINESS
REALITY IS ALWAYS CONTROLLED BY THE PEOPLE WHO ARE MOST INSANE.
© 1998 United Feature Syndicate, Inc.
6/14/98
EXAMPLE
THANKS FOR AGREEING TO WORK ON MY PROJECT.
I NEVER AGREED TO WORK ON YOUR PROJECT.
YOU CAN'T CHANGE YOUR MIND NOW! IT'S TOO LATE TO GET SOMEONE ELSE!
UM... I'M NOT CHANGING MY MIND. I CLEARLY SAID I WOULD NOT WORK ON YOUR PROJECT.
S.Adams
YOU LYING WEASEL! I'LL RUIN YOU!!
OKAY! OKAY! I'LL WORK ON YOUR PROJECT!
WALLY, THANKS FOR AGREEING TO DONATE YOUR COMPUTER TO MY PROJECT.
WHAT?

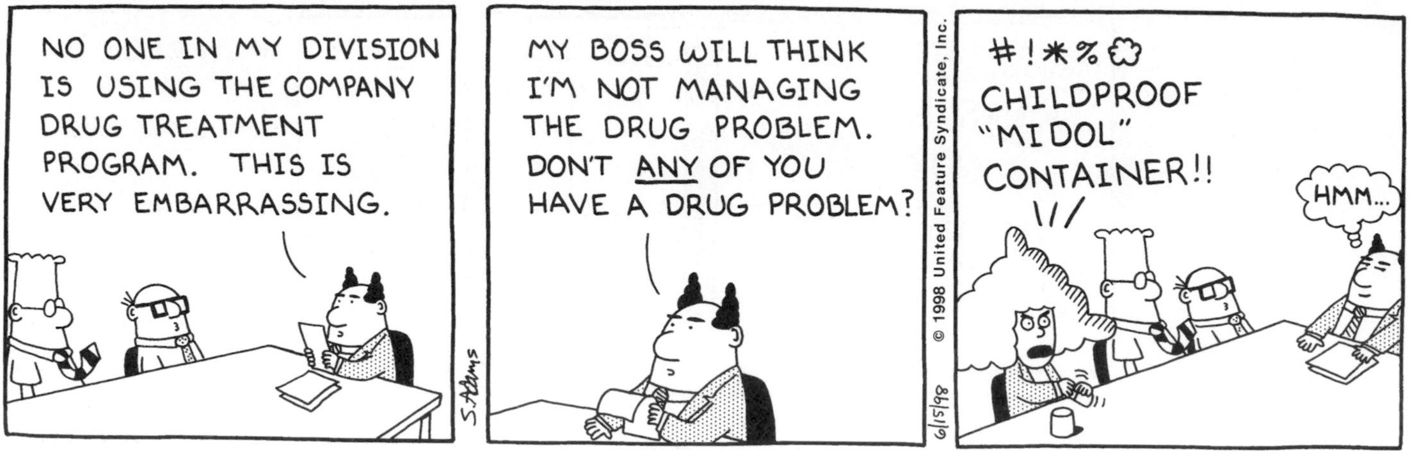
NO ONE IN MY DIVISION IS USING THE COMPANY DRUG TREATMENT PROGRAM. THIS IS VERY EMBARRASSING.
S. Adams
MY BOSS WILL THINK I'M NOT MANAGING THE DRUG PROBLEM. DON'T ANY OF YOU HAVE A DRUG PROBLEM?
© 1998 United Feature Syndicate, Inc.
6/15/98
#!*%
CHILDPROOF "MIDOL" CONTAINER!!
HMM...

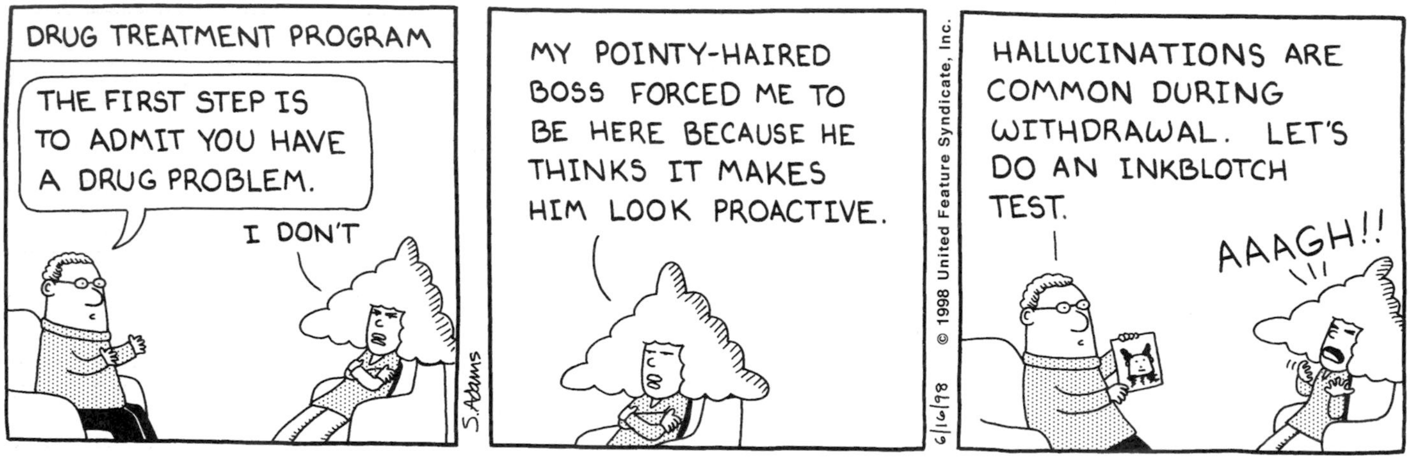
DRUG TREATMENT PROGRAM
THE FIRST STEP IS TO ADMIT YOU HAVE A DRUG PROBLEM.
I DON'T
S. Adams
MY POINTY-HAIRED BOSS FORCED ME TO BE HERE BECAUSE HE THINKS IT MAKES HIM LOOK PROACTIVE.
© 1998 United Feature Syndicate, Inc.
6/16/98
HALLUCINATIONS ARE COMMON DURING WITHDRAWAL. LET'S DO AN INKBLOTCH TEST.
AAAGH!!

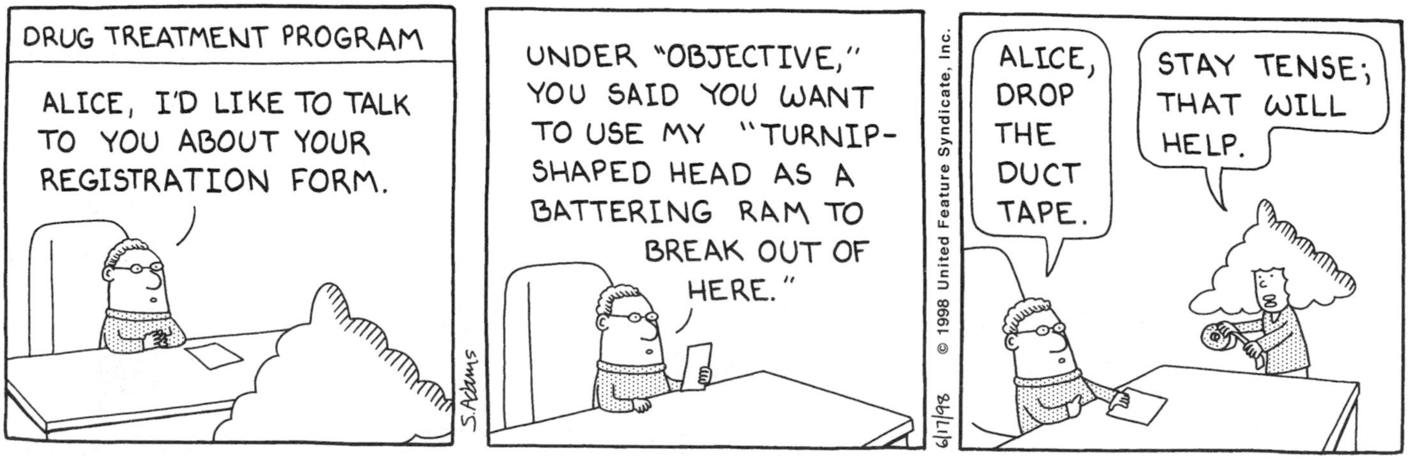
DRUG TREATMENT PROGRAM
ALICE, I'D LIKE TO TALK TO YOU ABOUT YOUR REGISTRATION FORM.
S. Adams
UNDER "OBJECTIVE," YOU SAID YOU WANT TO USE MY "TURNIP-SHAPED HEAD AS A BATTERING RAM TO BREAK OUT OF HERE."
© 1998 United Feature Syndicate, Inc.
6/17/98
ALICE, DROP THE DUCT TAPE.
STAY TENSE; THAT WILL HELP.

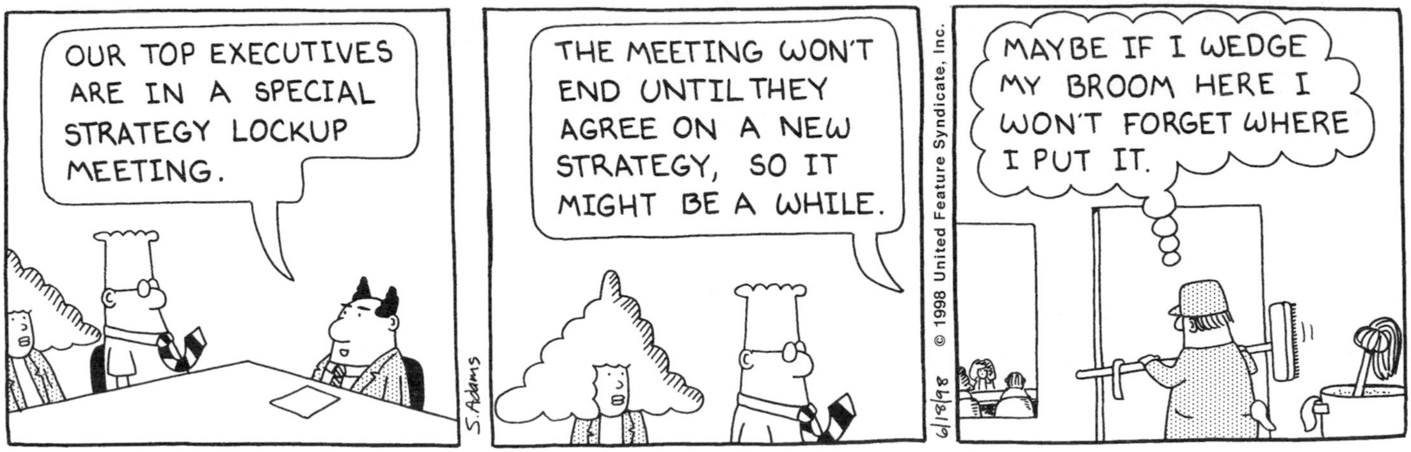
OUR TOP EXECUTIVES ARE IN A SPECIAL STRATEGY LOCKUP MEETING.
S. Adams
THE MEETING WON'T END UNTIL THEY AGREE ON A NEW STRATEGY, SO IT MIGHT BE A WHILE.
6/18/98 © 1998 United Feature Syndicate, Inc.
MAYBE IF I WEDGE MY BROOM HERE I WON'T FORGET WHERE I PUT IT.

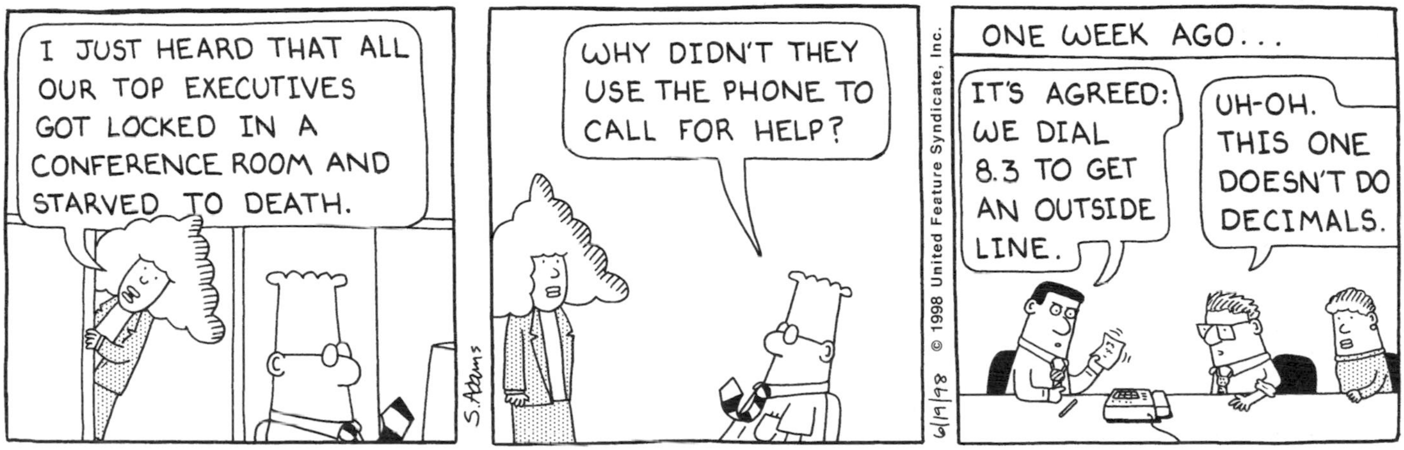
I JUST HEARD THAT ALL OUR TOP EXECUTIVES GOT LOCKED IN A CONFERENCE ROOM AND STARVED TO DEATH.
S. Adams
WHY DIDN'T THEY USE THE PHONE TO CALL FOR HELP?
6/19/98 © 1998 United Feature Syndicate, Inc.
ONE WEEK AGO...
IT'S AGREED: WE DIAL 8.3 TO GET AN OUTSIDE LINE.
UH-OH. THIS ONE DOESN'T DO DECIMALS.

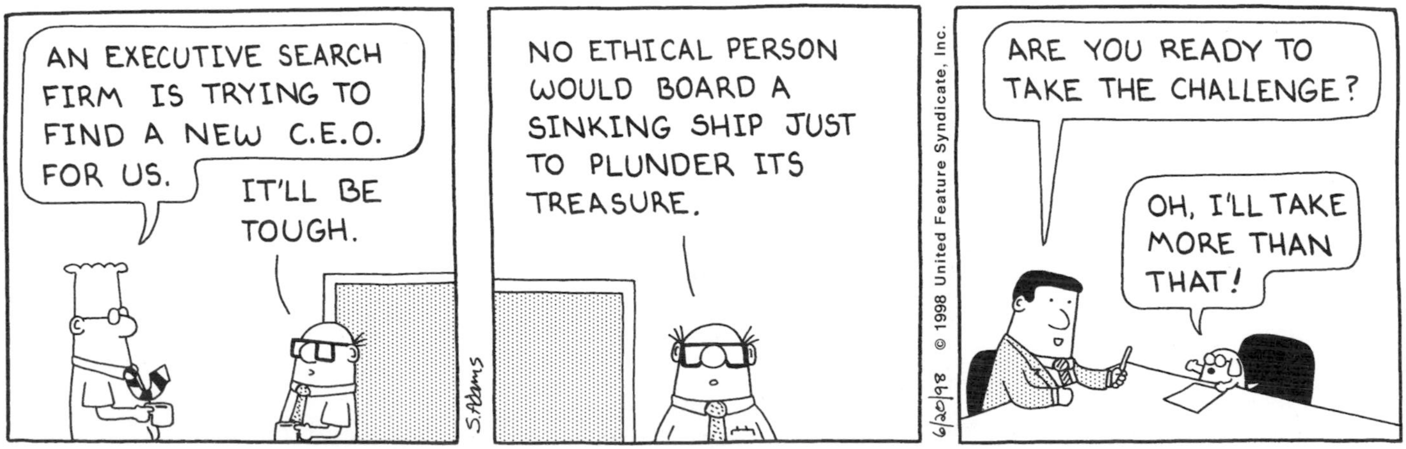
AN EXECUTIVE SEARCH FIRM IS TRYING TO FIND A NEW C.E.O. FOR US.
IT'LL BE TOUGH.
S. Adams
NO ETHICAL PERSON WOULD BOARD A SINKING SHIP JUST TO PLUNDER ITS TREASURE.
6/20/98 © 1998 United Feature Syndicate, Inc.
ARE YOU READY TO TAKE THE CHALLENGE?
OH, I'LL TAKE MORE THAN THAT!

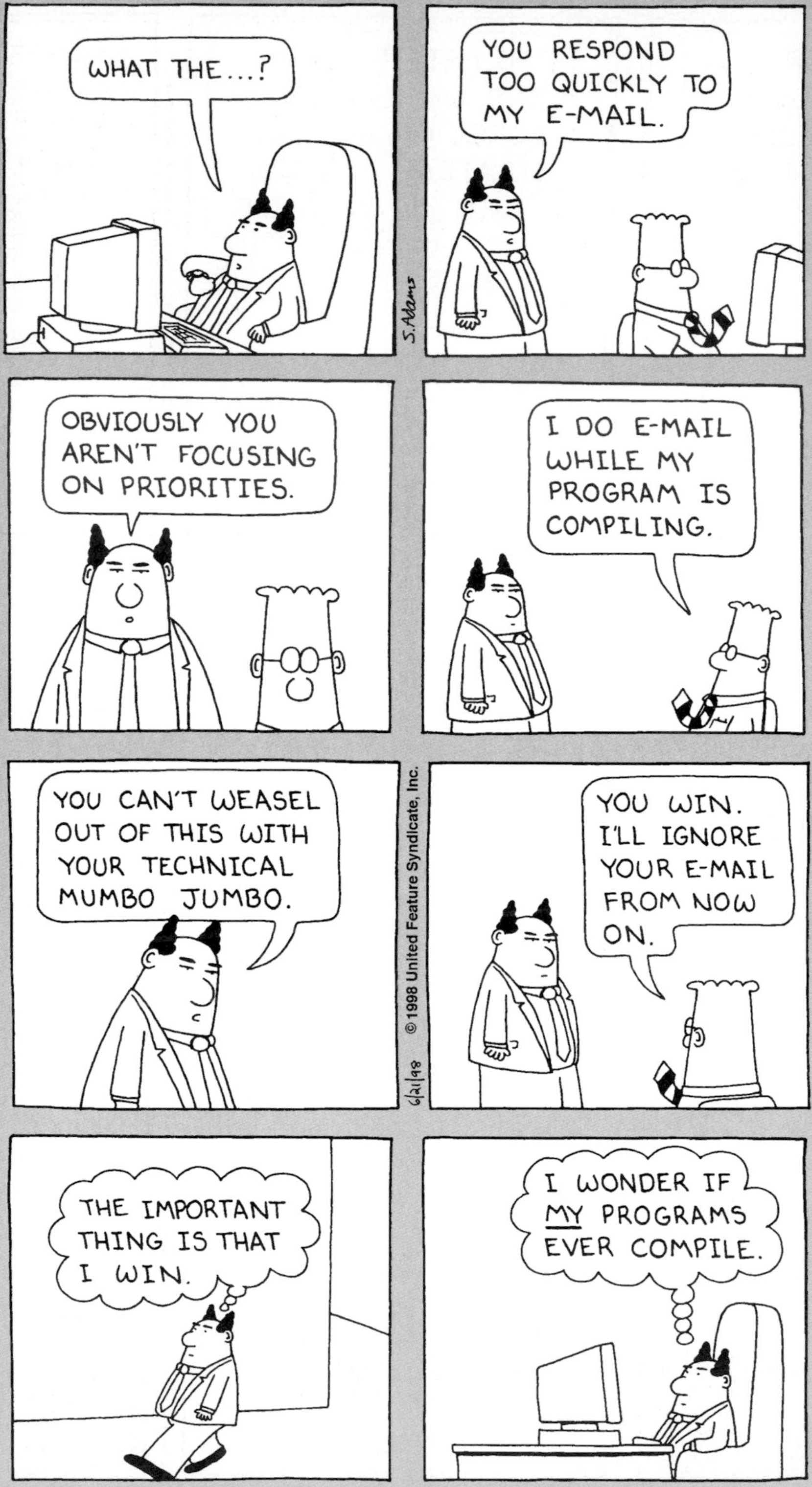
WHAT THE...?
YOU RESPOND TOO QUICKLY TO MY E-MAIL.
OBVIOUSLY YOU AREN'T FOCUSING ON PRIORITIES.
I DO E-MAIL WHILE MY PROGRAM IS COMPILING.
YOU CAN'T WEASEL OUT OF THIS WITH YOUR TECHNICAL MUMBO JUMBO.
YOU WIN. I'LL IGNORE YOUR E-MAIL FROM NOW ON.
THE IMPORTANT THING IS THAT I WIN.
I WONDER IF MY PROGRAMS EVER COMPILE.
© 1998 United Feature Syndicate, Inc.
6/21/98

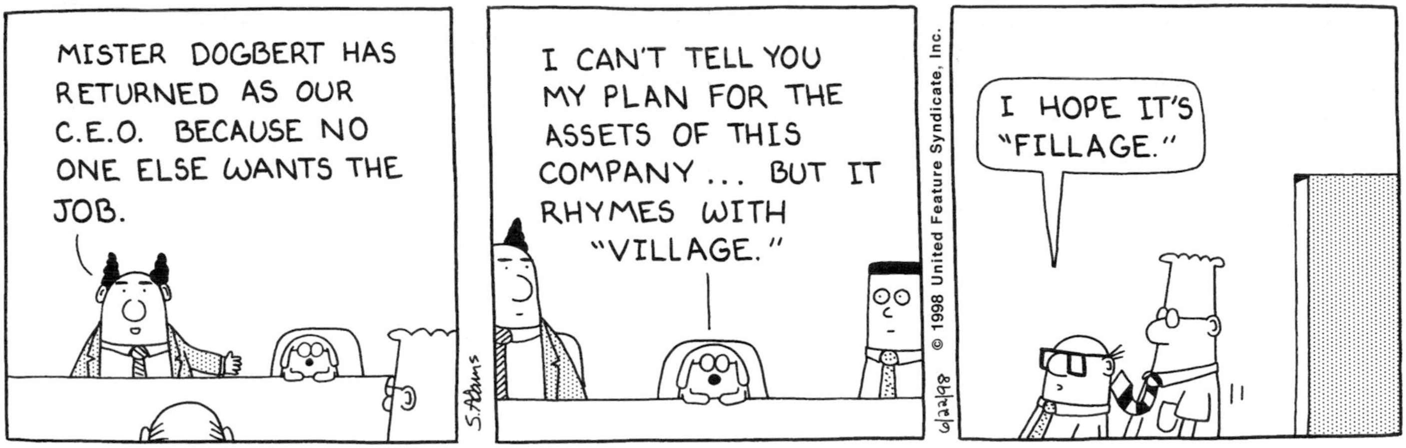
MISTER DOGBERT HAS RETURNED AS OUR C.E.O. BECAUSE NO ONE ELSE WANTS THE JOB.
I CAN'T TELL YOU MY PLAN FOR THE ASSETS OF THIS COMPANY ... BUT IT RHYMES WITH "VILLAGE."
I HOPE IT'S "FILLAGE."
S. Adams
6/22/98 © 1998 United Feature Syndicate, Inc.

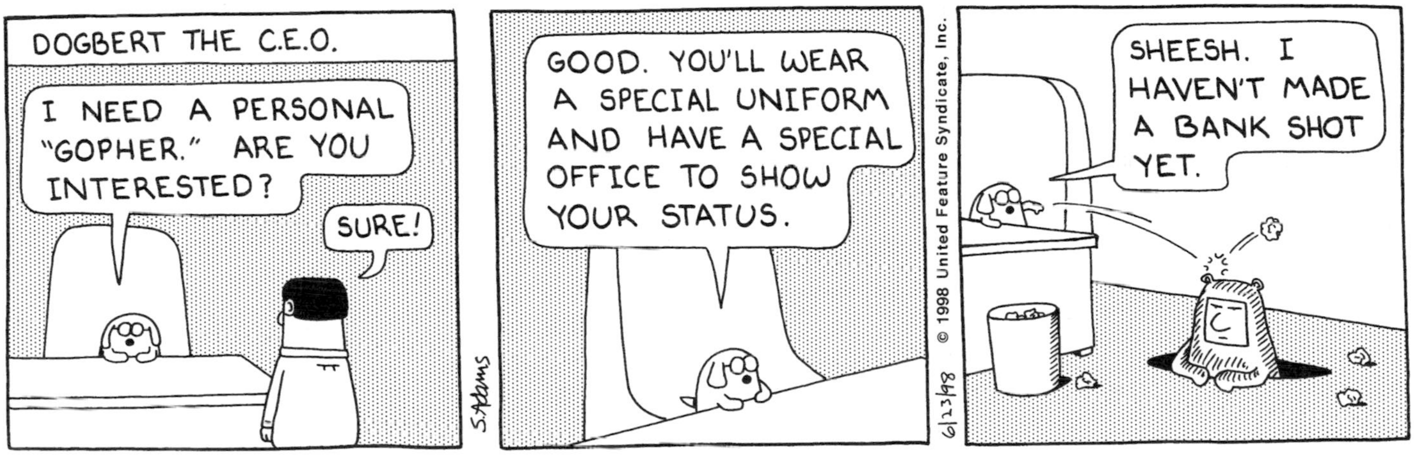
DOGBERT THE C.E.O.
I NEED A PERSONAL "GOPHER." ARE YOU INTERESTED?
SURE!
GOOD. YOU'LL WEAR A SPECIAL UNIFORM AND HAVE A SPECIAL OFFICE TO SHOW YOUR STATUS.
SHEESH. I HAVEN'T MADE A BANK SHOT YET.
S. Adams
6/23/98 © 1998 United Feature Syndicate, Inc.

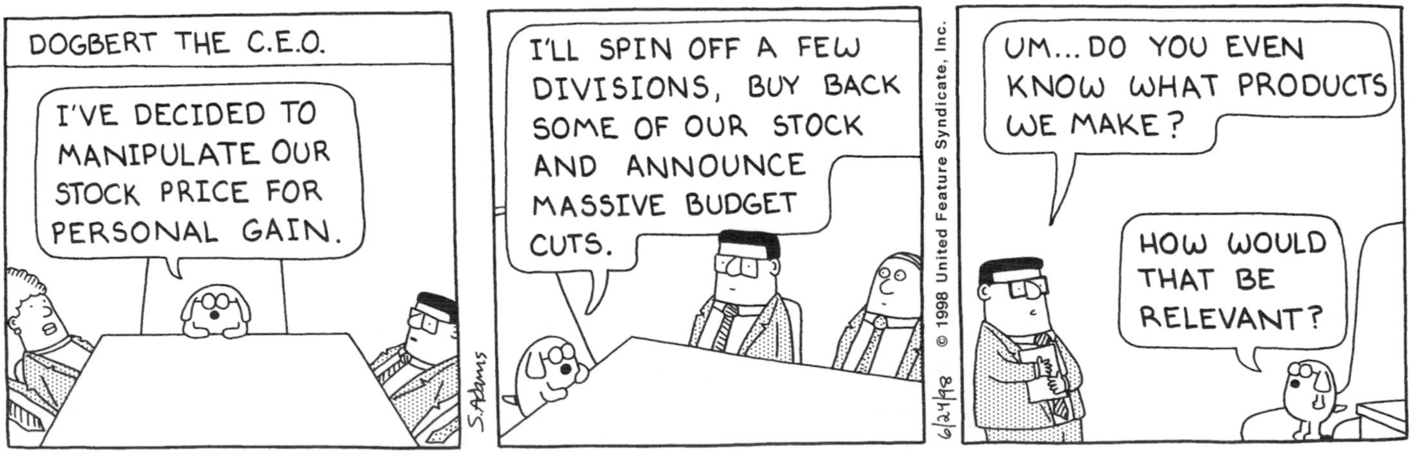
DOGBERT THE C.E.O.
I'VE DECIDED TO MANIPULATE OUR STOCK PRICE FOR PERSONAL GAIN.
I'LL SPIN OFF A FEW DIVISIONS, BUY BACK SOME OF OUR STOCK AND ANNOUNCE MASSIVE BUDGET CUTS.
UM... DO YOU EVEN KNOW WHAT PRODUCTS WE MAKE?
HOW WOULD THAT BE RELEVANT?
S. Adams
6/24/98 © 1998 United Feature Syndicate, Inc.

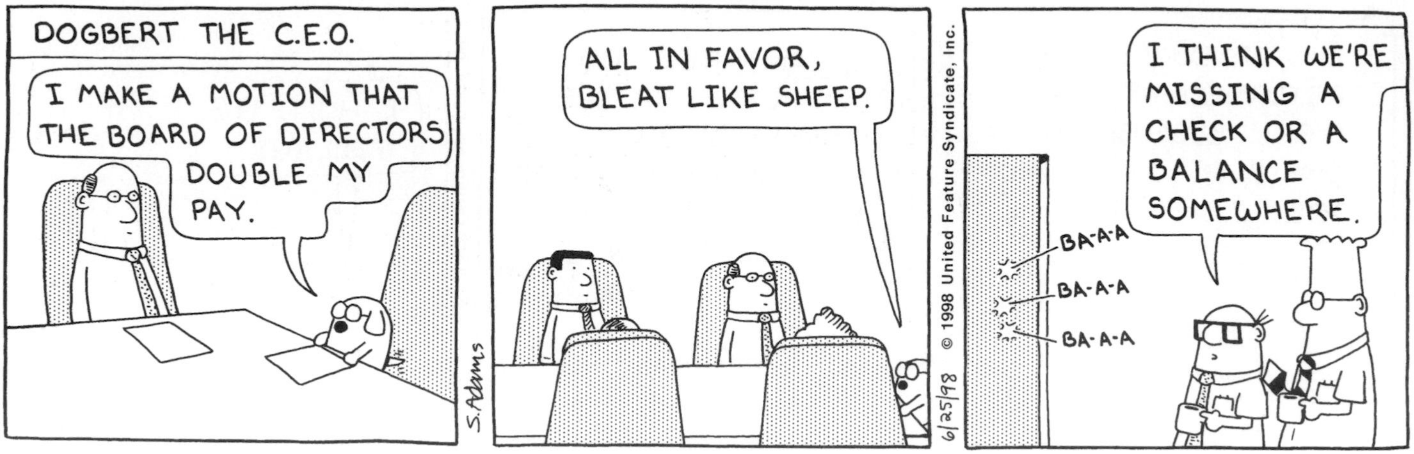
DOGBERT THE C.E.O.
I MAKE A MOTION THAT THE BOARD OF DIRECTORS DOUBLE MY PAY.
S. Adams
ALL IN FAVOR, BLEAT LIKE SHEEP.
6/25/98 © 1998 United Feature Syndicate, Inc.
BA-A-A
BA-A-A
BA-A-A
I THINK WE'RE MISSING A CHECK OR A BALANCE SOMEWHERE.

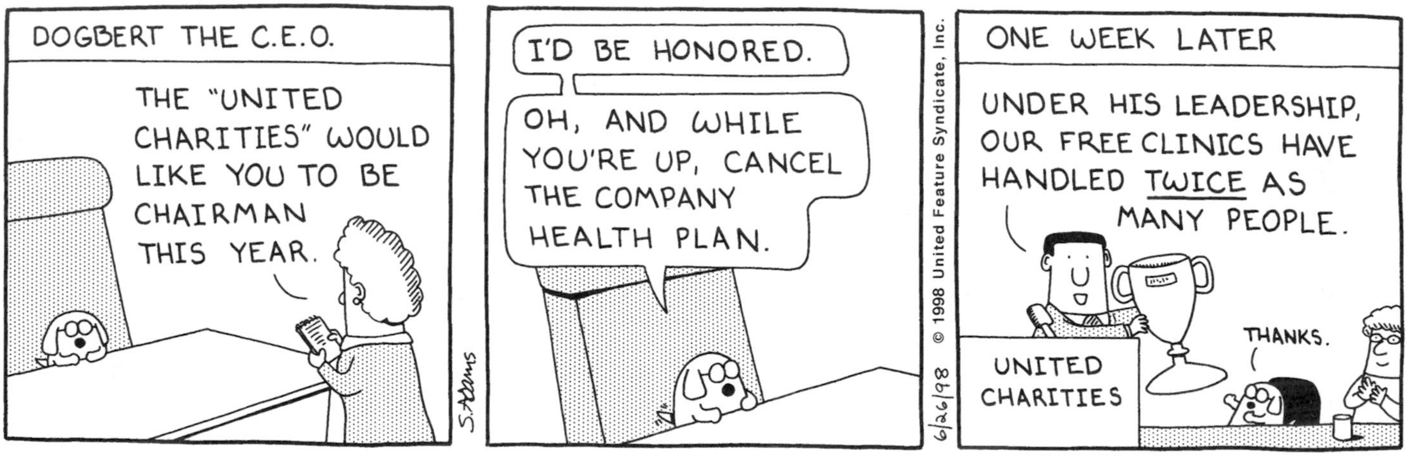
DOGBERT THE C.E.O.
THE "UNITED CHARITIES" WOULD LIKE YOU TO BE CHAIRMAN THIS YEAR.
S. Adams
I'D BE HONORED.
OH, AND WHILE YOU'RE UP, CANCEL THE COMPANY HEALTH PLAN.
6/26/98 © 1998 United Feature Syndicate, Inc.
ONE WEEK LATER
UNDER HIS LEADERSHIP, OUR FREE CLINICS HAVE HANDLED TWICE AS MANY PEOPLE.
UNITED CHARITIES
THANKS.

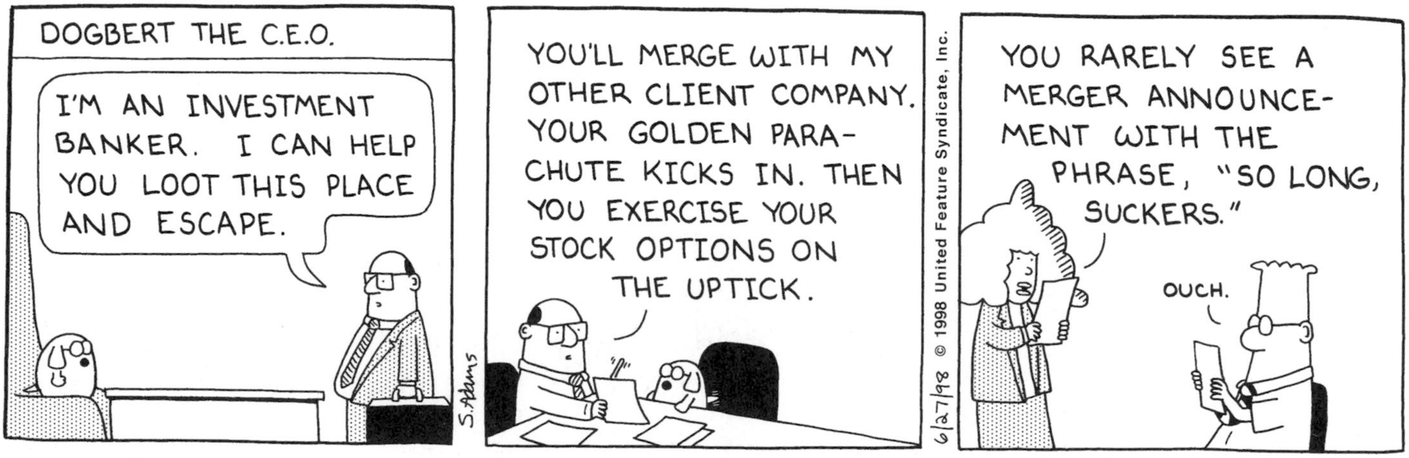
DOGBERT THE C.E.O.
I'M AN INVESTMENT BANKER. I CAN HELP YOU LOOT THIS PLACE AND ESCAPE.
S. Adams
YOU'LL MERGE WITH MY OTHER CLIENT COMPANY. YOUR GOLDEN PARA-CHUTE KICKS IN. THEN YOU EXERCISE YOUR STOCK OPTIONS ON THE UPTICK.
6/27/98 © 1998 United Feature Syndicate, Inc.
YOU RARELY SEE A MERGER ANNOUNCE-MENT WITH THE PHRASE, "SO LONG, SUCKERS."
OUCH.

OUR NEXT PRODUCT WILL DETERMINE THE FUTURE OF OUR COMPANY!
$
S. Adams
I NEED A PROJECT LEADER WHO HAS A PASSION FOR SUCCESS!
WOULD THAT LEADER GET EXTRA PAY?
IT'S NOT ABOUT MONEY, WALLY. IT'S ABOUT A PASSION FOR SUCCESS!
ALL I HAVE IS A VAGUE PREFERENCE. HOW ABOUT YOU?
6/28/98 © 1998 United Feature Syndicate, Inc.
YES, I'M FEELING SOMETHING . . . MAYBE IT'S . . .
NO, IT'S JUST MY ALLERGY MEDICATION.
WHAT WAS IT LIKE?
IT TINGLED.

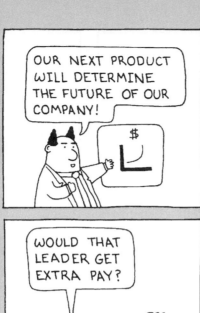

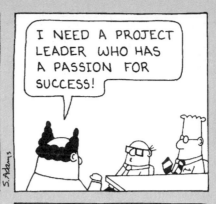

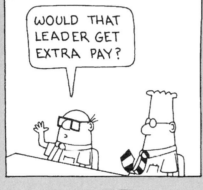

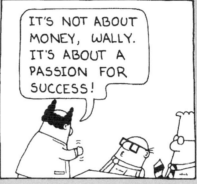

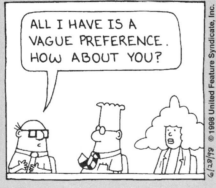

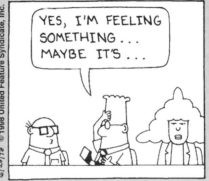

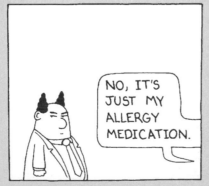

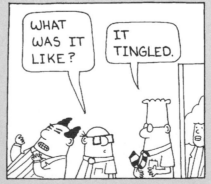

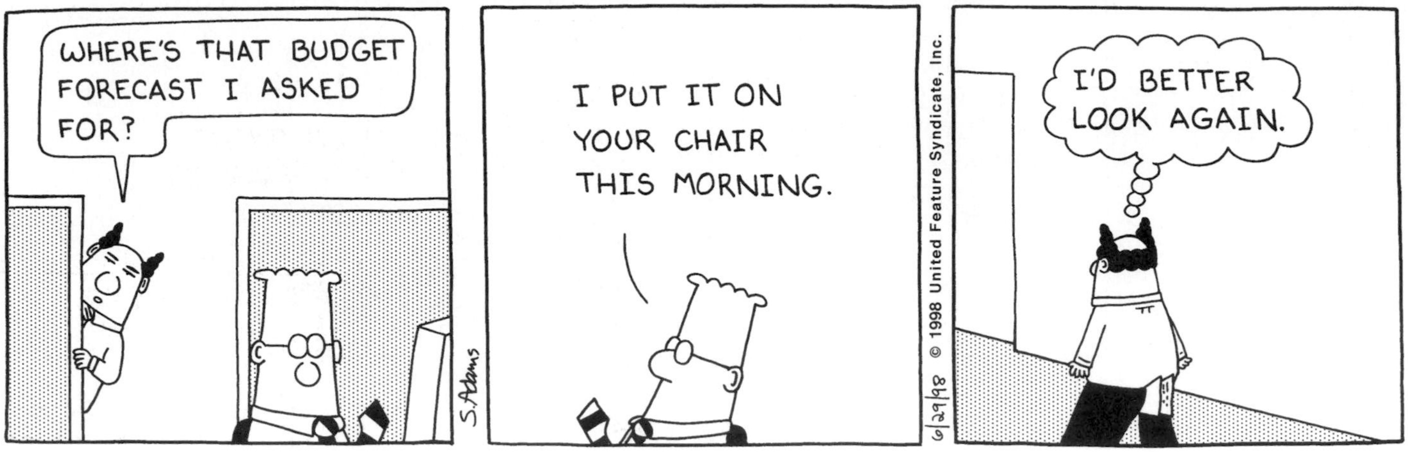
WHERE'S THAT BUDGET FORECAST I ASKED FOR?
I PUT IT ON YOUR CHAIR THIS MORNING.
I'D BETTER LOOK AGAIN.
S. Adams
6/29/98 © 1998 United Feature Syndicate, Inc.

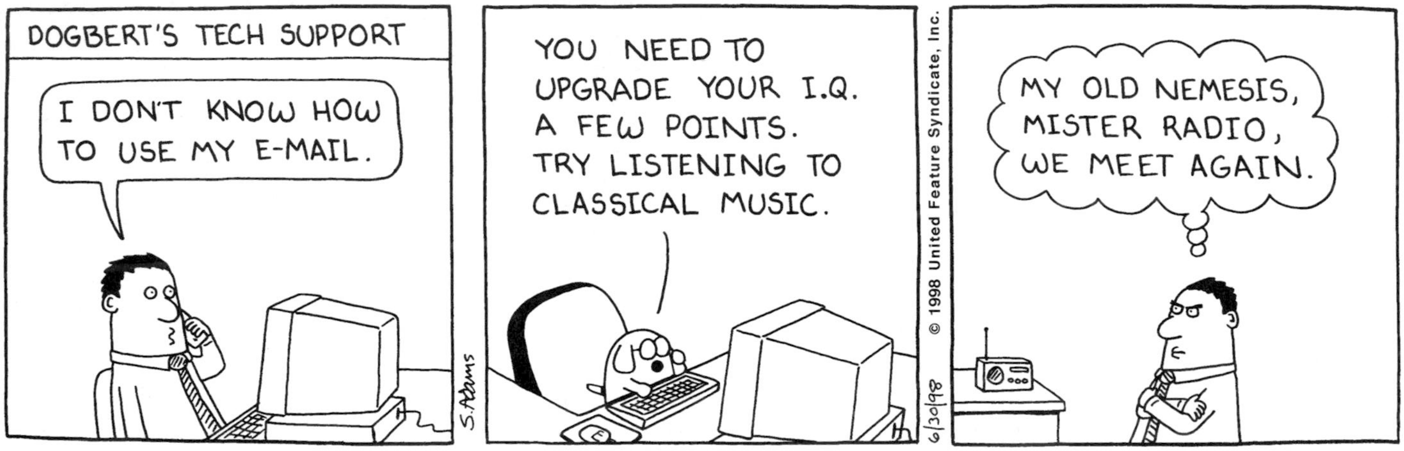
DOGBERT'S TECH SUPPORT
I DON'T KNOW HOW TO USE MY E-MAIL.
YOU NEED TO UPGRADE YOUR I.Q. A FEW POINTS. TRY LISTENING TO CLASSICAL MUSIC.
MY OLD NEMESIS, MISTER RADIO, WE MEET AGAIN.
S. Adams
6/30/98 © 1998 United Feature Syndicate, Inc.

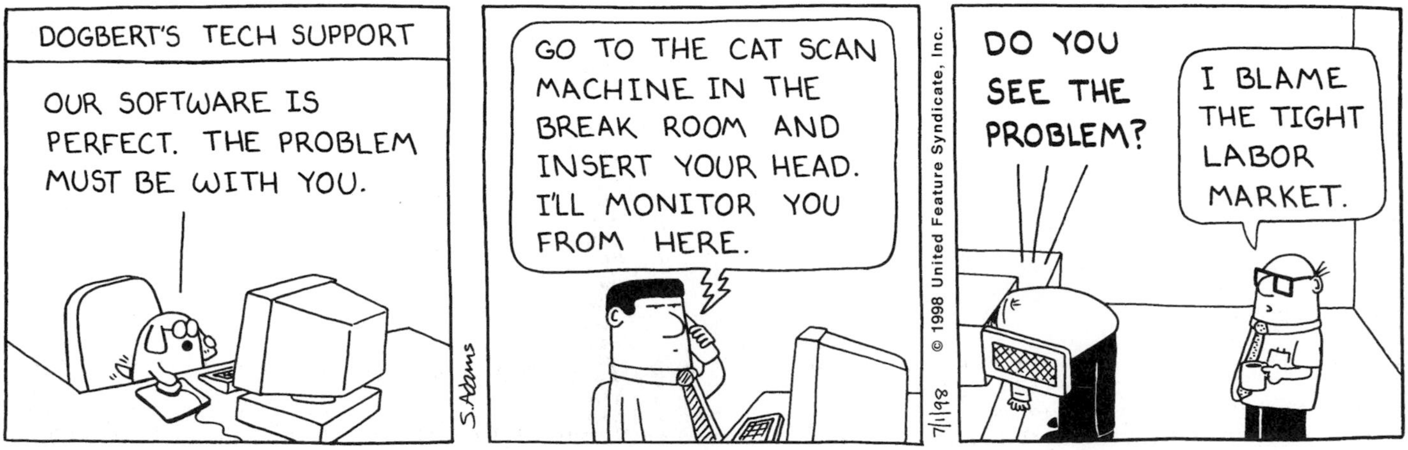
DOGBERT'S TECH SUPPORT
OUR SOFTWARE IS PERFECT. THE PROBLEM MUST BE WITH YOU.
GO TO THE CAT SCAN MACHINE IN THE BREAK ROOM AND INSERT YOUR HEAD. I'LL MONITOR YOU FROM HERE.
DO YOU SEE THE PROBLEM?
I BLAME THE TIGHT LABOR MARKET.
S. Adams
7/1/98 © 1998 United Feature Syndicate, Inc.

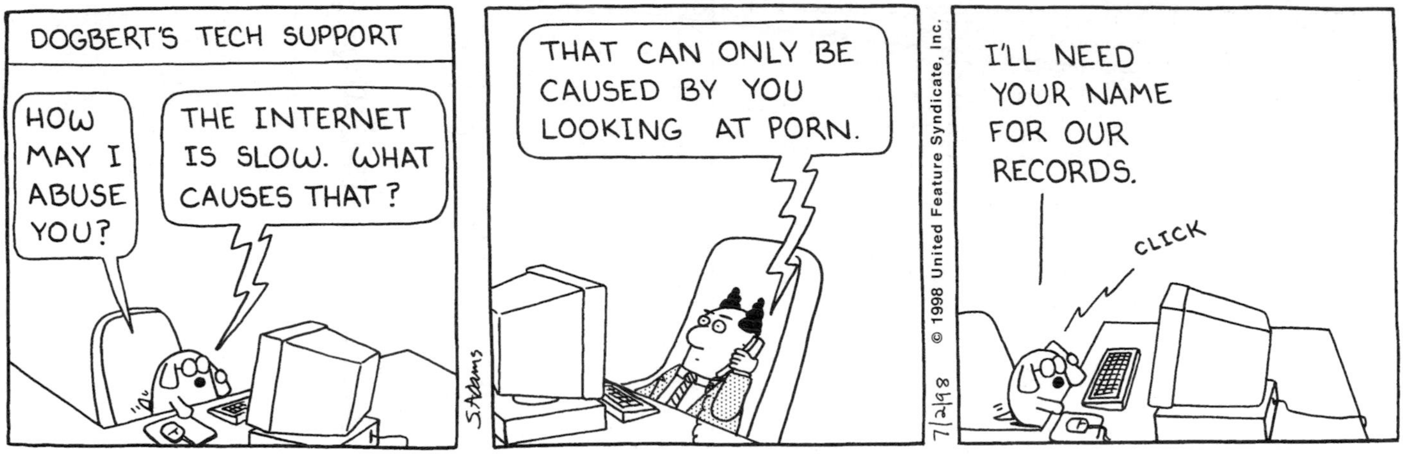
DOGBERT'S TECH SUPPORT
HOW MAY I ABUSE YOU?
THE INTERNET IS SLOW. WHAT CAUSES THAT?
THAT CAN ONLY BE CAUSED BY YOU LOOKING AT PORN.
I'LL NEED YOUR NAME FOR OUR RECORDS.
CLICK
7/2/98 © 1998 United Feature Syndicate, Inc.

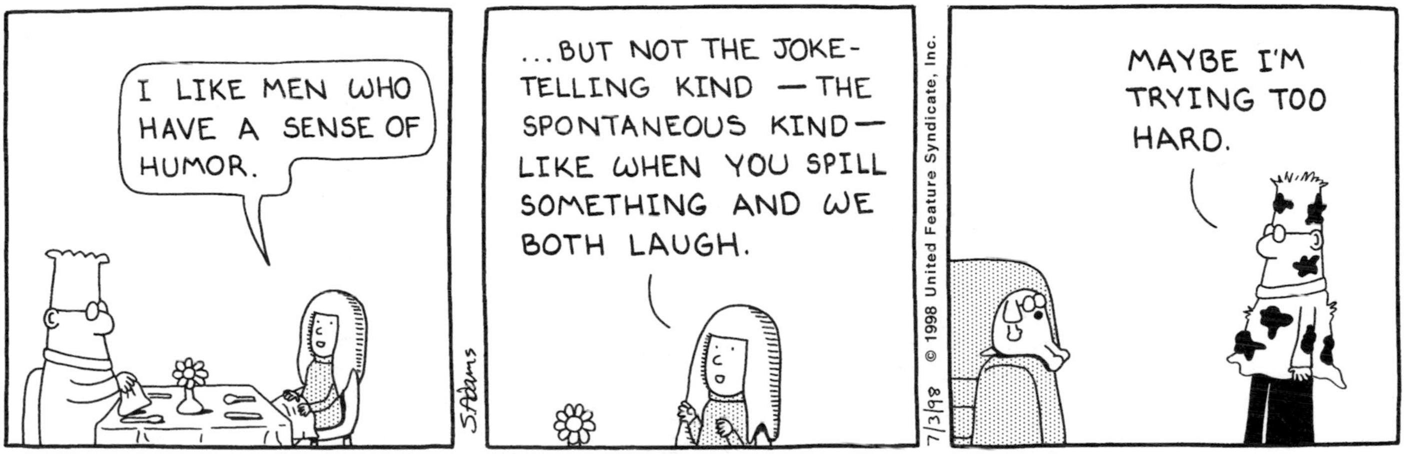
I LIKE MEN WHO HAVE A SENSE OF HUMOR.
...BUT NOT THE JOKE-TELLING KIND — THE SPONTANEOUS KIND — LIKE WHEN YOU SPILL SOMETHING AND WE BOTH LAUGH.
MAYBE I'M TRYING TOO HARD.
7/3/98 © 1998 United Feature Syndicate, Inc.

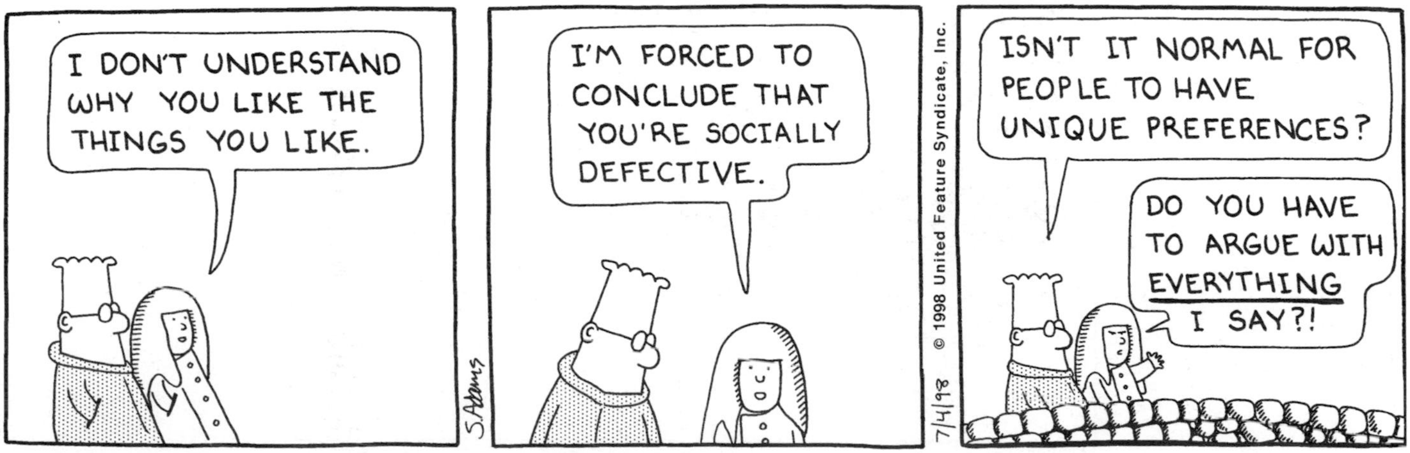
I DON'T UNDERSTAND WHY YOU LIKE THE THINGS YOU LIKE.
I'M FORCED TO CONCLUDE THAT YOU'RE SOCIALLY DEFECTIVE.
ISN'T IT NORMAL FOR PEOPLE TO HAVE UNIQUE PREFERENCES?
DO YOU HAVE TO ARGUE WITH EVERYTHING I SAY?!
7/4/98 © 1998 United Feature Syndicate, Inc.

MY POSTERIOR IS GROWING TO FIT THE SIZE OF MY CHAIR.
IS THAT POSSIBLE?
S. Adams
POSTERIORS ARE LIKE GOLDFISH. THEY GROW TO THE LIMIT OF THEIR ENVIRON-MENT.
THAT'S RIDICULOUS. I HAVE THE BIGGEST CHAIR. THAT WOULD MEAN...
FORGET I BROUGHT IT UP.
WELL, BACK TO WORK.
7/5/98 © 1998 United Feature Syndicate, Inc.
MISSION REPORT.
SUCCESS.
THE GLUE ON HIS CHAIR SHOULD BE SET BY NOW.
I GUESS THIS IS WHY GOLDFISHES DON'T USE CHAIRS.

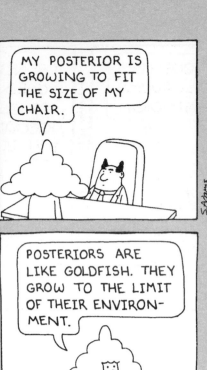

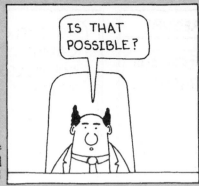

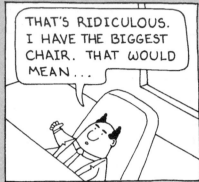

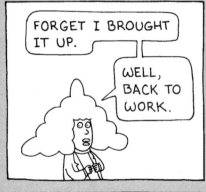

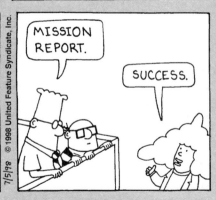

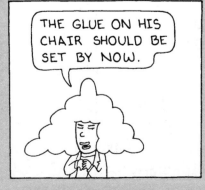

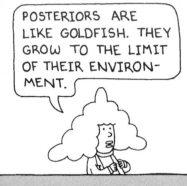

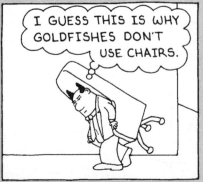

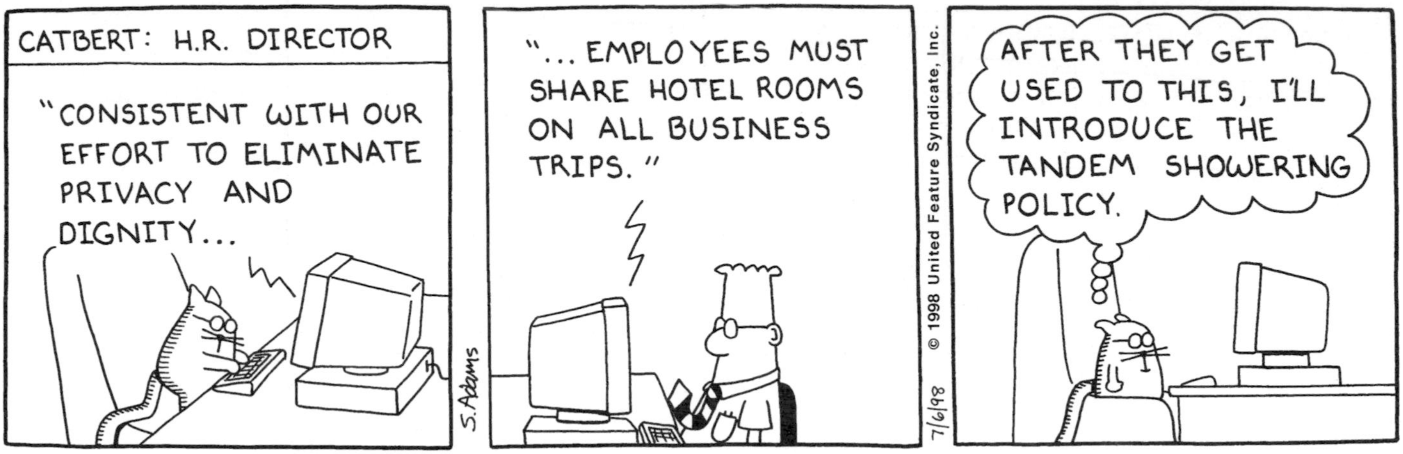
CATBERT: H.R. DIRECTOR
"CONSISTENT WITH OUR EFFORT TO ELIMINATE PRIVACY AND DIGNITY...
"... EMPLOYEES MUST SHARE HOTEL ROOMS ON ALL BUSINESS TRIPS."
AFTER THEY GET USED TO THIS, I'LL INTRODUCE THE TANDEM SHOWERING POLICY.
S. Adams
7/6/98 © 1998 United Feature Syndicate, Inc.

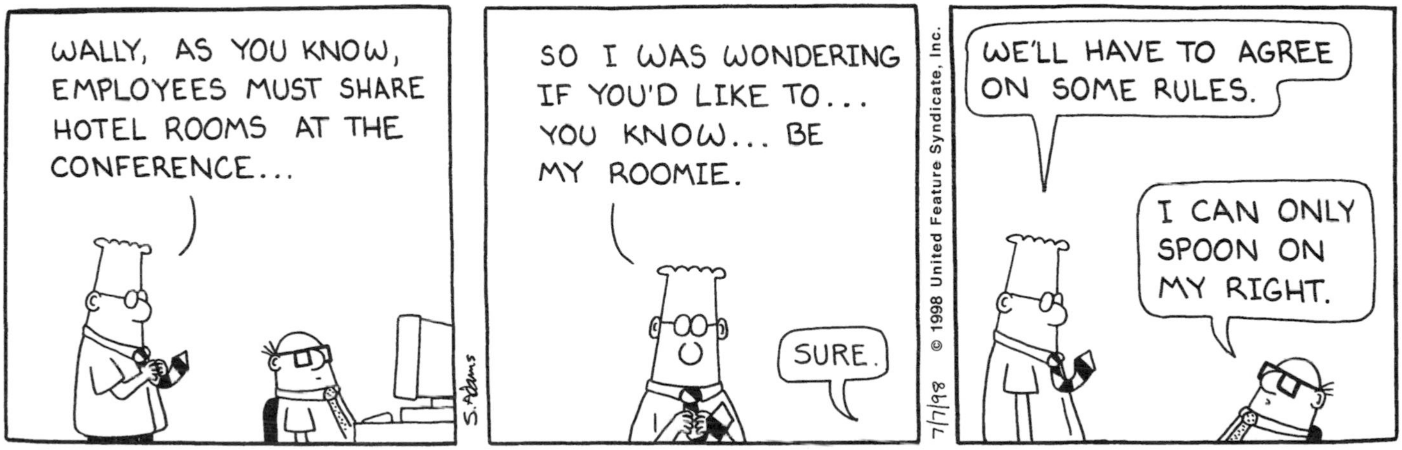
WALLY, AS YOU KNOW, EMPLOYEES MUST SHARE HOTEL ROOMS AT THE CONFERENCE...
SO I WAS WONDERING IF YOU'D LIKE TO... YOU KNOW... BE MY ROOMIE.
SURE.
WE'LL HAVE TO AGREE ON SOME RULES.
I CAN ONLY SPOON ON MY RIGHT.
S. Adams
7/7/98 © 1998 United Feature Syndicate, Inc.

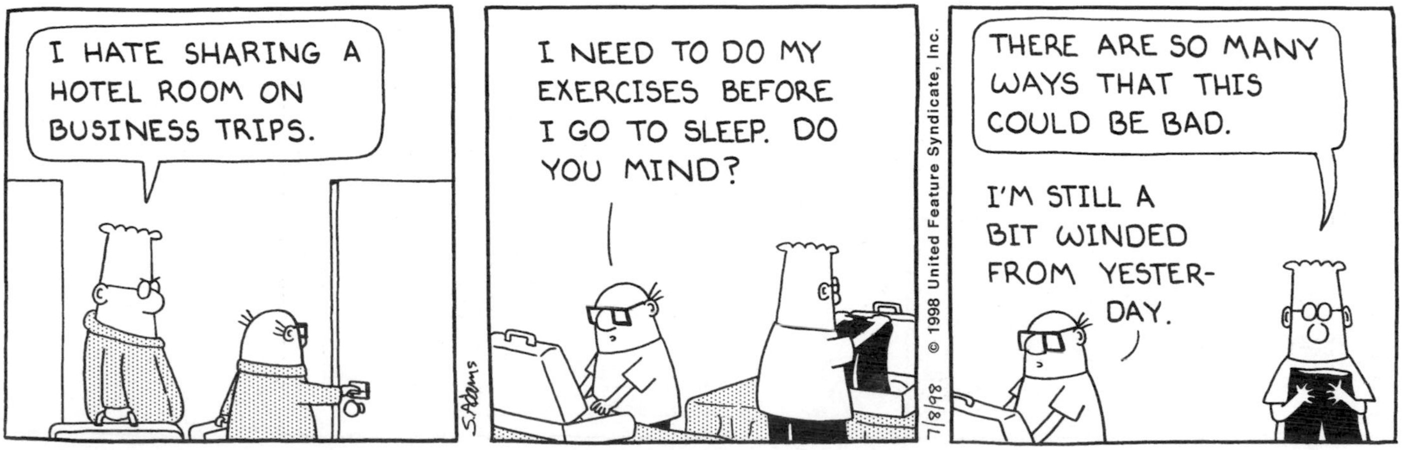
I HATE SHARING A HOTEL ROOM ON BUSINESS TRIPS.
I NEED TO DO MY EXERCISES BEFORE I GO TO SLEEP. DO YOU MIND?
THERE ARE SO MANY WAYS THAT THIS COULD BE BAD.
I'M STILL A BIT WINDED FROM YESTER-DAY.
S. Adams
7/8/98 © 1998 United Feature Syndicate, Inc.

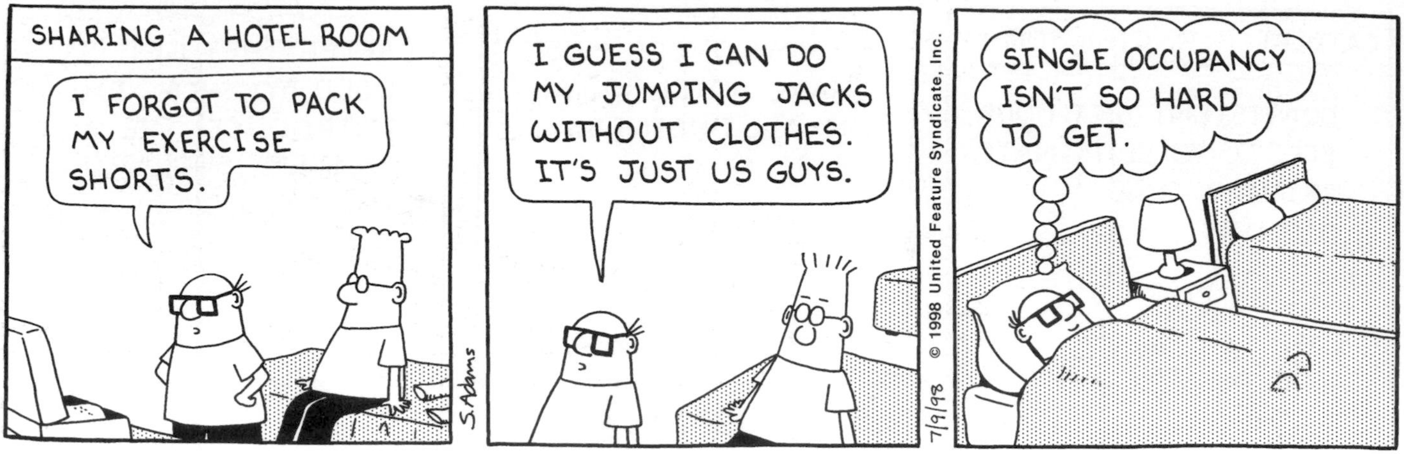
SHARING A HOTEL ROOM
I FORGOT TO PACK MY EXERCISE SHORTS.
I GUESS I CAN DO MY JUMPING JACKS WITHOUT CLOTHES. IT'S JUST US GUYS.
SINGLE OCCUPANCY ISN'T SO HARD TO GET.
S. Adams
7/9/98 © 1998 United Feature Syndicate, Inc.

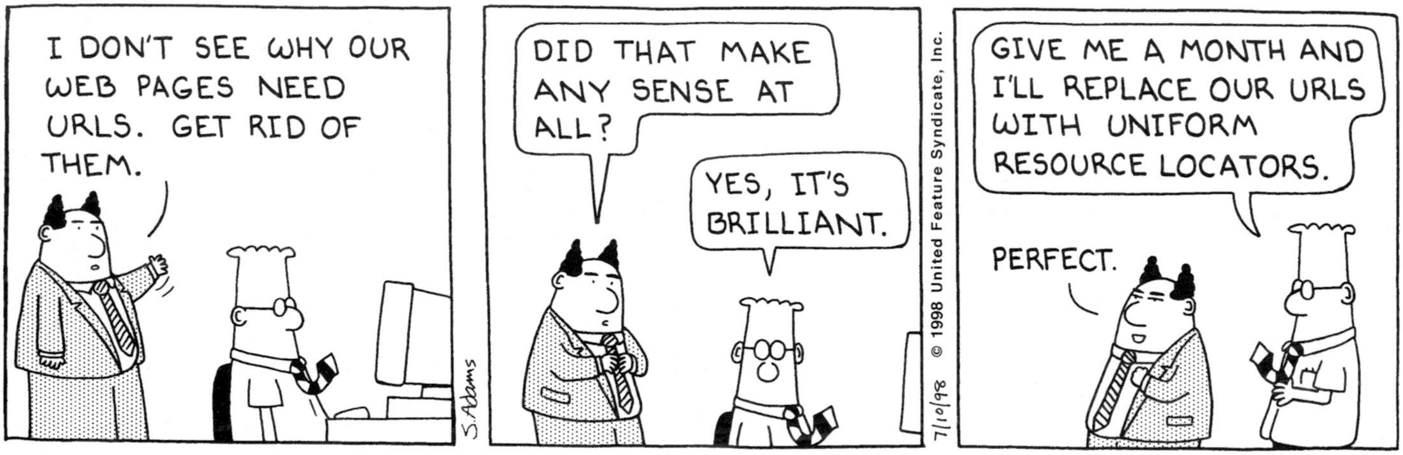
I DON'T SEE WHY OUR WEB PAGES NEED URLS. GET RID OF THEM.
DID THAT MAKE ANY SENSE AT ALL?
YES, IT'S BRILLIANT.
GIVE ME A MONTH AND I'LL REPLACE OUR URLS WITH UNIFORM RESOURCE LOCATORS.
PERFECT.
S. Adams
7/10/98 © 1998 United Feature Syndicate, Inc.

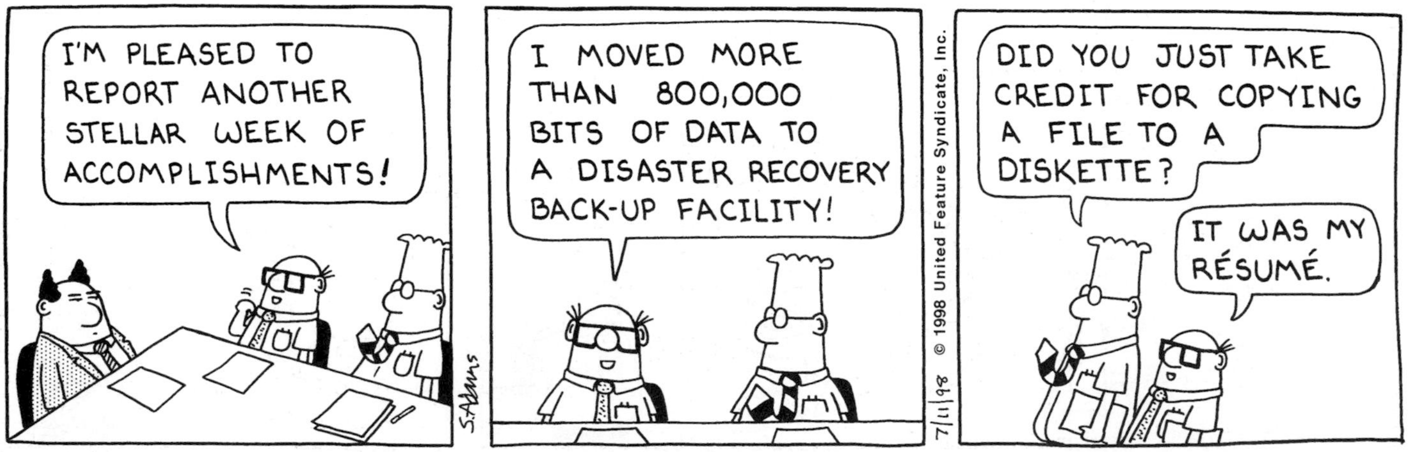
I'M PLEASED TO REPORT ANOTHER STELLAR WEEK OF ACCOMPLISHMENTS!
I MOVED MORE THAN 800,000 BITS OF DATA TO A DISASTER RECOVERY BACK-UP FACILITY!
DID YOU JUST TAKE CREDIT FOR COPYING A FILE TO A DISKETTE?
IT WAS MY RÉSUMÉ.
S. Adams
7/11/98 © 1998 United Feature Syndicate, Inc.

I CAN'T BELIEVE I GET PAID FOR THIS.
BLAH BLAH
S. Adams
THIS THING LASTS TWO MORE HOURS.
MAYBE I SHOULD FIDGET WITH MY PEN.
I'M TOO LATE. NOW I'D LOOK UNCREATIVE.
FIDGET.
I WONDER HOW LONG I CAN HOLD MY BREATH.
FIDGET.
© 1998 United Feature Syndicate, Inc.
7/12/98
FIDGET.
WHUMP!
OOH, TWO PENS. WHAT WOULD THAT BE LIKE?

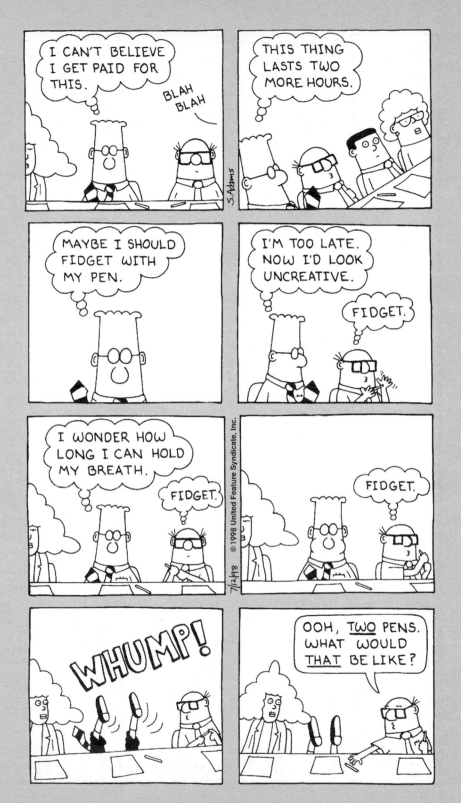

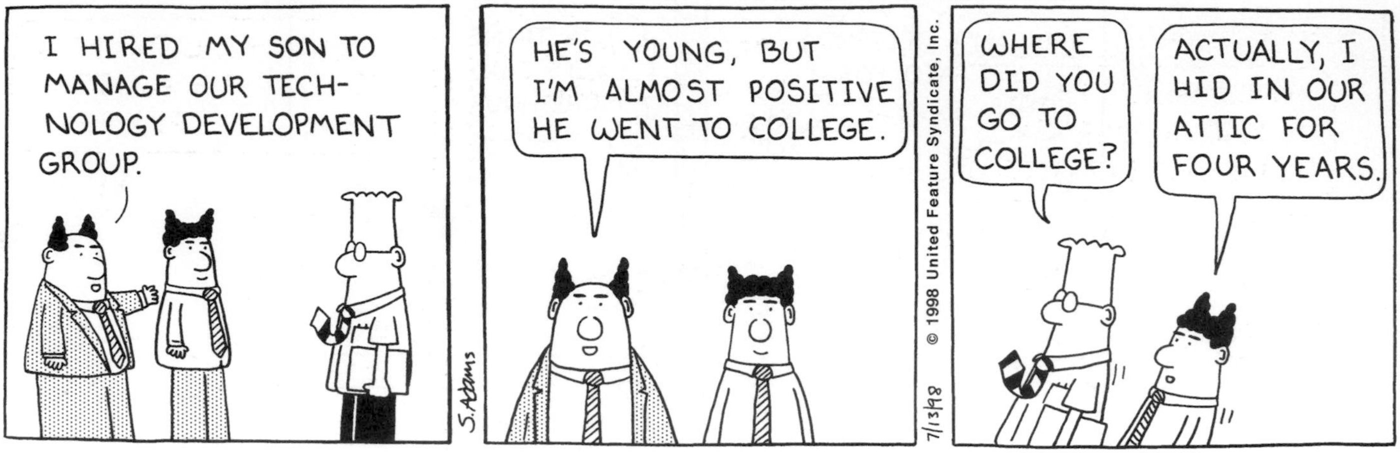
I HIRED MY SON TO MANAGE OUR TECH-NOLOGY DEVELOPMENT GROUP.
S. Adams
HE'S YOUNG, BUT I'M ALMOST POSITIVE HE WENT TO COLLEGE.
7/13/98 © 1998 United Feature Syndicate, Inc.
WHERE DID YOU GO TO COLLEGE?
ACTUALLY, I HID IN OUR ATTIC FOR FOUR YEARS.

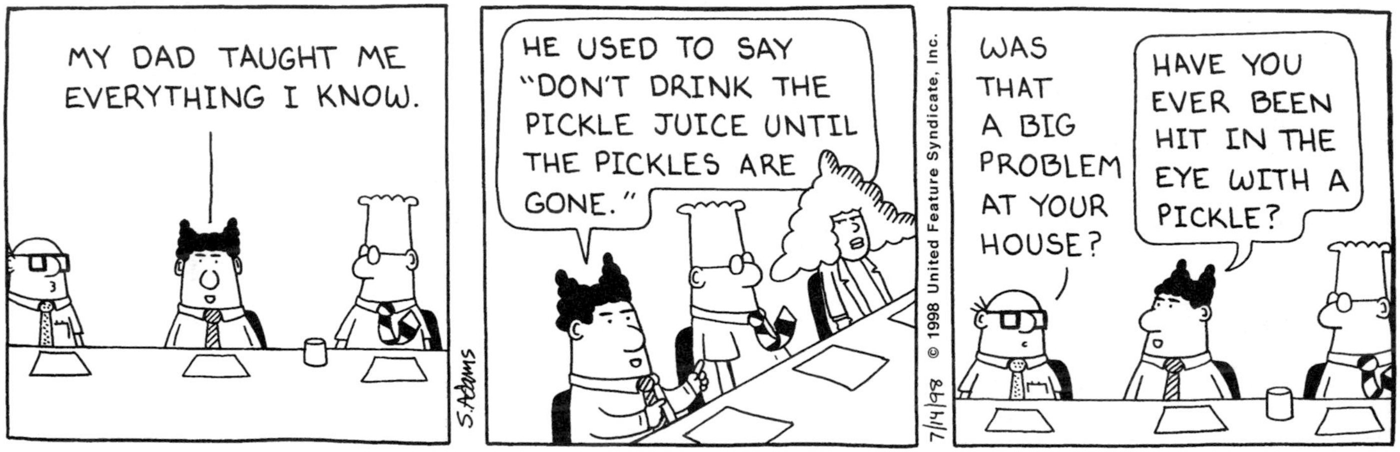
MY DAD TAUGHT ME EVERYTHING I KNOW.
S. Adams
HE USED TO SAY "DON'T DRINK THE PICKLE JUICE UNTIL THE PICKLES ARE GONE."
7/14/98 © 1998 United Feature Syndicate, Inc.
WAS THAT A BIG PROBLEM AT YOUR HOUSE?
HAVE YOU EVER BEEN HIT IN THE EYE WITH A PICKLE?

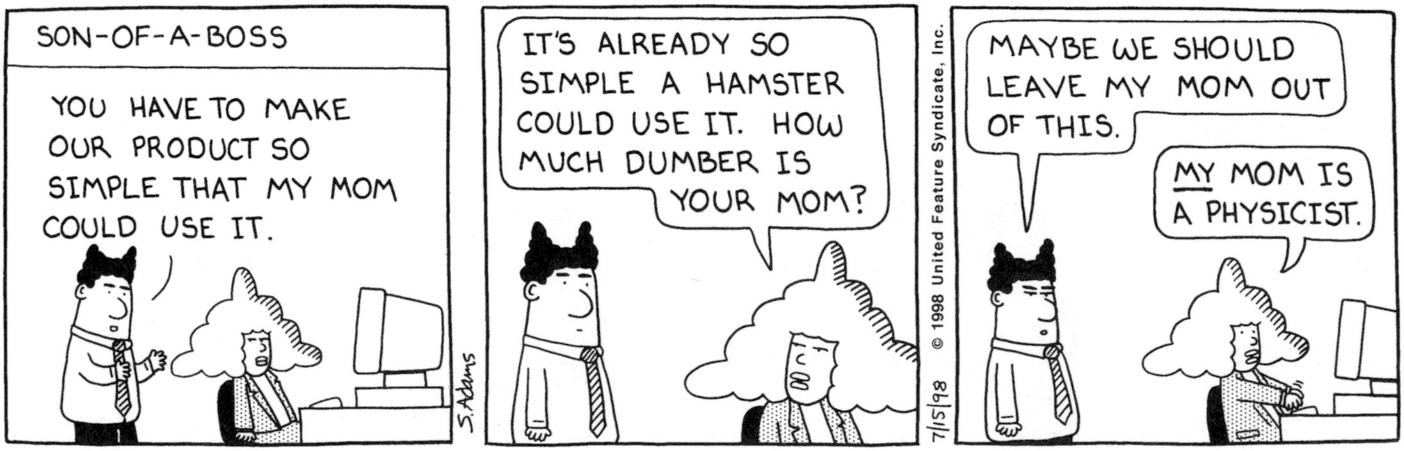
SON-OF-A-BOSS
YOU HAVE TO MAKE OUR PRODUCT SO SIMPLE THAT MY MOM COULD USE IT.
S. Adams
IT'S ALREADY SO SIMPLE A HAMSTER COULD USE IT. HOW MUCH DUMBER IS YOUR MOM?
7/15/98 © 1998 United Feature Syndicate, Inc.
MAYBE WE SHOULD LEAVE MY MOM OUT OF THIS.
MY MOM IS A PHYSICIST.

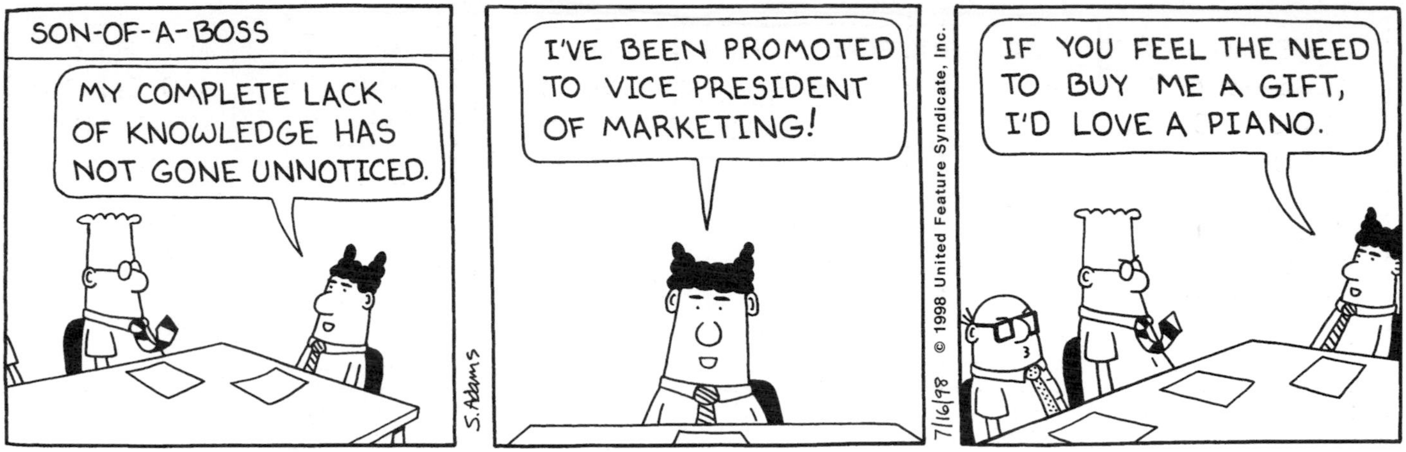
SON-OF-A-BOSS
MY COMPLETE LACK OF KNOWLEDGE HAS NOT GONE UNNOTICED.
I'VE BEEN PROMOTED TO VICE PRESIDENT OF MARKETING!
IF YOU FEEL THE NEED TO BUY ME A GIFT, I'D LOVE A PIANO.
S. Adams
7/16/98 © 1998 United Feature Syndicate, Inc.

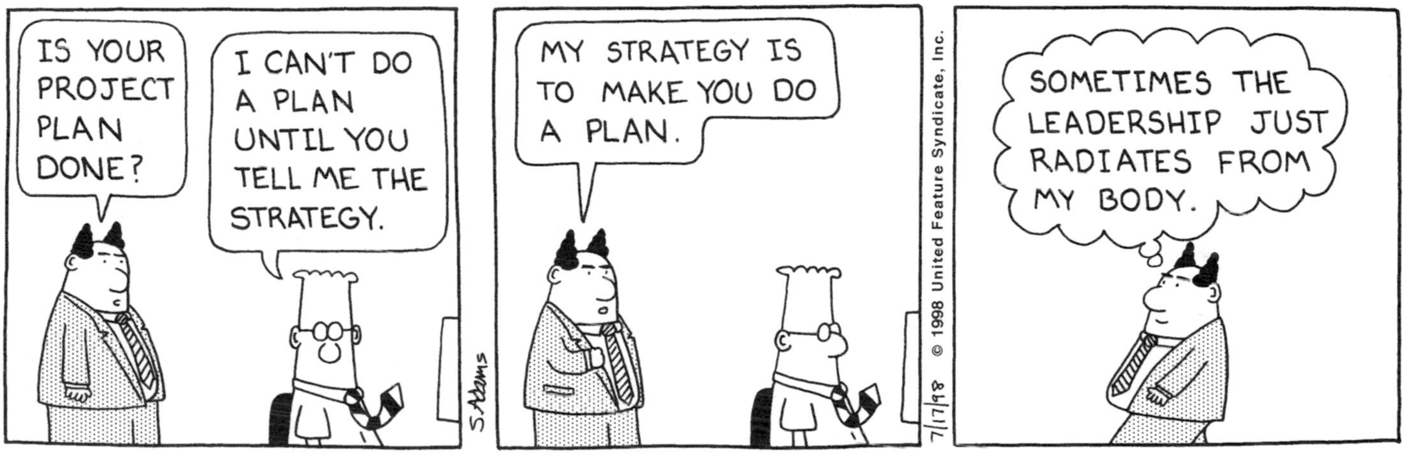
IS YOUR PROJECT PLAN DONE?
I CAN'T DO A PLAN UNTIL YOU TELL ME THE STRATEGY.
MY STRATEGY IS TO MAKE YOU DO A PLAN.
SOMETIMES THE LEADERSHIP JUST RADIATES FROM MY BODY.
S. Adams
7/17/98 © 1998 United Feature Syndicate, Inc.

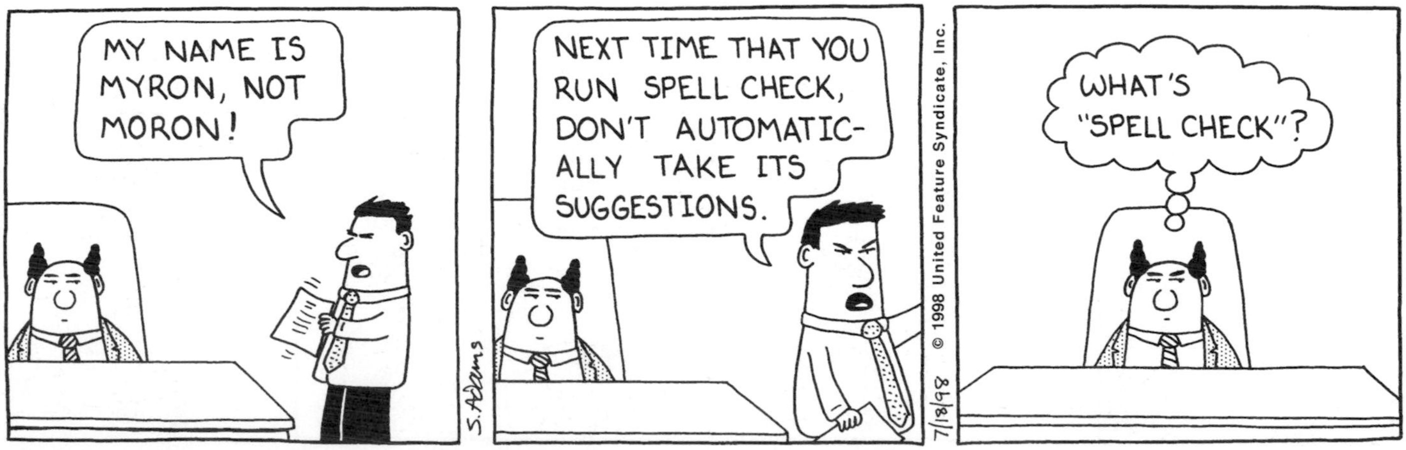
MY NAME IS MYRON, NOT MORON!
NEXT TIME THAT YOU RUN SPELL CHECK, DON'T AUTOMATIC-ALLY TAKE ITS SUGGESTIONS.
WHAT'S "SPELL CHECK"?
S. Adams
7/18/98 © 1998 United Feature Syndicate, Inc.

HERE'S THE GOAL THAT WILL MOTIVATE YOU FOR THE NEXT YEAR.
"BUILD A GLOBAL SATELLITE NETWORK. BUDGET: $12,000."
MOTIVATION FEELS MUCH DIFFERENT FROM WHAT I IMAGINED.
I WAS EXPECTING A LIGHT, ENERGETIC FEELING.
BUT IT'S MORE LIKE BEING PINNED UNDER A BURNING COUCH.
WHOO! I'M GETTING DIZZY.
I'D BETTER LIE DOWN UNTIL THE MOTIVATION WEARS OFF.
HE'S GOING TO BE TROUBLE DURING THE NEXT ROUND OF BUDGET CUTS.
S.Adams
7/19/98
© 1998 United Feature Syndicate, Inc.

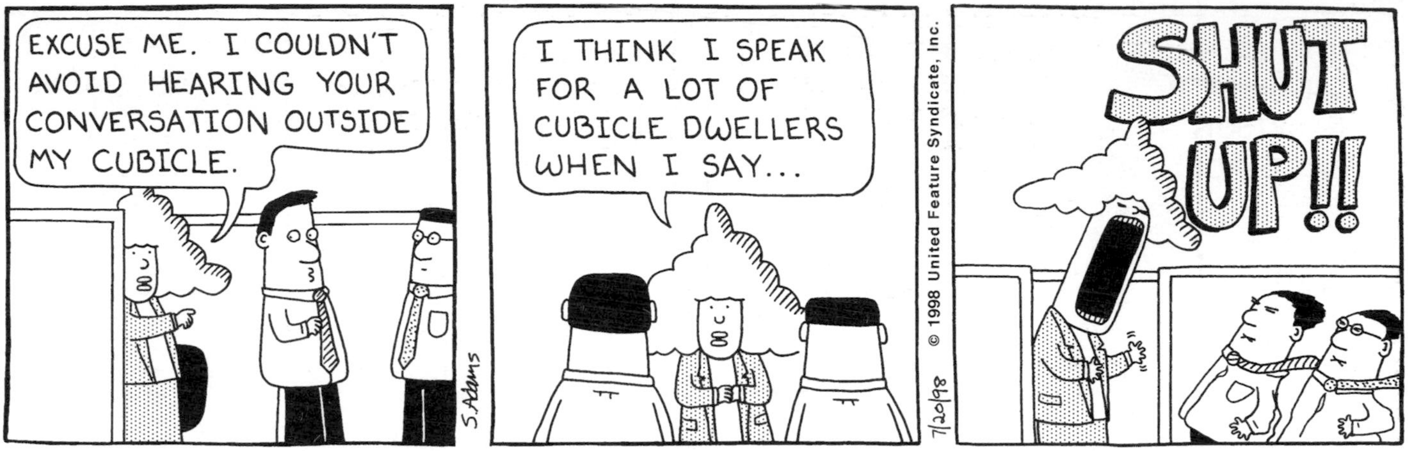
EXCUSE ME. I COULDN'T AVOID HEARING YOUR CONVERSATION OUTSIDE MY CUBICLE.
I THINK I SPEAK FOR A LOT OF CUBICLE DWELLERS WHEN I SAY...
SHUT UP!!
S. Adams
7/20/98 © 1998 United Feature Syndicate, Inc.

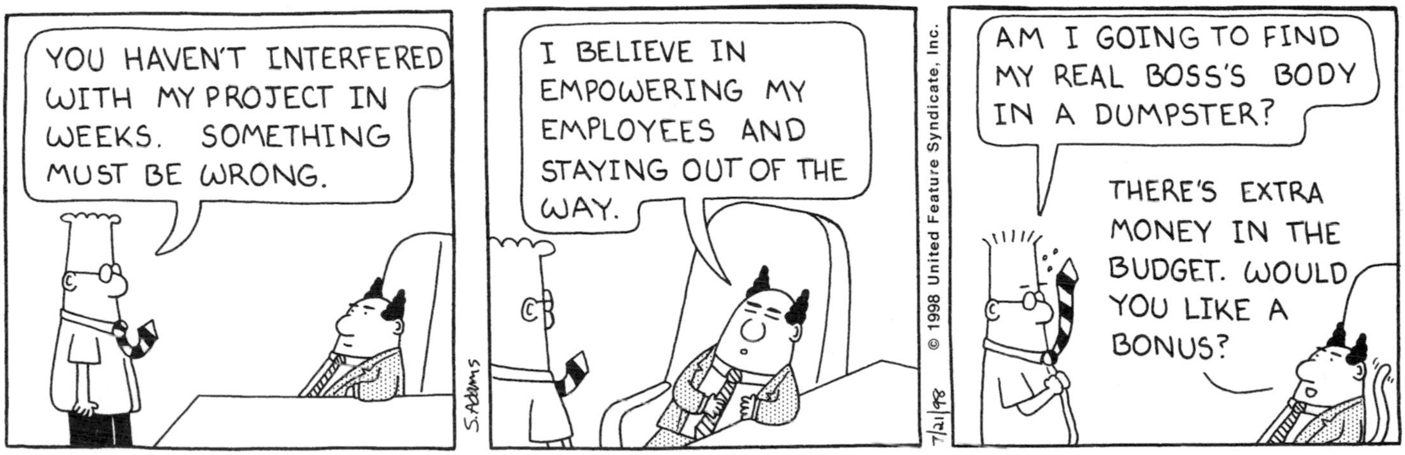
YOU HAVEN'T INTERFERED WITH MY PROJECT IN WEEKS. SOMETHING MUST BE WRONG.
I BELIEVE IN EMPOWERING MY EMPLOYEES AND STAYING OUT OF THE WAY.
AM I GOING TO FIND MY REAL BOSS'S BODY IN A DUMPSTER?
THERE'S EXTRA MONEY IN THE BUDGET. WOULD YOU LIKE A BONUS?
S. Adams
7/21/98 © 1998 United Feature Syndicate, Inc.

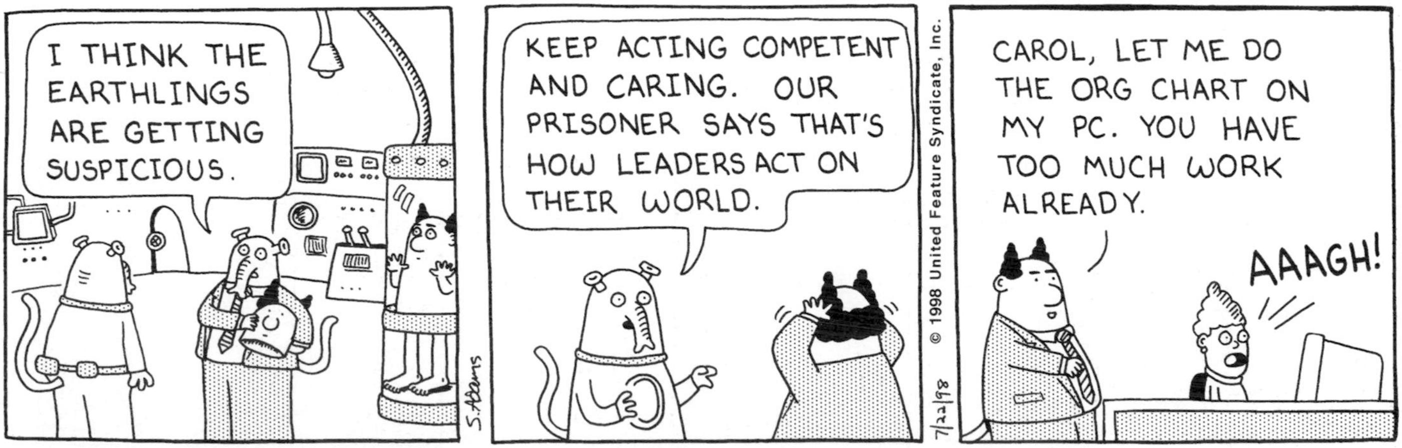
I THINK THE EARTHLINGS ARE GETTING SUSPICIOUS.
KEEP ACTING COMPETENT AND CARING. OUR PRISONER SAYS THAT'S HOW LEADERS ACT ON THEIR WORLD.
CAROL, LET ME DO THE ORG CHART ON MY PC. YOU HAVE TOO MUCH WORK ALREADY.
AAAGH!
S. Adams
7/22/98 © 1998 United Feature Syndicate, Inc.

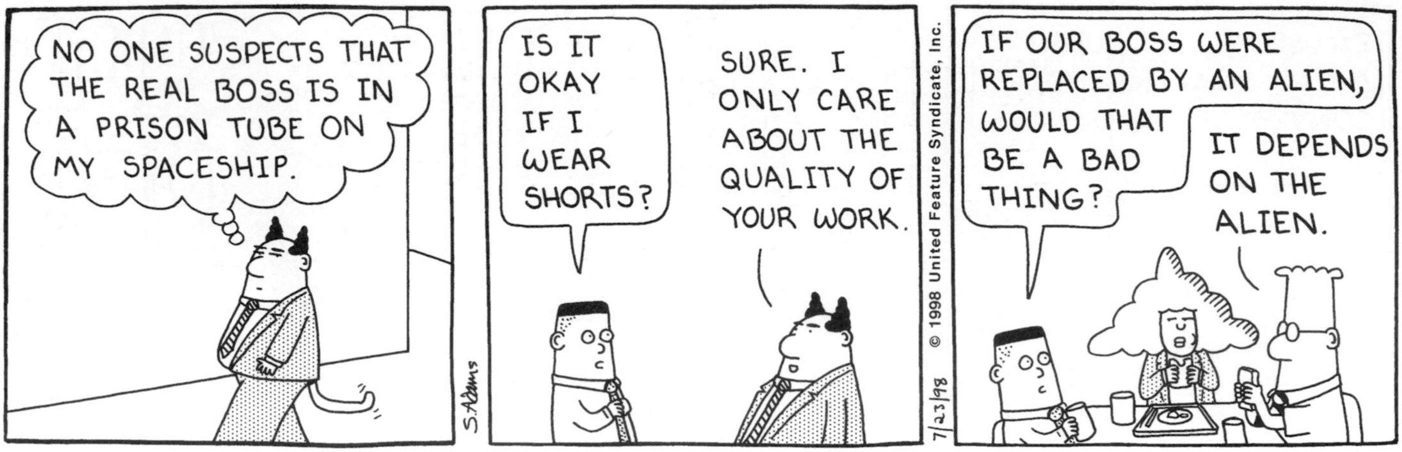
NO ONE SUSPECTS THAT THE REAL BOSS IS IN A PRISON TUBE ON MY SPACESHIP.
S. Adams
IS IT OKAY IF I WEAR SHORTS?
SURE. I ONLY CARE ABOUT THE QUALITY OF YOUR WORK.
7/23/98 © 1998 United Feature Syndicate, Inc.
IF OUR BOSS WERE REPLACED BY AN ALIEN, WOULD THAT BE A BAD THING?
IT DEPENDS ON THE ALIEN.

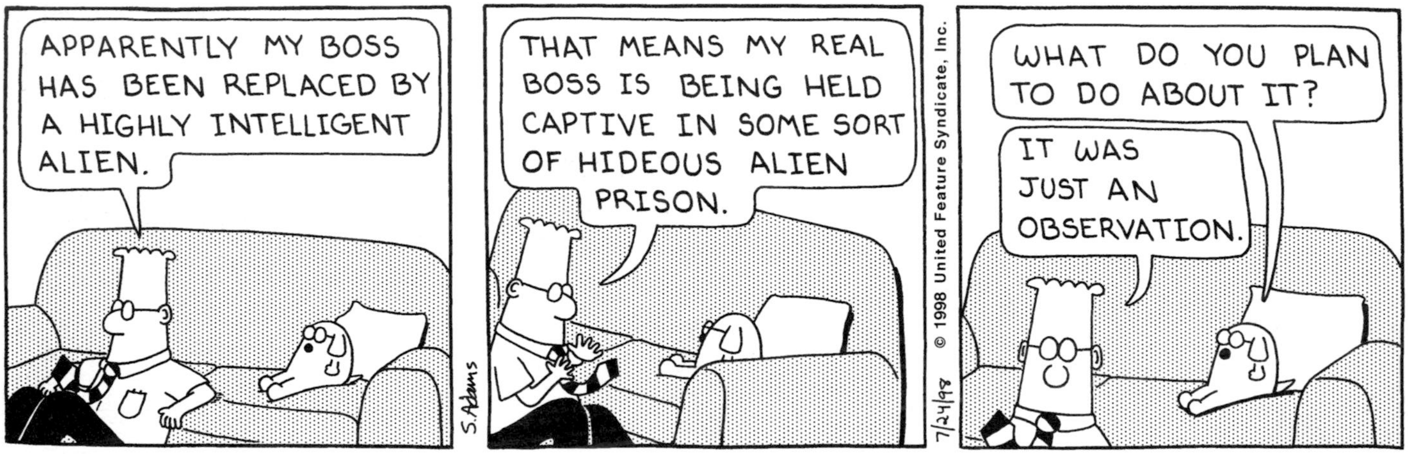
APPARENTLY MY BOSS HAS BEEN REPLACED BY A HIGHLY INTELLIGENT ALIEN.
S. Adams
THAT MEANS MY REAL BOSS IS BEING HELD CAPTIVE IN SOME SORT OF HIDEOUS ALIEN PRISON.
7/24/98 © 1998 United Feature Syndicate, Inc.
WHAT DO YOU PLAN TO DO ABOUT IT?
IT WAS JUST AN OBSERVATION.

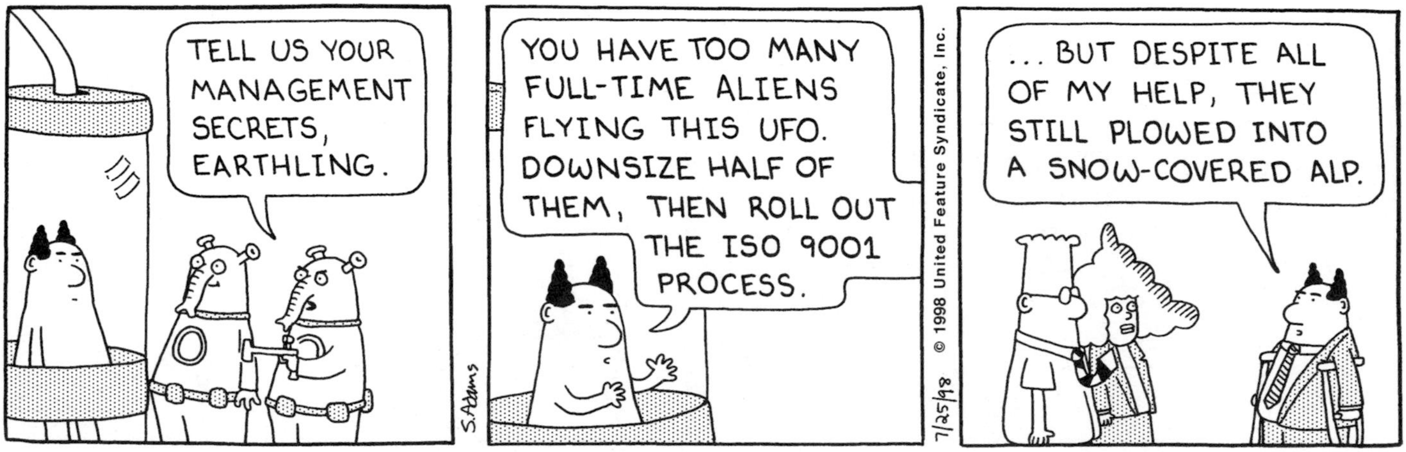
TELL US YOUR MANAGEMENT SECRETS, EARTHLING.
S. Adams
YOU HAVE TOO MANY FULL-TIME ALIENS FLYING THIS UFO. DOWNSIZE HALF OF THEM, THEN ROLL OUT THE ISO 9001 PROCESS.
7/25/98 © 1998 United Feature Syndicate, Inc.
... BUT DESPITE ALL OF MY HELP, THEY STILL PLOWED INTO A SNOW-COVERED ALP.

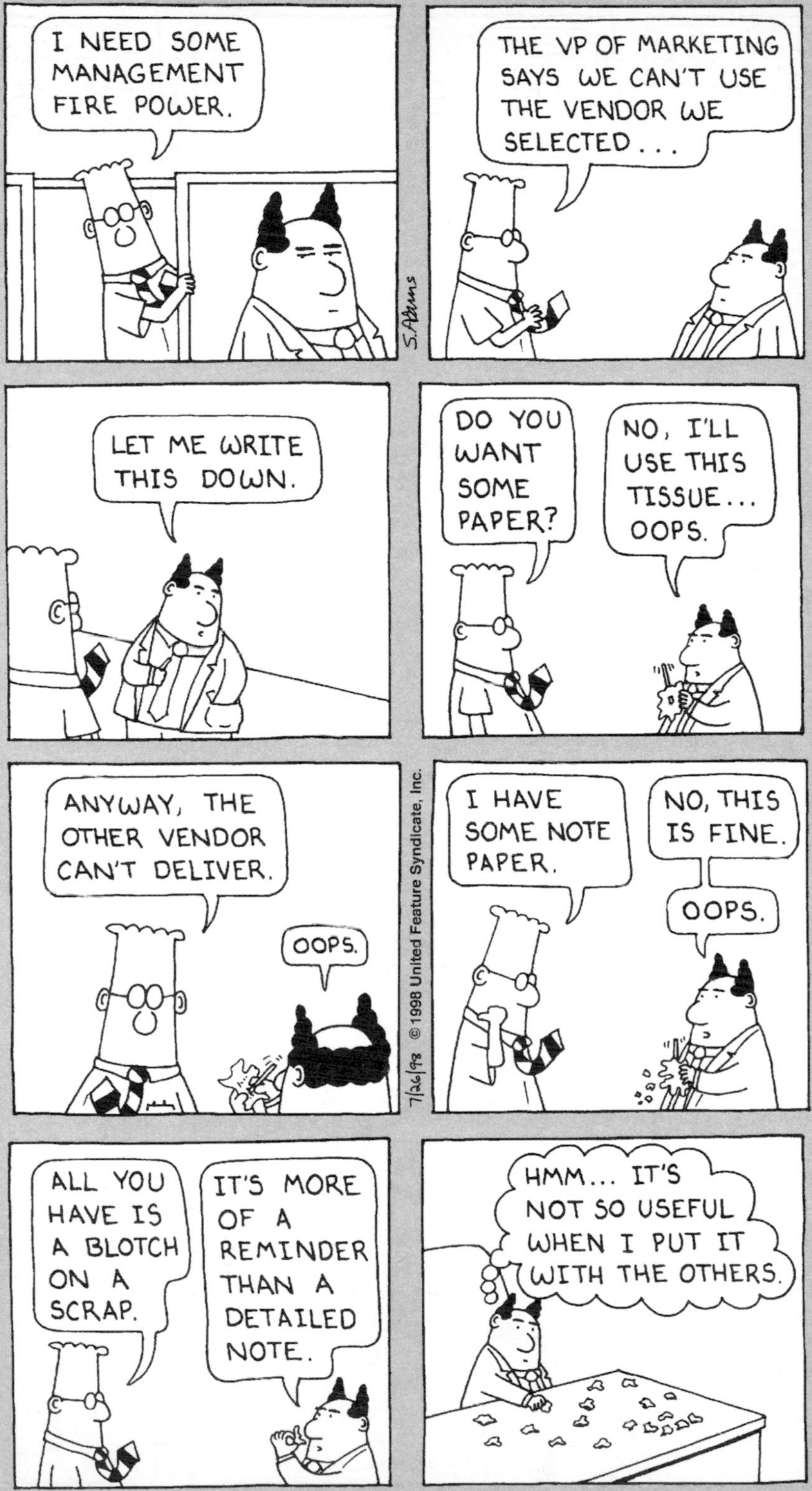
I NEED SOME MANAGEMENT FIRE POWER.
S. Adams
THE VP OF MARKETING SAYS WE CAN'T USE THE VENDOR WE SELECTED . . .
LET ME WRITE THIS DOWN.
DO YOU WANT SOME PAPER?
NO, I'LL USE THIS TISSUE... OOPS.
ANYWAY, THE OTHER VENDOR CAN'T DELIVER.
OOPS.
7/26/98 © 1998 United Feature Syndicate, Inc.
I HAVE SOME NOTE PAPER.
NO, THIS IS FINE.
OOPS.
ALL YOU HAVE IS A BLOTCH ON A SCRAP.
IT'S MORE OF A REMINDER THAN A DETAILED NOTE.
HMM... IT'S NOT SO USEFUL WHEN I PUT IT WITH THE OTHERS.

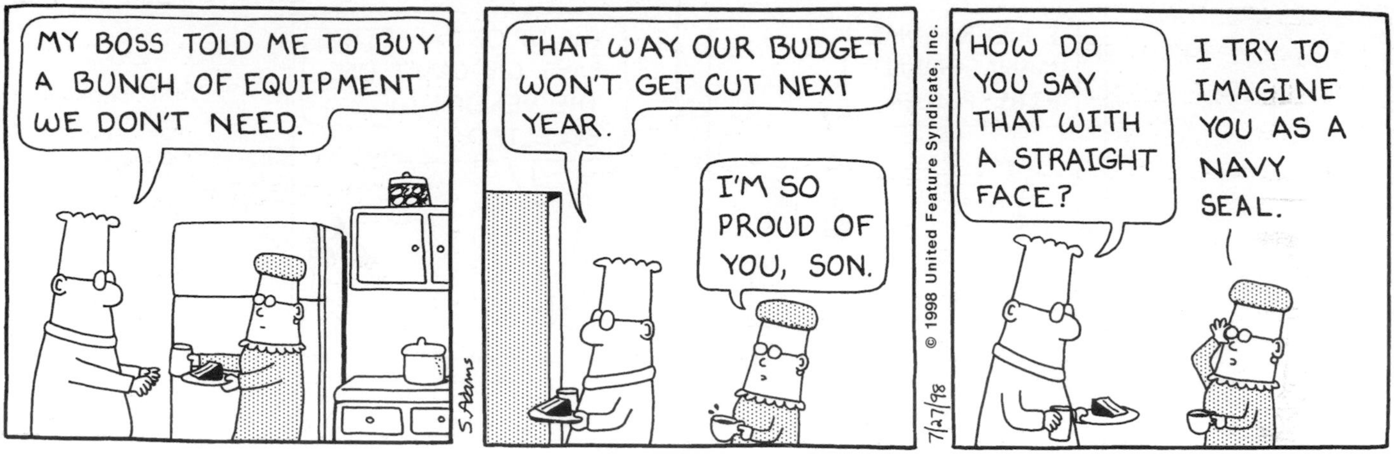
MY BOSS TOLD ME TO BUY A BUNCH OF EQUIPMENT WE DON'T NEED.
S. Adams
THAT WAY OUR BUDGET WON'T GET CUT NEXT YEAR.
I'M SO PROUD OF YOU, SON.
© 1998 United Feature Syndicate, Inc.
7/27/98
HOW DO YOU SAY THAT WITH A STRAIGHT FACE?
I TRY TO IMAGINE YOU AS A NAVY SEAL.

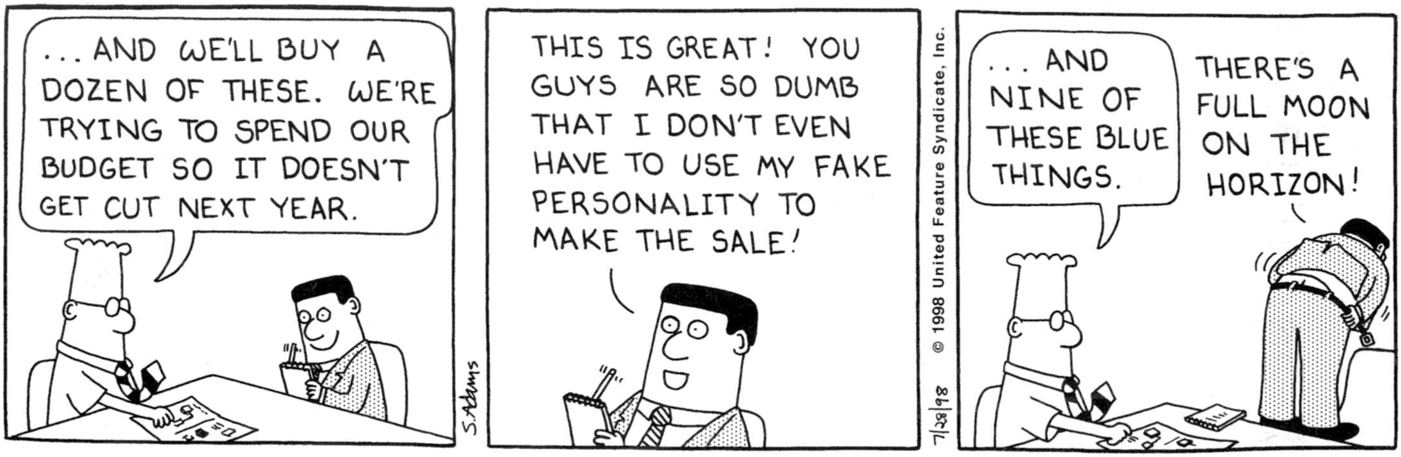
... AND WE'LL BUY A DOZEN OF THESE. WE'RE TRYING TO SPEND OUR BUDGET SO IT DOESN'T GET CUT NEXT YEAR.
S. Adams
THIS IS GREAT! YOU GUYS ARE SO DUMB THAT I DON'T EVEN HAVE TO USE MY FAKE PERSONALITY TO MAKE THE SALE!
© 1998 United Feature Syndicate, Inc.
7/28/98
... AND NINE OF THESE BLUE THINGS.
THERE'S A FULL MOON ON THE HORIZON!

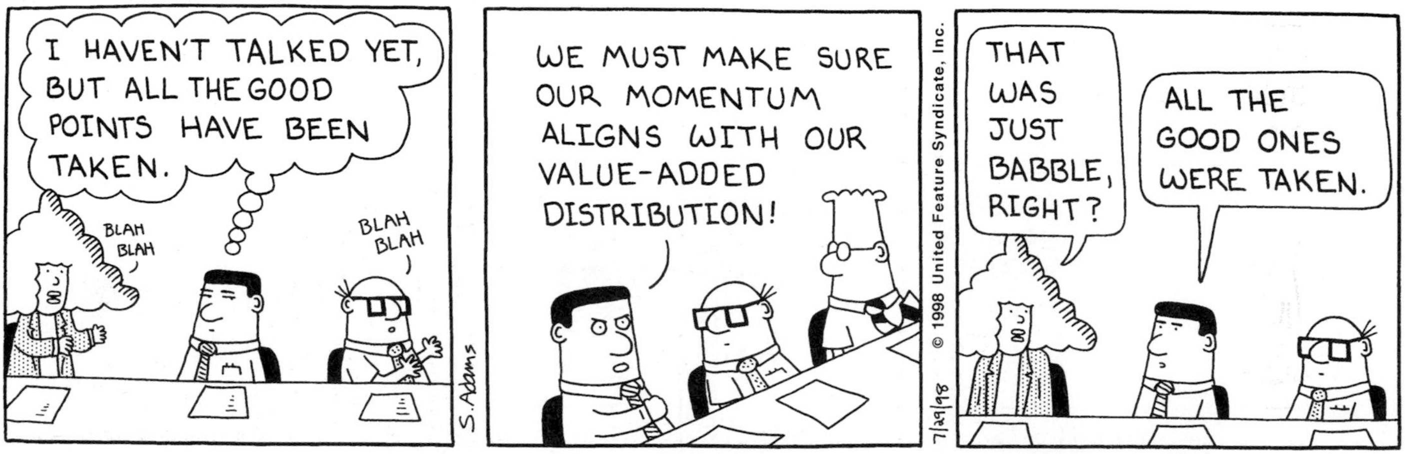
I HAVEN'T TALKED YET, BUT ALL THE GOOD POINTS HAVE BEEN TAKEN.
BLAH BLAH
BLAH BLAH
S. Adams
WE MUST MAKE SURE OUR MOMENTUM ALIGNS WITH OUR VALUE-ADDED DISTRIBUTION!
© 1998 United Feature Syndicate, Inc.
7/29/98
THAT WAS JUST BABBLE, RIGHT?
ALL THE GOOD ONES WERE TAKEN.

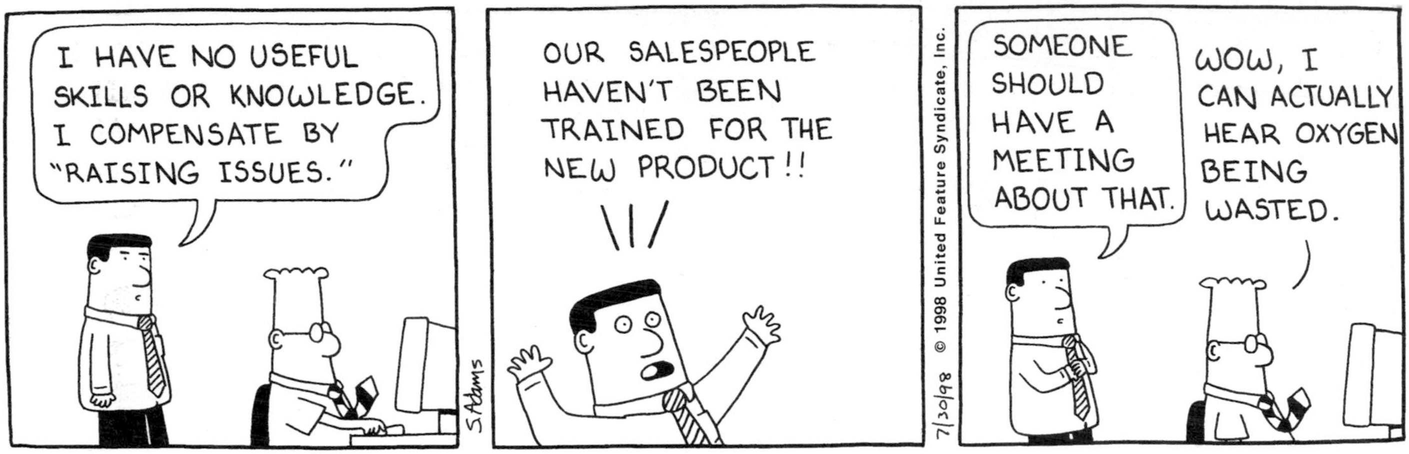
I HAVE NO USEFUL SKILLS OR KNOWLEDGE. I COMPENSATE BY "RAISING ISSUES."
OUR SALESPEOPLE HAVEN'T BEEN TRAINED FOR THE NEW PRODUCT!!
SOMEONE SHOULD HAVE A MEETING ABOUT THAT.
WOW, I CAN ACTUALLY HEAR OXYGEN BEING WASTED.
S. Adams
7/30/98 © 1998 United Feature Syndicate, Inc.

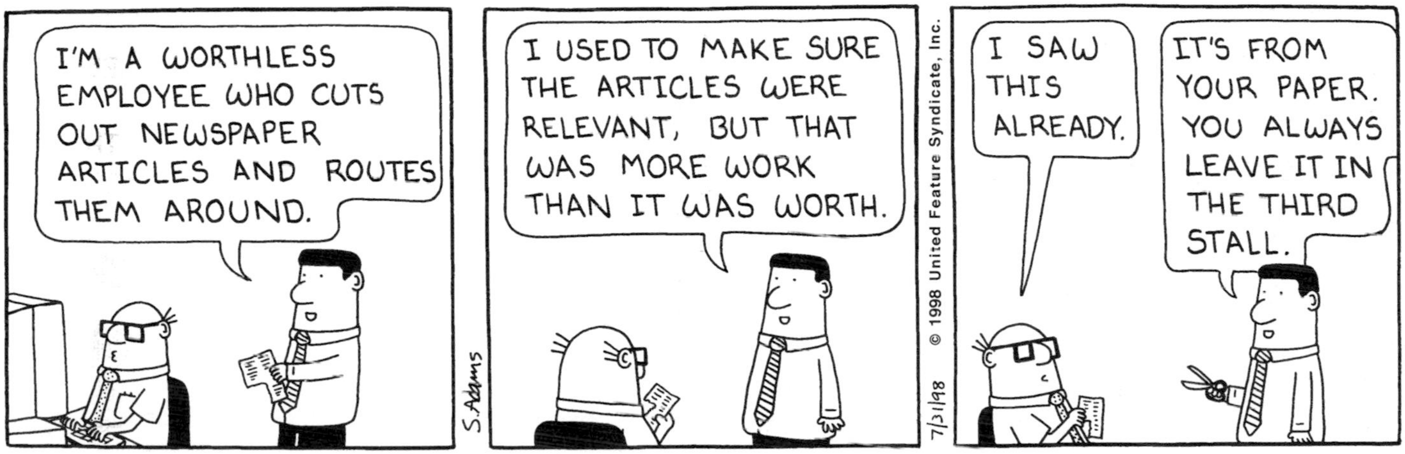
I'M A WORTHLESS EMPLOYEE WHO CUTS OUT NEWSPAPER ARTICLES AND ROUTES THEM AROUND.
I USED TO MAKE SURE THE ARTICLES WERE RELEVANT, BUT THAT WAS MORE WORK THAN IT WAS WORTH.
I SAW THIS ALREADY.
IT'S FROM YOUR PAPER. YOU ALWAYS LEAVE IT IN THE THIRD STALL.
S. Adams
7/31/98 © 1998 United Feature Syndicate, Inc.

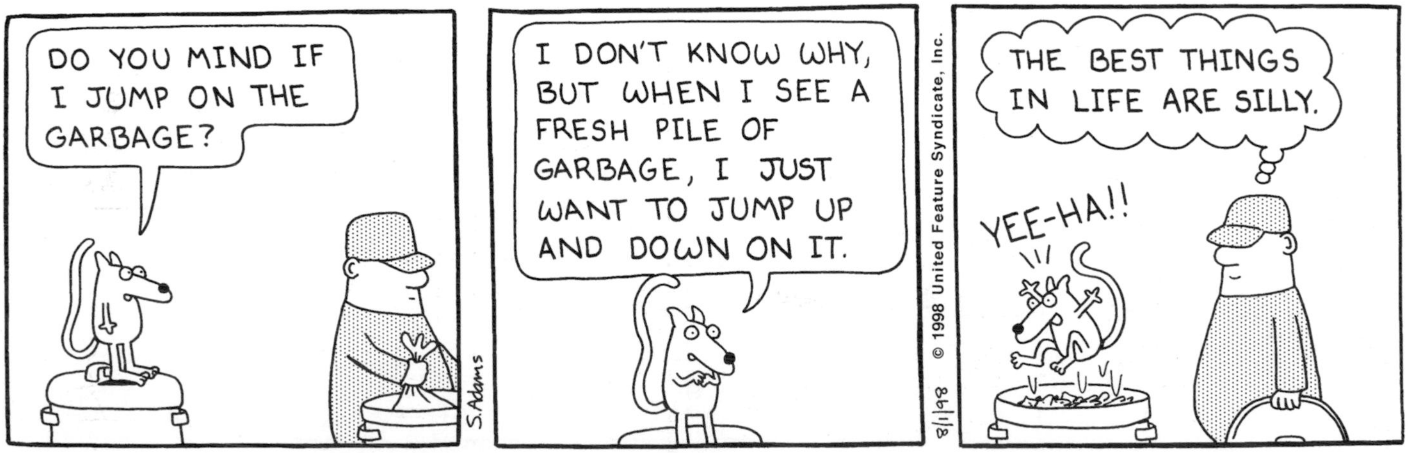
DO YOU MIND IF I JUMP ON THE GARBAGE?
I DON'T KNOW WHY, BUT WHEN I SEE A FRESH PILE OF GARBAGE, I JUST WANT TO JUMP UP AND DOWN ON IT.
THE BEST THINGS IN LIFE ARE SILLY.
YEE-HA!!
S. Adams
8/1/98 © 1998 United Feature Syndicate, Inc.

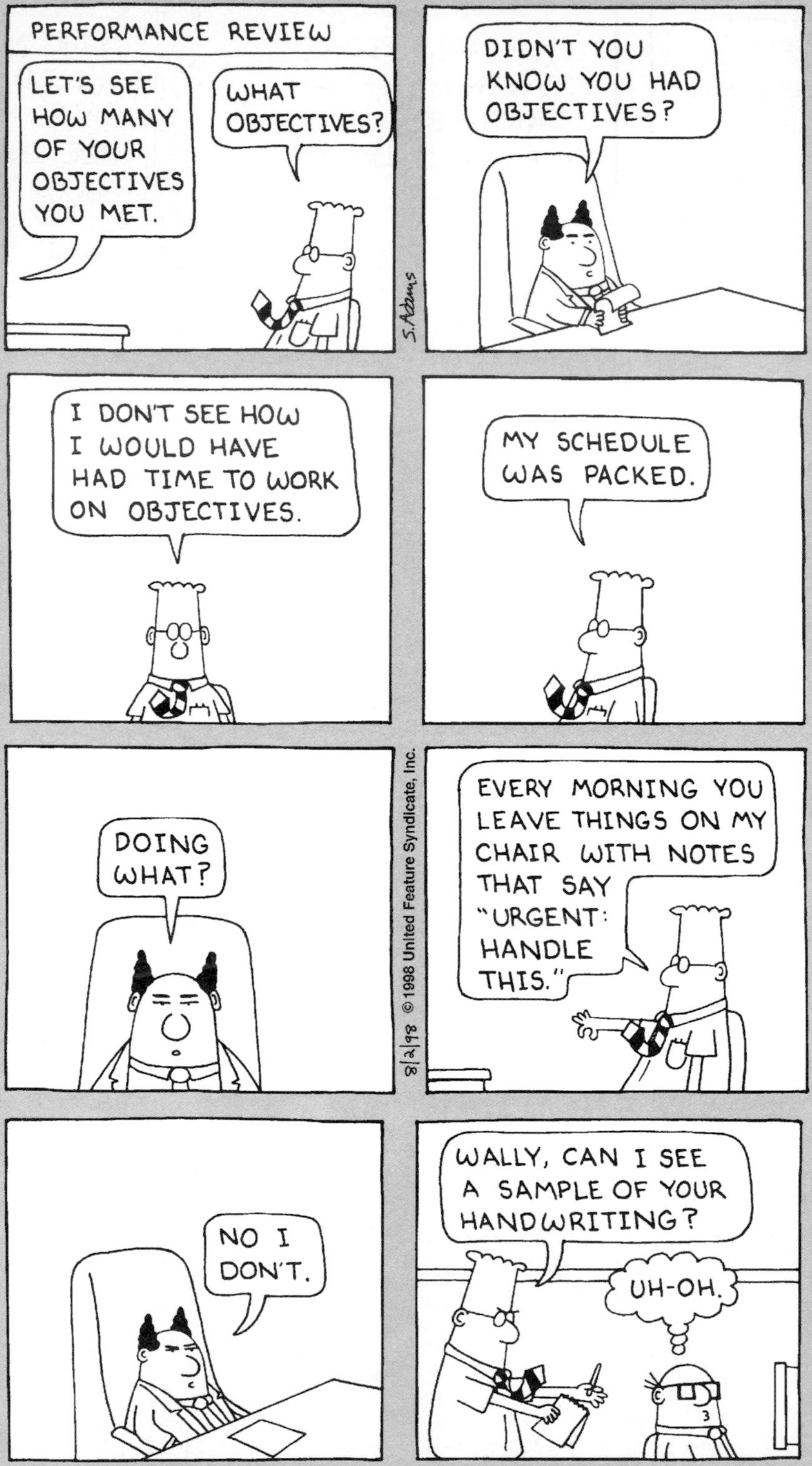
PERFORMANCE REVIEW
LET'S SEE HOW MANY OF YOUR OBJECTIVES YOU MET.
WHAT OBJECTIVES?
S. Adams
DIDN'T YOU KNOW YOU HAD OBJECTIVES?
I DON'T SEE HOW I WOULD HAVE HAD TIME TO WORK ON OBJECTIVES.
MY SCHEDULE WAS PACKED.
DOING WHAT?
8/2/98 © 1998 United Feature Syndicate, Inc.
EVERY MORNING YOU LEAVE THINGS ON MY CHAIR WITH NOTES THAT SAY "URGENT: HANDLE THIS."
NO I DON'T.
WALLY, CAN I SEE A SAMPLE OF YOUR HANDWRITING?
UH-OH.

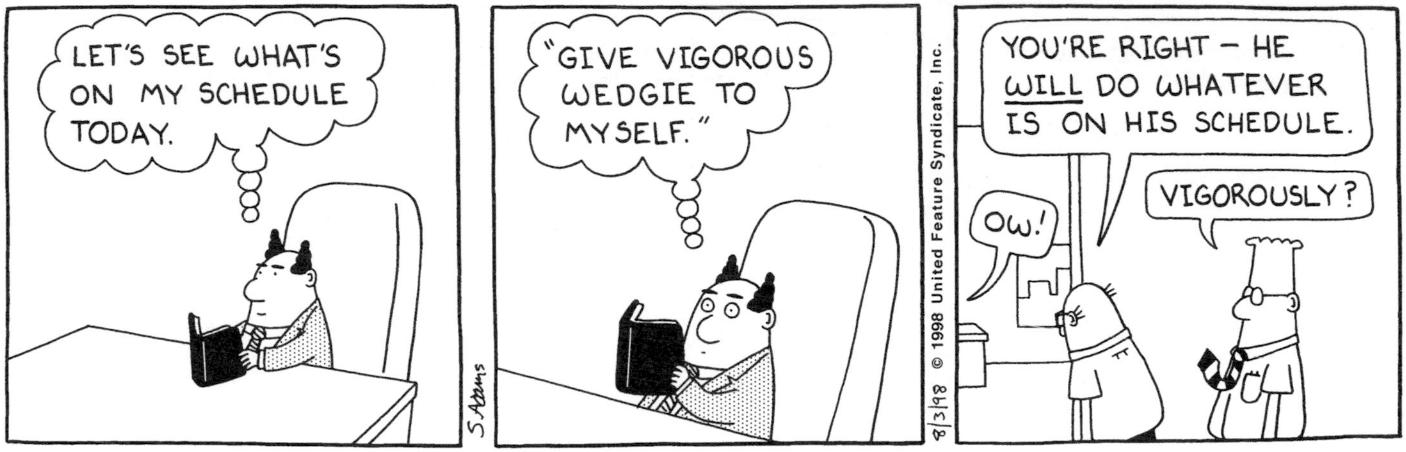
LET'S SEE WHAT'S ON MY SCHEDULE TODAY.
"GIVE VIGOROUS WEDGIE TO MYSELF."
S. Adams
8/3/98 © 1998 United Feature Syndicate, Inc.
YOU'RE RIGHT – HE WILL DO WHATEVER IS ON HIS SCHEDULE.
OW!
VIGOROUSLY?

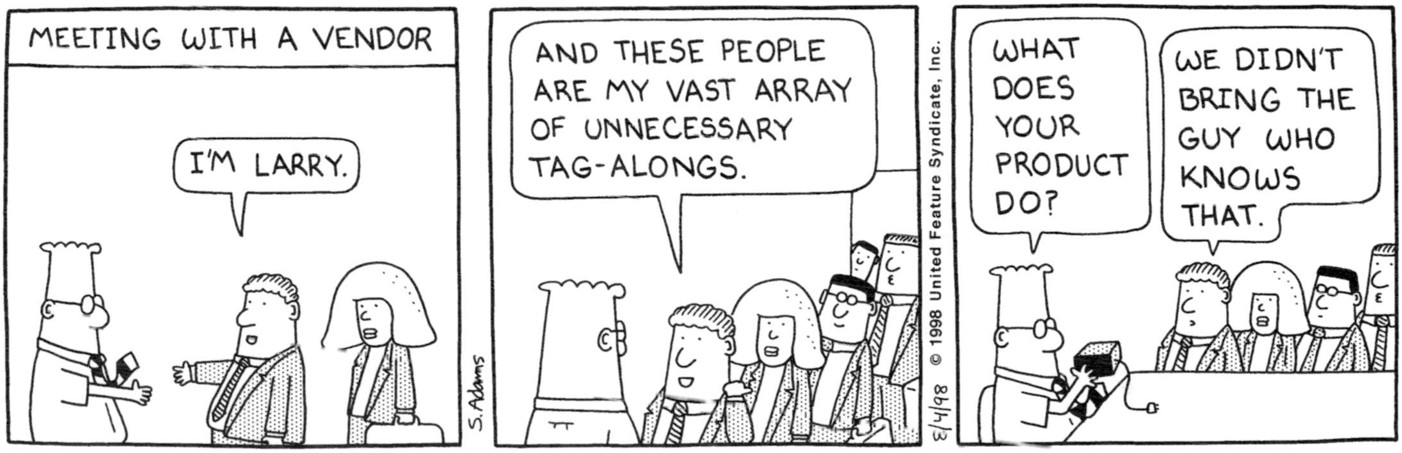
MEETING WITH A VENDOR
I'M LARRY.
S. Adams
AND THESE PEOPLE ARE MY VAST ARRAY OF UNNECESSARY TAG-ALONGS.
8/4/98 © 1998 United Feature Syndicate, Inc.
WHAT DOES YOUR PRODUCT DO?
WE DIDN'T BRING THE GUY WHO KNOWS THAT.

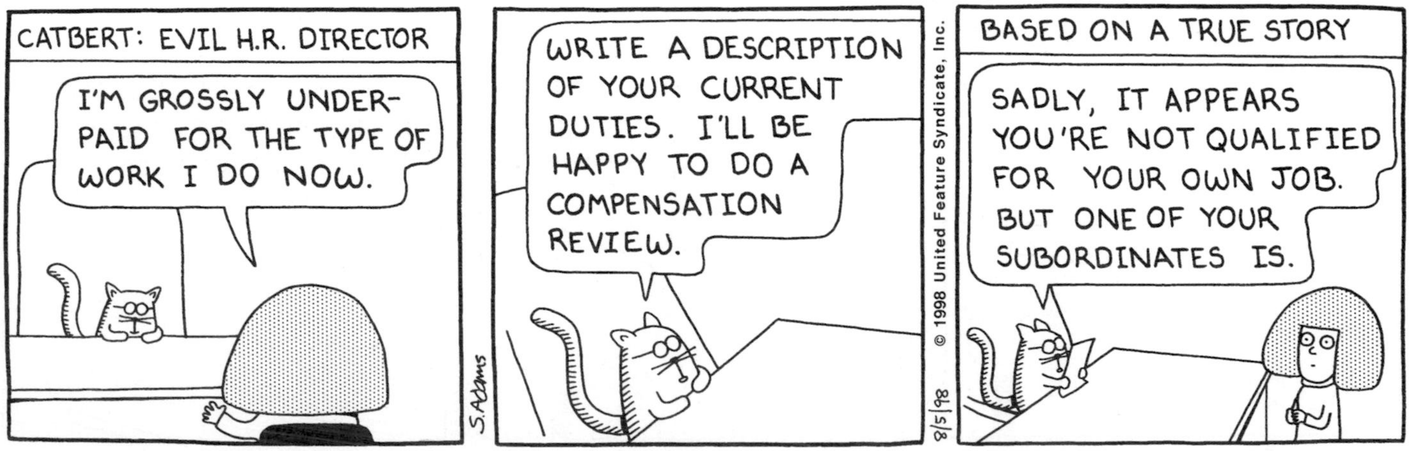
CATBERT: EVIL H.R. DIRECTOR
I'M GROSSLY UNDER-PAID FOR THE TYPE OF WORK I DO NOW.
S. Adams
WRITE A DESCRIPTION OF YOUR CURRENT DUTIES. I'LL BE HAPPY TO DO A COMPENSATION REVIEW.
8/5/98 © 1998 United Feature Syndicate, Inc.
BASED ON A TRUE STORY
SADLY, IT APPEARS YOU'RE NOT QUALIFIED FOR YOUR OWN JOB. BUT ONE OF YOUR SUBORDINATES IS.

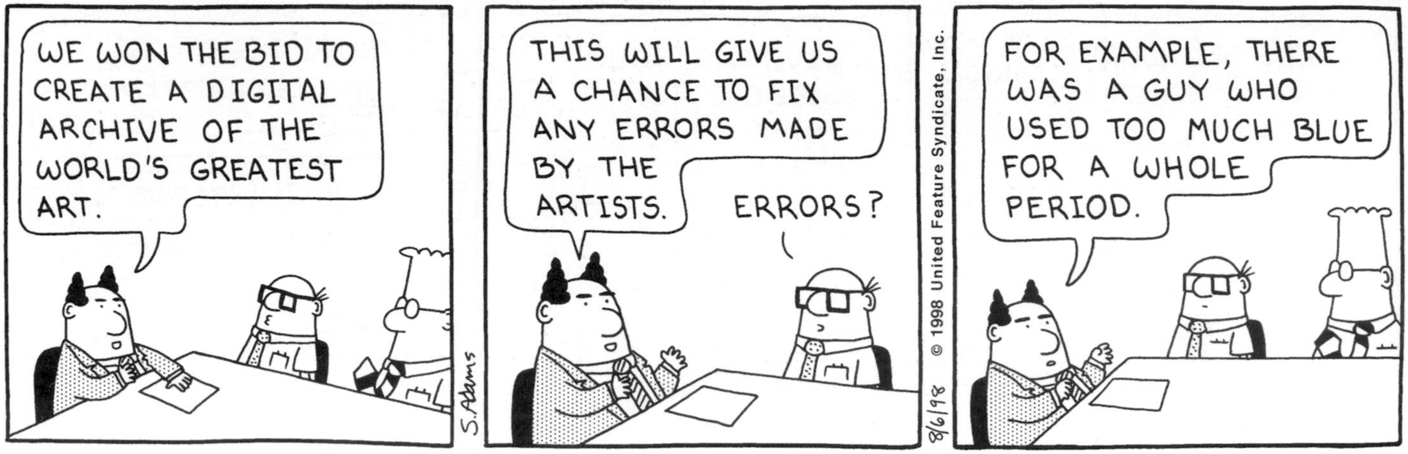
WE WON THE BID TO CREATE A DIGITAL ARCHIVE OF THE WORLD'S GREATEST ART.
THIS WILL GIVE US A CHANCE TO FIX ANY ERRORS MADE BY THE ARTISTS.
ERRORS?
FOR EXAMPLE, THERE WAS A GUY WHO USED TOO MUCH BLUE FOR A WHOLE PERIOD.
S. Adams
8/6/98
© 1998 United Feature Syndicate, Inc.

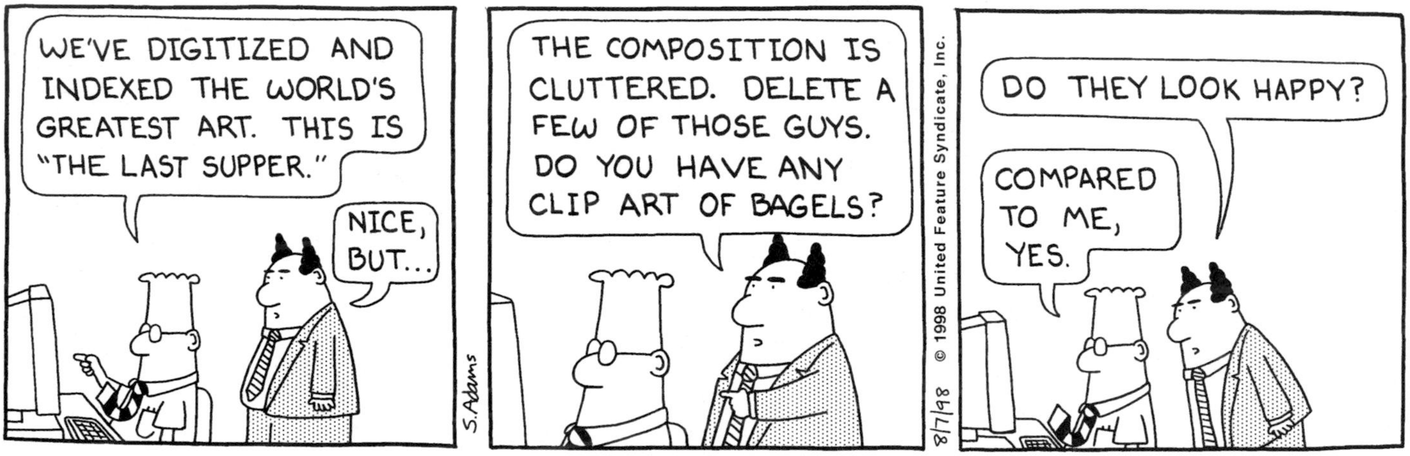
WE'VE DIGITIZED AND INDEXED THE WORLD'S GREATEST ART. THIS IS "THE LAST SUPPER."
NICE, BUT...
THE COMPOSITION IS CLUTTERED. DELETE A FEW OF THOSE GUYS. DO YOU HAVE ANY CLIP ART OF BAGELS?
DO THEY LOOK HAPPY?
COMPARED TO ME, YES.
S. Adams
8/7/98
© 1998 United Feature Syndicate, Inc.

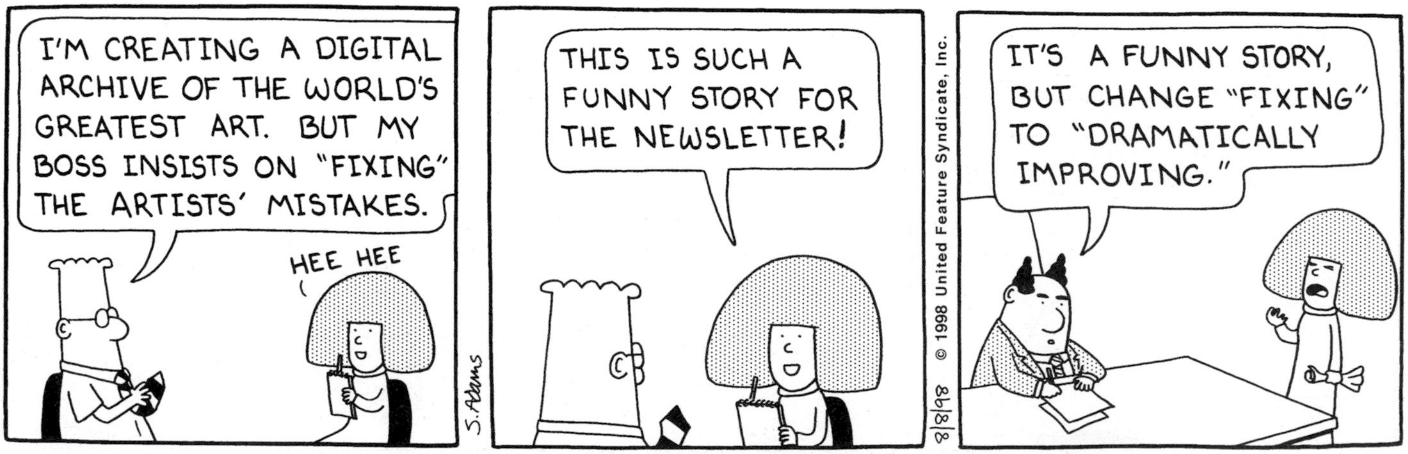
I'M CREATING A DIGITAL ARCHIVE OF THE WORLD'S GREATEST ART. BUT MY BOSS INSISTS ON "FIXING" THE ARTISTS' MISTAKES.
HEE HEE
THIS IS SUCH A FUNNY STORY FOR THE NEWSLETTER!
IT'S A FUNNY STORY, BUT CHANGE "FIXING" TO "DRAMATICALLY IMPROVING."
S. Adams
8/8/98
© 1998 United Feature Syndicate, Inc.

WE'RE DISCONTINUING TECHNICAL SUPPORT OF ALL OUR PRODUCTS.
S. Adams
A RECORDED MESSAGE WILL EXPLAIN IT TO THE CALLER THIS WAY...
"IN ORDER TO SERVE CUSTOMERS BETTER, WE'VE DISCONTINUED TECHNICAL SUPPORT."
HOW DOES THAT SERVE CUSTOMERS BETTER?
WE'LL REDIRECT THOSE RESOURCES TO OTHER AREAS.
WHAT OTHER AREAS?
8/9/98 © 1998 United Feature Syndicate, Inc.
PROFITS.
THAT MAKES YOUR BONUS LARGER.
ANY OTHER QUESTIONS?
APPARENTLY I'M ENGULFED IN EVIL.
THAT'S THE SPIRIT!

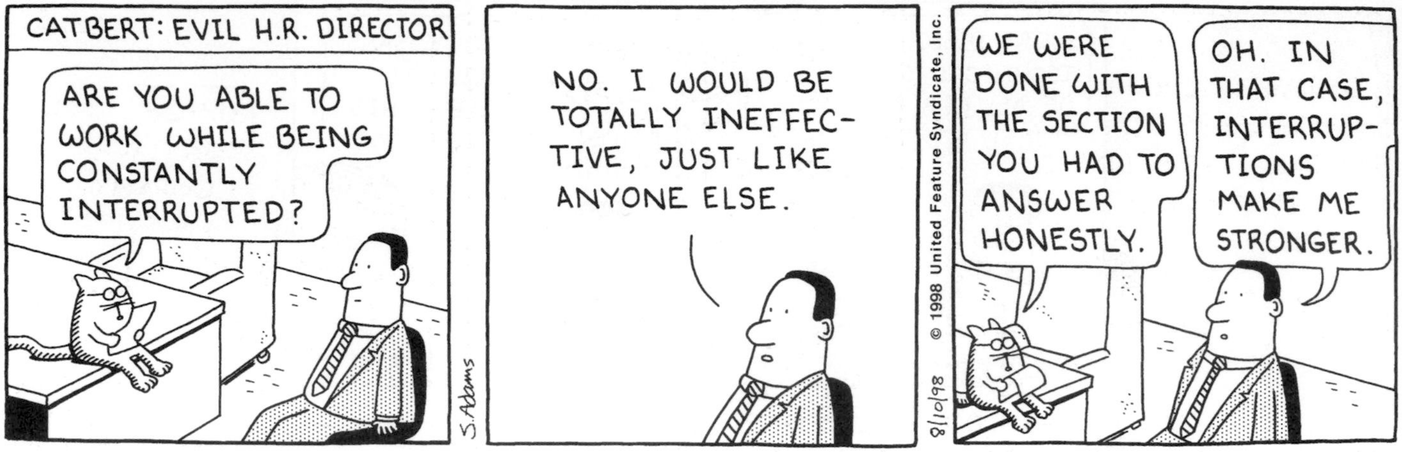
CATBERT: EVIL H.R. DIRECTOR
ARE YOU ABLE TO WORK WHILE BEING CONSTANTLY INTERRUPTED?
S. Adams
NO. I WOULD BE TOTALLY INEFFECTIVE, JUST LIKE ANYONE ELSE.
8/10/98 © 1998 United Feature Syndicate, Inc.
WE WERE DONE WITH THE SECTION YOU HAD TO ANSWER HONESTLY.
OH. IN THAT CASE, INTERRUPTIONS MAKE ME STRONGER.

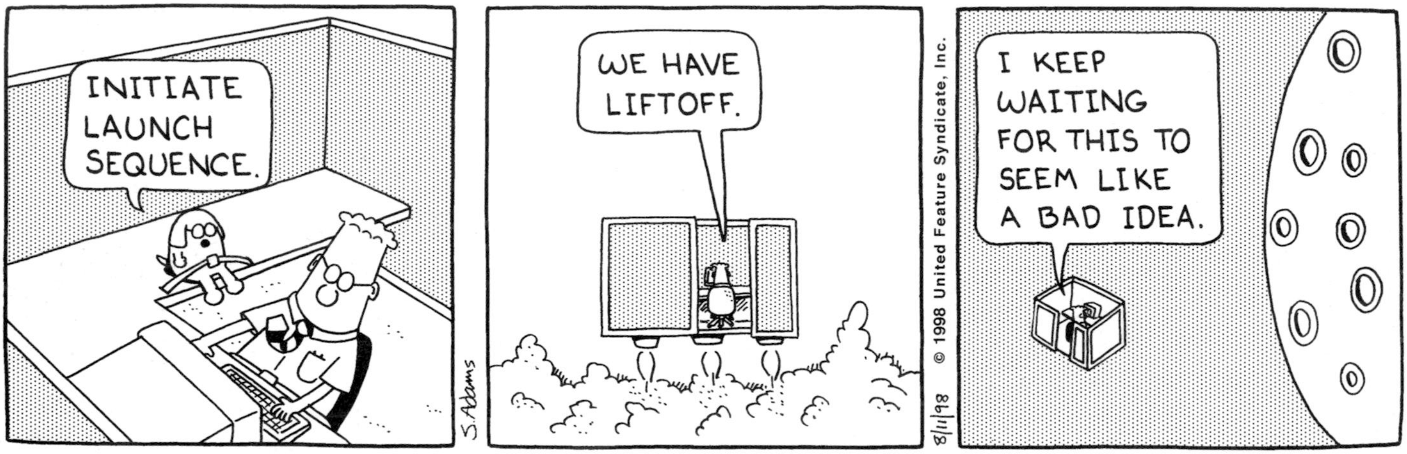
INITIATE LAUNCH SEQUENCE.
S. Adams
WE HAVE LIFTOFF.
8/11/98 © 1998 United Feature Syndicate, Inc.
I KEEP WAITING FOR THIS TO SEEM LIKE A BAD IDEA.

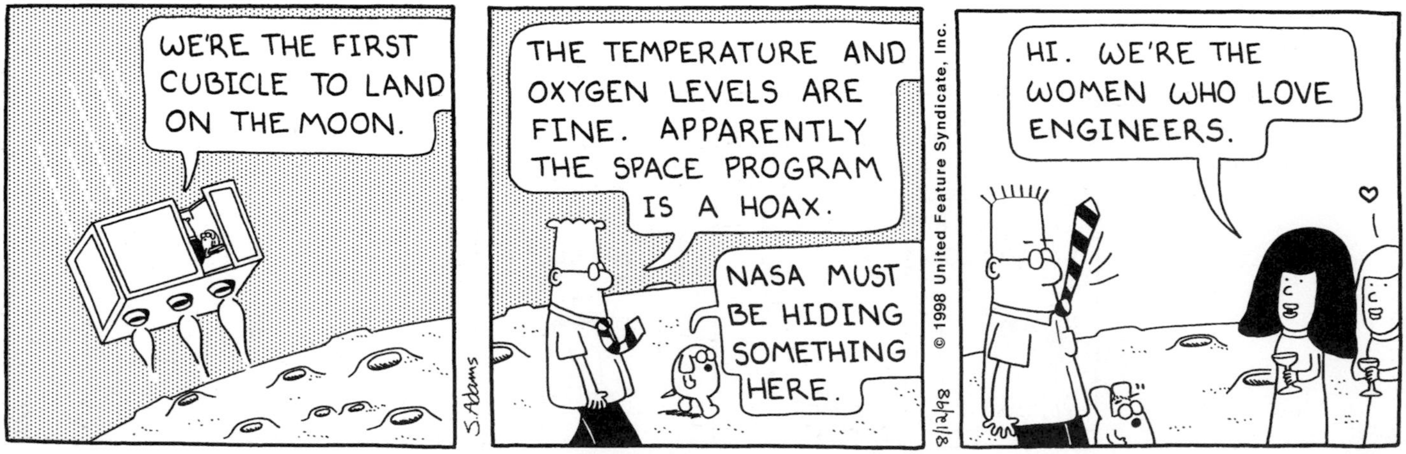
WE'RE THE FIRST CUBICLE TO LAND ON THE MOON.
S. Adams
THE TEMPERATURE AND OXYGEN LEVELS ARE FINE. APPARENTLY THE SPACE PROGRAM IS A HOAX.
NASA MUST BE HIDING SOMETHING HERE.
8/12/98 © 1998 United Feature Syndicate, Inc.
HI. WE'RE THE WOMEN WHO LOVE ENGINEERS.

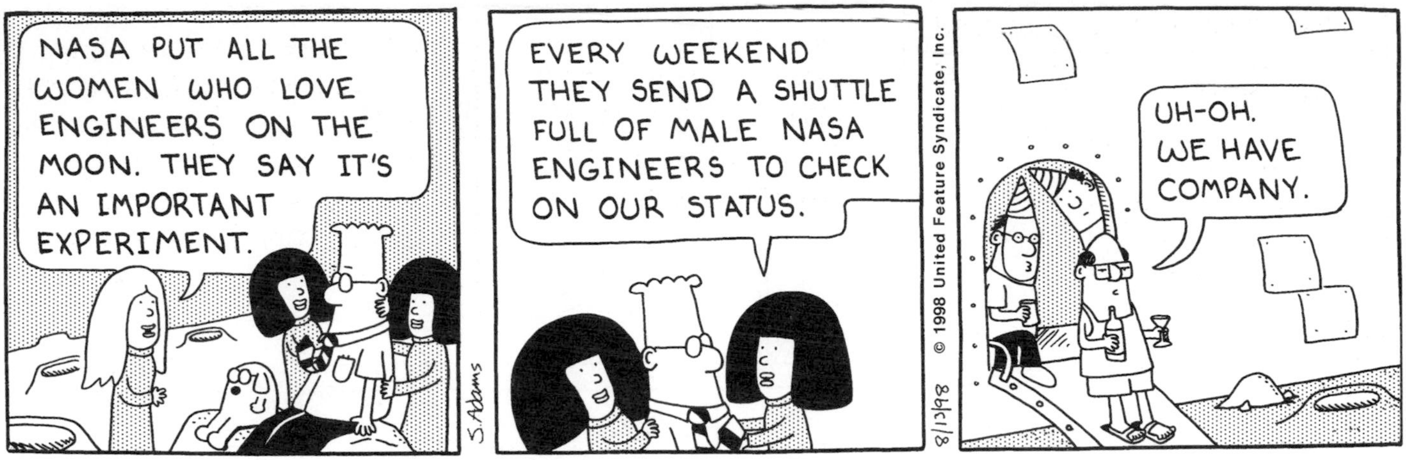
NASA PUT ALL THE WOMEN WHO LOVE ENGINEERS ON THE MOON. THEY SAY IT'S AN IMPORTANT EXPERIMENT.
EVERY WEEKEND THEY SEND A SHUTTLE FULL OF MALE NASA ENGINEERS TO CHECK ON OUR STATUS.
UH-OH. WE HAVE COMPANY.
© 1998 United Feature Syndicate, Inc.
8/13/98

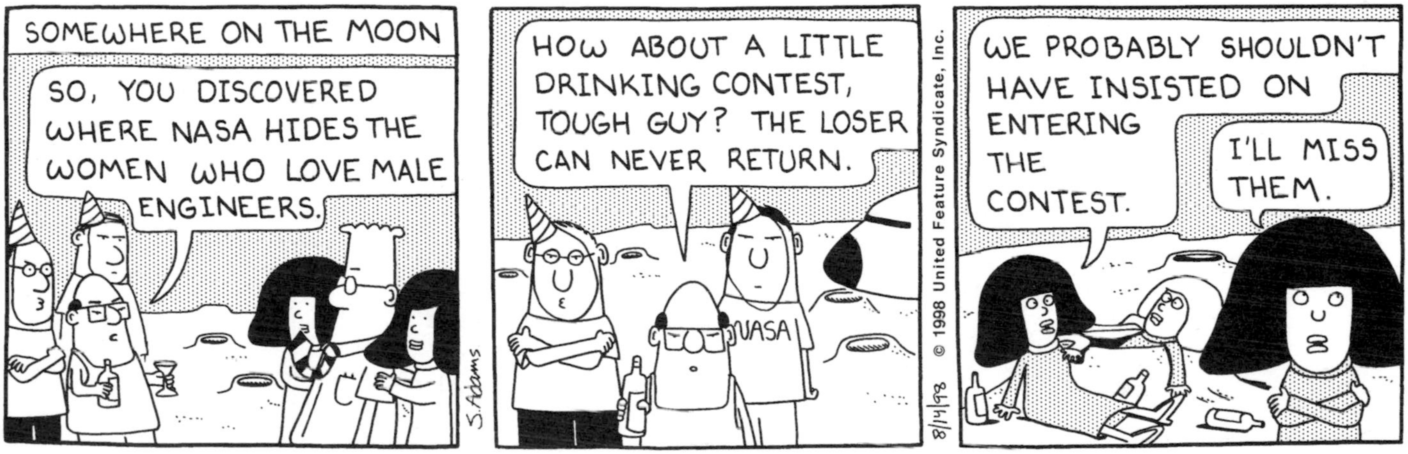
SOMEWHERE ON THE MOON
SO, YOU DISCOVERED WHERE NASA HIDES THE WOMEN WHO LOVE MALE ENGINEERS.
HOW ABOUT A LITTLE DRINKING CONTEST, TOUGH GUY? THE LOSER CAN NEVER RETURN.
NASA
WE PROBABLY SHOULDN'T HAVE INSISTED ON ENTERING THE CONTEST.
I'LL MISS THEM.
© 1998 United Feature Syndicate, Inc.
8/14/98

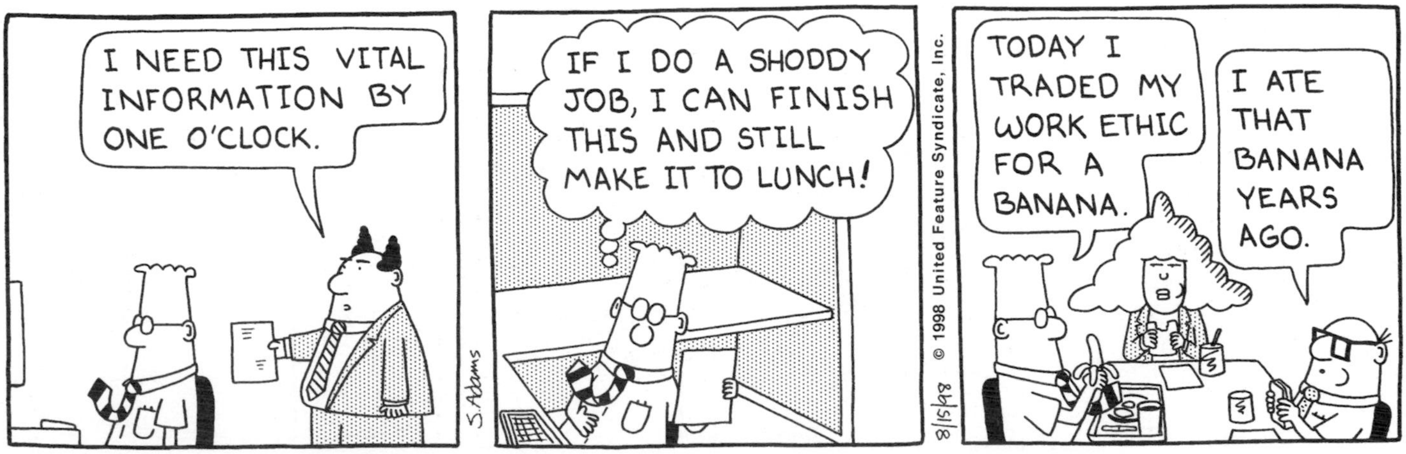
I NEED THIS VITAL INFORMATION BY ONE O'CLOCK.
IF I DO A SHODDY JOB, I CAN FINISH THIS AND STILL MAKE IT TO LUNCH!
TODAY I TRADED MY WORK ETHIC FOR A BANANA.
I ATE THAT BANANA YEARS AGO.
© 1998 United Feature Syndicate, Inc.
8/15/98

THE EVIL DIRECTOR OF HUMAN RESOURCES SPOTS HIS PREY.
S. Adams
WALLY, YOU HAVEN'T FILLED OUT A VACATION REQUEST FORM YET.
IF WE DON'T GET IT BY TOMORROW, YOU LOSE YOUR VACATION.
WHERE DO I GET A FORM?
WE'RE ALL OUT.
DID THEY EVER EXIST?
8/16/98 © 1998 United Feature Syndicate, Inc.
WALLY, DOES ANY-THING REALLY EXIST, OR IS IT ALL JUST SHADOWS ON A CUBICLE WALL?
I LEAVE YOU WITH THAT THOUGHT.
WHO SAYS PHILOSOPHY IS USELESS?
BONK
BONK

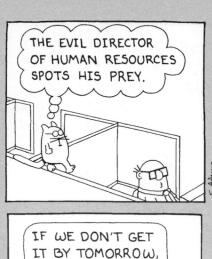

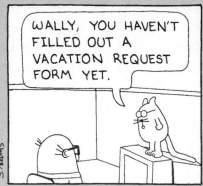

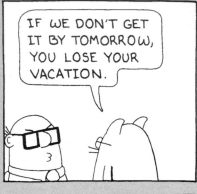

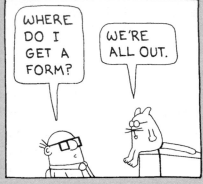

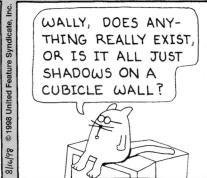

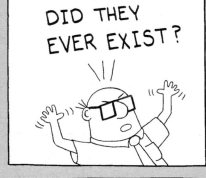

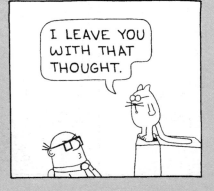

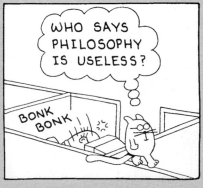

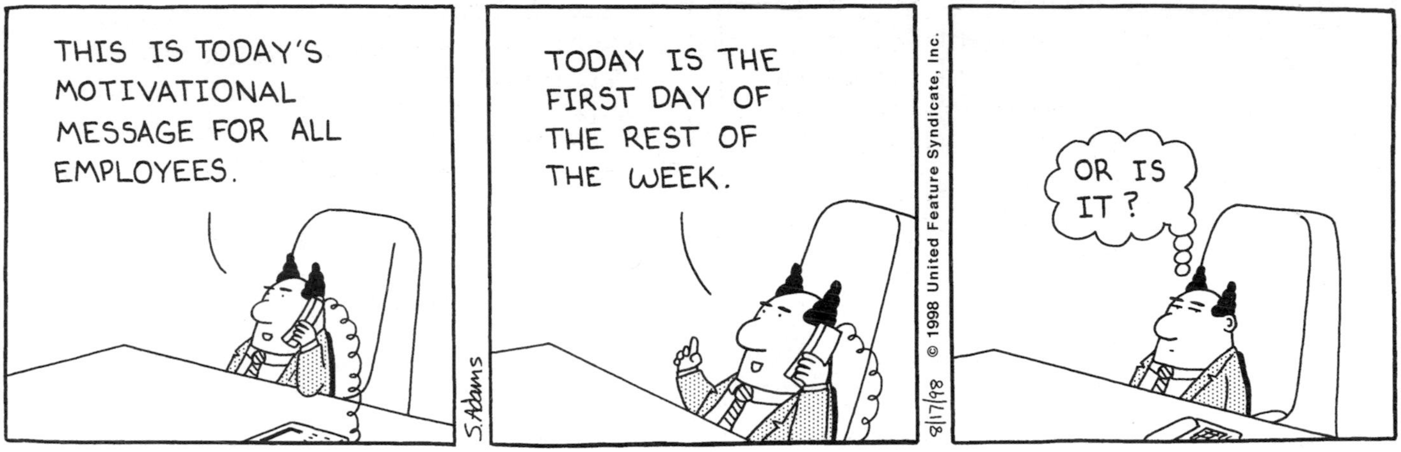
THIS IS TODAY'S MOTIVATIONAL MESSAGE FOR ALL EMPLOYEES.
S. Adams
TODAY IS THE FIRST DAY OF THE REST OF THE WEEK.
8/17/98 © 1998 United Feature Syndicate, Inc.
OR IS IT?

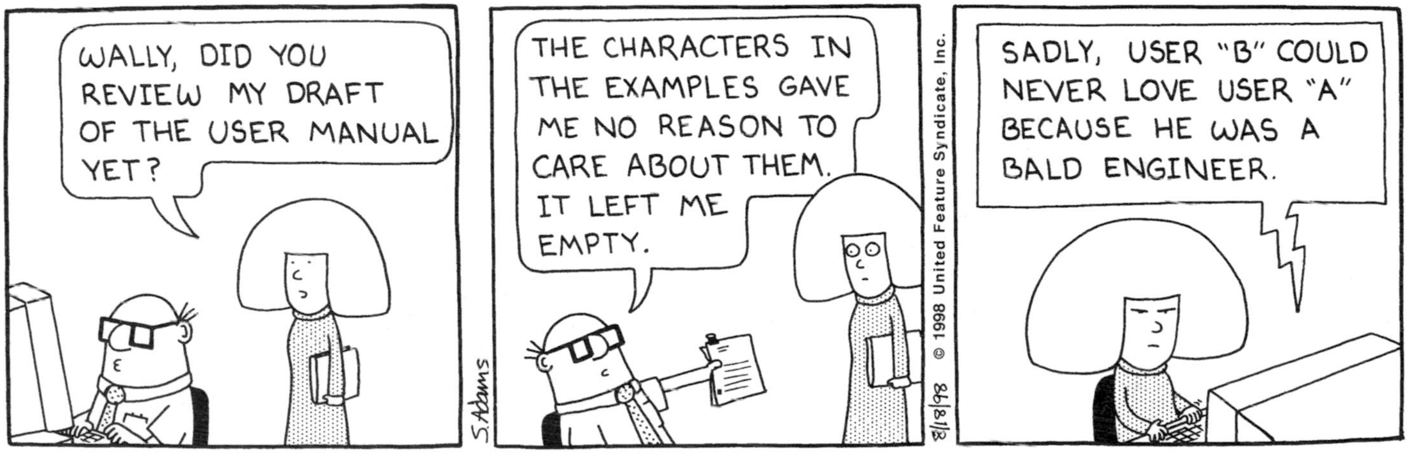
WALLY, DID YOU REVIEW MY DRAFT OF THE USER MANUAL YET?
S. Adams
THE CHARACTERS IN THE EXAMPLES GAVE ME NO REASON TO CARE ABOUT THEM. IT LEFT ME EMPTY.
8/18/98 © 1998 United Feature Syndicate, Inc.
SADLY, USER "B" COULD NEVER LOVE USER "A" BECAUSE HE WAS A BALD ENGINEER.

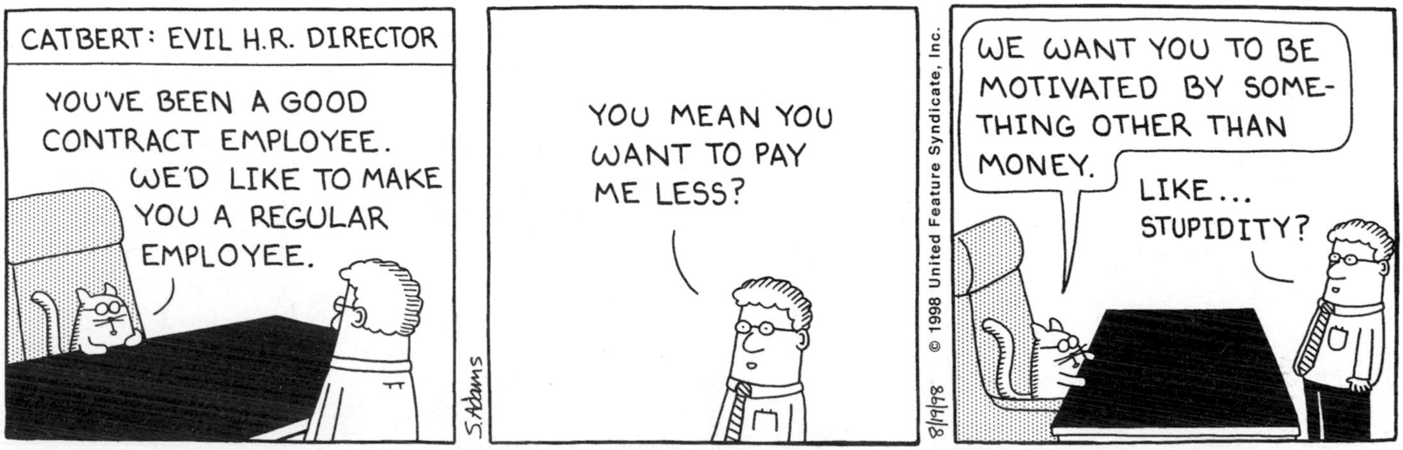
CATBERT: EVIL H.R. DIRECTOR
YOU'VE BEEN A GOOD CONTRACT EMPLOYEE.
WE'D LIKE TO MAKE YOU A REGULAR EMPLOYEE.
S. Adams
YOU MEAN YOU WANT TO PAY ME LESS?
8/19/98 © 1998 United Feature Syndicate, Inc.
WE WANT YOU TO BE MOTIVATED BY SOME-THING OTHER THAN MONEY.
LIKE... STUPIDITY?

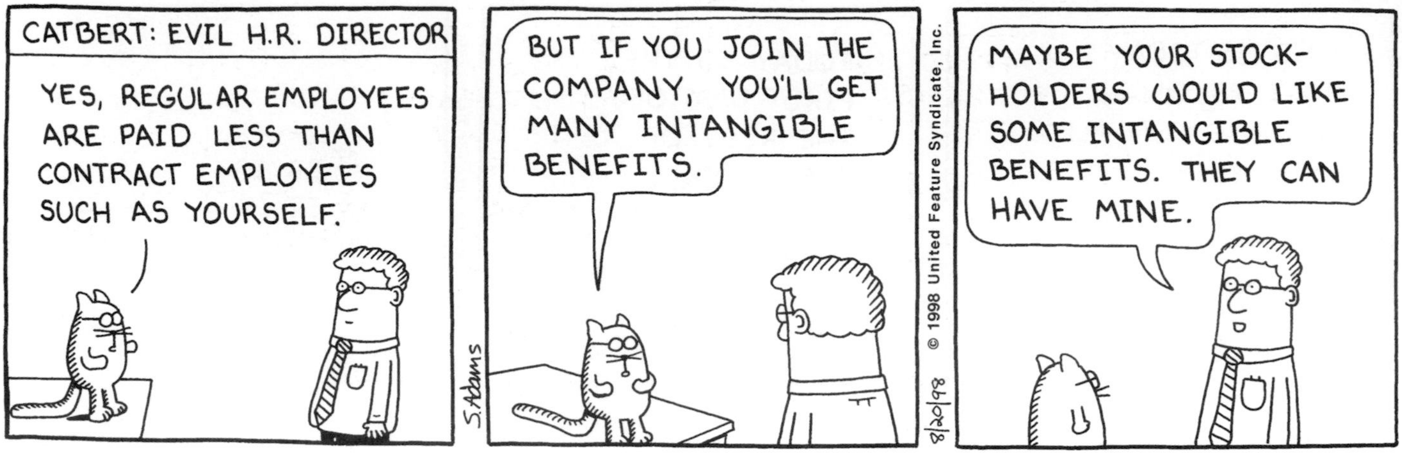
CATBERT: EVIL H.R. DIRECTOR
YES, REGULAR EMPLOYEES ARE PAID LESS THAN CONTRACT EMPLOYEES SUCH AS YOURSELF.
S.Adams
BUT IF YOU JOIN THE COMPANY, YOU'LL GET MANY INTANGIBLE BENEFITS.
8/20/98 © 1998 United Feature Syndicate, Inc.
MAYBE YOUR STOCK-HOLDERS WOULD LIKE SOME INTANGIBLE BENEFITS. THEY CAN HAVE MINE.

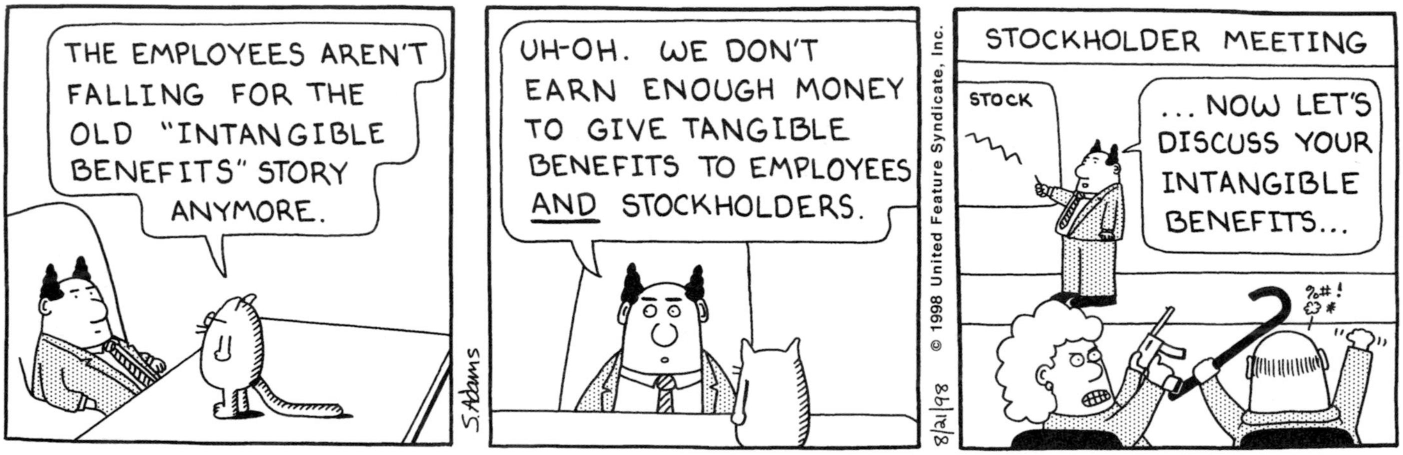
THE EMPLOYEES AREN'T FALLING FOR THE OLD "INTANGIBLE BENEFITS" STORY ANYMORE.
S.Adams
UH-OH. WE DON'T EARN ENOUGH MONEY TO GIVE TANGIBLE BENEFITS TO EMPLOYEES AND STOCKHOLDERS.
8/21/98 © 1998 United Feature Syndicate, Inc.
STOCKHOLDER MEETING
STOCK
...NOW LET'S DISCUSS YOUR INTANGIBLE BENEFITS...

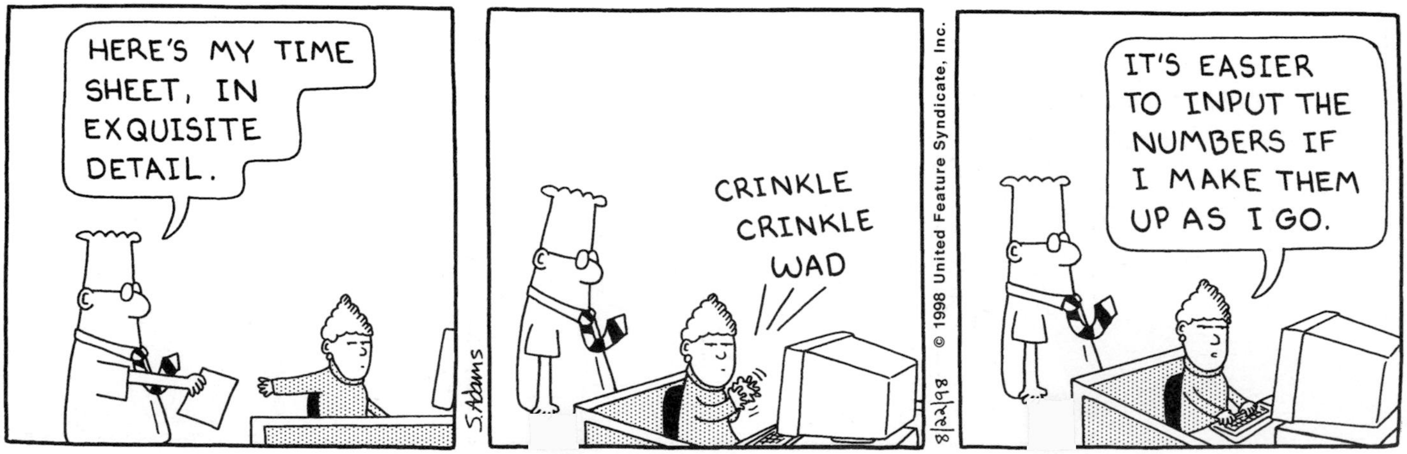
HERE'S MY TIME SHEET, IN EXQUISITE DETAIL.
S.Adams
CRINKLE CRINKLE WAD
8/22/98 © 1998 United Feature Syndicate, Inc.
IT'S EASIER TO INPUT THE NUMBERS IF I MAKE THEM UP AS I GO.

HAPPY COMBINED BIRTHDAYS.
S. Adams
TODAY WE HONOR THE EMPLOYEES WHO HAD BIRTHDAYS WITHIN THE PAST YEAR.
THAT'S DILBERT... ALICE... ASOK... DID I MISS ANYONE?
UM... YOU MISSED ME.
YOU TOO? THAT'S SPOOKY.
8/23/98 © 1998 United Feature Syndicate, Inc.
I'D CUT THE CAKE BUT IT'S A PLASTIC PROP.
LET'S SING. DOES ANYONE KNOW THE WORDS TO "HAPPY BIRTHDAY"?
I'LL BET THOSE WEREN'T THE REAL WORDS.

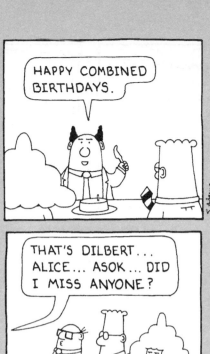

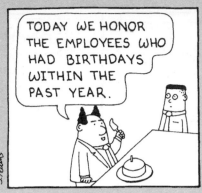

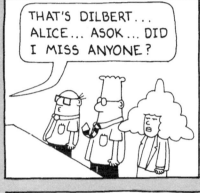

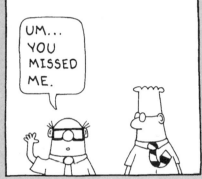

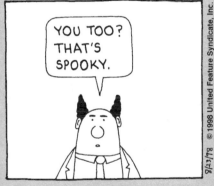

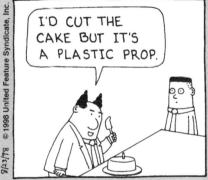

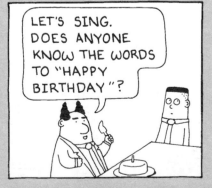

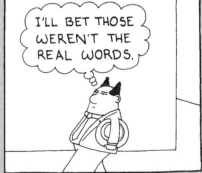

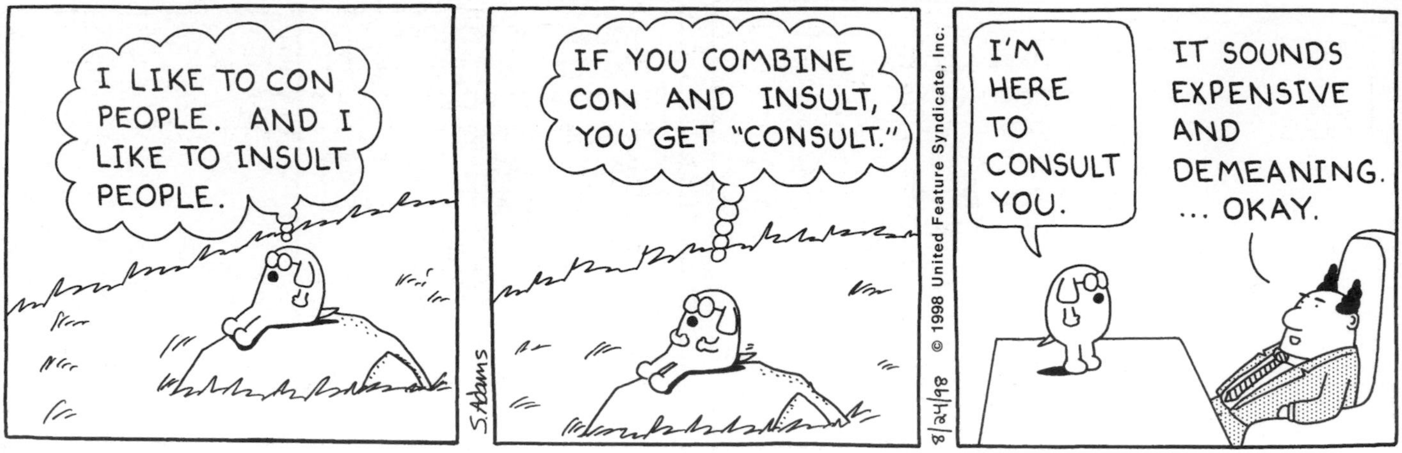
I LIKE TO CON PEOPLE. AND I LIKE TO INSULT PEOPLE.
IF YOU COMBINE CON AND INSULT, YOU GET "CONSULT."
I'M HERE TO CONSULT YOU.
IT SOUNDS EXPENSIVE AND DEMEANING. ... OKAY.
S. Adams
8/24/98 © 1998 United Feature Syndicate, Inc.

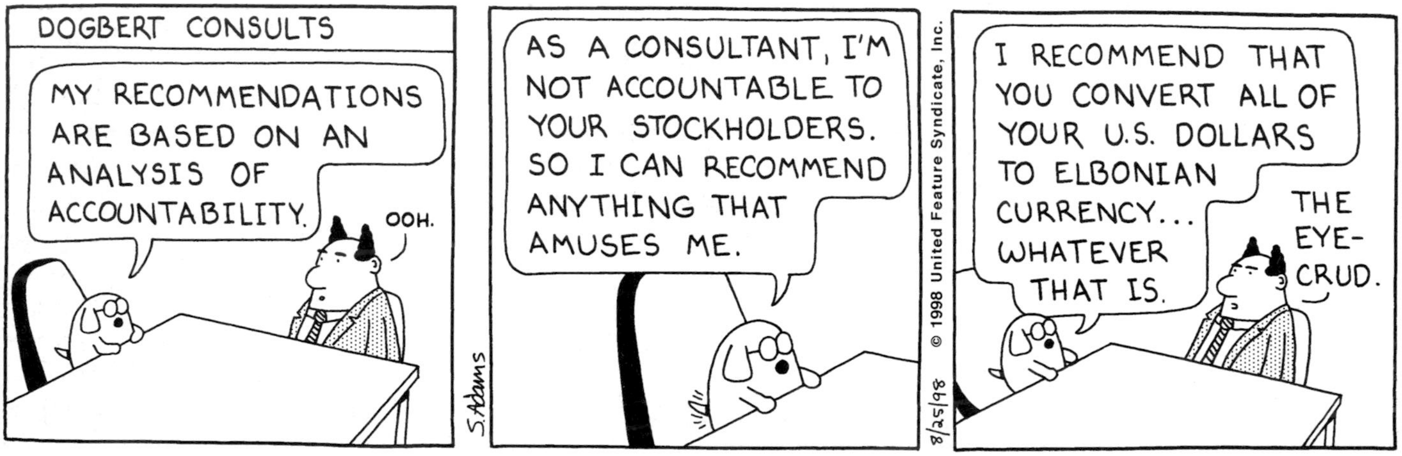
DOGBERT CONSULTS
MY RECOMMENDATIONS ARE BASED ON AN ANALYSIS OF ACCOUNTABILITY.
OOH.
AS A CONSULTANT, I'M NOT ACCOUNTABLE TO YOUR STOCKHOLDERS. SO I CAN RECOMMEND ANYTHING THAT AMUSES ME.
I RECOMMEND THAT YOU CONVERT ALL OF YOUR U.S. DOLLARS TO ELBONIAN CURRENCY... WHATEVER THAT IS.
THE EYE-CRUD.
S. Adams
8/25/98 © 1998 United Feature Syndicate, Inc.

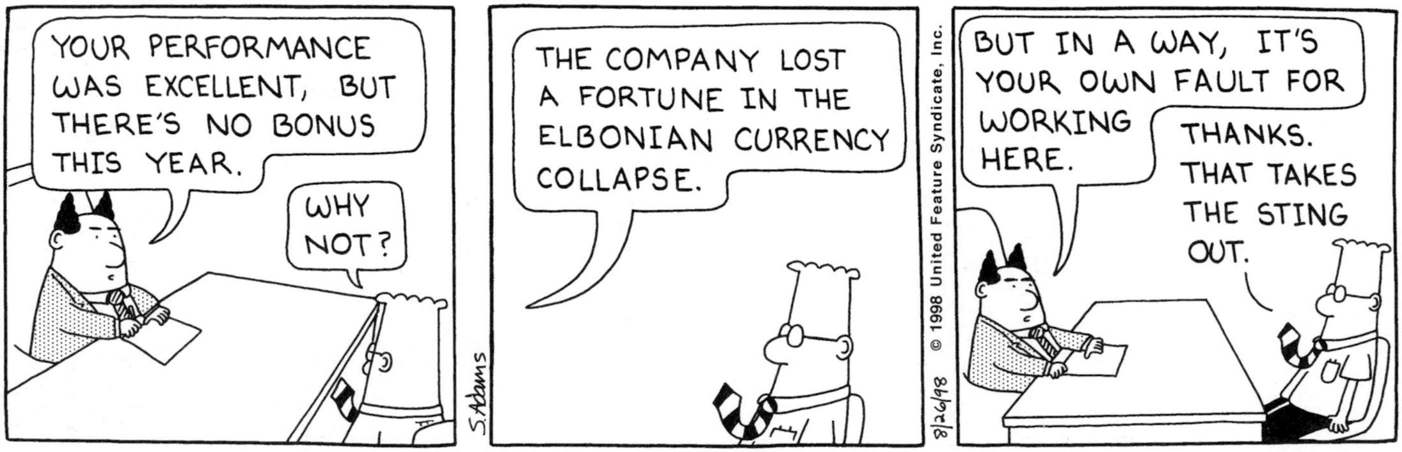
YOUR PERFORMANCE WAS EXCELLENT, BUT THERE'S NO BONUS THIS YEAR.
WHY NOT?
THE COMPANY LOST A FORTUNE IN THE ELBONIAN CURRENCY COLLAPSE.
BUT IN A WAY, IT'S YOUR OWN FAULT FOR WORKING HERE.
THANKS. THAT TAKES THE STING OUT.
S. Adams
8/26/98 © 1998 United Feature Syndicate, Inc.

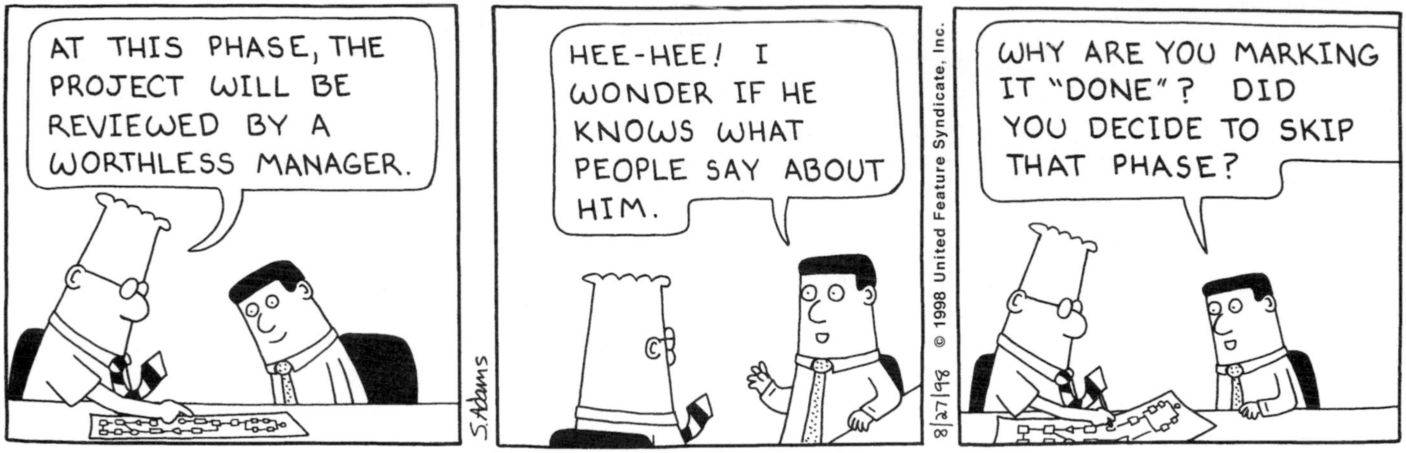
AT THIS PHASE, THE PROJECT WILL BE REVIEWED BY A WORTHLESS MANAGER.
HEE-HEE! I WONDER IF HE KNOWS WHAT PEOPLE SAY ABOUT HIM.
WHY ARE YOU MARKING IT "DONE"? DID YOU DECIDE TO SKIP THAT PHASE?
S.Adams
8/27/98 © 1998 United Feature Syndicate, Inc.

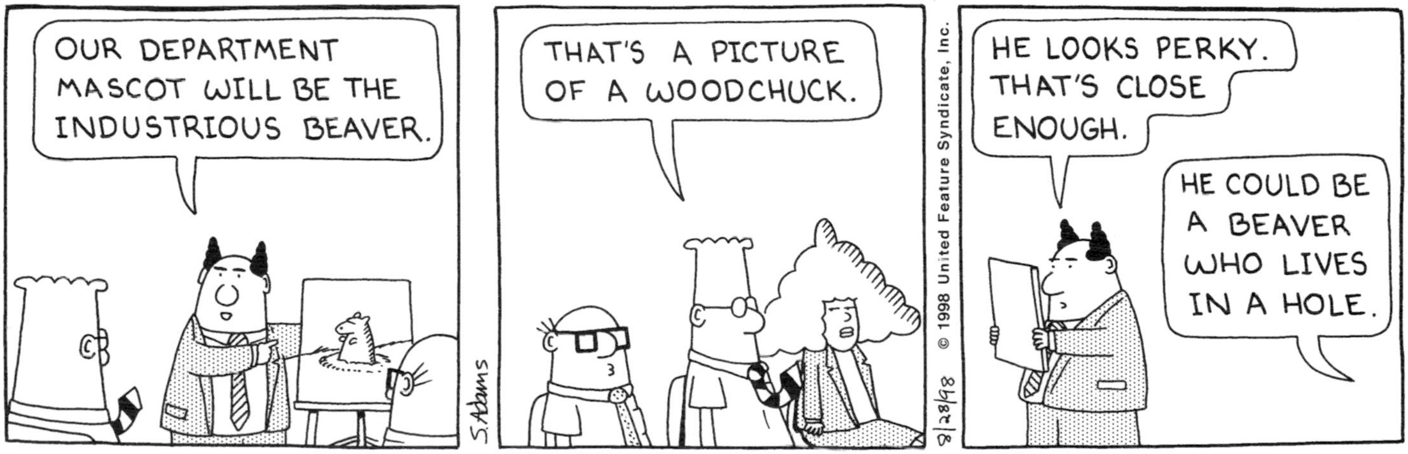
OUR DEPARTMENT MASCOT WILL BE THE INDUSTRIOUS BEAVER.
THAT'S A PICTURE OF A WOODCHUCK.
HE LOOKS PERKY. THAT'S CLOSE ENOUGH.
HE COULD BE A BEAVER WHO LIVES IN A HOLE.
S.Adams
8/28/98 © 1998 United Feature Syndicate, Inc.

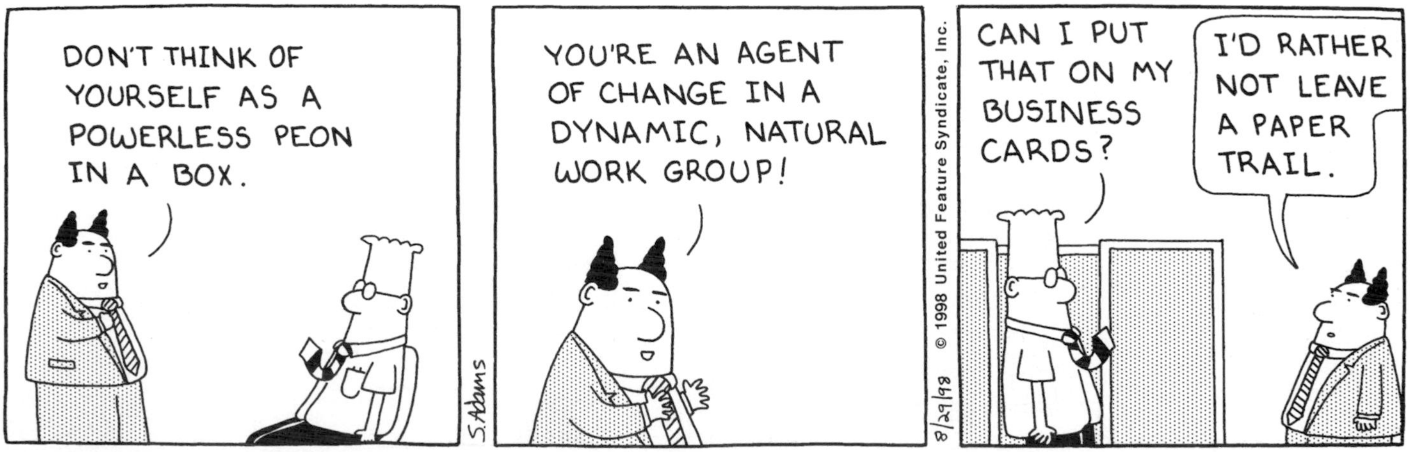
DON'T THINK OF YOURSELF AS A POWERLESS PEON IN A BOX.
YOU'RE AN AGENT OF CHANGE IN A DYNAMIC, NATURAL WORK GROUP!
CAN I PUT THAT ON MY BUSINESS CARDS?
I'D RATHER NOT LEAVE A PAPER TRAIL.
S.Adams
8/29/98 © 1998 United Feature Syndicate, Inc.

I NEED TO DOCUMENT YOUR PROCEDURES. IT'S AN ISO 9000 REQUIREMENT.
SO... THE ENGINEERS SUBMIT THEIR TIME CARDS AND THEN YOU DO WHAT?
I PUT THEM IN A PILE UNTIL I'M SURE THEY'RE ALL HERE.
THEN I MOVE THEM TO THE MAGIC CYLINDER.
THE TRASH CAN?
NO, IT'S A MAGIC CYLINDER. I PUT MY WORK IN THERE AND BY MORNING IT'S GONE.
I'VE BEEN GIVING YOU MY TIME CARDS FOR FIVE YEARS.
NO ONE HAS COMPLAINED YET.
AFTER TODAY, I AM NOT ROUNDING TO THE NEAREST FIFTEEN MINUTES.
8/30/98

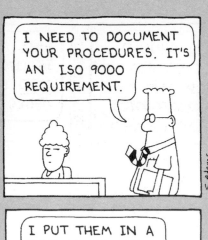

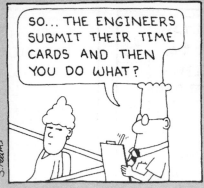

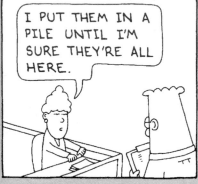

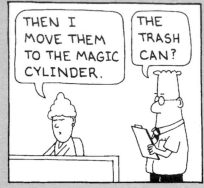

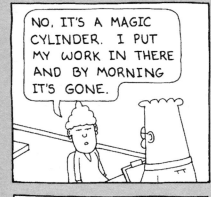

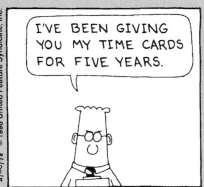

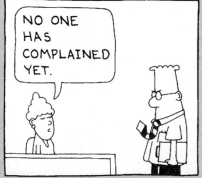

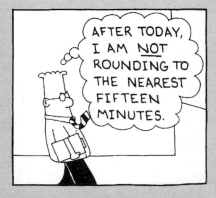

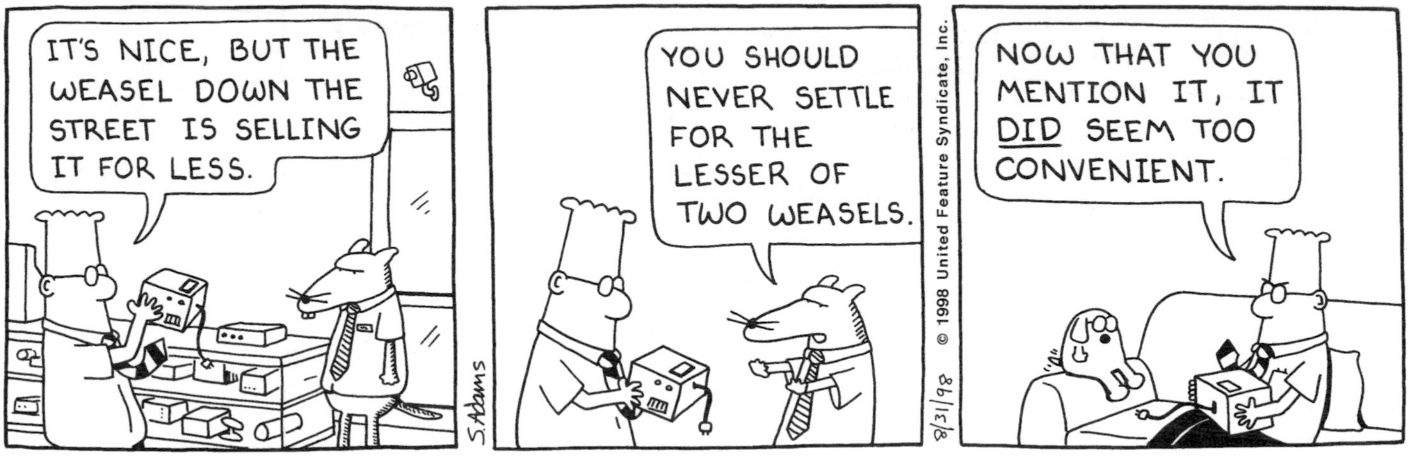
IT'S NICE, BUT THE WEASEL DOWN THE STREET IS SELLING IT FOR LESS.
S. Adams
YOU SHOULD NEVER SETTLE FOR THE LESSER OF TWO WEASELS.
8/31/98 © 1998 United Feature Syndicate, Inc.
NOW THAT YOU MENTION IT, IT DID SEEM TOO CONVENIENT.

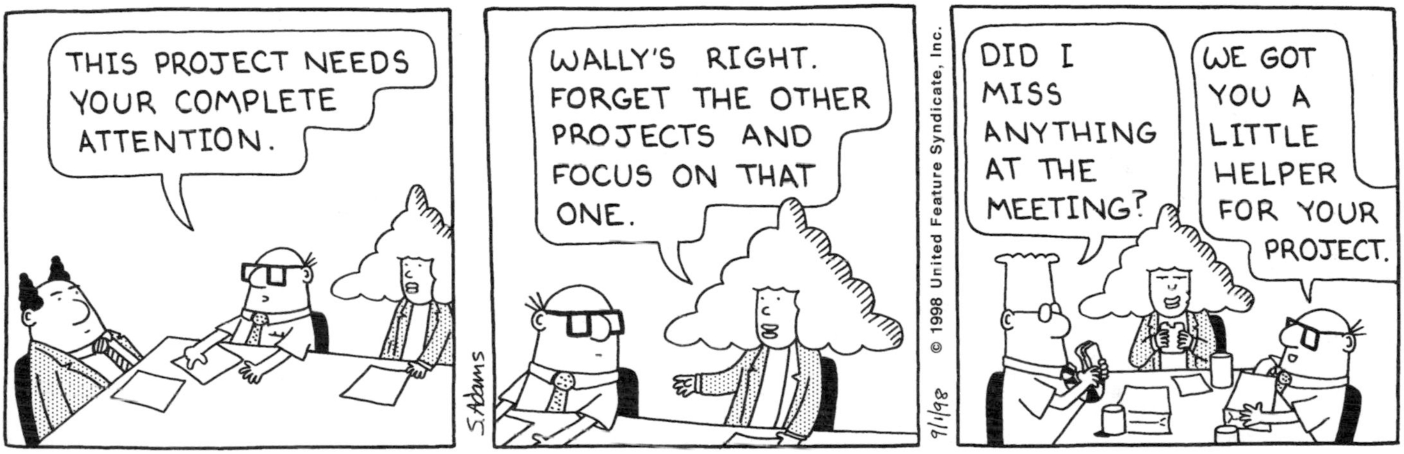
THIS PROJECT NEEDS YOUR COMPLETE ATTENTION.
S. Adams
WALLY'S RIGHT. FORGET THE OTHER PROJECTS AND FOCUS ON THAT ONE.
9/1/98 © 1998 United Feature Syndicate, Inc.
DID I MISS ANYTHING AT THE MEETING?
WE GOT YOU A LITTLE HELPER FOR YOUR PROJECT.

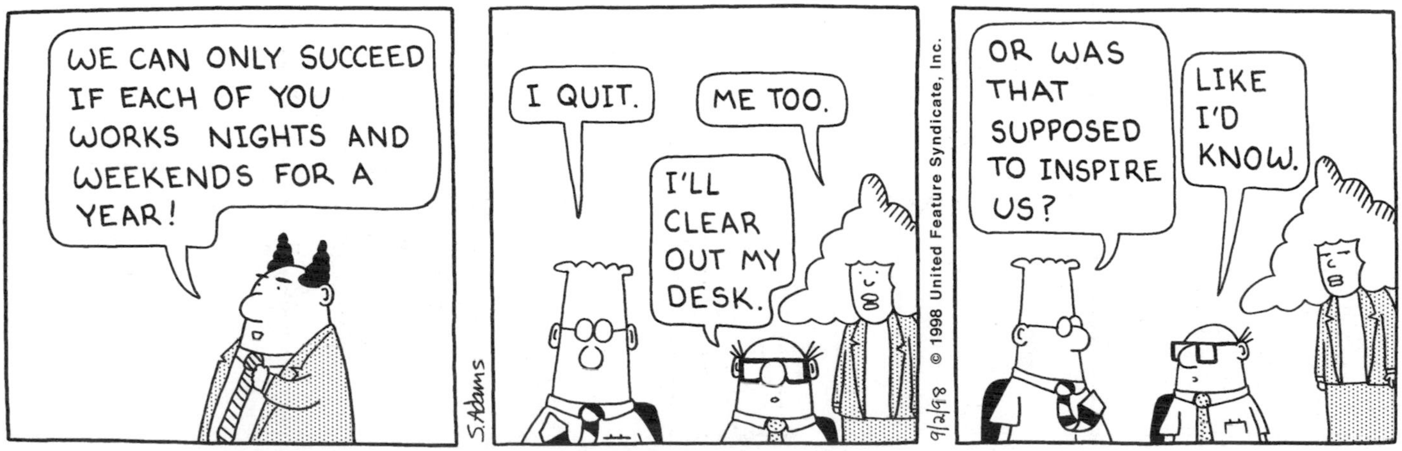
WE CAN ONLY SUCCEED IF EACH OF YOU WORKS NIGHTS AND WEEKENDS FOR A YEAR!
S. Adams
I QUIT.
ME TOO.
I'LL CLEAR OUT MY DESK.
9/2/98 © 1998 United Feature Syndicate, Inc.
OR WAS THAT SUPPOSED TO INSPIRE US?
LIKE I'D KNOW.

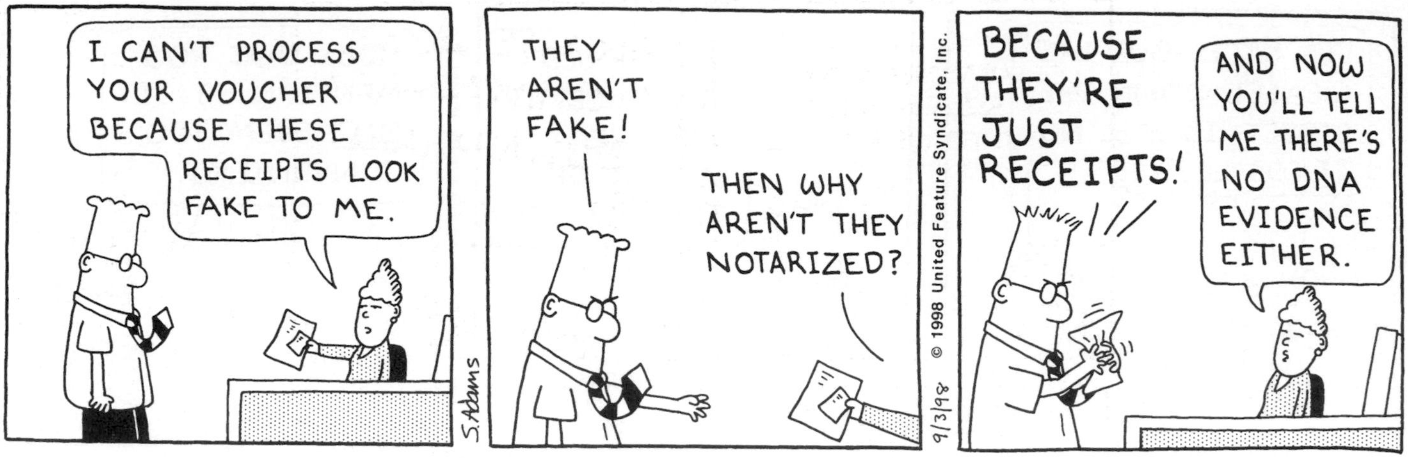
I CAN'T PROCESS YOUR VOUCHER BECAUSE THESE RECEIPTS LOOK FAKE TO ME.
S.Adams
THEY AREN'T FAKE!
THEN WHY AREN'T THEY NOTARIZED?
9/3/98 © 1998 United Feature Syndicate, Inc.
BECAUSE THEY'RE JUST RECEIPTS!
AND NOW YOU'LL TELL ME THERE'S NO DNA EVIDENCE EITHER.

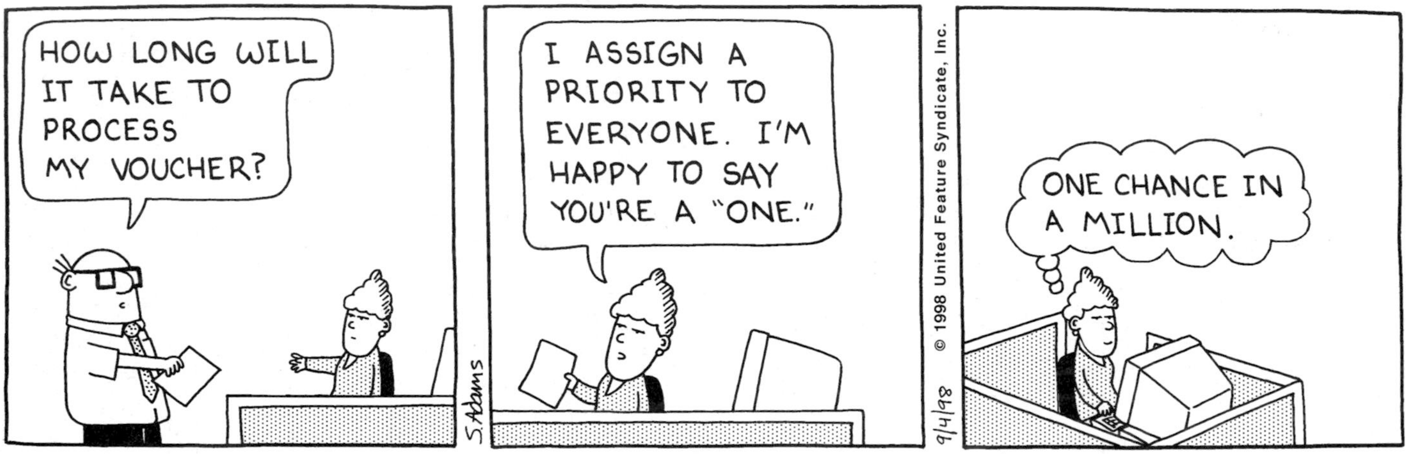
HOW LONG WILL IT TAKE TO PROCESS MY VOUCHER?
S.Adams
I ASSIGN A PRIORITY TO EVERYONE. I'M HAPPY TO SAY YOU'RE A "ONE."
9/4/98 © 1998 United Feature Syndicate, Inc.
ONE CHANCE IN A MILLION.

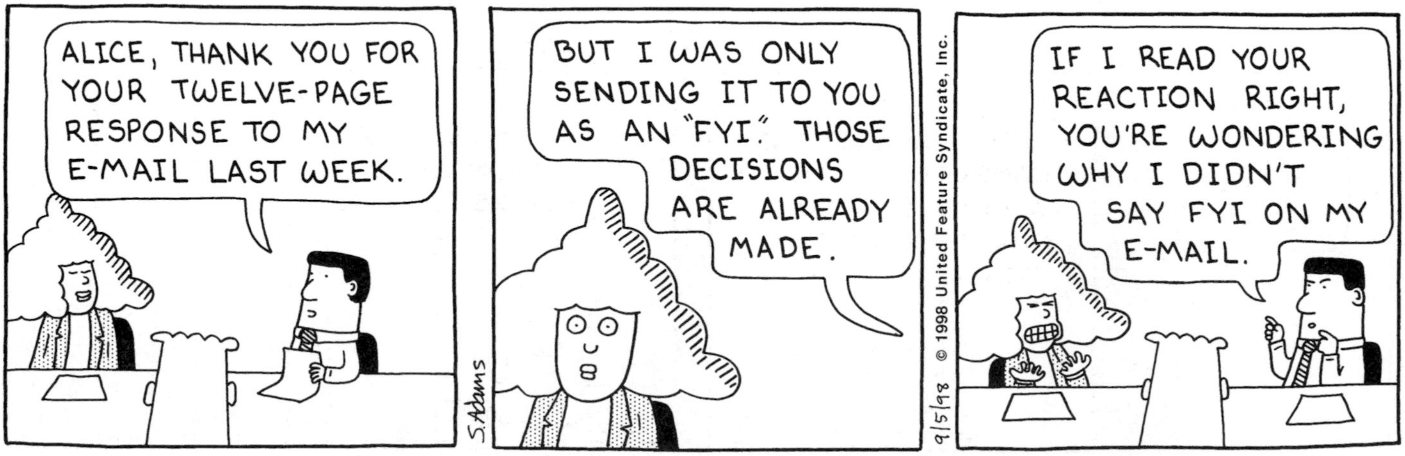
ALICE, THANK YOU FOR YOUR TWELVE-PAGE RESPONSE TO MY E-MAIL LAST WEEK.
S.Adams
BUT I WAS ONLY SENDING IT TO YOU AS AN "FYI." THOSE DECISIONS ARE ALREADY MADE.
9/5/98 © 1998 United Feature Syndicate, Inc.
IF I READ YOUR REACTION RIGHT, YOU'RE WONDERING WHY I DIDN'T SAY FYI ON MY E-MAIL.

WHY DID THE I.S. DEPARTMENT DENY MY REQUEST FOR A PC UPGRADE?
BECAUSE WE ARE EVIL INCARNATE!! BUWAHAHAHA!!
S. Adams
I WAS LOOKING FOR SOMETHING MORE SPECIFIC.
YOU DIDN'T PROVIDE A DOLLAR ESTIMATE OF THE BENEFITS.
THAT'S RIDICULOUS. I CAN'T PUT A VALUE ON EVERY TOOL I NEED TO DO MY JOB.
© 1998 United Feature Syndicate, Inc.
9/6/98
IF YOU CAN'T QUANTIFY IT, THEN IT MUST NOT BE NECESSARY.
THEN WHY DOES THE COMPANY GIVE ME A CHAIR? I CAN'T QUANTIFY THAT EITHER!
HERE'S ONE MORE REASON WHY IT STINKS TO BE ME.

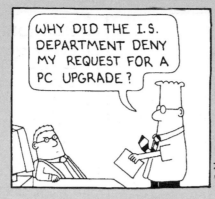

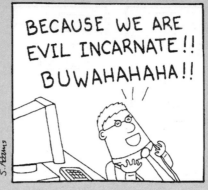

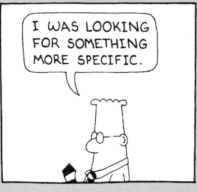

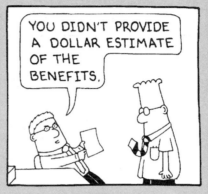

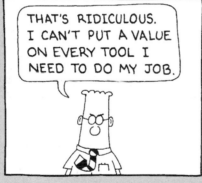

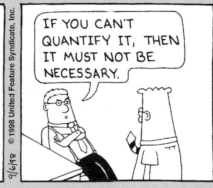

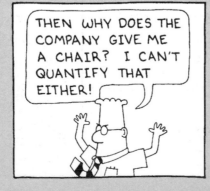

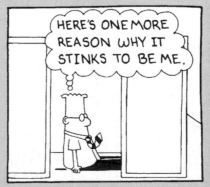

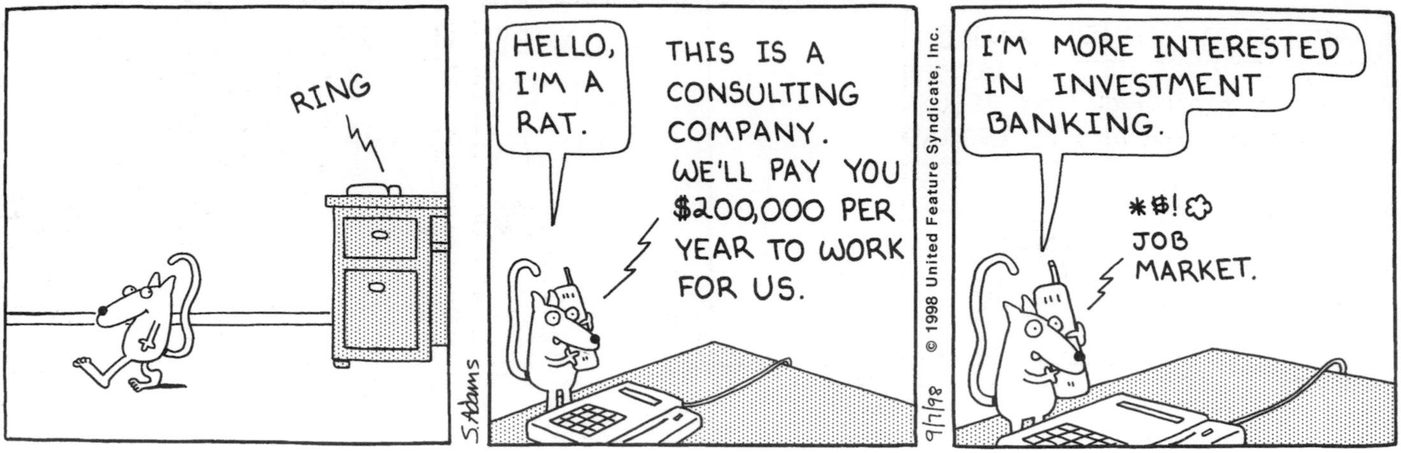
RING
HELLO, I'M A RAT.
THIS IS A CONSULTING COMPANY. WE'LL PAY YOU $200,000 PER YEAR TO WORK FOR US.
I'M MORE INTERESTED IN INVESTMENT BANKING.
*$! JOB MARKET.
S. Adams
9/7/98
© 1998 United Feature Syndicate, Inc.

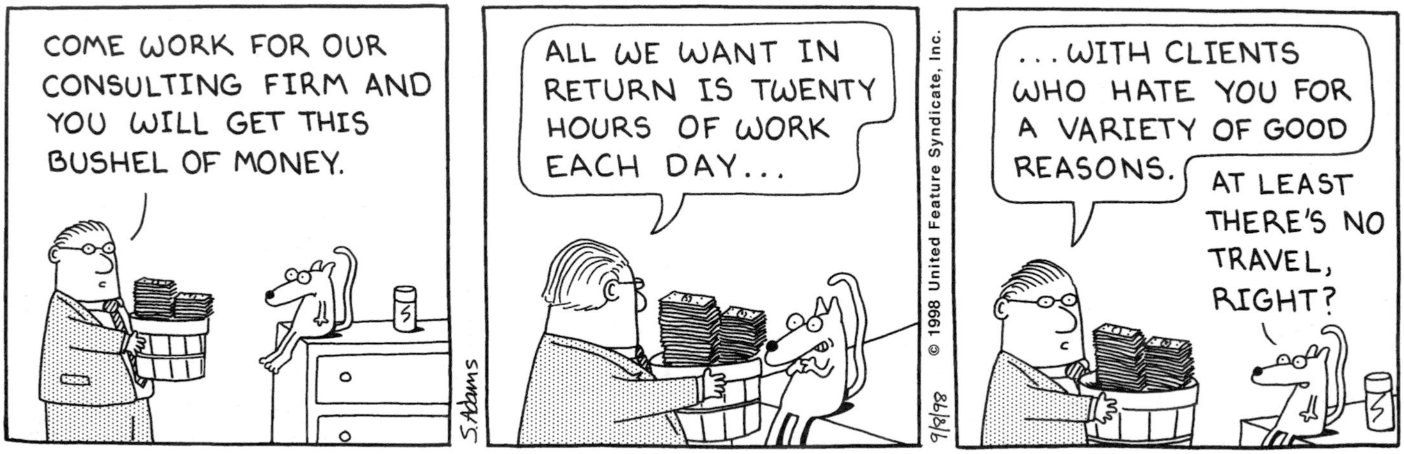
COME WORK FOR OUR CONSULTING FIRM AND YOU WILL GET THIS BUSHEL OF MONEY.
ALL WE WANT IN RETURN IS TWENTY HOURS OF WORK EACH DAY...
...WITH CLIENTS WHO HATE YOU FOR A VARIETY OF GOOD REASONS.
AT LEAST THERE'S NO TRAVEL, RIGHT?
S. Adams
9/8/98
© 1998 United Feature Syndicate, Inc.

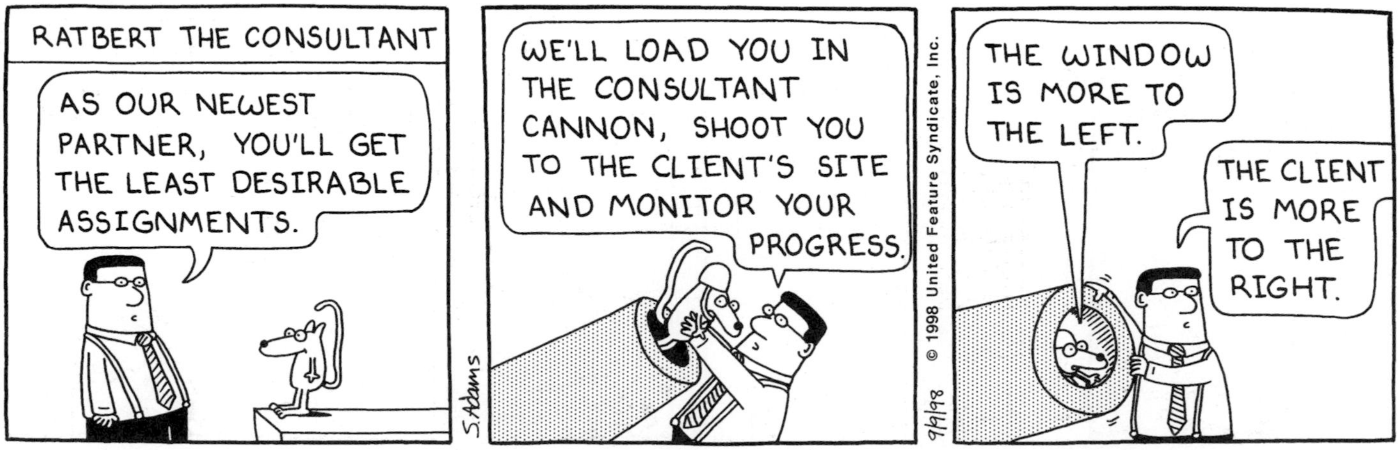
RATBERT THE CONSULTANT
AS OUR NEWEST PARTNER, YOU'LL GET THE LEAST DESIRABLE ASSIGNMENTS.
WE'LL LOAD YOU IN THE CONSULTANT CANNON, SHOOT YOU TO THE CLIENT'S SITE AND MONITOR YOUR PROGRESS.
THE WINDOW IS MORE TO THE LEFT.
THE CLIENT IS MORE TO THE RIGHT.
S. Adams
9/9/98
© 1998 United Feature Syndicate, Inc.

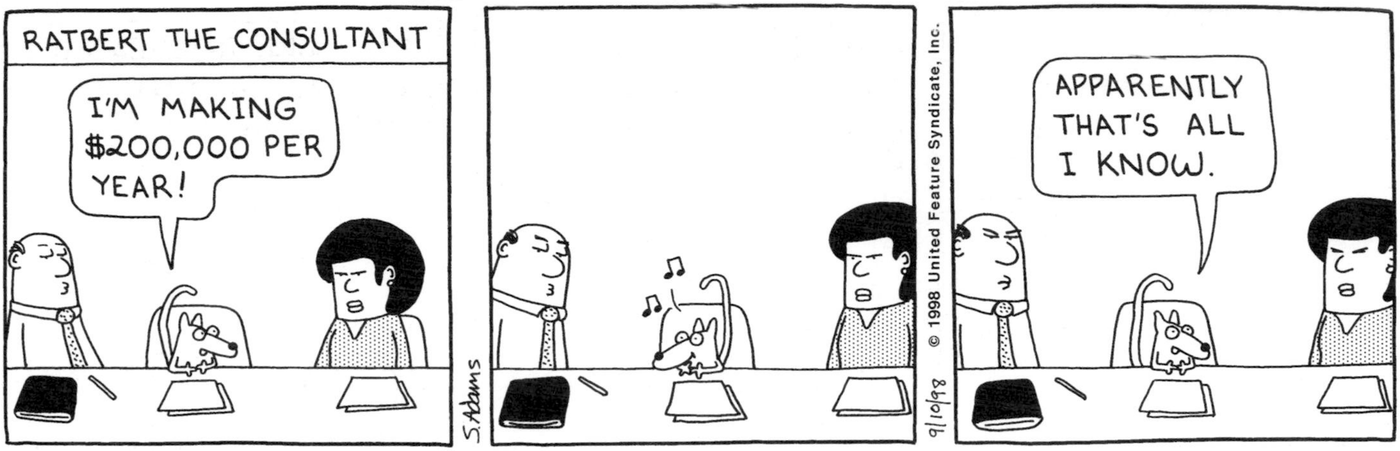
RATBERT THE CONSULTANT
I'M MAKING $200,000 PER YEAR!
APPARENTLY THAT'S ALL I KNOW.
© 1998 United Feature Syndicate, Inc.

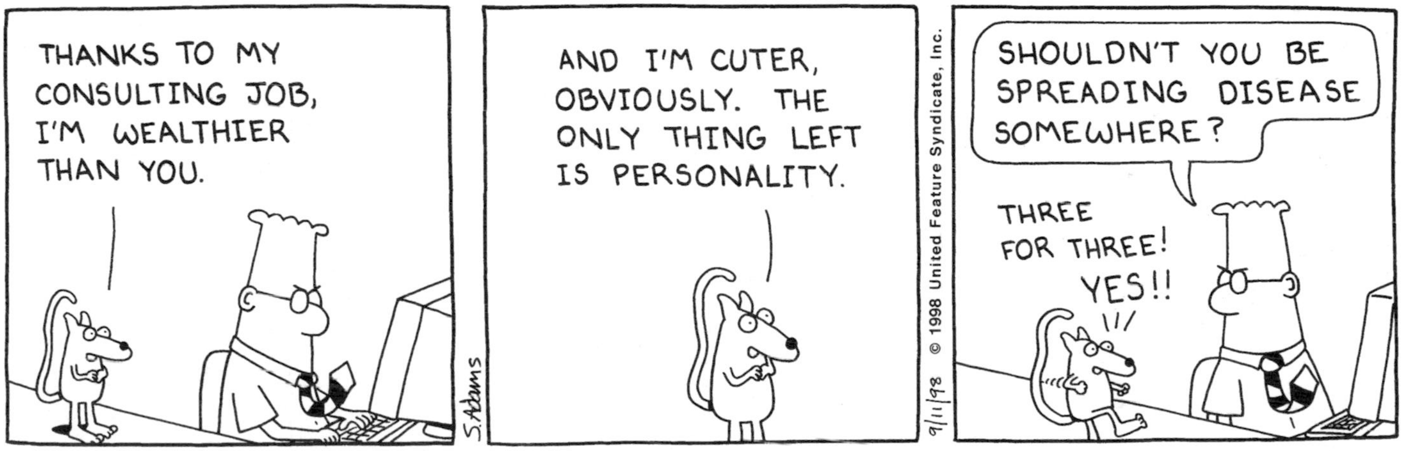
THANKS TO MY CONSULTING JOB, I'M WEALTHIER THAN YOU.
AND I'M CUTER, OBVIOUSLY. THE ONLY THING LEFT IS PERSONALITY.
SHOULDN'T YOU BE SPREADING DISEASE SOMEWHERE?
THREE FOR THREE!
YES!!
© 1998 United Feature Syndicate, Inc.

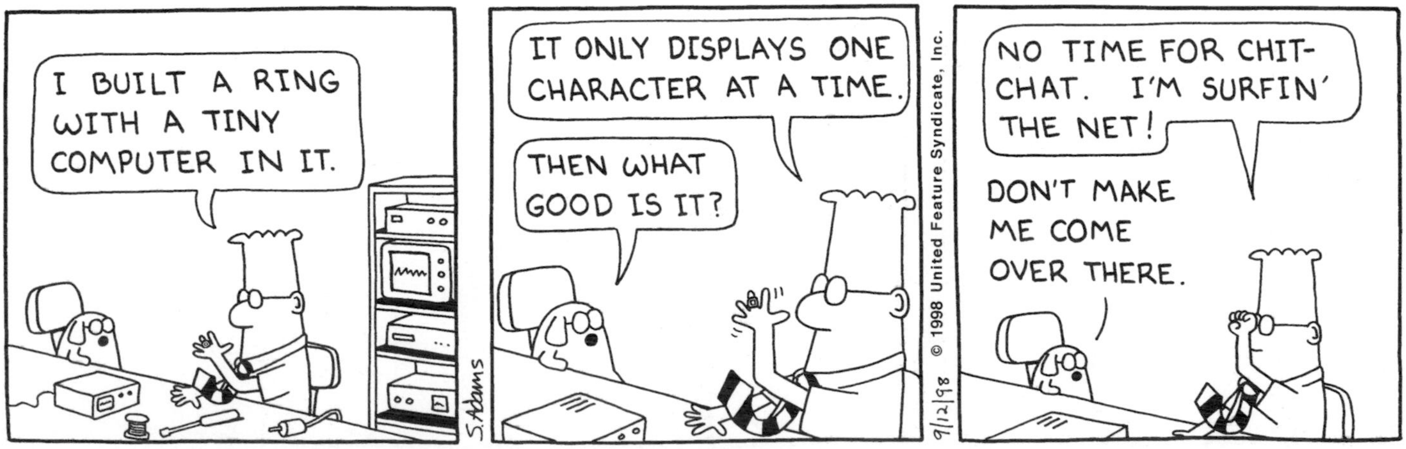
I BUILT A RING WITH A TINY COMPUTER IN IT.
IT ONLY DISPLAYS ONE CHARACTER AT A TIME.
THEN WHAT GOOD IS IT?
NO TIME FOR CHIT-CHAT. I'M SURFIN' THE NET!
DON'T MAKE ME COME OVER THERE.
© 1998 United Feature Syndicate, Inc.

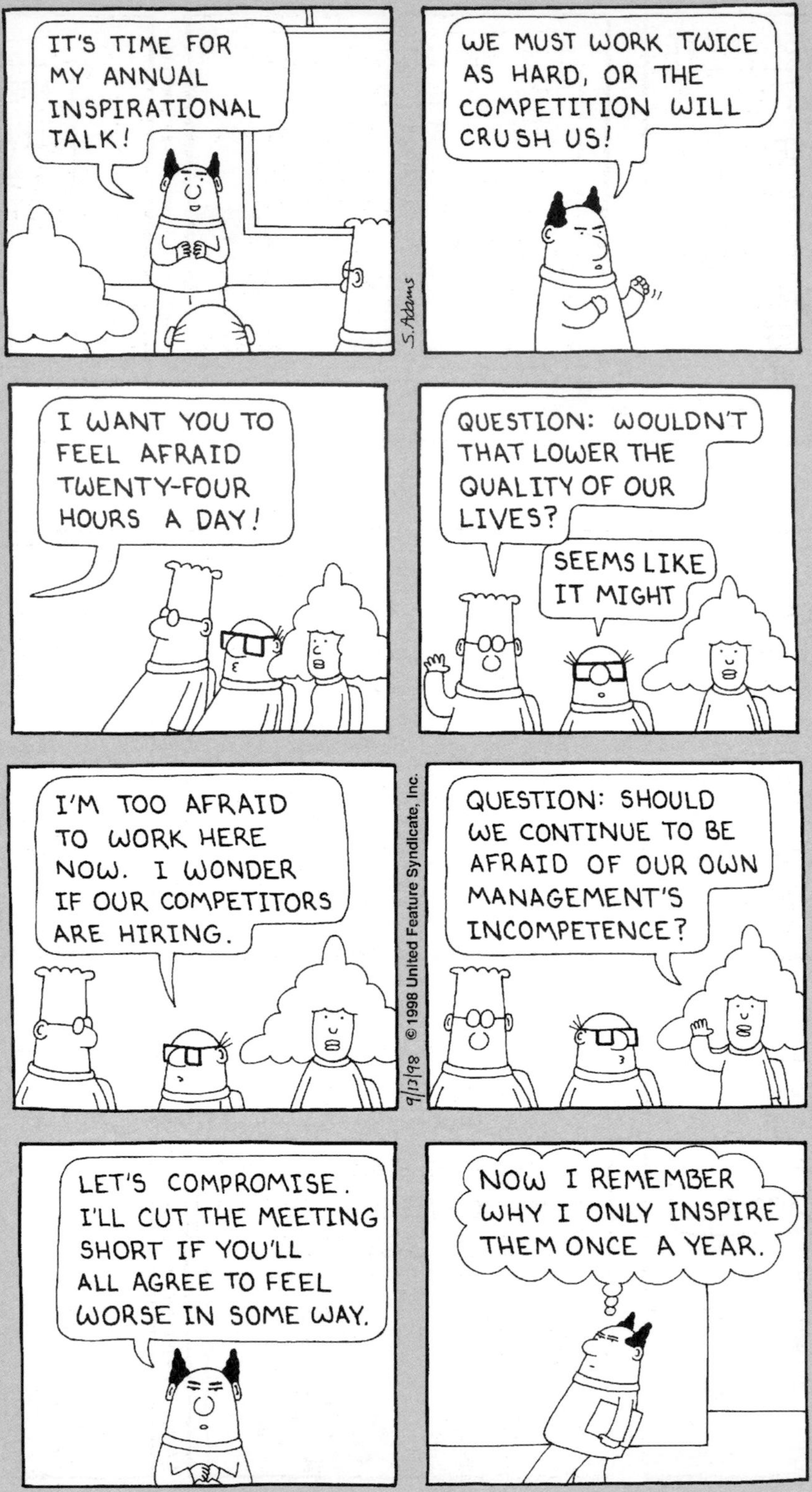
IT'S TIME FOR MY ANNUAL INSPIRATIONAL TALK!
WE MUST WORK TWICE AS HARD, OR THE COMPETITION WILL CRUSH US!
S. Adams
I WANT YOU TO FEEL AFRAID TWENTY-FOUR HOURS A DAY!
QUESTION: WOULDN'T THAT LOWER THE QUALITY OF OUR LIVES?
SEEMS LIKE IT MIGHT
I'M TOO AFRAID TO WORK HERE NOW. I WONDER IF OUR COMPETITORS ARE HIRING.
QUESTION: SHOULD WE CONTINUE TO BE AFRAID OF OUR OWN MANAGEMENT'S INCOMPETENCE?
9/13/98 © 1998 United Feature Syndicate, Inc.
LET'S COMPROMISE. I'LL CUT THE MEETING SHORT IF YOU'LL ALL AGREE TO FEEL WORSE IN SOME WAY.
NOW I REMEMBER WHY I ONLY INSPIRE THEM ONCE A YEAR.

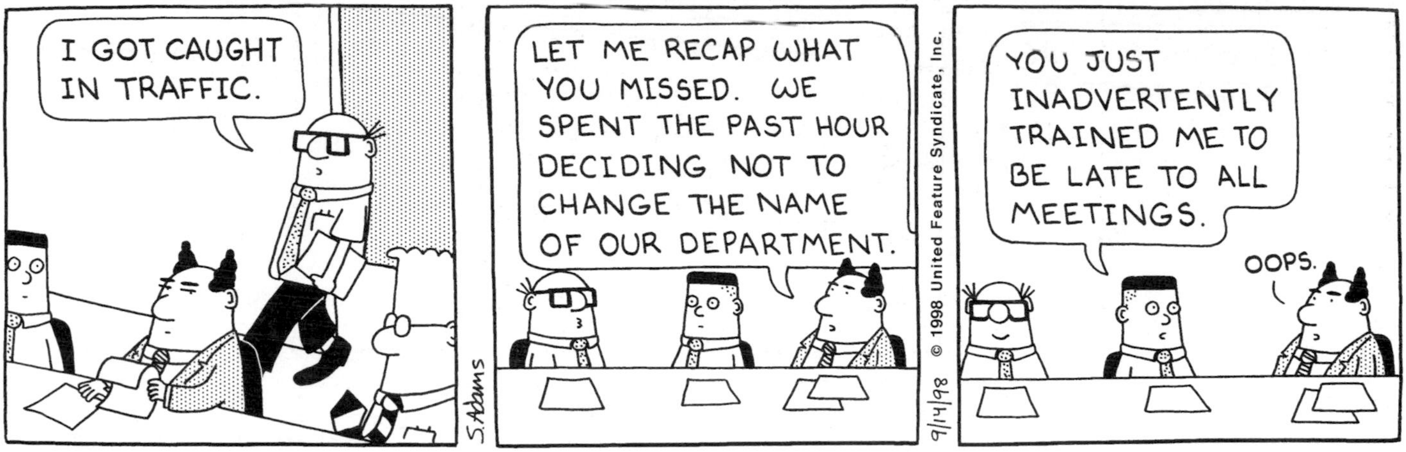
I GOT CAUGHT IN TRAFFIC.
S.Adams
LET ME RECAP WHAT YOU MISSED. WE SPENT THE PAST HOUR DECIDING NOT TO CHANGE THE NAME OF OUR DEPARTMENT.
9/14/98
© 1998 United Feature Syndicate, Inc.
YOU JUST INADVERTENTLY TRAINED ME TO BE LATE TO ALL MEETINGS.
OOPS.

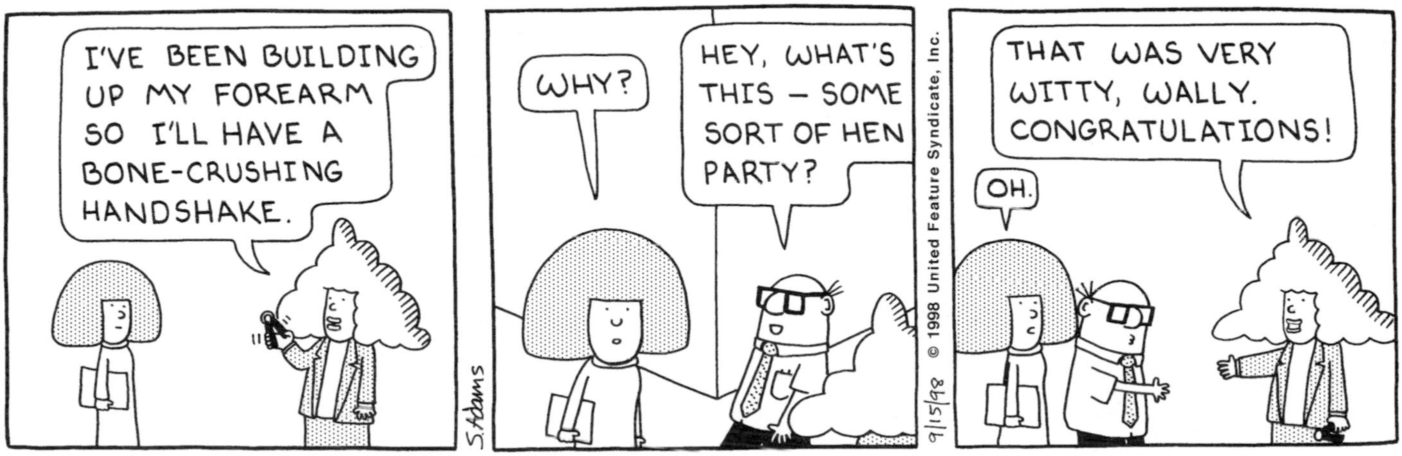
I'VE BEEN BUILDING UP MY FOREARM SO I'LL HAVE A BONE-CRUSHING HANDSHAKE.
S.Adams
WHY?
HEY, WHAT'S THIS – SOME SORT OF HEN PARTY?
9/15/98
© 1998 United Feature Syndicate, Inc.
THAT WAS VERY WITTY, WALLY. CONGRATULATIONS!
OH.

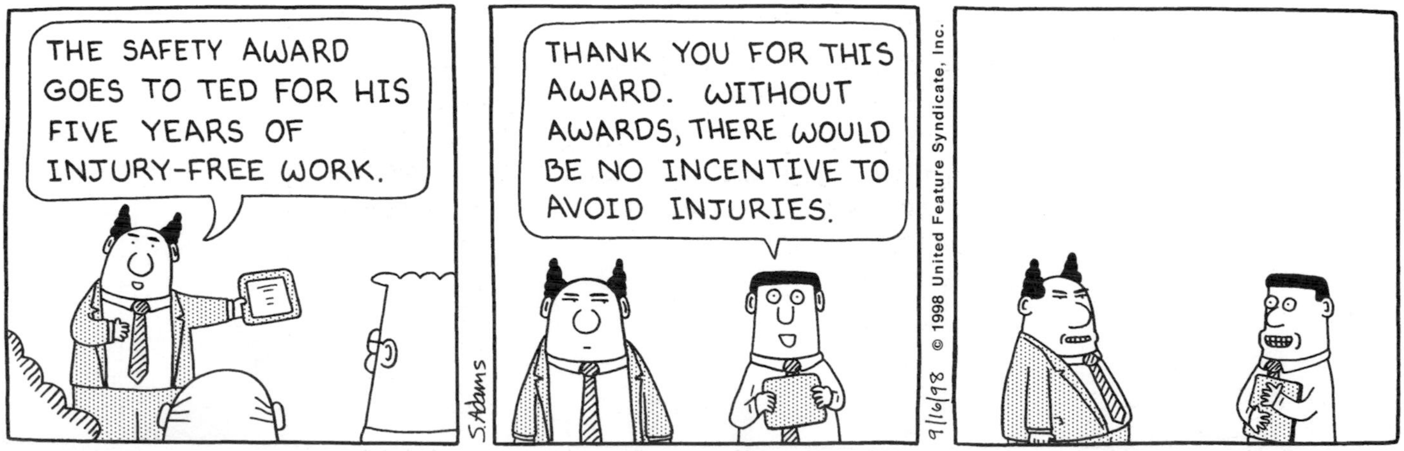
THE SAFETY AWARD GOES TO TED FOR HIS FIVE YEARS OF INJURY-FREE WORK.
S.Adams
THANK YOU FOR THIS AWARD. WITHOUT AWARDS, THERE WOULD BE NO INCENTIVE TO AVOID INJURIES.
9/16/98
© 1998 United Feature Syndicate, Inc.

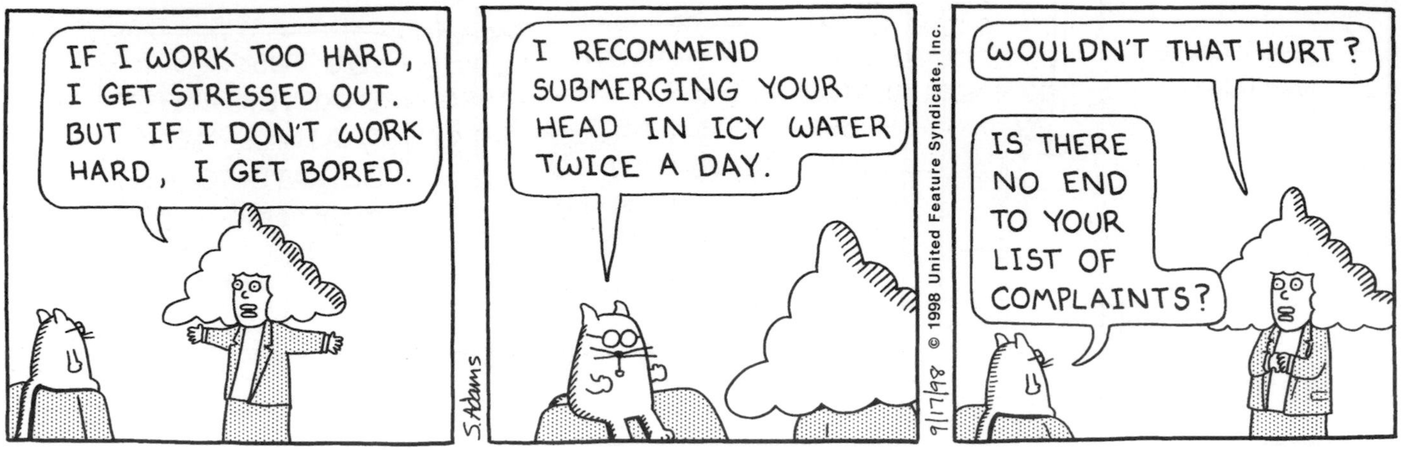
IF I WORK TOO HARD, I GET STRESSED OUT. BUT IF I DON'T WORK HARD, I GET BORED.
I RECOMMEND SUBMERGING YOUR HEAD IN ICY WATER TWICE A DAY.
WOULDN'T THAT HURT?
IS THERE NO END TO YOUR LIST OF COMPLAINTS?
S. Adams
9/17/98 © 1998 United Feature Syndicate, Inc.

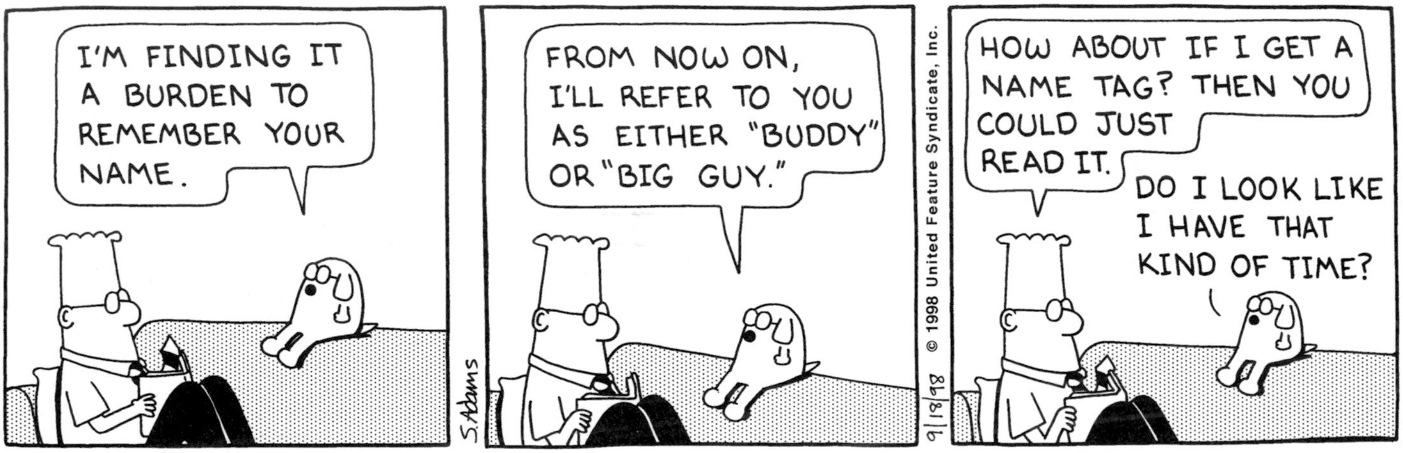
I'M FINDING IT A BURDEN TO REMEMBER YOUR NAME.
FROM NOW ON, I'LL REFER TO YOU AS EITHER "BUDDY" OR "BIG GUY."
HOW ABOUT IF I GET A NAME TAG? THEN YOU COULD JUST READ IT.
DO I LOOK LIKE I HAVE THAT KIND OF TIME?
S. Adams
9/18/98 © 1998 United Feature Syndicate, Inc.

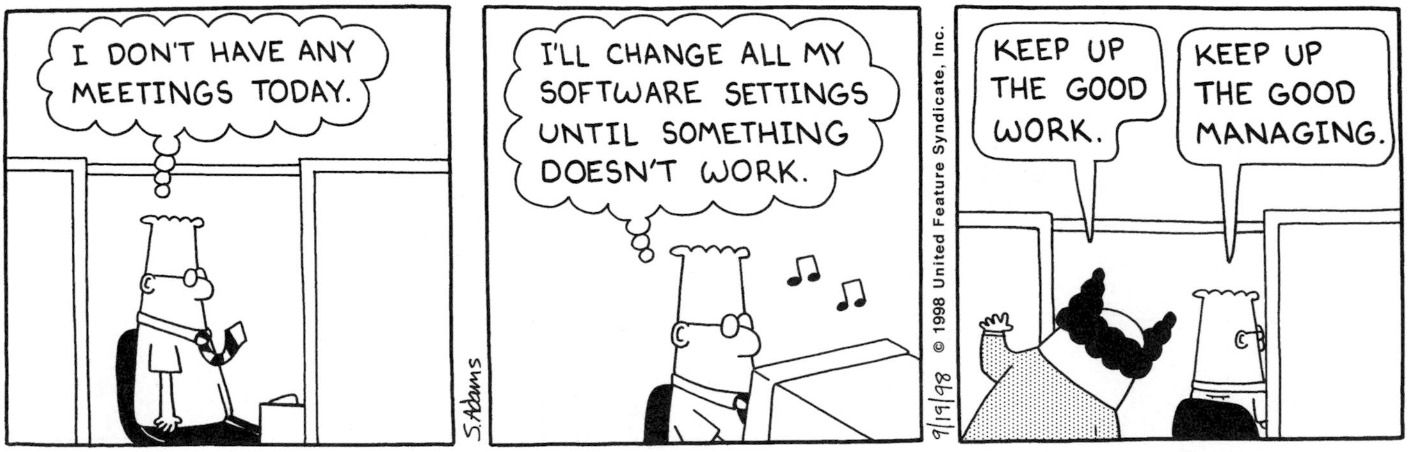
I DON'T HAVE ANY MEETINGS TODAY.
I'LL CHANGE ALL MY SOFTWARE SETTINGS UNTIL SOMETHING DOESN'T WORK.
KEEP UP THE GOOD WORK.
KEEP UP THE GOOD MANAGING.
S. Adams
9/19/98 © 1998 United Feature Syndicate, Inc.

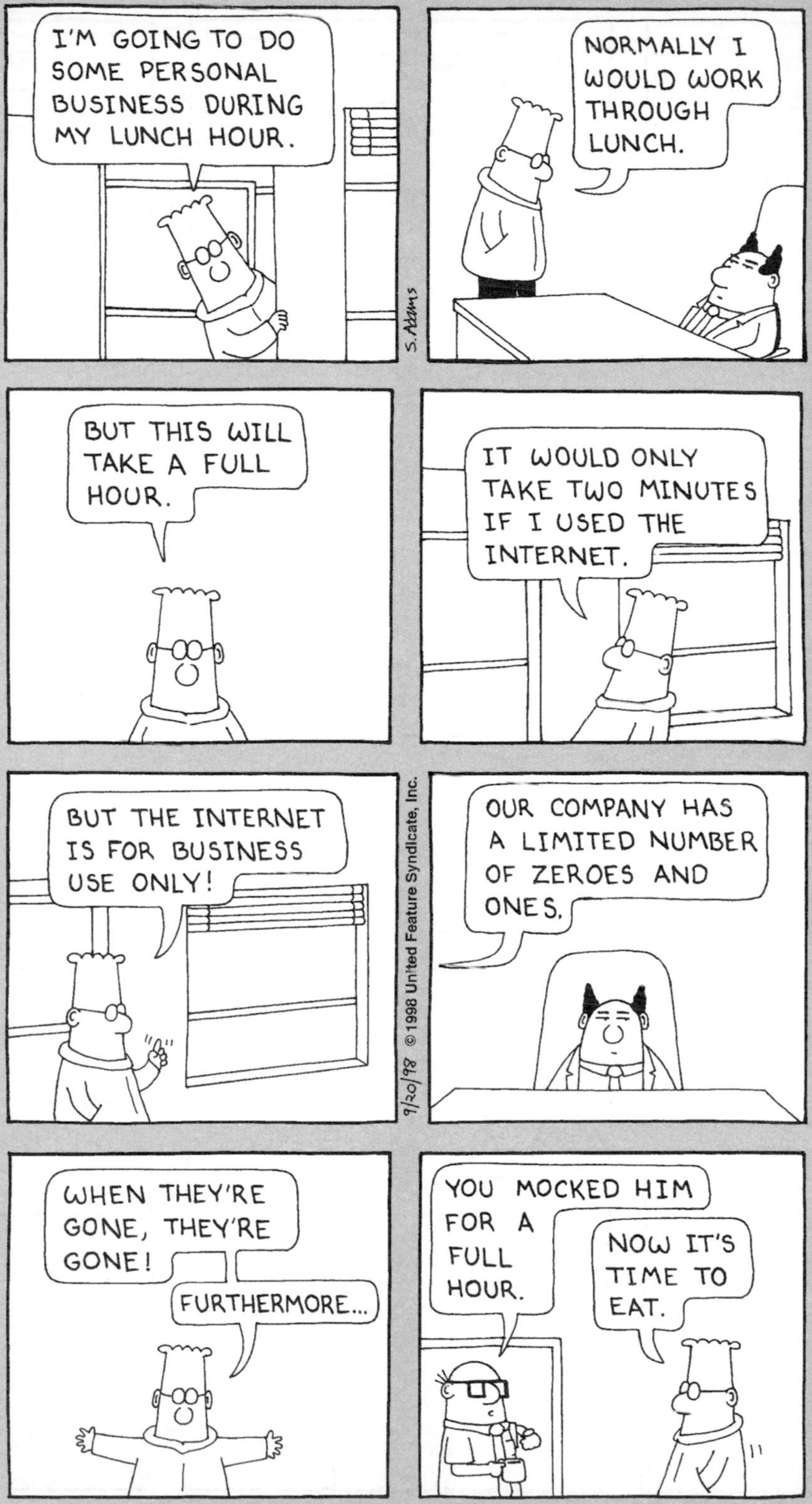
I'M GOING TO DO SOME PERSONAL BUSINESS DURING MY LUNCH HOUR.
NORMALLY I WOULD WORK THROUGH LUNCH.
S. Adams
BUT THIS WILL TAKE A FULL HOUR.
IT WOULD ONLY TAKE TWO MINUTES IF I USED THE INTERNET.
BUT THE INTERNET IS FOR BUSINESS USE ONLY!
9/20/98 © 1998 United Feature Syndicate, Inc.
OUR COMPANY HAS A LIMITED NUMBER OF ZEROES AND ONES.
WHEN THEY'RE GONE, THEY'RE GONE!
FURTHERMORE...
YOU MOCKED HIM FOR A FULL HOUR.
NOW IT'S TIME TO EAT.

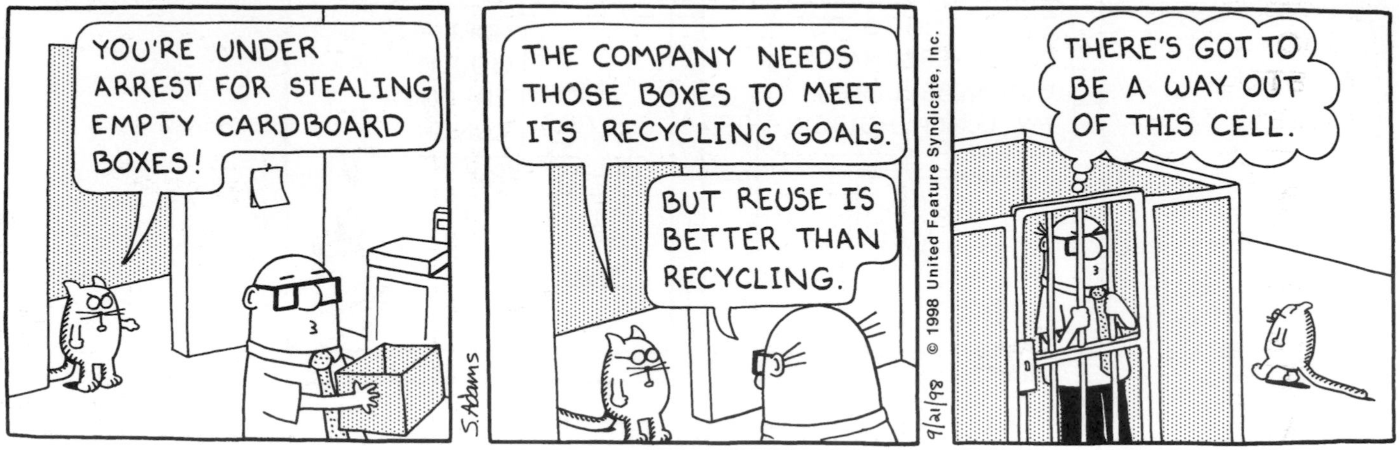
YOU'RE UNDER ARREST FOR STEALING EMPTY CARDBOARD BOXES!
S. Adams
THE COMPANY NEEDS THOSE BOXES TO MEET ITS RECYCLING GOALS.
BUT REUSE IS BETTER THAN RECYCLING.
9/21/98 © 1998 United Feature Syndicate, Inc.
THERE'S GOT TO BE A WAY OUT OF THIS CELL.

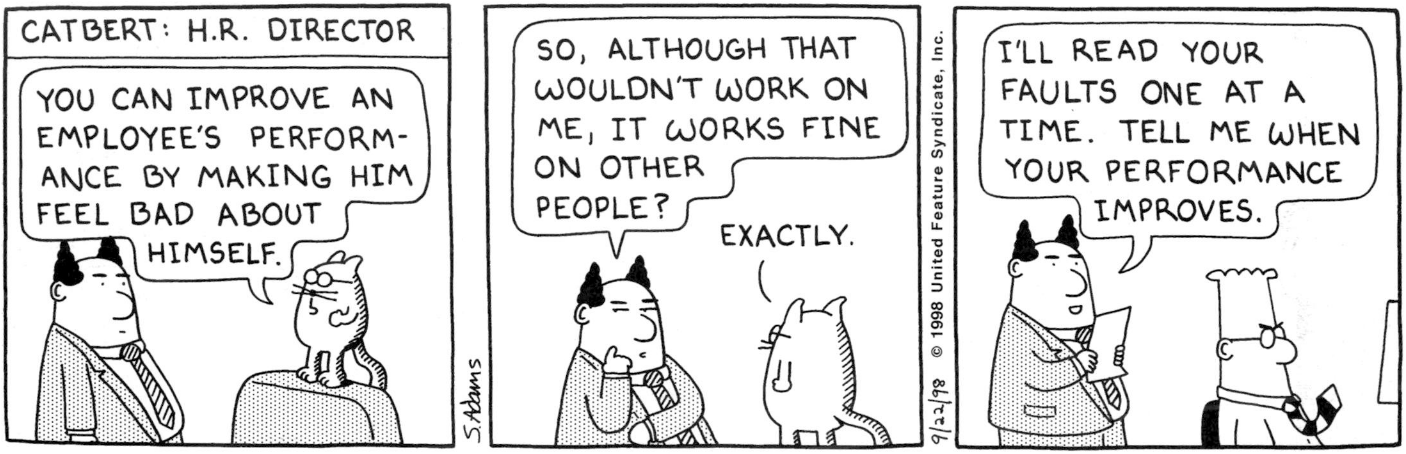
CATBERT: H.R. DIRECTOR
YOU CAN IMPROVE AN EMPLOYEE'S PERFORMANCE BY MAKING HIM FEEL BAD ABOUT HIMSELF.
S. Adams
SO, ALTHOUGH THAT WOULDN'T WORK ON ME, IT WORKS FINE ON OTHER PEOPLE?
EXACTLY.
9/22/98 © 1998 United Feature Syndicate, Inc.
I'LL READ YOUR FAULTS ONE AT A TIME. TELL ME WHEN YOUR PERFORMANCE IMPROVES.

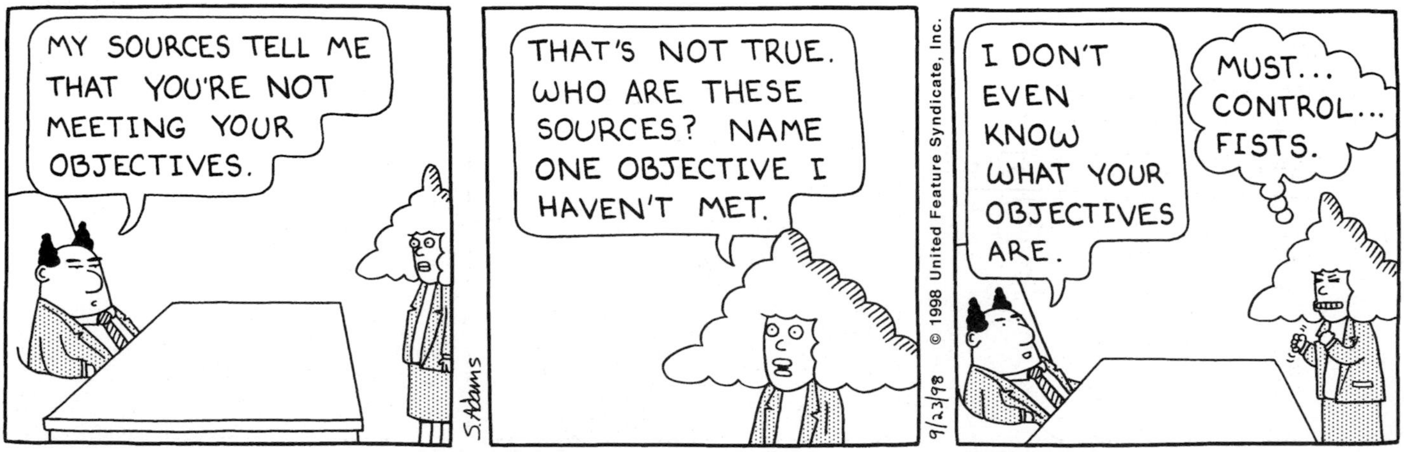
MY SOURCES TELL ME THAT YOU'RE NOT MEETING YOUR OBJECTIVES.
S. Adams
THAT'S NOT TRUE. WHO ARE THESE SOURCES? NAME ONE OBJECTIVE I HAVEN'T MET.
9/23/98 © 1998 United Feature Syndicate, Inc.
I DON'T EVEN KNOW WHAT YOUR OBJECTIVES ARE.
MUST... CONTROL... FISTS.

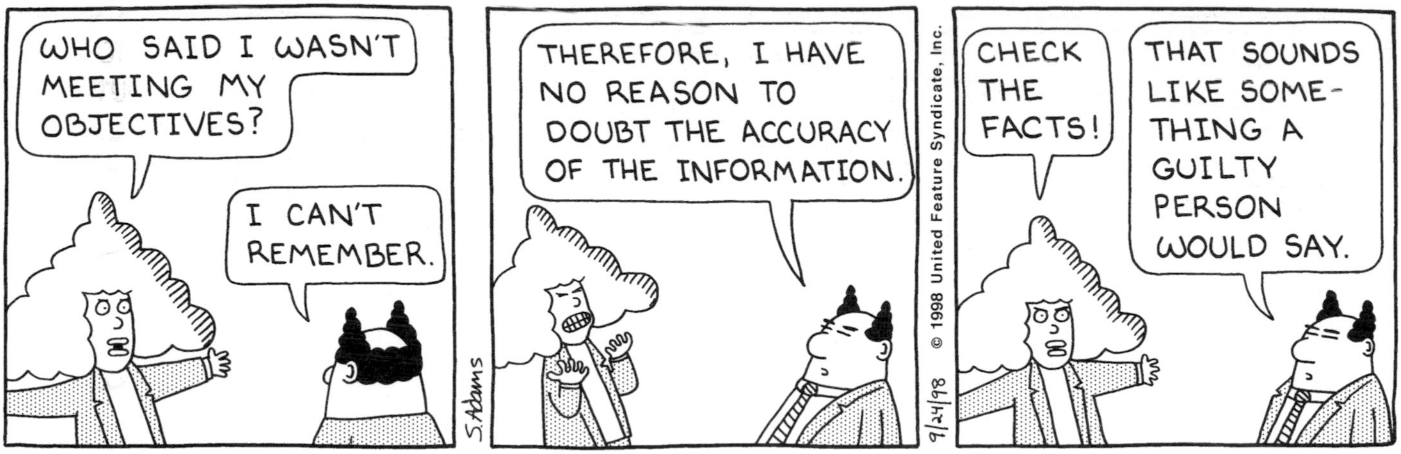
WHO SAID I WASN'T MEETING MY OBJECTIVES?
I CAN'T REMEMBER.
S.Adams
THEREFORE, I HAVE NO REASON TO DOUBT THE ACCURACY OF THE INFORMATION.
9/24/98 © 1998 United Feature Syndicate, Inc.
CHECK THE FACTS!
THAT SOUNDS LIKE SOME-THING A GUILTY PERSON WOULD SAY.

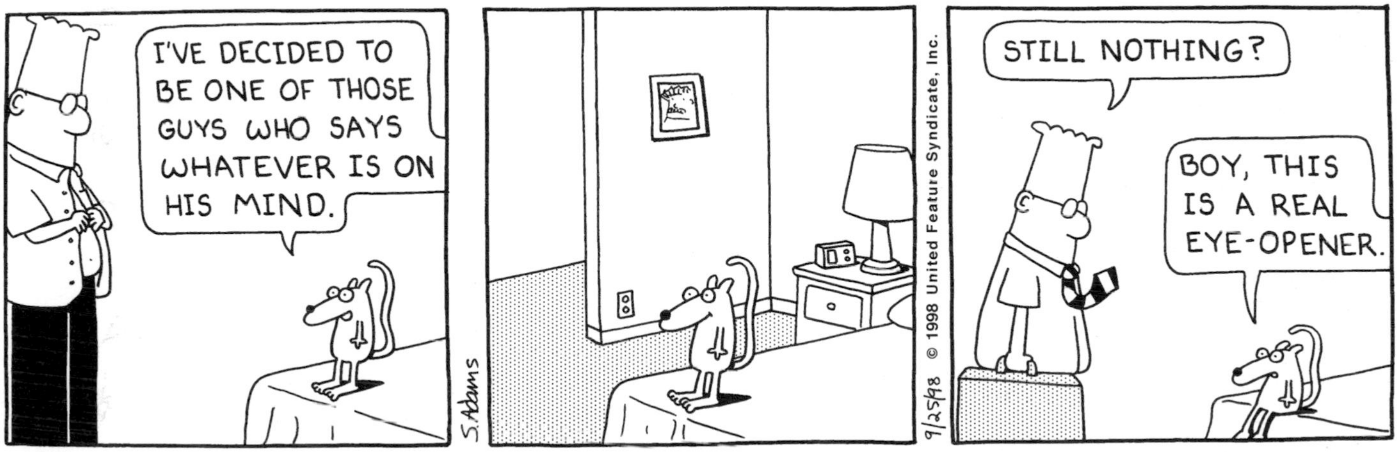
I'VE DECIDED TO BE ONE OF THOSE GUYS WHO SAYS WHATEVER IS ON HIS MIND.
S.Adams
9/25/98 © 1998 United Feature Syndicate, Inc.
STILL NOTHING?
BOY, THIS IS A REAL EYE-OPENER.

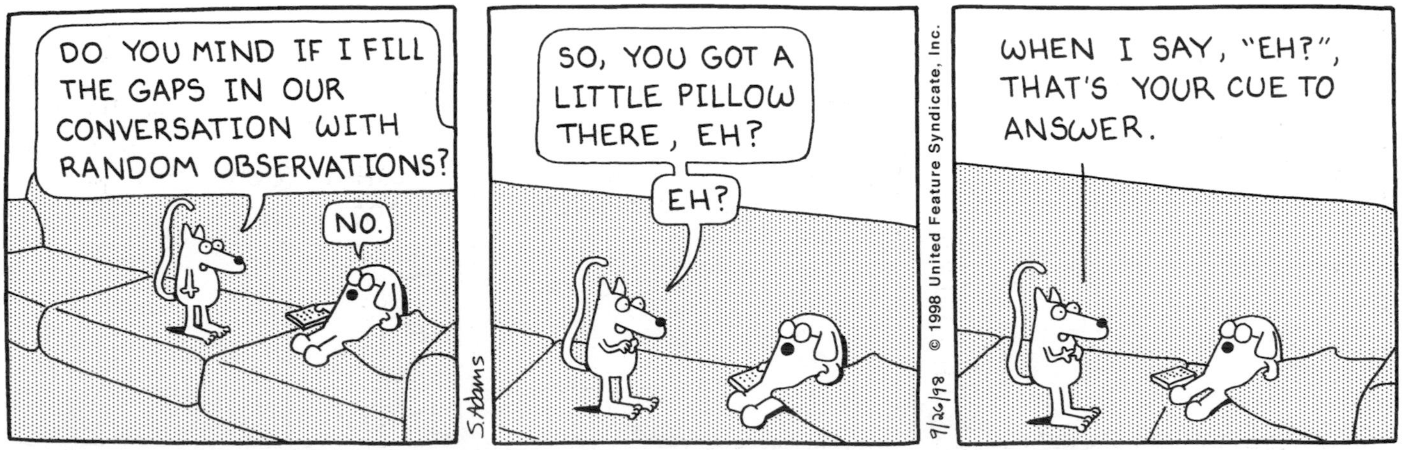
DO YOU MIND IF I FILL THE GAPS IN OUR CONVERSATION WITH RANDOM OBSERVATIONS?
NO.
S.Adams
SO, YOU GOT A LITTLE PILLOW THERE, EH?
EH?
9/26/98 © 1998 United Feature Syndicate, Inc.
WHEN I SAY, "EH?", THAT'S YOUR CUE TO ANSWER.

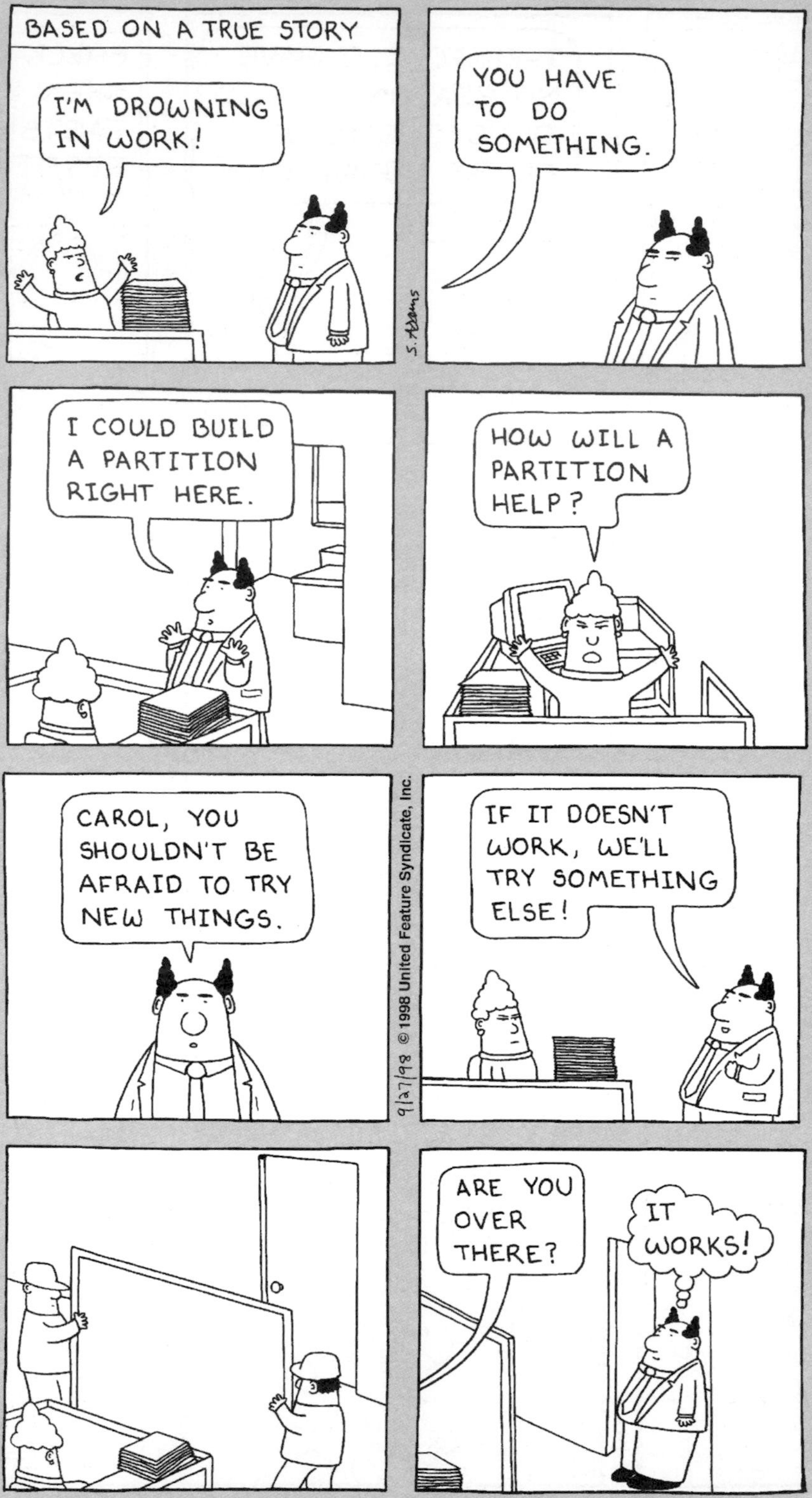
BASED ON A TRUE STORY
I'M DROWNING IN WORK!
S. Adams
YOU HAVE TO DO SOMETHING.
I COULD BUILD A PARTITION RIGHT HERE.
HOW WILL A PARTITION HELP?
CAROL, YOU SHOULDN'T BE AFRAID TO TRY NEW THINGS.
9/27/98 © 1998 United Feature Syndicate, Inc.
IF IT DOESN'T WORK, WE'LL TRY SOMETHING ELSE!
ARE YOU OVER THERE?
IT WORKS!

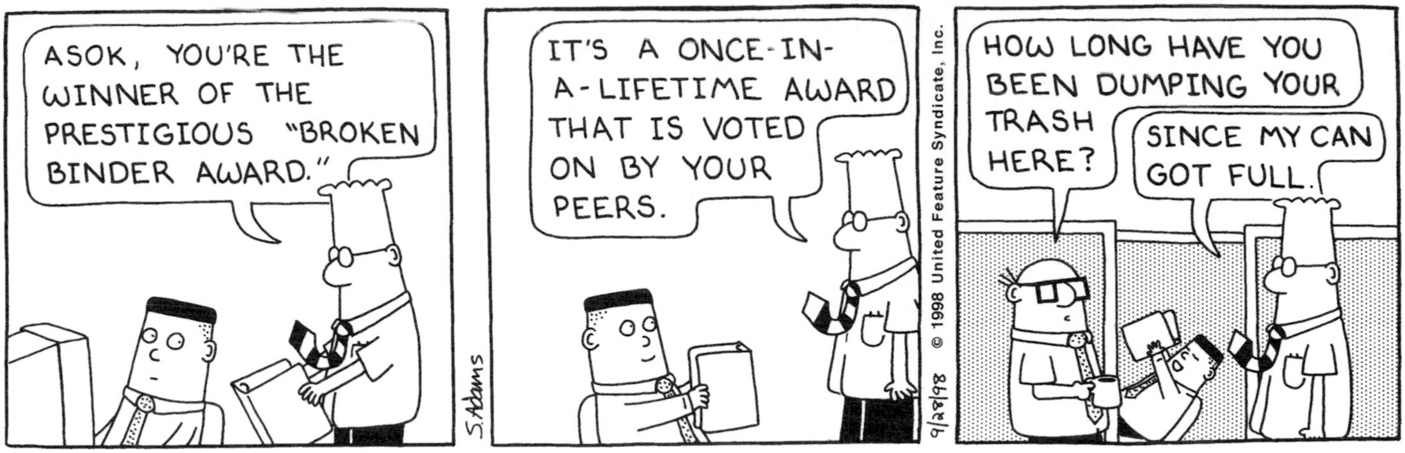
ASOK, YOU'RE THE WINNER OF THE PRESTIGIOUS "BROKEN BINDER AWARD."
IT'S A ONCE-IN-A-LIFETIME AWARD THAT IS VOTED ON BY YOUR PEERS.
HOW LONG HAVE YOU BEEN DUMPING YOUR TRASH HERE?
SINCE MY CAN GOT FULL.
S.Adams 9/28/98 © 1998 United Feature Syndicate, Inc.

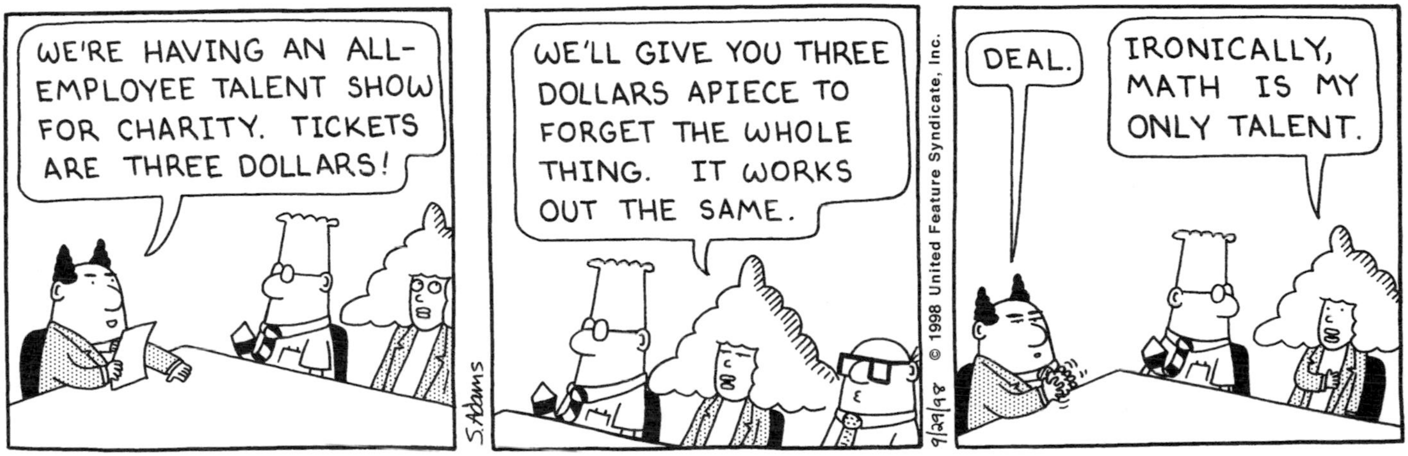
WE'RE HAVING AN ALL-EMPLOYEE TALENT SHOW FOR CHARITY. TICKETS ARE THREE DOLLARS!
WE'LL GIVE YOU THREE DOLLARS APIECE TO FORGET THE WHOLE THING. IT WORKS OUT THE SAME.
DEAL.
IRONICALLY, MATH IS MY ONLY TALENT.
S.Adams 9/29/98 © 1998 United Feature Syndicate, Inc.

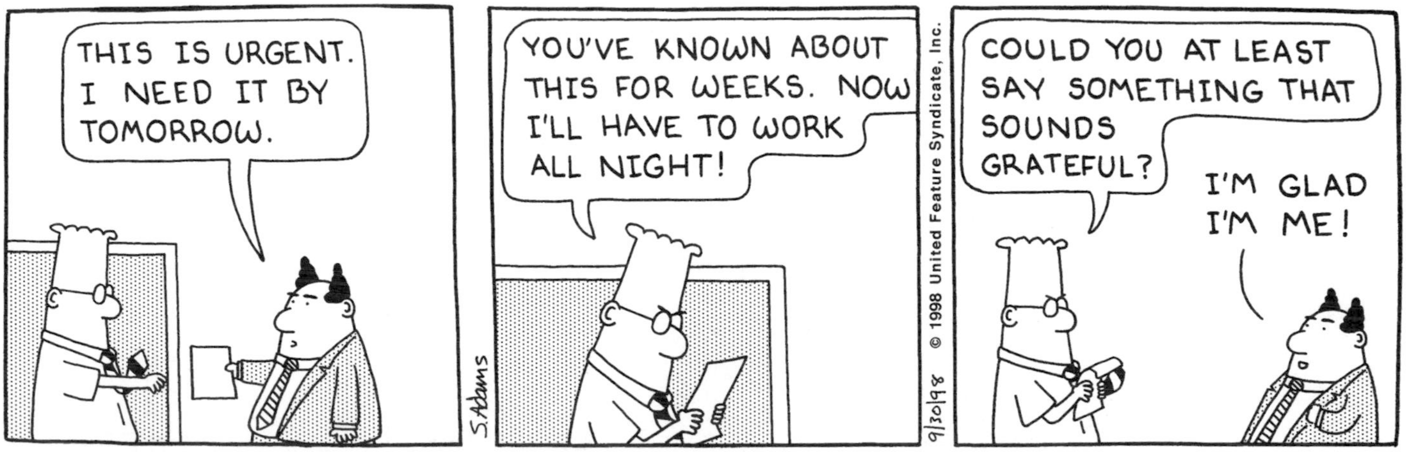
THIS IS URGENT. I NEED IT BY TOMORROW.
YOU'VE KNOWN ABOUT THIS FOR WEEKS. NOW I'LL HAVE TO WORK ALL NIGHT!
COULD YOU AT LEAST SAY SOMETHING THAT SOUNDS GRATEFUL?
I'M GLAD I'M ME!
S.Adams 9/30/98 © 1998 United Feature Syndicate, Inc.

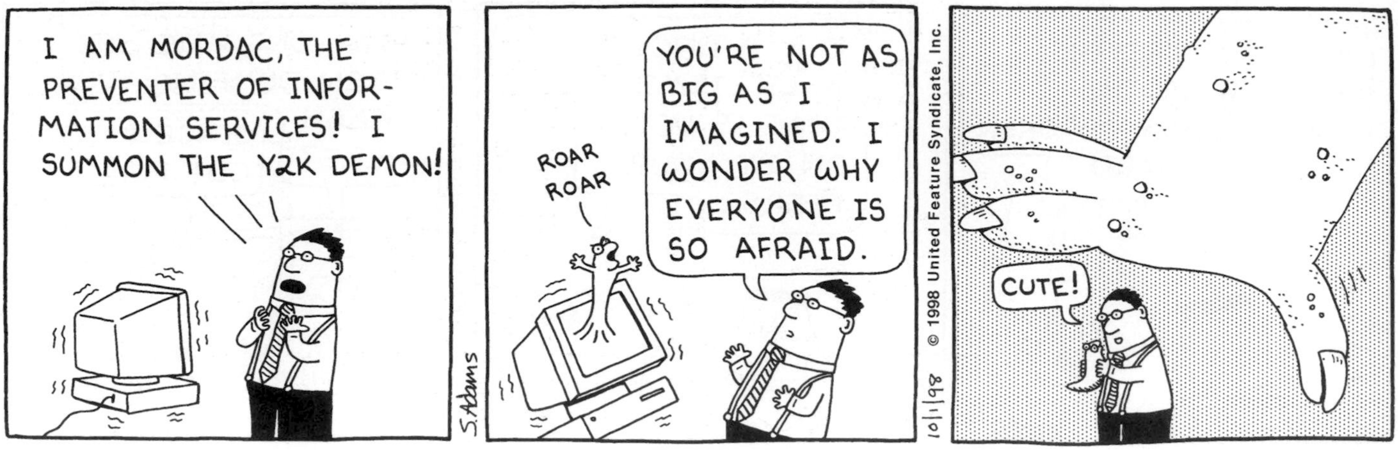
I AM MORDAC, THE PREVENTER OF INFORMATION SERVICES! I SUMMON THE Y2K DEMON!
S. Adams
ROAR ROAR
YOU'RE NOT AS BIG AS I IMAGINED. I WONDER WHY EVERYONE IS SO AFRAID.
10/1/98 © 1998 United Feature Syndicate, Inc.
CUTE!

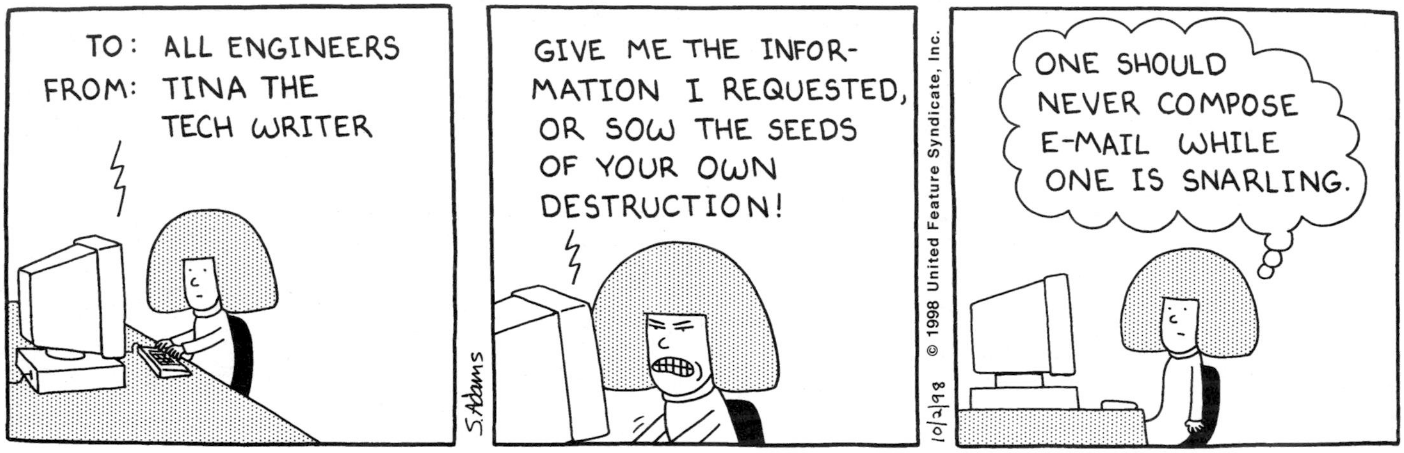
TO: ALL ENGINEERS
FROM: TINA THE TECH WRITER
S. Adams
GIVE ME THE INFORMATION I REQUESTED, OR SOW THE SEEDS OF YOUR OWN DESTRUCTION!
10/2/98 © 1998 United Feature Syndicate, Inc.
ONE SHOULD NEVER COMPOSE E-MAIL WHILE ONE IS SNARLING.

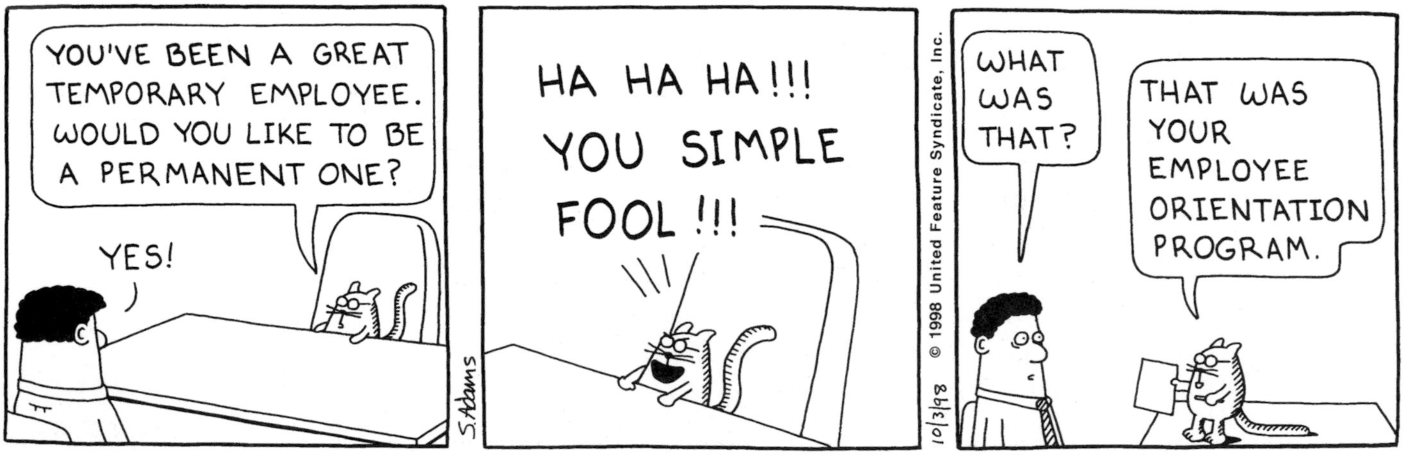
YOU'VE BEEN A GREAT TEMPORARY EMPLOYEE. WOULD YOU LIKE TO BE A PERMANENT ONE?
YES!
S. Adams
HA HA HA!!! YOU SIMPLE FOOL!!!
10/3/98 © 1998 United Feature Syndicate, Inc.
WHAT WAS THAT?
THAT WAS YOUR EMPLOYEE ORIENTATION PROGRAM.

THIS BELL WILL IMPROVE YOUR MORALE.
S. Adams
YOU RING THE BELL WHENEVER YOU ACHIEVE A GOAL.
THEN YELL YOUR ACCOMPLISHMENT TO THE REST OF THE OFFICE
I KNOW IT SOUNDS CORNY, BUT THE BELL HAS WORKED AT OTHER COMPANIES.
DOES YOUR INFORMATION COME FROM THE BOSSES OF THOSE OTHER COMPANIES?
10/4/98 © 1998 United Feature Syndicate, Inc.
NO.
IT COMES FROM A MAGAZINE THAT INTERVIEWED THOSE BOSSES.
I'LL GO FIRST.
CLANG CLANG
I RESISTED KILLING MY BOSS WITH A STUPID BELL!!

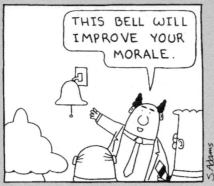

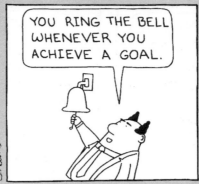

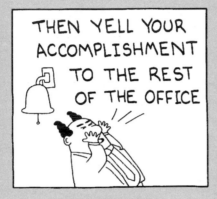

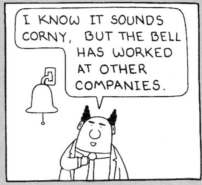

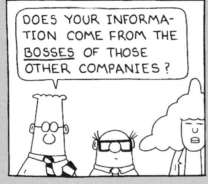

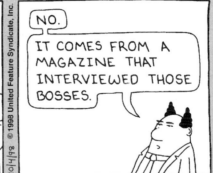

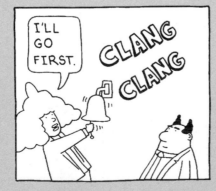

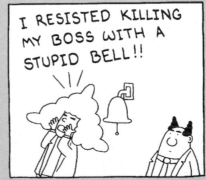

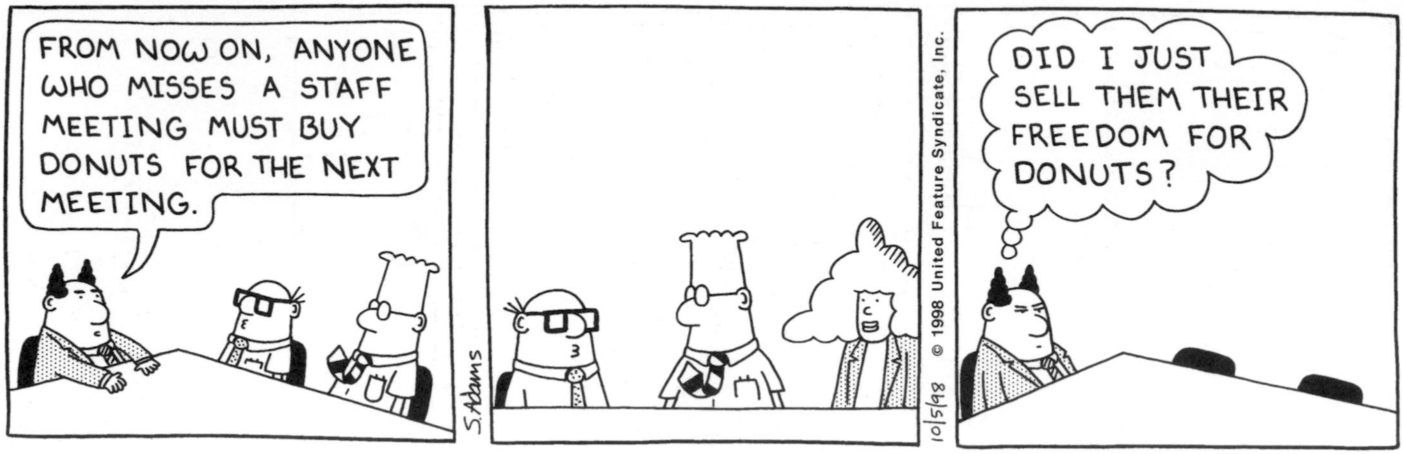
FROM NOW ON, ANYONE WHO MISSES A STAFF MEETING MUST BUY DONUTS FOR THE NEXT MEETING.
S.Adams
10/5/98 © 1998 United Feature Syndicate, Inc.
DID I JUST SELL THEM THEIR FREEDOM FOR DONUTS?

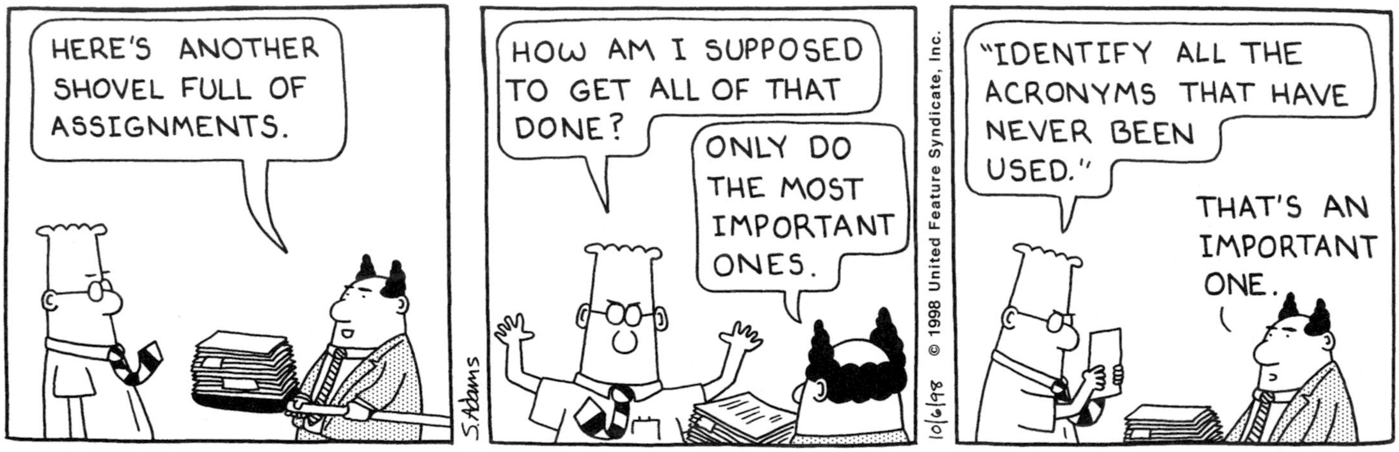
HERE'S ANOTHER SHOVEL FULL OF ASSIGNMENTS.
S.Adams
HOW AM I SUPPOSED TO GET ALL OF THAT DONE?
ONLY DO THE MOST IMPORTANT ONES.
10/6/98 © 1998 United Feature Syndicate, Inc.
"IDENTIFY ALL THE ACRONYMS THAT HAVE NEVER BEEN USED."
THAT'S AN IMPORTANT ONE.

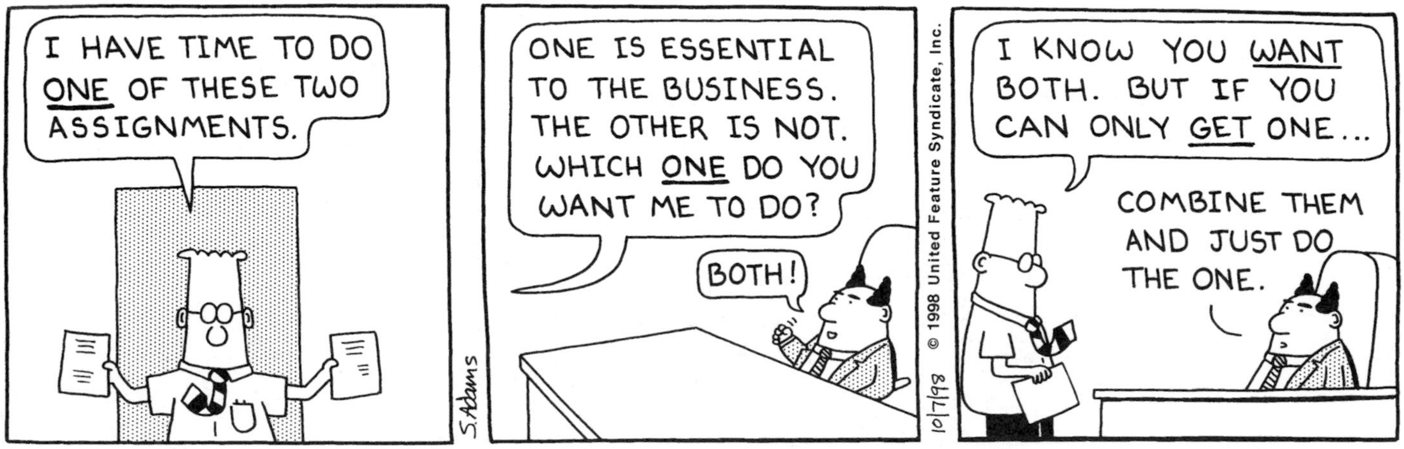
I HAVE TIME TO DO ONE OF THESE TWO ASSIGNMENTS.
S.Adams
ONE IS ESSENTIAL TO THE BUSINESS. THE OTHER IS NOT. WHICH ONE DO YOU WANT ME TO DO?
BOTH!
10/7/98 © 1998 United Feature Syndicate, Inc.
I KNOW YOU WANT BOTH. BUT IF YOU CAN ONLY GET ONE...
COMBINE THEM AND JUST DO THE ONE.

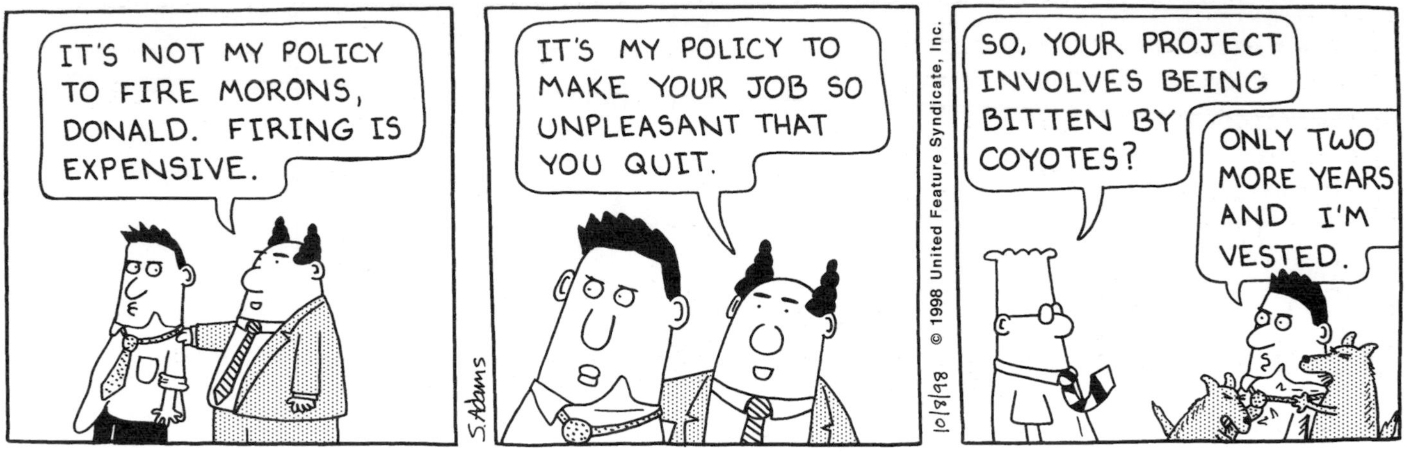
IT'S NOT MY POLICY TO FIRE MORONS, DONALD. FIRING IS EXPENSIVE.
IT'S MY POLICY TO MAKE YOUR JOB SO UNPLEASANT THAT YOU QUIT.
S.Adams
10/8/98 © 1998 United Feature Syndicate, Inc.
SO, YOUR PROJECT INVOLVES BEING BITTEN BY COYOTES?
ONLY TWO MORE YEARS AND I'M VESTED.

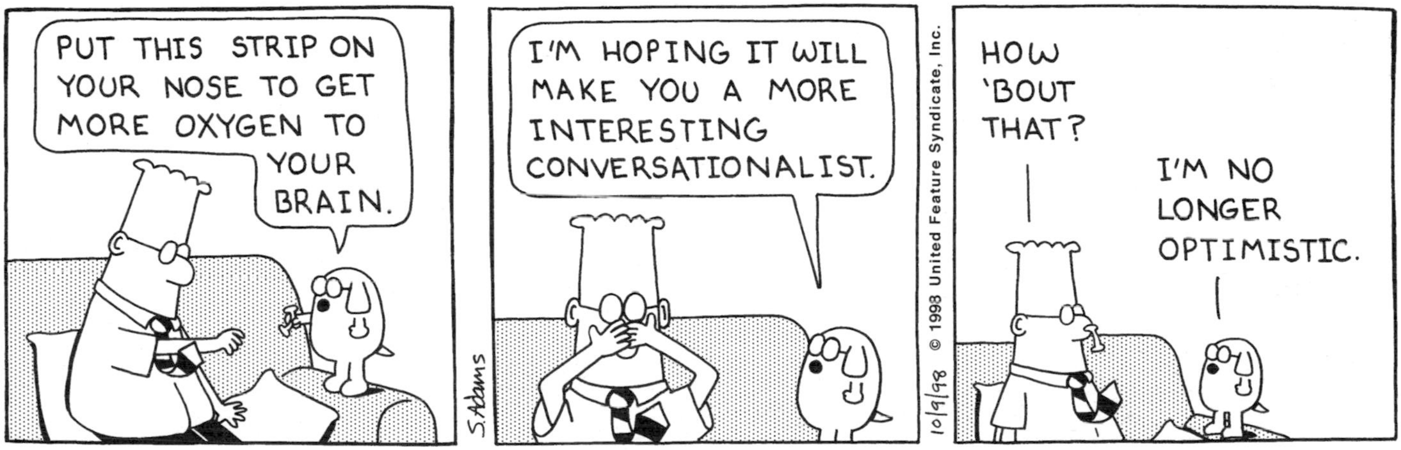
PUT THIS STRIP ON YOUR NOSE TO GET MORE OXYGEN TO YOUR BRAIN.
I'M HOPING IT WILL MAKE YOU A MORE INTERESTING CONVERSATIONALIST.
S.Adams
10/9/98 © 1998 United Feature Syndicate, Inc.
HOW 'BOUT THAT?
I'M NO LONGER OPTIMISTIC.

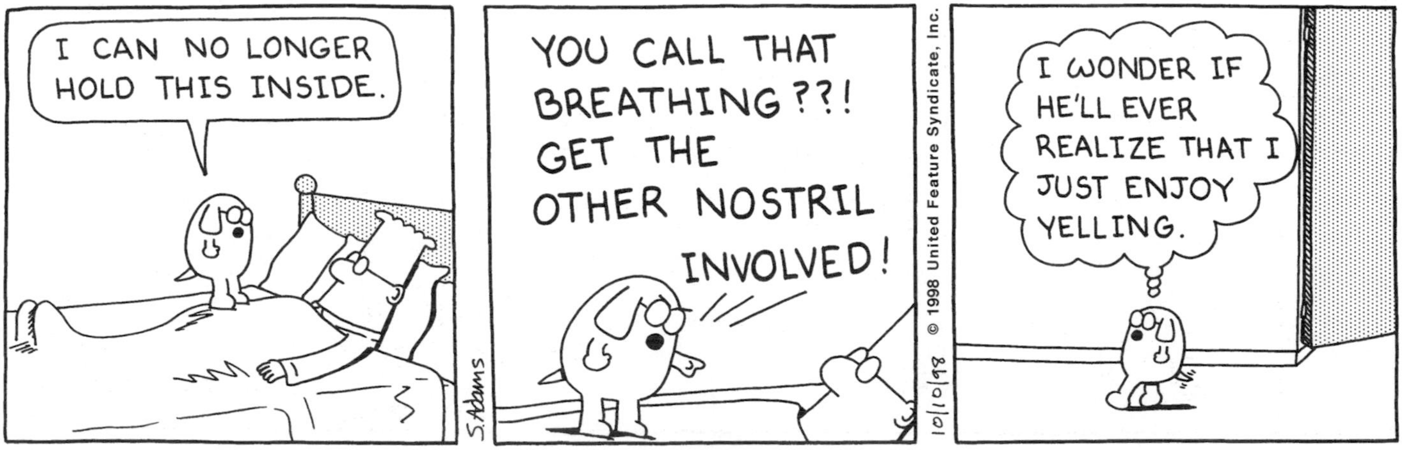
I CAN NO LONGER HOLD THIS INSIDE.
YOU CALL THAT BREATHING??! GET THE OTHER NOSTRIL INVOLVED!
S.Adams
10/10/98 © 1998 United Feature Syndicate, Inc.
I WONDER IF HE'LL EVER REALIZE THAT I JUST ENJOY YELLING.

IT'S NOT ENOUGH TO "SERVE" OUR CUSTOMERS...
WE MUST DELIGHT THEM!
S. Adams
YOU MEAN WE HAVE TO STOP PRICE-GOUGING?
NO, I THINK WE CAN STILL DO THAT.
OOH OOH! I KNOW!
10/1/98 © 1998 United Feature Syndicate, Inc.
WE COULD STOP SELLING PRODUCTS WITH KNOWN DEFECTS.
I'M TALKING ABOUT CUSTOMERS, NOT PRODUCTS!!
DO YOU FEEL LIKE DELIGHTING CUSTOMERS?
I BARELY HAVE THE EMPATHY TO PITY THEM.

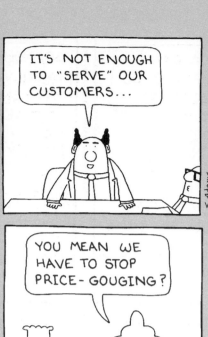

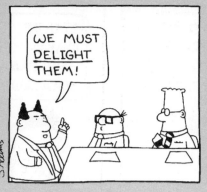

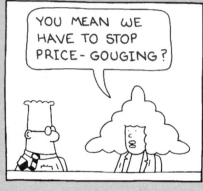

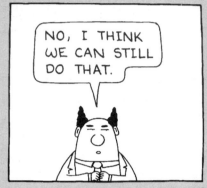

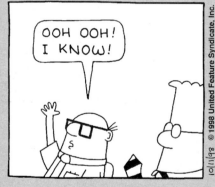

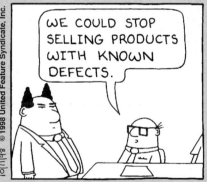

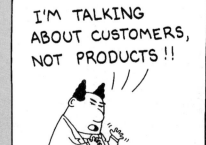

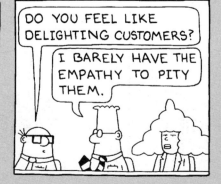

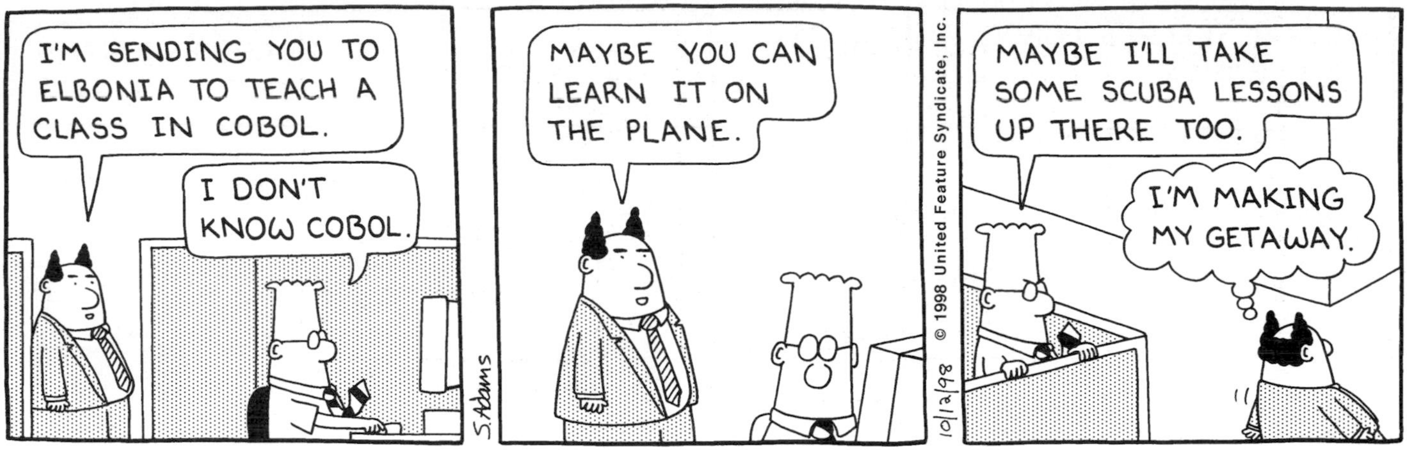
I'M SENDING YOU TO ELBONIA TO TEACH A CLASS IN COBOL.
I DON'T KNOW COBOL.
S. Adams
MAYBE YOU CAN LEARN IT ON THE PLANE.
10/12/98 © 1998 United Feature Syndicate, Inc.
MAYBE I'LL TAKE SOME SCUBA LESSONS UP THERE TOO.
I'M MAKING MY GETAWAY.

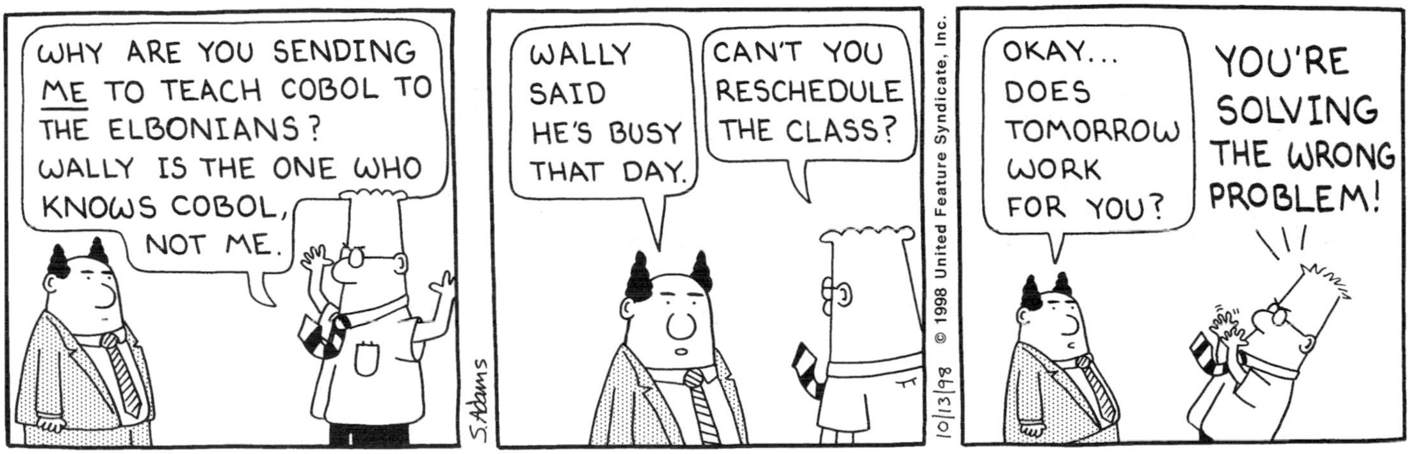
WHY ARE YOU SENDING ME TO TEACH COBOL TO THE ELBONIANS? WALLY IS THE ONE WHO KNOWS COBOL, NOT ME.
S. Adams
WALLY SAID HE'S BUSY THAT DAY.
CAN'T YOU RESCHEDULE THE CLASS?
10/13/98 © 1998 United Feature Syndicate, Inc.
OKAY... DOES TOMORROW WORK FOR YOU?
YOU'RE SOLVING THE WRONG PROBLEM!

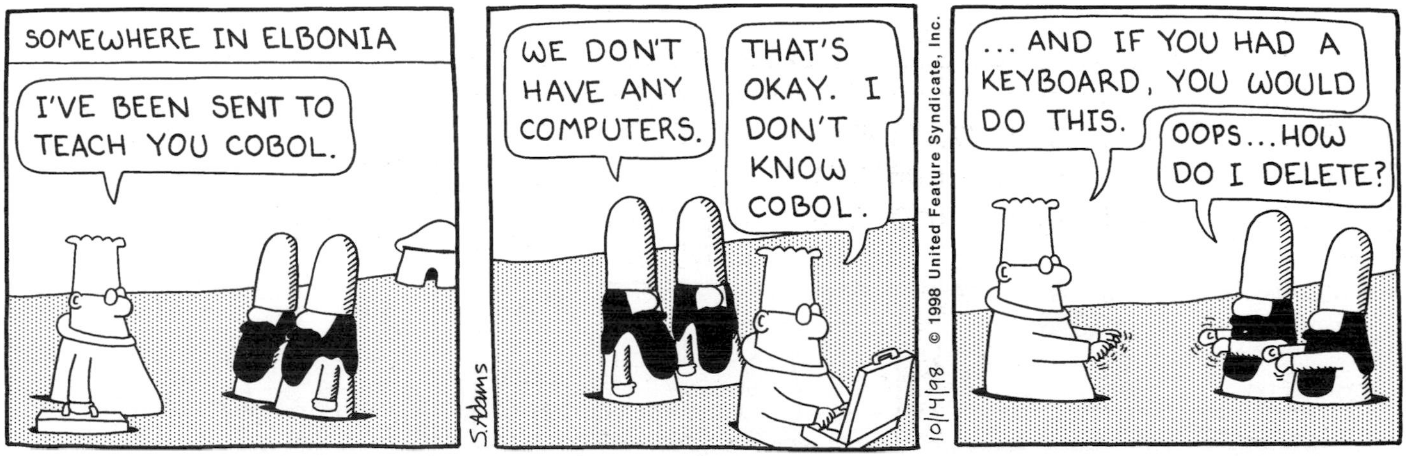
SOMEWHERE IN ELBONIA
I'VE BEEN SENT TO TEACH YOU COBOL.
S. Adams
WE DON'T HAVE ANY COMPUTERS.
THAT'S OKAY. I DON'T KNOW COBOL.
10/14/98 © 1998 United Feature Syndicate, Inc.
... AND IF YOU HAD A KEYBOARD, YOU WOULD DO THIS.
OOPS... HOW DO I DELETE?

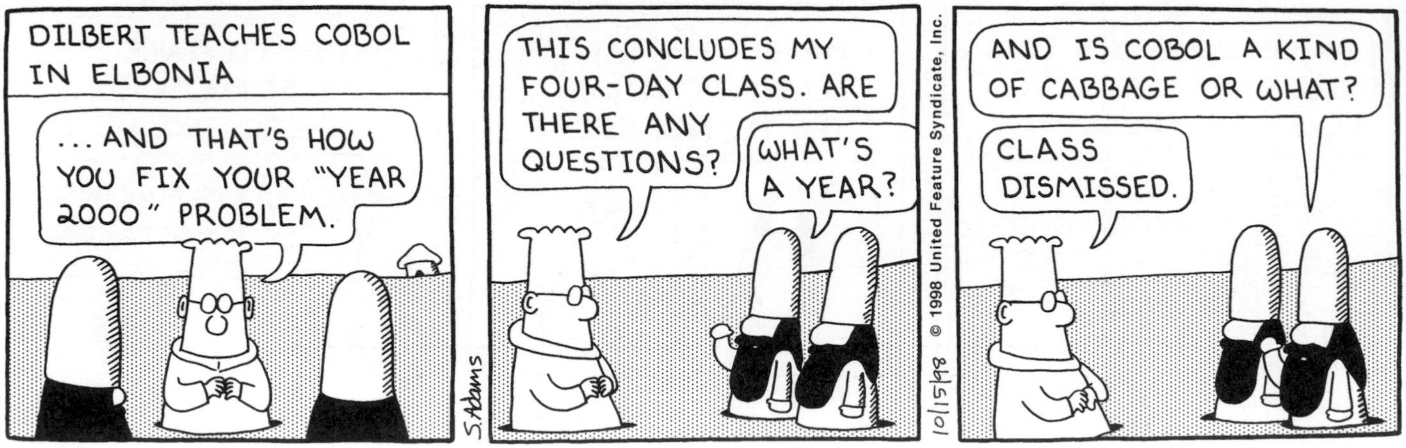
DILBERT TEACHES COBOL IN ELBONIA
... AND THAT'S HOW YOU FIX YOUR "YEAR 2000" PROBLEM.
S. Adams
THIS CONCLUDES MY FOUR-DAY CLASS. ARE THERE ANY QUESTIONS?
WHAT'S A YEAR?
10/15/98 © 1998 United Feature Syndicate, Inc.
AND IS COBOL A KIND OF CABBAGE OR WHAT?
CLASS DISMISSED.

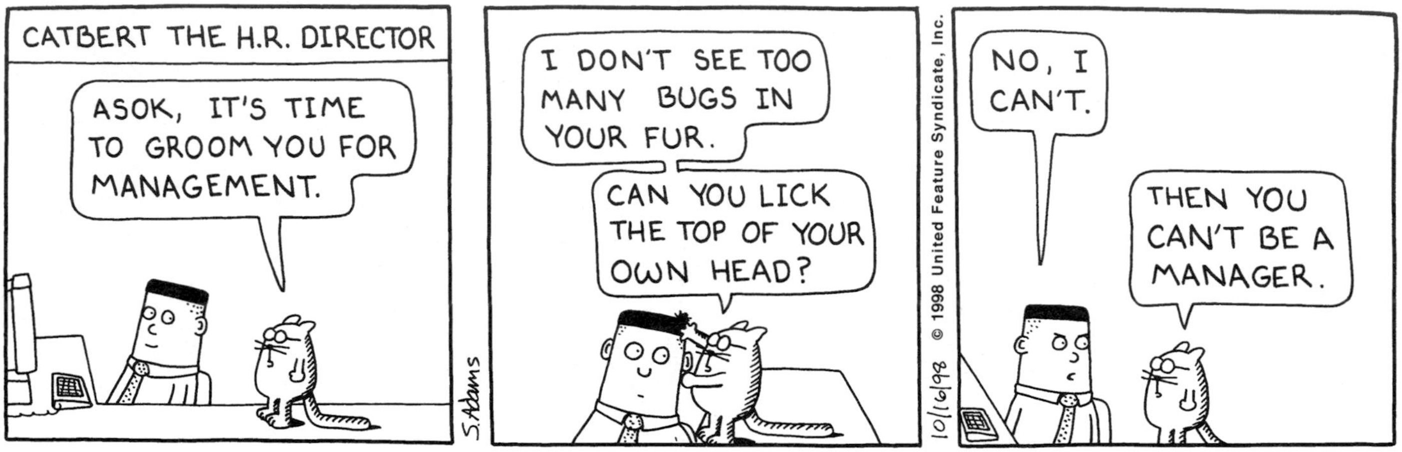
CATBERT THE H.R. DIRECTOR
ASOK, IT'S TIME TO GROOM YOU FOR MANAGEMENT.
S. Adams
I DON'T SEE TOO MANY BUGS IN YOUR FUR.
CAN YOU LICK THE TOP OF YOUR OWN HEAD?
10/16/98 © 1998 United Feature Syndicate, Inc.
NO, I CAN'T.
THEN YOU CAN'T BE A MANAGER.

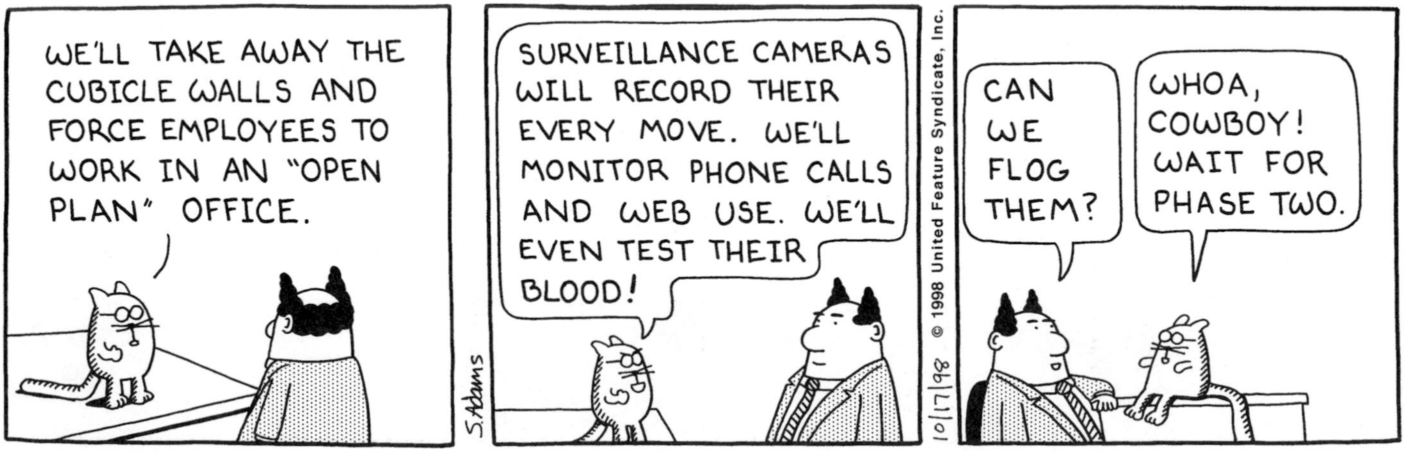
WE'LL TAKE AWAY THE CUBICLE WALLS AND FORCE EMPLOYEES TO WORK IN AN "OPEN PLAN" OFFICE.
S. Adams
SURVEILLANCE CAMERAS WILL RECORD THEIR EVERY MOVE. WE'LL MONITOR PHONE CALLS AND WEB USE. WE'LL EVEN TEST THEIR BLOOD!
10/17/98 © 1998 United Feature Syndicate, Inc.
CAN WE FLOG THEM?
WHOA, COWBOY! WAIT FOR PHASE TWO.

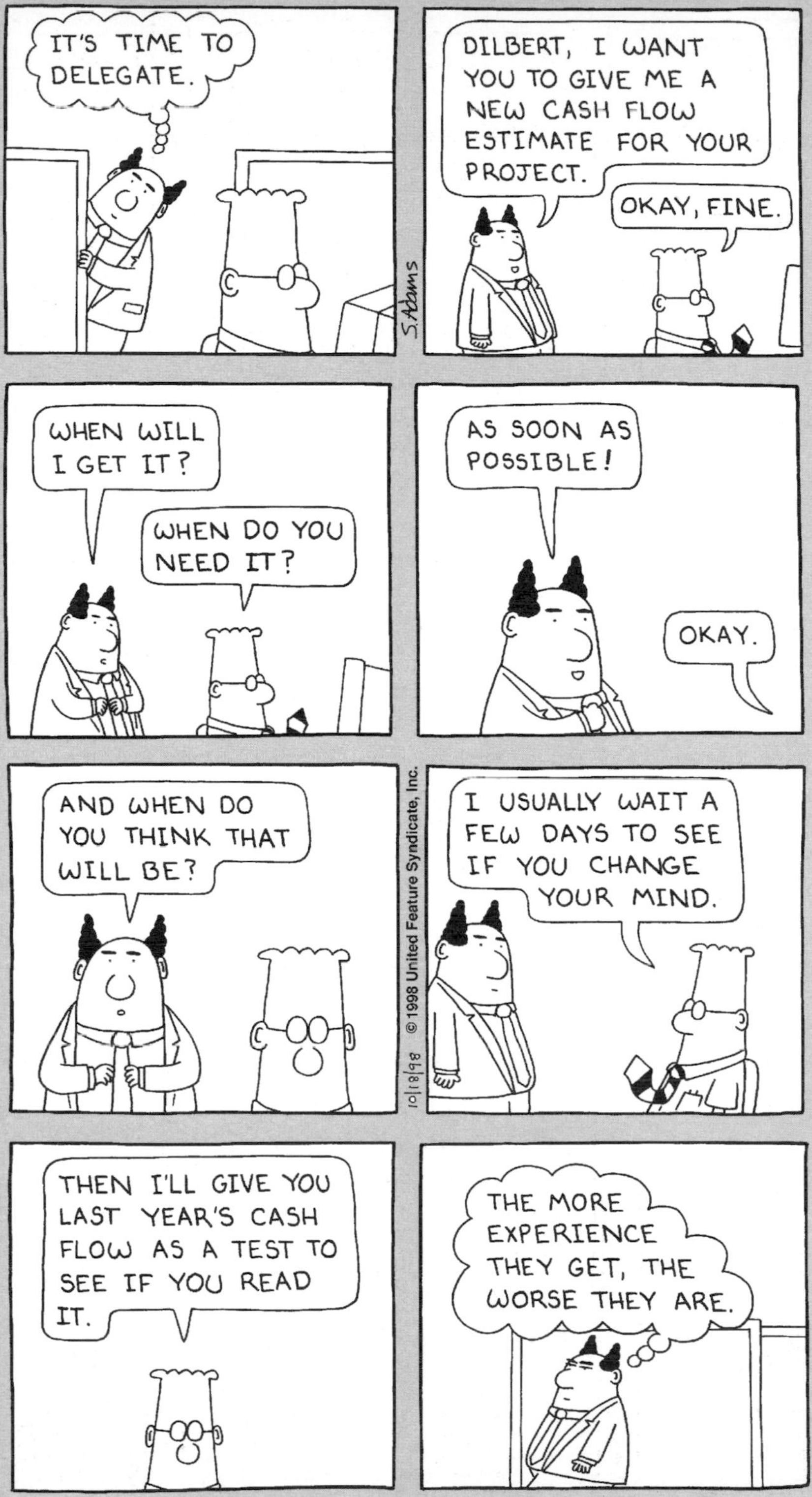
IT'S TIME TO DELEGATE.
S. Adams
DILBERT, I WANT YOU TO GIVE ME A NEW CASH FLOW ESTIMATE FOR YOUR PROJECT.
OKAY, FINE.
WHEN WILL I GET IT?
WHEN DO YOU NEED IT?
AS SOON AS POSSIBLE!
OKAY.
AND WHEN DO YOU THINK THAT WILL BE?
10/18/98 © 1998 United Feature Syndicate, Inc.
I USUALLY WAIT A FEW DAYS TO SEE IF YOU CHANGE YOUR MIND.
THEN I'LL GIVE YOU LAST YEAR'S CASH FLOW AS A TEST TO SEE IF YOU READ IT.
THE MORE EXPERIENCE THEY GET, THE WORSE THEY ARE.